OXFORD LIBRARY OF
AFRICAN LITERATURE

General Editors

E. E. EVANS-FRITCHARD
G. LIENHARDT
W. H. WHITELEY

LITHOKO

SOTHO PRAISE-POEMS

Edited and Translated
with an Introduction and Notes
_by_
M. DAMANE
and
P. B. SANDERS

CLARENDON PRESS · OXFORD

1974

Oxford University Press, Ely House, London W.1

GLASGOW NEW YORK TORONTO MELBOURNE WELLINGTON
CAPE TOWN IBADAN NAIROBI DAR ES SALAAM LUSAKA ADDIS ABABA
DELHI BOMBAY CALCUTTA MADRAS KARACHI LAHORE DACCA
KUALA LUMPUR SINGAPORE HONG KONG TOKYO

ISBN 0 19 815143 8

*Printed in Great Britain
by William Clowes & Sons, Limited
London, Beccles and Colchester*

HO MOTLOTLEHI MOSHOESHOE II

PREFACE

THE noun *lithoko* (praise-poems) is formed from the verb *ho roka* (to praise). The Sotho compose *lithoko* on many subjects, among them chiefs and warriors, politicians and footballers, animals and plants, and trains, cars and bicycles. Moreover boys at the initiation school have always been expected to compose their own *lithoko*. This volume is confined to *lithoko tsa marena* (praise-poems of chiefs), which, together with the praise-poems of ordinary warriors, which are of much the same character, are generally regarded as the Sotho's finest creations in this field.

In the early years of this century a collection of such *lithoko* was made by Z. D. Mangoaela (1883–1962), who had previously been working as a teacher, but who was then helping the French Protestant missionaries at Morija in the production of their newspaper, *Leselinyana la Lesotho*. Some of these *lithoko* he recorded himself: others were recorded for him by friends, or were sent to him by chiefs. Between 1919 and 1921 they were published in *Leselinyana*, and in the latter year they were published in book form at Morija under the title *Lithoko tsa Marena a Basotho tse boleketsoeng ke Z. D. Mangoaela* (The Praise-Poems of the Chiefs of the Sotho collected by Z. D. Mangoaela), although in fact they also included a few praise-poems of ordinary warriors. Further editions of this book have since appeared, the last being the seventh in 1965. Mangoaela's original collection has been slightly expanded, and this last edition contains the *lithoko*, complete or in part, of eighty-two chiefs and warriors. The earliest date from the second half of the eighteenth century, the latest from the 1920s.

Mangoaela's collection is our most valuable source for praise-poems of this type, but there are other sources too. In 1841 the French missionary Casalis published his *Études sur la Langue Séchuana* (Séchuana being the name then given to the Sotho language), in which he presented French translations of five *lithoko*, together with explanatory notes, but without the original Sotho. In 1858 Tlali, a son of Moshoeshoe, wrote a brief history of his people

in which he gave quotations from a few *lithoko*.[1] Furthermore, over
and above Mangoaela's work, several *lithoko* have been published
in *Leselinyana*, and many fragments of them are to be found in
A. M. Sekese's historical articles, which appeared in that newspaper between 1890 and 1930. In 1940 George Lerotholi
published his own compositions, *Lithoko tsa Morena e Moholo
Seeiso Griffith* (The Praise-Poems of Paramount Chief Seeiso
Griffith), which were revised in 1956; and these were followed in
1964 by the same author's *Lithoko tsa Motlotlehi Moshoeshoe II*
(The Praise-Poems of His Majesty King Moshoeshoe II). Finally
there are *lithoko* which have never been reduced to writing, but
which may still be heard in Lesotho today. Some of these are
lithoko tsa khale (praise-poems of long ago), which have been
passed on by word of mouth over many years. Because of lapses
of memory they are usually much shorter than those recorded by
Mangoaela, but even so they can sometimes be used to supplement or correct them. Others are *lithoko tse ncha* (recent praise-
poems), and may relate, for example, to the life of the present
King of Lesotho.

Most of the translations in this volume are based on texts provided by Mangoaela and George Lerotholi, and, since these are
readily available from the Sesuto Book Depot in Morija, they are
not reprinted here. No significant variations are made from
Mangoaela's texts except on very good authority, and all such
variations are indicated in footnotes. Texts which are not so
readily available, i.e. the third of Moshoeshoe I's poems and the
only poem of Moshoeshoe II, are given in an Appendix.

In 1971 D. P. Kunene's study, *Heroic Poetry of the Basotho*,
was published in this series. Before then, with the exception of
Casalis's work, a few scattered observations in *Leselinyana*, and some
detailed Sotho notes in the first volume of M. Damane's *Marath'a
Lilepe a Puo ea Sesotho* (Fragments of Sotho Language) (Morija,
1960), no significant attempt had been made either to translate or
to interpret any of the *lithoko*. Moreover, even Kunene has been
concerned more with analysis than with translation and interpretation. Broadly speaking, this volume, with its emphasis on the last

---

[1] Tlali's history, which he called 'Litaba tsa Mofuta oa Basuthu', 'The Story
of the Sotho People', survives as a manuscript in the Grey Library, Cape Town.

two aspects, though without, we hope, any undue neglect of the first, may be said to supplement Kunene's study.

The *lithoko* translated here have been drawn from every period, our selection being based on aesthetic excellence and historical interest. Using these criteria, we would have wished to have added other *lithoko*, but were deterred from doing so by the obscurity of many of their allusions and the difficulty of much of their language, which, even with the assistance of others, we were unable to understand. It is partly for this reason that our selection has been confined to the *lithoko* of chiefs who belonged to the royal family.

In preparing our translations and notes we have consulted not only written sources, both published and unpublished, but also many Sotho who are rightly regarded as experts on their language and history. Our profound indebtedness to them is obvious throughout our work. In particular, we wish to acknowledge the exceptionally valuable assistance given by Chief 'Mako Moliboea Molapo, with whom we spent many days at his village of Likhakeng. We also wish to express our gratitude to Captain R. S. Webb, M.B.E., for his generous help in matters of topography, and to Mr. D. Ambrose (of the University of Botswana, Lesotho, and Swaziland), Mr. A. Brutsch (of the Church of Lesotho), Professor W. D. Hammond-Tooke (of the University of the Witwatersrand), and Dr. C. Saunders (of the University of Cape Town), for their help on several points of detail. Finally we wish to thank the Administrators of the Beit Fund in Oxford, without whose liberal financial support this work could not have been completed.

CONTENTS

NOTE ON NAMES, ORTHOGRAPHY AND PRONUNCIATION   xiv

MAP   *facing p. 1*

INTRODUCTION

I. THE HISTORICAL BACKGROUND TO THE PRAISE-
POEMS

  1. The Independent Chiefdoms   1

  2. The *Lifaqane* and the Emergence of the Sotho Chief-
dom   2

  3. The Growth of the Sotho Chiefdom and the Distur-
bances of the Orange River Sovereignty   3

  4. The Wars with the Orange Free State and the Intervention of Sir Philip Wodehouse   5

  5. Annexation to the Cape Colony and the Gun War   6

  6. The British Colony of Basutoland and the Indepen-
dent Kingdom of Lesotho   8

II. THE SOCIAL AND CULTURAL BACKGROUND TO THE
PRAISE-POEMS

  1. Ecological Factors   10

  2. Education   12

  3. Warfare   13

  4. Marriage   14

  5. The Position of the Chief   15

  6. Religious Beliefs   16

  7. Witchcraft, Divination, Rainmaking and Medicine   16

III. THE PRAISE-POEMS IN SOTHO LIFE

  1. The Poet   18

2. The Occasions of Composition 23
3. Chanting 24
4. Functions 27

IV. AN ANALYSIS OF THE PRAISE-POEMS
1. Theme and Structure 34
2. The Eulogue 40
3. The Stanza 43
4. The Line and the Rhythm 52
5. Poetic Qualities 54
6. The Praise-Poems and the Historian 59
   Notes on the Sotho Texts and the English Translations 61
   Genealogical Table 61

THE PRAISE-POEMS

1. Peete 63
2. Mokhachane 64
3. Moshoeshoe I 65
4. Makhabane 75
5. Posholi 79
6. Mopeli 96
7. Letsie I 106
8. Molapo 110
9. Masopha 115
10. Lerotholi 136
11. Maama 154
12. Jonathan 168
13. Joel 187
14. Letsie II 208
15. Griffith 213
16. Lerotholi Mojela 234

Contents

17. Seeiso   242
18. Moshoeshoe II   266

APPENDIX   270
SELECT BIBLIOGRAPHY   274
INDEX   275

NOTE ON NAMES,
ORTHOGRAPHY AND PRONUNCIATION

THE Africans who now live in Lesotho and the neighbouring areas of the Republic of South Africa generally refer to themselves as *Basotho*. Among historians they have often beeen referred to as the Basuto, or the Basutos, and among anthropologists as the Southern Sotho, in order to distinguish them from the Northern and the Western Sotho, although these divisions were not very marked until the second half of the nineteenth century. Since the practice of dispensing with prefixes is now being widely adopted, and since most of the Northern Sotho may be called the Pedi and the Western Sotho may be called the Tswana, we here refer to them simply as the Sotho. Following common usage, however, we also use this term to refer in particular to those Sotho who came under the rule of Moshoeshoe, who may be regarded as the founder of the Sotho chiefdom, although in fact there were many Sotho, like Sekonyela's Tlokoa, who at first remained independent.

In the translations of the praise-poems, but not elsewhere, we use the terms 'Bushmen' and 'Boers' to refer to the San and Afrikaners.

The Sotho language has two systems of orthography, one of which is used in Lesotho and the other in the Republic of South Africa. We use the former because it is naturally more acceptable to the people of Lesotho, with whose history the *lithoko* are so closely connected.

Generally words are pronounced as they are written, but there are exceptions to this rule. The most important of these are as follows:

When placed before another vowel *e* should often be pronounced as *y*.

L before *i* or *u* should be pronounced as *d*.

'*M* at the beginning of a word represents *Mm*, the first *m* being a syllable in itself, and the second being the first letter in the second syllable.

Similarly '*N* at the beginning of a word represents *Nn*, the first *n* being a syllable in itself, and the second being the first letter in the second syllable.

When placed before another vowel *o* should usually be pronounced as *w*. For example, the name Moshoeshoe should be pronounced as Moshweshwe.

Ph represents an aspirated *p*.

Q represents a click.

Qh represents an aspirated click.

Th represents an aspirated *t*.

In *tš* the *s* sound is aspirated.

The accent in words of more than one syllable is almost invariably upon the penultimate syllable. *Ng*, however, is a syllable in itself, and so in Tlokoeng, for example, the accent is on the *e*.

INTRODUCTION

I

THE HISTORICAL BACKGROUND
TO THE PRAISE-POEMS

1. *The Independent Chiefdoms*

TODAY the Sotho number roughly 1,500,000 people. Of these a
little more than 1,000,000 belong to the Kingdom of Lesotho:
the rest live mainly in the adjacent areas of the Republic of South
Africa. Although it is now possible to refer to them by a single
name, in fact they are the descendants of many different groups,
which, broadly speaking, remained independent of each other
until the 1820s. Each of these groups had its own name, which was
usually formed from that of one of its chiefs, past or present, or
from that of the animal or object which it revered as its totem.
In the course of time, however, they generally became known to
outsiders as the Sotho and came to think of themselves as such.
They spoke the same language, though with varying dialects,
and they followed very much the same way of life. Their villages
extended over a wide area of the High Veld of southern Africa.
Below the Drakensberg lived the various Nguni peoples, whose
language and customs were very different. There were a few Nguni
groups, however, which were intermingled with the Sotho on the
High Veld, and, because of the historical processes which will be
described below, there is a large Nguni element in the present
Sotho nation.

The Sotho had no over-all ruler, but in the late eighteenth and
early nineteenth centuries Mohlomi, a Monaheng chief, was
exerting a strong influence among his neighbours because of his
wealth in cattle and his reputation for wisdom. He died *c.* 1815,
when Moshoeshoe, later the founder of the Sotho chiefdom, was

still a young man. Moshoeshoe was then living at Menkhoaneng
in the valley of the Hlotse, a tributary of the Caledon, and had no
more exciting prospect than that of succeeding his father, Mokhachane, as chief of the insignificant Mokoteli, a very junior Koena
group. In or around 1820 he moved away from his father and
established his own village nearby at the foot of Botha-Bothe
mountain. By this time he had made a name for himself as a
successful cattle-raider, and was therefore widely respected,
but he had not established any form of paramountcy.

2. *The* Lifaqane *and the Emergence of the Sotho Chiefdom*

Meanwhile, below the Drakensberg, the Zulu chief Shaka was
rapidly building up his power, mainly by wars of conquest. In
1822 the Hlubi of Mpangazitha and the Ngwane of Matiwane
fled from that troubled area, crossed over the mountain passes,
and invaded the High Veld. The Tlokoa, whose villages lay
immediately in their path, took to flight, and soon these three
hordes were pouring down into the Caledon valley. All the Sotho
chiefdoms were caught up in the subsequent turmoil, which became known to them as the *lifaqane*. Thousands were killed in
battle or died of starvation, and thousands more fled to the Cape
Colony or elsewhere. Others tried to eke out a living by hunting
and gathering, and others, more desperate still, turned to the
horrors of cannibalism. At Botha-Bothe Moshoeshoe and his followers took refuge on the summit of the mountain, but even there
they were far from secure, and in 1824 they migrated to the mountain fortress of Thaba Bosiu. (It was on this journey that Moshoeshoe's grandfather, Peete, was captured and killed by cannibals.)
By this time Moshoeshoe had assumed the leadership of the
Mokoteli. Moreover he had succeeded in maintaining the numbers
of his herds and flocks at a time when many of the chiefs around
him had been totally impoverished. Several groups had already
joined him, and others, attracted by reports of his wealth and of
his new-found strength on Thaba Bosiu, now began to follow
their example. In due course he became known, not as chief of the
Mokoteli, but as chief of the Sotho.

Not far from Thaba Bosiu were the villages of Matiwane's
Ngwane, who had earlier defeated the Hlubi, and who were now
dominant in the area. In 1828 some of their regiments moved
against the Sotho, but were decisively driven back. Shortly after-

wards, having suffered heavy losses at the hands of Ndebele raiders, Matiwane led his people into the country now known as the Transkei. There his power was broken by British troops from the Cape Colony, and eventually he made his way back to Zululand, where he was put to death by Shaka's successor, Dingane.

There were now only two chiefdoms of any importance in the Caledon valley, namely Moshoeshoe's Sotho at Thaba Bosiu and Sekonyela's Tlokoa at Marabeng. In 1829 Moshoeshoe twice plundered cattle from the Thembu below the Drakensberg, and so was able to attract yet more followers to himself. While he was absent on the second expedition, Sekonyela seized the opportunity to attack Thaba Bosiu, only to be beaten off by the boys and the old men who had been left behind. Two years later the Sotho repelled a fierce onslaught by some of Mzilikazi's far-ranging Ndebele regiments. Meanwhile, however, new enemies had appeared, small groups of Kora and men of mixed breed, many of whom were mounted on horses and armed with guns. At first they raided and killed the Sotho almost at will, but their boldness decreased as Moshoeshoe's people acquired horses and guns of their own. In 1835 the chief felt confident enough to conduct his third campaign against the Thembu, but this resulted in the death of his brother, Makhabane, and was almost a total failure. In the following year he took the initiative against the Kora when he attacked and routed some of their bands along the Riet River, and after this victory his followers could at last enjoy a respite from hostilities.

3. *The Growth of the Sotho Chiefdom and the Disturbances of the Orange River Sovereignty*

With the advent of peace many Sotho who had been uprooted from their homes came to live under Moshoeshoe's hegemony, so that between 1833 and 1848 the number of his adherents rose from about 25,000 to about 80,000. In June 1833 Casalis and Arbousset of the Paris Evangelical Missionary Society arrived at Thaba Bosiu, and in the following month they established their first station at Morija, about fifteen miles to the south. By 1848 there were eight French stations among Moshoeshoe's followers, and more than 1,000 people had been converted to the Christian faith.

Although the years between 1836 and 1848 were, on the whole, a period of tranquillity and prosperity for the Sotho, it was natural that, as they increased in numbers and expanded territorially, so they should become involved in disputes with their neighbours, many of whom had settled on land which they themselves had occupied before the *lifaqane* and which they still regarded as their own. Indeed Moshoeshoe's birth-place of Menkhoaneng was under the control of Sekonyela's Tlokoa.

Initially Letsie and Molapo, the two eldest sons in Moshoeshoe's senior house, had gone to join the missionaries at Morija. It was unusual, however, for two important chiefs to live so close to each other, and quarrels inevitably arose. Eventually, in the mid-1840s, Molapo left Morija and moved northwards to establish his village at Peka. There he was settling on land that was claimed by Sekonyela, and, as his following grew, and as other chiefs too moved into the disputed area, so the Sotho and the Tlokoa gradually became embroiled in raiding and counter-raiding.

Meanwhile, in the south-west, towards the junction of the Caledon and the Orange, the Afrikaners were steadily encroaching on land claimed by Moshoeshoe. It was partly for this reason that in February 1848 Sir Harry Smith, the Governor and High Commissioner at the Cape, annexed all the territory lying between the Orange, the Vaal and the Drakensberg, and this was given the name of the Orange River Sovereignty.

Seven months later Sekonyela's son, Maketekete, burned down the village of Kali, one of Moshoeshoe's subordinates, whereupon the Sotho rushed to arms and swept off many of the Tlokoa's flocks and herds. Major Warden, the British Resident at Bloemfontein, was now responsible for maintaining peace in the Sovereignty. With Smith's approval he intervened between the contestants, persuaded Moshoeshoe to restore the Tlokoa's livestock, and ordered him to withdraw his people from the disputed territory. The Sotho resented this interference, for in their eyes it was Sekonyela who was the intruder.

They were equally dissatisfied with some of Warden's other decisions. In 1833 and 1834 the Rolong of Moroka, the Kora of Jan Kaptein (who was soon succeeded by Gert Taaibosch), the Bastards of Carolus Baatje and the Griqua of Pieter Davids had moved down from the Vaal valley and had settled, with Moshoeshoe's permission, among his own followers. The Griqua had since departed, but the other chiefs now rejected Moshoeshoe's claims to the land which they occupied, and Warden accepted their case without holding a proper investigation. Moreover the boundary which he proposed in the south-west between the Sotho and the Afrikaners—the notorious Warden Line—was entirely in favour of the latter; and Smith accepted it without demur.

For these and other reasons the Sotho found themselves at war both with their neighbours and with the British. By now they were sufficiently powerful to hold their own. In 1851 they inflicted a sharp defeat on a combined force at Viervoet, and in the following year, when the High Commissioner, now Sir George Cathcart, came up from the Cape with a strong detachment of British troops, they held him at bay at the Berea plateau with a combination of hard fighting and brilliant diplomacy. In 1853 they completely overwhelmed the Tlokoa of Sekonyela and the Kora of Gert Taaibosch, and so recovered much of their land in the north.

By this time the British were weary of the troubles and expenses of the Orange River Sovereignty, and in 1854 they abandoned the territory, having prevailed upon Moshoeshoe's European neighbours to organize themselves into a new and independent nation, the Orange Free State, and having informed the Sotho, though not in so many words, that they were now being left to their own devices.

4. *The Wars with the Orange Free State and the Intervention of Sir Philip Wodehouse*

The manner of the British withdrawal was not calculated to ensure a lasting peace between the Sotho and the Afrikaners. Sir George Clerk, the officer who had been responsible for arranging the abandonment, had freely admitted that the Warden Line was unfair to the Sotho and had declared that it no longer existed. But he had neglected to lay down a new boundary and the Afrikaners, under President Boshof, resolved to maintain the old one. The Sotho expressed their frustration in cattle-raiding and encroachment; Moshoeshoe frequently agreed to restore the plundered stock but rarely did so in full or in time; and in 1858 the Free State declared war. As the Afrikaners invaded Lesotho, Moshoeshoe withdrew his forces to Thaba Bosiu; and as the commandos gathered below the mountain some of his regiments swept round behind them, raided deep into the Free State, and captured large numbers of cattle, sheep and goats. The Afrikaners, disturbed by reports of these raids, and deterred by the mountain's formidable defences, broke up camp and returned to their homes. At Boshof's request, and with Moshoeshoe's consent, the High Commissioner, now Sir George Grey, acted as mediator. Through him the Sotho recovered some land in the south-west, but even so they were bitterly disappointed.

Subsequently the Sotho began to move onto Afrikaner farms in the north, where the ruins of many of their former villages were still to be seen. By 1865 the Free Staters were again exasperated, and again they declared war. This time their forces were more powerful, and their Government, under President Brand, more determined. Although Thaba Bosiu itself was never taken, the Sotho suffered a string of heavy defeats. In March 1866 Molapo made a separate peace with the enemy, in which he signed away most of the north of Lesotho, and in the following month Moshoeshoe was forced to come to terms in the Treaty of Thaba Bosiu, in which he relinquished most of his remaining arable land. However, the Sotho then refused to evacuate the conquered territory, and so fighting was renewed. Again they were heavily defeated, and indeed they might well have been destroyed as a unified chiefdom had not the High Commissioner, now Sir Philip Wodehouse, intervened for their protection. In March 1868 he proclaimed them British subjects and their territory British territory. In the Treaty of Aliwal North in the following year they recovered some but not all of their land, and, broadly speaking, the boundaries of Basutoland, as the British called Lesotho, have remained unchanged since then to the present day.

In 1870 Moshoeshoe died in his sleep, being about eighty-four years of age, and was succeeded by his son Letsie.

5. *Annexation to the Cape Colony and the Gun War*

Initially Basutoland was under the control of the High Commissioner, but in 1871 it was annexed to the Cape Colony, which was granted responsible government in the following year. The officer in charge of the territory was the Governor's Agent, Colonel Griffith, whose administrative headquarters were at Maseru. The country was divided into four districts, some of which were later subdivided, and in each of these there was a magistrate supported by a small band of police. In spite of the paucity of its resources, the administration attempted to introduce several radical reforms in Sotho custom, but these, on the whole, the people were able to ignore. Indeed real power in the country stayed mainly in the hands of the chiefs.

Although the Sotho had lost much of their land to the Free State, they quickly recovered their former prosperity. This was enhanced by the opening up of the diamond mines at Kimberley, which gave them new opportunities, not only as labourers and transport drivers, but also in trade. With their wages they were allowed to purchase firearms and ammunition, and soon almost every man in the country was the proud possessor of a gun.

There was little danger at first that they would turn these weapons against their European rulers. In 1873, when the Hlubi chief, Langalibalele, fled with his followers from Natal into the Maloti mountains, Molapo and his son Jonathan quietly co-operated with the Government in arresting him. And when, in 1879, Moorosi and his Phuthi defied the authorities in the south of the country, most of the chiefs agreed to send warriors, albeit reluctantly in many cases, to assist in the investment and capture of his mountain.

In 1878, however, the Cape Government had been empowered to order total disarmament in any district under its control, and in 1880 J. G. Sprigg, the Prime Minister, rashly attempted to apply this measure to Basutoland. The Sotho's loathing of disarmament was universal, but their response to the Government's demands varied from chief to chief. Even under Moshoeshoe they had been far from united, and Letsie was now totally incapable of exercising any over-all control. From his village of Matsieng he dutifully sent off his guns in a cart for Maseru, but within a few hundred yards they were waylaid and captured on the orders of his son, Lerotholi. In this policy Lerotholi was fully supported by his powerful brothers, Bereng, Maama and Seeiso. In the central parts of the country Masopha, the third son in Moshoeshoe's senior house, also refused to surrender his arms; and when one of his headmen, Tokonya, failed to follow his example, he drove him and his followers into the Free State. In the north Molapo had just died, and his family was split between his sons Jonathan, who supported the Government, and Joel, who supported the rebels.

Faced with such widespread resistance Sprigg resolved to send in his troops. The Gun War, or the Basutoland Rebellion as it was also known, began in September 1880 and ended in April 1881. The Cape forces were unequal to the task of defeating the Sotho, and indeed for much of the war they were confined to the defence of three of the border magistracies. Ultimately a compromise agreement was reached whereby the Sotho were to retain their weapons but were to pay an annual licence of £1 for each gun; they were also to pay a fine in cattle and were to compensate traders and 'loyalists' who had suffered loss. In the event only part of the cattle fine was paid. The rest of the agreement was virtually ignored. Clearly the Gun War had been an almost unqualified triumph for the rebels. The Cape's prestige had been shattered, and in 1884, after three years of demoralized and ineffective government, Basutoland was disannexed from the Colony and came under direct imperial rule.

6. *The British Colony of Basutoland and the Independent Kingdom of Lesotho*

After the disasters of the Cape's administration the first Resident Commissioner, Marshall Clarke, and his successors, Lagden and Sloley, knew better than to force the Sotho along paths which they had no wish to take. Rather they sought to keep the peace by winning the confidence of the chiefs and by building up the paramountcy. In this they were largely successful, especially after 1891, when Letsie died, and his son Lerotholi came to power.

Their policy was severely tested, however, in 1898, when Moeketsi, one of Masopha's sons, created a disturbance in the Free State, and when his father, always the most intransigent of the chiefs, refused to hand him over for trial. At Lagden's request Lerotholi enforced obedience, but only after fierce fighting in which fifty-five men were killed. Masopha's pride was broken, and he died a few months later.

There were still minor disturbances from time to time, usually because long-established chiefs reacted violently when the latest scions of the royal house were placed above them in their own areas. In general, however, the Sotho were at peace and were content. During the Anglo-Boer War they remained loyal to the Crown, with the unimportant exception of Joel Molapo in the north, and during the First World War they provided 1,400 men for the Native Labour Corps.

When Lerotholi died in 1905 he was succeeded by his son, Letsie II; and when Letsie II died in 1913 he was succeeded by his younger brother, Griffith, who enjoyed a relatively quiet reign until his death in 1939. Throughout this period progress was slowly being made in the fields of health and education. The latter was financed mainly by Christian missions, the French Protestants now finding themselves in competition with the Roman Catholics and, to a lesser extent, with the Anglicans. Agricultural output was increasing, and soon the country had added wool and mohair to its already existing exports of grain and livestock. Equally important, it was receiving an even larger income from its labourers in South Africa, many of whom were now employed at the gold mines on the Rand. Such was the prosperity of the country that in the early years of this century it was sometimes referred to as a model colony.

Yet even then it was possible, in theory at least, to foresee the plight in which the territory finds itself today. Soil erosion was first officially noted in 1902, and since that time, in spite of the efforts of devoted agricultural officers, many of the country's richest acres have been totally ruined. One of the main reasons for this has been the rapid increase in population. According to census figures it was 128,000 in 1875; 349,000 in 1904; 635,000 in 1946; and 970,000 in 1966. Although roughly half of the adult males are working in the Republic at any given time, the land available cannot support so many people without industrial development, in which possibilities are extremely limited, and without intensive agriculture, in which progress is extremely slow. Today the Sotho are no longer exporters of food, but importers, at least on balance, and the incidence of malnutrition is tragically high.

During the Second World War more than 20,000 Sotho volunteered to serve abroad, being encouraged to do so first by their Paramount Chief, Seeiso, who died young in 1940, and then by his widow, 'MaNtšebo, who acted as regent for his son. After the war, however, the nationalism which was soon to sweep away colonial rule in so much of Africa began to make itself felt in Basutoland too. Political parties and trade unions were formed, and, in spite of their parlous economic position, and in spite of being completely surrounded by South Africa, the Sotho demanded nothing less than full autonomy. In October 1966 the British Colony of Basutoland became the independent Kingdom of Lesotho.

II

THE SOCIAL AND CULTURAL
BACKGROUND TO THE PRAISE-POEMS

1. *Ecological Factors*

MODERN Lesotho, which is much smaller than Moshoeshoe's territory at the height of his power, has an area of approximately 11,720 square miles. Roughly three-quarters of the country is covered by the Maloti, the dark, basalt mountains which rise to over 11,000 feet in parts, and by the buttressing foothills, which send their spurs far out into the lowlands. These ranges are intersected by innumerable streams, which ultimately flow into the Caledon in the north and into the Orange in the south.

Before the 1870s the Maloti were inhabited mainly, if not exclusively, by small groups of San, who had found a refuge there as the Sotho had moved onto their hunting grounds below. Even in the mountains, however, game became scarce, and the San constantly irritated Moshoeshoe's people by plundering their horses and cattle. In 1871 and 1872 Molapo sent his sons Jonathan and Joel against them in successive campaigns. Their chief, Soai, was shot dead, several of their women and children were taken prisoner, and the remainder scattered and fled.

At first the Sotho used the mountains mainly for the pasturing of their cattle in the summer months, but in 1881 the Tlokoa of Lelingoana, Sekonyela's grandson, who had joined the Sotho rebels in the Gun War, were rewarded with the grant of an extensive area in what is now the Mokhotlong District. Subsequently, as the pressure of population built up in the lowlands, so more and more people went to settle permanently in the foothills and the Maloti, and today these areas support well over half of the country's inhabitants.

The so-called lowlands, which nowhere fall much below 5,000 feet, consist of valleys and plains, interrupted by sandstone hills and table-lands. Several of the smaller plateaux, encircled by precipitous cliffs and well endowed with grazing and fresh water, provided the Sotho with the defensive fortresses of which they made such effective use during the nineteenth century. In the valleys and plains the soil was once extremely rich and fertile, but it has now been impoverished by continuous cultivation and deeply scored by erosion.

Even so Lesotho is still one of the most favoured parts of southern Africa, for its rainfall is comparatively heavy, being in the region of thirty inches a year. Most of this falls in the summer months, from October to March, but often it comes in violent thunderstorms, and sometimes it is interrupted by lengthy droughts. By contrast the winter is dry and cold, with clear blue skies predominating by day and frosts by night. During these months the veld slowly turns from green to gold, and then to an empty, lifeless brown. The rivers dwindle to small streams, and the streams to chains of disconnected pools. In August and September the country is frequently swept by fierce dust-storms, and even on calmer days spiralling dust-devils may be seen teetering along until their cohesive rhythm is lost and they are dispersed. At other times the Maloti may be blanketed in snow, and on rare occassions even the lowlands may be covered.

Outside the district headquarters—and even these are not large—the Sotho tend to live in small, compact villages. In Moshoeshoe's time their usual habitation was the *mohlongoafatše*, a hut rather like a beehive in shape, with a basic structure of poles overlaid by thatching grass, and with a low tunnel jutting out from one side through which the occupants had to crawl when entering or leaving, and which was designed to thwart the attacks of wild animals. Today such huts are no longer seen, for they have given way to a variety of other styles. The most common of these is the *mokhoro*, or *rondavel*, which has cylindrical walls with doors and windows and a cone-shaped roof of thatch. Rectangular houses made of the local sandstone or of brick are also becoming increasingly popular, and so too are roofs of corrugated iron.

Most villages are situated on hillsides, for the valleys and the plains are given over almost entirely to cultivation. Before the *lifaqane* the Sotho concentrated very heavily on the growing of millet, from which they prepared several types of bread and porridge, as well as a light beer called *leting* and a strong beer called *joala*. Before the introduction of ploughs by Europeans they had to rely on their hoes alone, and so the area of land which they could break up was very limited; and there were the constant hazards of untimely frosts, devastating hailstorms, prolonged droughts and plagues of locusts. The possibility of famine could never be ignored. Maize was introduced by the Nguni invaders in the 1820s, and has now replaced millet as the Sotho's main crop. Moreover an increasing area is being placed under wheat, oats and barley, as well as under peas and beans.

Although agriculture is the mainstay of the Sotho's economy, their cattle have always been particularly precious to them. The reasons for this are in part social and political, although the latter at least are far less valid today than in the past. As will be seen, at one time a chief's power depended very largely on the size of his herds, and, although this is no longer the case, for many people cattle are still the main indicator of a man's wealth and status. Indeed the cow is almost revered among the Sotho. It is, as they say, *molimo o nko e metsi* (a god—or, more accurately, an ancestral spirit—with a wet nose), and once it was common for praise-poems to be composed for the best animals, and these would be chanted as they were brought back to the kraal in the evening. Large flocks of sheep and goats are also kept, and provide valuable exports in wool and mohair; and, in spite of the advent of the car, the bus and the lorry, horses, mules and donkeys are still very useful, especially in the mountain areas.

In the past, when cattle raiding was common, herding was the responsibility of the grown men. Today it is the task of the boys, for the danger of attack is negligible, and many of the men are working in the Republic of South Africa.

Another important prop of the Sotho's economy used to be hunting, for in Moshoeshoe's youth large herds of buck, zebra and quagga roamed through the valleys, hippopotami wallowed in the rivers, and lions, leopards, jackals and hyaenas infested the hills and the mountains. By the late nineteenth century, however, such game had almost been hunted out in the lowlands, and today it is rare even in the Maloti.

2. *Education*

Before the arrival of the missionaries it was the general practice for boys to be initiated when they reached the age of seventeen or eighteen years. All the youths who were ready to undergo this rite would live at the *mophato*, or initiation school, far away from their village, for about six months. Apart from being circumcised, they would receive military training and would be subjected to severe tests of physical endurance, and they would also be instructed in the history of their people and in the type of behaviour which would be expected of them as men. At the close of their training they would burn down the *mophato* and return to the village, where they would chant the praise-poems which they had composed for themselves. Normally, if the son of an important chief was among their number, they would thereafter form his personal regiment, and their regimental name would be derived from one of his praise-names. Moshoeshoe, for example, gave himself the name of Letlama (the Binder), presumably because of the way in which he would 'bind' his enemies and so bring them under control: his regiment was known as the Matlama (the Binders). Regiments formed at subsequent initiation schools might also be attached to the same man, but they would not be bound to him by such strong personal ties.

Girls too underwent a rite of initiation, but in their case the training was related to their future duties as wives and mothers.

Nowadays the initiation schools seem to be slowly disappearing, although they are still held from time to time in some areas. For most children their place has been taken by the mission schools, which receive financial assistance from the Government. Indeed Lesotho has a literacy rate of nearly fifty per cent, which is exceptionally high for an African country. Above the primary level, however, the results are not so impressive.

3. *Warfare*

After initiation the young warriors were expected to prove their manhood, and before the *lifaqane*, and indeed for many years afterwards, they generally did this by cattle-raiding. Sometimes a few adventurous individuals would set out, sometimes as many men as could be mustered. They would each be armed with a bunch of long spears, a knobkerrie and a light, oxhide shield, and normally they would approach the enemy's herds under cover, relying partly on surprise to achieve their ends. Occasionally the opposing herdsmen would have been warned of the attack, in which case they would have been specially reinforced and would offer a spirited resistance; but more often they would be taken unawares, and would then retreat to their village and sound the alarm. Thereupon all the able-bodied men available would join together in pursuit of the raiders and their plundered stock. If the warriors of two chiefdoms clashed they would hurl their spears at each other from a distance; but if they went on and came to grips at close quarters they would rely equally on their knob-kerries.

Moshoeshoe's Sotho never adopted the large oval shield and the short heavy stabbing spear of the Zulu, nor did they copy their strict military discipline. But they did make use of the battle-axe, which was introduced into the Caledon valley by the Tlokoa and was wielded at close quarters, together with the knobkerries and spears. More significantly, they were quick to realize the value of the Kora's horses and guns, and by the early 1840s they were probably the best-mounted and best-armed chiefdom in southern Africa. Even so most of their guns were old flintlock muskets, and after 1851 the restrictions imposed by the British and the Afri-kaners prevented them from procuring arms and ammunition through legitimate trade. It was mainly because of the disparity between their arms and ammunition and the Afrikaners' that they fared so badly in the second Free State war. After 1870, however, they were able to acquire excellent rifles at the diamond diggings, and they used these to good effect during the Gun War.

4. *Marriage*

Women were usually married almost as soon as they had been initiated, whereas men tended to wait until they were about twenty-four or twenty-five. Most marriages were arranged by the parents, and the central feature of the ceremony was the transfer of *bohali* (marriage cattle) from the groom's family to the bride's. Polygamy was common, especially among chiefs, some of whom had as many as sixty wives, or even more. For a commoner to have many wives was a symbol of wealth and standing. For a chief it was more besides, for these women enabled him to provide the hospitality that was so essential for maintaining his popularity and power. Moreover, since they were almost invariably the daughters of other chiefs, their presence at his home strengthened both the loyalty of his subordinates and the friendship of his neighbours.

Today, for several reasons—social and religious, but mainly

economic—polygamy is rapidly dying out. The payment of *bohali*, however, is still the general practice, even in church marriages.

5. *The Position of the Chief*

Chieftainship in Lesotho may be likened to a pyramid in structure, with the Paramount Chief, now styled as the King, at the top; with his senior relatives and subordinates, now styled as Principal and Ward Chiefs, immediately below him; and with a host of lesser authorities at the base. Although the chiefs are still of considerable importance, their powers have been drastically curtailed over the last hundred years, firstly by the colonial authorities, and lately by the democratically elected Government.

Broadly speaking, the chief of each village may still indicate the land where his followers should grow their crops and pasture their cattle. In Moshoeshoe's time he also acted as a magistrate and arbitrator in all disputes that were brought before him, and the Paramount Chief had the right of decision in all matters affecting his people as a whole. Every chief could send his subjects on errands and summon them to *matsema* (working-parties) on his lands. He could also require firewood and thatching grass from them, as well as the skins of certain animals. His herds were constantly being augmented by court fines, by stray stock, and, in some cases, by booty. Individuals who disobeyed him were liable to be 'eaten up', that is, their stock would be seized, their houses burnt, and they themselves banished or killed.

Yet he was never a despot. On every issue he was bound to consult his advisers in the *khotla* (court), and on matters of outstanding importance he was expected to summon all his followers to a *pitso* (assembly) at which they could express their views with almost total freedom. Admittedly he was not obliged to follow either his counsellors' advice or his people's wishes, but he knew that if he consistently ignored them, then aggrieved and discontented individuals might well begin intriguing against him with a more popular member of his family, or might even desert him completely and join another chief. Moreover his control over his most powerful subordinates was never absolute, and there were innumerable occasions when the orders of a chief, even of Moshoeshoe himself, were openly defied with impunity.

Furthermore his powers and privileges were matched by his responsibilities. For example, his lands were cultivated by his followers, but with their produce he was expected to feed guests and paupers. His cattle were numerous, but most of them he was expected to entrust to his subjects under the *mafisa* system, whereby he himself retained ownership of them while their care-takers were allowed their milk. It was for this reason that the size of his following was largely determined by the size of his herds, and, although this is no longer true today, a commoner may still greet a chief with the words *Likhomo tseo* (Those cattle), which probably refer to the animals which were once expected from the chief's hands.

6. *Religious Beliefs*

The Sotho had a very strong sense of community with the dead. Their ancestors, they believed, were worthy of reverence, and, if neglected in any way, would visit them with misfortune. In times of crisis they could be looked to for encouragement and inspira-tion, and even for active assistance. At such times the chief was expected to intercede with his own ancestors on behalf of the people as a whole.

Today Christianity is the professed religion of more than half of Lesotho's inhabitants. The Anglican Church is flourishing, and the French Protestant Mission has given birth to the powerful and independent Church of Lesotho. Yet both churches have been outstripped by the Roman Catholics. In 1912 Griffith was ad-mitted to the Roman Church shortly before becoming Paramount Chief, and since then his successors at Matsieng have all been Catholics.

The adoption of Christianity has not always resulted in the abandonment of earlier beliefs. Indeed many Sotho see their convictions about their ancestors strikingly confirmed in the Christian doctrine of the communion of saints, and the outcome of such thinking is the sort of syncretism which is so well illustrated, for example, in the praise-poems of Seeiso.

7. *Witchcraft, Divination, Rainmaking and Medicine*

Misfortune, according to the Sotho, could be sent by the ances-tors, but it could also be sent by witchcraft. If this was so a diviner would be able to 'smell out' the witch, who would then be punished by a heavy fine, banishment, or even death. A diviner might also be called upon to provide factual information, such as the whereabouts of stray stock, or to give advice about a proposed course of action, such as a migration or a military campaign.

In times of drought rainmakers were in great demand, and some of them, no doubt through a mixture of sound observation, careful ambiguity and good luck, were reputed to be very successful.

The same man could combine the functions of a diviner and a rainmaker, and he could be a doctor as well. In this capacity he would administer medicines, not only for the curing of illnesses, but also for the attainment of certain desired ends. No doubt some of his medicines would be genuinely beneficial. The effect of others, however, could only have been psychological—for example, those medicines which were believed to give a man eloquence in court, or to render him invisible when cattle-raiding.

Each chief had his own doctor, who kept the medicines of the chiefdom in various horns. The ingredients of these were culled from many sources. The hairs from the base of a bull's horn, for example, were believed to impart strength, and various organs cut from the bodies of slain enemies were believed to impart bravery. (It was only when wars ceased and the bodies of enemy warriors were no longer available for this purpose that the notorious medicine murders began.) Such ingredients would normally be burnt down into ashes and mixed with fat, and the medicines so prepared would then be ready for their various uses. Some, for example, would be given to boys in the initiation school or to warriors about to set out for battle, and they would be administered by being rubbed into light incisions in the flesh. Others would be smeared on pegs which would then be driven into the ground near the village in order to protect its inhabitants against misfortune.

Today belief in witchcraft is still strong, although witchcraft itself has long since ceased to be a punishable offence. Although full advantage is taken of the medical facilities provided by the Government, Sotho doctors relying mainly on traditional medicines are also widely consulted. Divination and rainmaking, however, are very much on the decline.

III

THE PRAISE-POEMS IN SOTHO LIFE

1. *The Poet*

THE French missionary, Casalis, who first arrived in Lesotho in 1833, has given the following account of the way in which praise-poems were composed during the early years of his residence there:

> The hero of the piece is almost always the author of it. On his return from war he cleanses himself in the neighbouring river, and then places his lance and his shield in safety in his hut. His friends surround him, and beg him to relate his exploits. He recounts them in a high-flown manner. He is carried away by the ardour of his feelings, and his expressions become poetical. The memory of the young takes hold of the most striking points: they are repeated to the delighted author, who ponders over them, and connects them in his mind during his leisure hours.[1]

Casalis is correct when he states that in most praise-poems the hero is the author. The exceptions, however, are particularly important, for they are the praises of certain chiefs, which were composed for them by their more gifted retainers, who thus became known as their *liroki* (sing. *seroki*) (praise-poets). Some chiefs, it is true, preferred to compose their own, and were highly respected for doing so. 'Nowadays the chiefs of the Sotho are praised just like cattle', one chief remarked to us, with obvious contempt; 'but', he added, with equally obvious approval, 'Chief Maama and Chief Lerotholi used to praise themselves.' Chiefs who rely on *liroki*, however, sometimes justify this by pointing out that self-praise is no recommendation. In several cases, such as those of Posholi and Lerotholi, praises appear to have been composed both by the chief and by some of his followers, and then to have been jumbled together.

For the more recent *lithoko* there is nearly always external evidence in the form of oral tradition to indicate whether a poem,

---

[1] *The Basutos* (1861), pp. 328–9: translated from *Les Bassoutos* (1859), p. 346. These lines are based on a similar passage in the same author's *Études sur la langue séchuana* (1841), p. 53.

or a part of a poem, has been composed by a chief himself or by one of his followers. For the earlier *lithoko* such evidence is usually lacking, and the internal evidence of the poems themselves is often inconclusive. Occasionally a poet may indicate his own position in such a way as to reveal that he is someone other than the chief. For example, in the praises of Posholi (iii. 44–6) he refers to himself and others as watching the lightning's rays clothing the mountain of Sekonyela. Since the lightning here is Posholi, the composer of this stanza at least must have been someone else. But although such clues are perversely common in the more recent *lithoko*,[1] they are extremely rare in the earlier ones.

It might be thought that the use of the first person singular to refer to the chief, outside his own quoted speeches, would indicate that he himself was the poet; that the use of the second person singular would indicate that it was one of his *liroki*, and that so too would the use of the third person singular. This assumption may be set out as three propositions, and it will be seen that the first, when suitably amended, can provide a useful guide, but that there are so many exceptions to the second and third that they serve no useful purpose.

(1) *If the chief is referred to in the first person singular, outside his own quoted speeches, then he himself is the poet.* To this proposition there are two types of exception, neither of them common.

First, a *seroki* may, in his imagination, temporarily identify himself with the chief. For example, in the praises of Griffith, which are known to have been composed by his *liroki*, the following line appears:

> Now I, 'MaNthe's son, became angry.
> (Griffith, ii. 153)

Similarly, in the praises of Seeiso, which are known to have been composed by George Lerotholi, there is the following stanza:

> Now it is that these troubles are begun,
> Being caused by Molise and my uncle,
> In particular I mean by Sekhonyana.
> They console me by disputing, Koena,
> They'd like to seize hold of my father's authority!
> (Seeiso, ii. 55–9)

---

[1] See, e.g., the praises of Lerotholi Mojela, line 15; Seeiso, i. 65–6; Moshoeshoe II, lines 57–8.

Further examples of such identification may be found in the praises
of Seeiso, i. 136–42; iii. 85–91; and iii. 102–5. Other passages,
however, which at first appear to be similar examples, e.g. in the
praises of Posholi and Lerotholi, may well be fragments of poems
composed by chiefs which have been embedded in poems composed by their *liroki*.

Second, a chief may chant praise-poems which have been composed for him by one of his *liroki*, and in doing so may transpose
them from the third person to the first. This, however, does not
happen very often, and there are no known examples of it recorded
in this volume.

In view of these exceptions, however, this first proposition must
obviously be amended. The most that can be argued is that the
frequent use in a poem of the first person singular to refer to a
chief, outside his own quoted speeches, is very strong evidence
that he himself composed at least substantial passages in that poem.

(2) *If the chief is referred to in the second person singular, then the
poet is one of his* liroki. Exceptions to this proposition are very
common, and they usually take the form of exhortations which the
chief addresses to himself. For example, in one of Maama's
praise-poems, which is known to have been composed by the
chief, he says:

> Maama, strike, that the Young Vultures may strike,
> That Sethobane and RaPontšo may strike,
> That the Dogeaters may stab them with spears!
>
> (Maama, ii. 89–91)

And again:

> Son of Letsie, stopper of the oxen,
> Stop the oxen as they run below Qeme:
> . . .
>
> (Maama, iv. 73–4)

He may also use the second person with the indicative mood, as
in the following example:

> In surpassing 'Matšoana you've excelled,
> You've surpassed Sethobane and RaPontšo!
>
> (Maama, ii. 40–1)

No doubt the second person singular may also be used in this way
with the interrogative mood, although there are no certain
examples of this in the present volume.

(3) *If the chief is referred to in the third person singular, then the poet is one of his* liroki. There are two types of exception to this proposition, both extremely common, and they may be regarded as the converse of the exceptions to the first rule.

First, a chief who composes his own praises may frequently refer to himself in the third person, especially when using metaphors. In the first praise-poem of Maama, for example, there are many passages like the following:

> A man's been devoured by Letsie's Vulture,
> He's been devoured by RaSenate's Young Vulture,
> The Vulture of Sekhobe and Makhabane,
> The child of the heavenly lightning, Maama the Kindler of Fires.
> (Maama, i. 16–19)

Second, praise-poems composed by a chief are often chanted by his followers. Sometimes they merely introduce them with the words 'Chief So-and-So says', and then leave them unchanged in the first person. Sometimes, however, they transpose them wherever necessary from the first person to the third. In several cases, therefore, we have two versions of the same lines, one in the first person and the other in the third. In the famous praises in which Moshoeshoe gave himself his name, these two versions are as follows:

(a)   It is I, Moshoeshoe, the Barber from Kali's,
              The Shaver who's shaved off RaMonaheng's beard.

(b)   It is he, Moshoeshoe, the Barber from Kali's,
              The Shaver, he's shaved off RaMonaheng's beard.[1]

Similarly one may compare the praises of Maama as chanted by the chief himself with the same praises as chanted by Mr. Kolobe Moerane, a commoner at the village of Chief Molapo Maama, in November 1968.[2] The differences between the two versions are best illustrated by the following extract:

(a)   I, the young cub, have been sired by the strong,
              And so I'm a mighty warrior:

---

[1] The first version is taken from D. F. Ellenberger's *Histori ea Basotho, Buka ea Pele* (1917), p. 107, the second from the same author's *History of the Basuto* (translated by J. C. Macgregor, 1912), p. 107.

[2] The first version was recorded by Chief Molapo at his father's dictation for Mangoaela's collection, and is reproduced in this volume. The second version we recorded on tape.

I was sired by bulls that were strong,
I've been sired by Peete and Mokhachane;
I was sired by Libe, the child of Matlole,
And Mohato, Thesele's boy.
   RaMatiea, go and report,
You who like taking news,
Go and inform Letsie,
   . . .

(b)   The young cub, he's been sired to be strong,
And so he's a mighty warrior:
He was sired by bulls that were strong,
He was sired by Peete and Mokhachane;
He was sired by Libe, the child of Matlole,
And Mohato, Thesele's boy.
   He says: 'RaMatiea, go and report,
You who like taking news,
Go and inform Letsie,
   . . .'

(Maama, ii. 59–67)[1]

As far as is known, the praises of chiefs and warriors, being inspired mainly by war, have been composed only by men and never by women. At one time almost every adult male Sotho was able to compose and chant his own *lithoko*, although only a man of outstanding ability would become a *seroki* for his chief. He would be drawn to this task partly by the material rewards which he could expect; partly by the prestige which he would gain; partly, perhaps, by genuine personal devotion, for many *liroki* are known to have been close and loyal adherents of their chiefs, and to have fought alongside them in their regiments; and partly, no doubt, by the sheer pleasure which he derived from it. In this century several chiefs have held competitions for the best praises composed in their honour, and have invited men from all over the country to take part.

Today, for reasons which are indicated below,[2] there are very few *liroki*, and, almost without exception, those who still practise the art are relatively uneducated men. Indeed we know of no *liroki* who are highly qualified teachers, top-level civil servants, or full-time ministers of religion, for, it seems, such men have been

---

[1] Differences between the two versions, other than the change in person, may be attributed to lapses of memory.

[2] See p. 32.

educated out of the culture in which the *lithoko* thrive, and the tasks of composition and chanting are now alien to them.

Although *liroki* were once highly esteemed among the Sotho, their names appear to have been quickly forgotten. For example, we found it impossible to discover who had composed the *lithoko* of Moshoeshoe's brothers, Makhabane (died 1835) and Posholi (died 1868), or of his sons, Letsie (died 1891) and Molapo (died 1880); while the names of the *liroki* of his grandson, Jonathan Molapo (died 1928), are now remembered only by a few elderly inhabitants of the Leribe District. Generally praises are designated, not by the name of the man who composed them, but by the name of the chief whom they extol; and no doubt the poets themselves would have regarded this as correct and fitting.

2. *The Occasions of Composition*

According to Casalis, praise-poems were 'inspired by the emotions of war or of the chase'.[1] But in none of the poems recorded either by himself or by anyone else are there any but incidental references to hunting, and it would appear that, until the end of the nineteenth century at least, most poems were inspired by war and were composed during periods of leisure and reflection in the aftermath of battle. Although Moshoeshoe lived until 1870, the last event mentioned in his *lithoko* is the war against the Kora in 1836, for this was the last occasion on which he fought in person.[2] And similarly the only incident which is described in the praises of Letsie II is the war with Masopha in 1898, for this was the only fighting in which he took part. Moreover it is significant in this context that the poets have devoted so much attention to events which occurred when the warriors returned home. Mokhachane, for example, tells how his followers were surprised by his own tardy return after he had been captured by the enemy, and how the more malevolent among them grumbled that he ought to have been killed; and Molapo's *seroki* complains about the way in which the plundered cattle were distributed after the campaign against the Thembu in 1835.

In this century, however, the Sotho have been involved in only two major conflicts, the First and Second World Wars, and even in

---

[1] *The Basutos*, p. 328. Cp. the same author's *Études*, p. 53.

[2] The reference may be found, not in the poems reproduced in this volume, but in that recorded by Casalis in his *Études*, pp. 63–7.

these very few of the leading chiefs have taken an active part. For most *liroki*, therefore, wars have been replaced as the normal stimuli for composition by crises in internal chieftainship disputes, for these often give rise to much the same emotions. Towards the end of Griffith's praises, for example, the poet refers to the quarrel which broke out between the chief and his brother, Letsie II, on the death of their father; and, in the praises of Seeiso, George Lerotholi refers time and time again to the main confrontations in his dispute over the succession with his brother Bereng. But Lerotholi also makes use of other themes—Seeiso's accession to the paramountcy, for example, and his visit to the British High Commissioner in Pretoria—and during Seeiso's brief reign (1939–40) he was almost beginning to assume the functions of a Poet Laureate, composing praises to mark important state occasions. Later, in his praises of Seeiso's son, Bereng, who took the title of Moshoeshoe II, he not only commemorated state occasions, such as Bereng's accession to the paramountcy and his wedding, but also composed poems of a more general nature, describing, for example, the chief's appearance, his religious faith, and the difficulties which he had experienced in his youth. Similarly the praises composed for the chief by David RaMaema, which are published here for the first time, cannot be said to have been inspired by any particular event or events. For praises of this nature, of course, no occasion is required, and they are very different in character from the war-inspired compositions of the nineteenth century.

3. *Chanting*

Initially praise-poems would be chanted by the man who composed them, and this is reflected in the dictionary definition of a *seroki* as a 'poet, one who composes or recites praises'.[1] In the poet's absence, or after his death, the same *lithoko* would be chanted by others who had heard and memorized them, often with unintentional variations and omissions, but very rarely with deliberate additions.[2]

Lithoko were most commonly chanted at *lipitso* (assemblies),

[1] All dictionary definitions quoted in this volume are taken from the *Southern Sotho–English Dictionary*, by A. Mabille and H. Dieterlen, reclassified, revised and enlarged by R. A. Paroz (Morija, 1961). This will be referred to simply as 'Paroz'.

[2] The only poem in this volume to which additions are known to have been made is the third poem of Moshoeshoe I.

usually before business was conducted, but sometimes afterwards
as well, and at *matsema* (work-parties), as the people rested after
labouring on the chief's lands. Often, however, a *seroki* would rise
early in the morning, make his way to the court, and there begin a
recitation which might last several hours; and all the men in the
village would be aroused and go to listen to him. Or sometimes, by
way of announcing his arrival, he would chant his chief's praises
as he approached his court. Similarly, when one chief visited
another, one of his *liroki* would begin reciting his *lithoko* as he
entered his host's village. Less dramatically, allusions to chiefs
and warriors in everyday conversation would be enlivened by
snatches from their praises, and there were many other circumstances in which the poems, or parts of them, would be heard.
Chief Jonathan Molapo, for example, would often feel moved to
recite his own praises as he sat in court with his men, usually
because something which had been said had reminded him of the
turbulent events to which they alluded. And if he saw some boys
misbehaving themselves in the village he would say: 'Where were
your fathers when . . .'—and then begin chanting.[1]

Today praises may still be heard at *lipitso* and *matsema*, though
not very often, and fragments of them may still be quoted in
ordinary conversation. But no *seroki* would think of waking up his
neighbours in the early hours of the morning; no one would chant
lithoko in order to announce his arrival; and any chief who recited
his praises in an endeavour to put young boys to shame would be
dismissed as an amiable eccentric.

One of the earliest accounts of an occasion on which praises
were chanted has been left by the French Protestant missionary,
Théophile Jousse. In 1868, as he and the High Commissioner, Sir
Philip Wodehouse, were travelling from Thaba Bosiu to Leribe,
they heard the sound of celebrations coming from the village of
Lesaoana, Moshoeshoe's nephew. When they went near to see
what was happening, they found the chief and his warriors per-
forming what appears to have been the *mokorotlo*, or war-dance.
At least, Jousse describes how they were standing in a circle,
with their spears, knobkerries and shields, and how they were
singing and stamping rhythmically on the ground.

The bravest [he continues] come out from the ranks, one after another,
and, as they walk, they chant of their own exploits. When one of them

[1] Information from Chief 'Mako Moliboea Molapo, who knew Jonathan well.

has finished the other warriors strike up a chant of which these are the words: 'We're going to devour you, we're devourers of men.' If the hero is really a brave man they respond to his account with a chant of approval: if the contrary is the case a terrible din commences and lasts a good while; one can scarcely catch what is said, with everybody shouting out at the same time, but one catches phrases like this: 'You're only a braggart devoid of courage, all the praises which you've just uttered are pure lies alone.' And the hero goes back, somewhat embarrassed, into the ranks. When the courage of a hero has been acknowledged by the assembly, he then devotes himself to a simulated combat in which he certainly gives proof of agility. Alternately striking and warding off the blows of an enemy, he makes prodigious leaps, then, suddenly stopping, he strikes the earth with his spear and the assembly calls out in a deep, strong voice: Heu! Each blow of the spear indicates a victim of his courage and is received with a hui! Then, as he shakes his spear in the direction where he has killed his enemies, the assembly answers him with dreadful 'ha's, which are repeated according to the number of deaths. After this pantomime, the hero goes back into the ranks, and another begins.[1]

Another account of the chanting of *lithoko* has been given to us by Chief Molapo Maama, who was often present when his father, Maama Letsie (died 1924), the celebrated warrior of the Gun War, regaled his followers with beer and meat after they had been working on his lands. At such times everyone in the village would be happy and relaxed, and would look to their chief with an up-lifting sense of gratitude and devotion. Perhaps the men would sing the *mokorotlo*, itself a deeply moving experience, and then Maama would rise and call for silence: '*Tsie, lala*' (literally, 'Locust, go to sleep'). Taking up his weapons, he would begin chanting his own praises, and the people would listen in rapt attention. At first he would walk slowly and recite carefully, but gradually he would quicken both his movement and his delivery, until after a while he would be almost trotting and would be chant-ing half as fast again as normal speech. As he moved around some of his old comrades in arms would follow him, occasionally patting him on the back and calling out: '*Ke ne ke le teng! Ke ne ke le teng!*' ('I was there! I was there!'). Listening to his exalted language, with its pulsating rhythms and its evocation of a glorious

---

[1] T. Jousse to E. Casalis, 20 May 1868, in file entitled 'Lessouto: 1867 janv.–1869 janv.' in the Archives of the Paris Evangelical Missionary Society (here-after P.E.M.S.), Paris. Translated from the French.

past, many of his followers would weep with emotion; and when at last he had stabbed the ground with his spear, there would be deafening shouts and whistles from the men, and long, trilling ululations from the women. Then the *lithoko* of Moshoeshoe and Letsie would be chanted, perhaps by Maama himself, perhaps by one of his followers; and after that some of his warriors might come forward and recite their own praises. So the festivities would go on into the night.

Nowadays it is most unusual to see a warrior striking the ground with his spear—an action known as *ho tlala*—or pointing it towards the scene of his opponent's death, for only those who have actually killed in battle have the right to do this. And it is equally unusual to hear a chief praising himself, for most are content to listen to their *liroki*, and to interject occasionally with the cry: '*U tseba 'na! U tseba 'na!*' ('You know me! You know me!', i.e. 'You know that what is being said about me is true!'). Moreover many *liroki* stand still when praising a chief, and even argue that it is wrong to move around except when praising oneself. But for all this it is still possible to witness spectacles which are not very different from those described by Jousse and Molapo Maama.

4. *Functions*

For the Sotho, war was the supreme test of manhood. For a chief, however, it was more besides, for it was also the supreme test of his leadership, and by boasting of his courage and success he was in effect recommending himself to his people. Similarly, when a *seroki* praised a chief, he was not merely showering him with personal flattery: he was also presenting him to his followers as a leader worthy of their loyalty and support. It was partly for this reason that he always chanted in public, and that he always insisted on being heard, often prefacing his recitations with the cry: '*Thea tšebe u mamele*' ('Pay heed and listen').

In some passages the poet merely draws attention to the chief's physical beauty. In the following stanza from the praises of Letsie II, the chief is likened to a ratel and to a guinea-fowl, both of which are greatly admired for their colouring:

> RaLetšabisa, the chief, begets,
> He's begotten a ratel with a beautiful colour.
> The child of the chief is a bright-coloured guinea-fowl,

The child of the chief is a wonderful monster,
He's just like a guinea-fowl hopping to the veld!
(Letsie II, lines 14–18)

And Griffith, in his praises, is compared with the moon, with the stars, and with the dawn:

He was like the moon that appears o'er snowy mountains,
He was like the stars of the morning when they appear,
Appearing at Makholo, in the mountains,
Appearing at Kokobe, at 'Malifatjana,
A rosy dawn that vies with the Pleiades.
(Griffith, i. 35–9)

More significant are those allusions which link the chief with his relatives, both past and present; with his comrades in his regiment; and with the places of his home. Most of these allusions are of the type that Kunene has classified as 'eulogues of associative reference'. Moshoeshoe, for example, is described, *inter alia*, as the child of Mokhachane; one who has cattle killed for the Koena; the Chooser of the people from Kali's (an ancestor); the comrade of Shakhane and Makoanyane; the father of Mohato (i.e. Letsie) and Masopha; the husband of Mokali and RaNtheosi; the man of Kholu (his mother); and the Lion of the Binders (his regiment). Similarly his brother Posholi is described, *inter alia*, as the Lion of Mangolo and Mangolonyane (two hills near his home); the young chief of Makhabane (his brother) and his people; the husband of Nkopi and 'MaBotle; and the Hungry One of the Claws (his regiment). And in the praises of Lerotholi Mojela such allusions are piled one on top of the other as he is referred to as:

The Crocodile, the otter of Tšakholo, the child of the mighty chief,
The Crocodile, the otter of your family, Seeiso,
Of the family of Nkoebe and Maama,
Of the family of Thaabe and Sekhobe,
Of the family of Peete and Mokhachane,
Of the family of Moholobela and Theko,
Of the family of Masopha and Lepolesa,
Of the family of Sempe and Mohlakana!
(Lerotholi Mojela, lines 46–53)

In many passages the association is established, not through eulogues, but through what may loosely be termed the narrative.

Relatives, friends and the places of home must naturally be mentioned in any account of a chief's exploits, but in many instances they appear to be introduced solely for the purpose of emphasizing the chief's connection with them. This is particularly true of references to ancestors in later poems. The following three examples are taken from the praises of Lerotholi (the son of Letsie I, not Lerotholi Mojela), Seeiso and Bereng (i.e. Moshoeshoe II).

(1)   The child resembles Chief Posholi,
By his voice you'd say he was RaMathalea,
                              even when giving commands,
When saying that RaNneela should give medicines for binding,
That with them he should bind the various peoples;
And that RaMahlolela should give him medicines
                              for making his enemies blind.
                                        (Lerotholi, v. 37–41)

(2)   The child of the bulls of the Beoana, Seeiso,
          Was begotten by hardy bulls,
          He was begotten by Griffith and Letsie,
          And so it was that he became a leopard.
          He was begotten by Api and Makhaola,
          By Marakabei and Teko,
          By Tau and Motsarapane,
          And so it was that he became a leopard!
                                        (Seeiso, i. 1–8)

(3)   When first he was born, the Chief Bereng,
          Trumpets were heard to sound afar off,
          At Thaba Bosiu a paean was begun,
          The tenor was sung by RaLetšabisa,
          The bass was taken up by Chief Moshoeshoe.
                                        (Moshoeshoe II, lines 8–12)

In building up these associations the poet is deepening his audience's awareness of itself as an historically continuous community, with a powerful attachment to its land, and with a proud tradition that is embodied, above all, in its chief, the heir and descendant of the great rulers of the past. The names of his relatives and comrades are clustered around his as if to support and strengthen him. Resplendent in his own glory, he can yet receive added lustre from theirs. The poet is also reminding his listeners that they are part of a community that consists of both the living

and the dead, for the ancestors are still thought of as being some-
how present, inspiring their descendants by their encouragement
and constantly reminding them of their duty. This is why it is so
important that their praises too should be chanted; and it was not
merely by chance that at Maama's village, for example, the praises
which followed his own were those of Moshoeshoe, his grandfather, and of Letsie, his father.

Equally important are eulogies of the chief's character and
actions, for, apart from ennobling him in the eyes of his followers,
they also have the function, as Cope has pointed out in his dis-
cussion of Zulu praises, of bringing about 'conformity to the
approved modes of behaviour'.[1] Thus, for example, when a
seroki praises a chief for being brave in battle, he is in effect
preaching the cause of military valour. Conversely, when he
ridicules the chief's enemies for running away, he is warning his
listeners against being cowards themselves. Indeed, in very
exceptional circumstances, he may even criticize a chief for a lapse
or failure.

Since the *lithoko* of the nineteenth century were inspired mainly
by war, 'the approved modes of behaviour' with which they are
concerned are almost exclusively military. Moreover such has been
the strength of this tradition that the same is true of most of the
twentieth-century *lithoko*, in which the various chieftainship disputes are depicted almost as battles, and the chiefs themselves are extolled as great warriors. In general, of course, a chief is expected to
strike hard at his enemies and to afford his own followers a sure
defence. Masopha, for example, is praised for the part which he
and his men played in an attack on the Mpondomise in 1861:

> As the battle caught light and burned,
> And became almost a fiery blaze,
> In went the falcon of Mokhachane,
> In went the falcon, the bird of prey,
> This bird of prey of my master.
> As it went in its eyes were glaring,
> Its teeth were bared in its open mouth,
> Its teeth were bared in its gaping mouth;
> As it entered it spoke to the Hawks,
> Saying to the dogs: 'Devour them, they're there!'
> (Masopha, iv. 45–54)

[1] T. Cope, *Izibongo: Zulu Praise-Poems* (1968), p. 31.

And Joel Molapo is praised for his uncompromising resistance during the Gun War:

> Mohato's Protector, Mokhachane's Tough Warrior,
> Fortress of the old, of the men and of the children,
> Of the people who remain at the ruins!
> If you hadn't been brave, Moshoeshoe's Tough Warrior,
> Your family's village wouldn't be here.
>
> (Joel, i. 1–5)

No chief is openly criticized for cowardice. It is still widely believed, however, that, had he wished to do so, Moshoeshoe could have saved his brother, Makhabane, who was killed in the Sotho's third campaign against the Thembu in 1835, but that instead he deliberately abandoned him; and, given this background, it may well be permissible to detect a veiled accusation in the tragic and beautiful lines which close his praises on this occasion. He has brought grief and distress, says the poet, and the cattle which he has plundered should not be allowed to mingle with the Sotho's herds.

> Black white-spotted ox, though you've come with gladness,
> Yet you have come with grief,
> You have come with cries of lamentation,
> You have come as the women hold their heads
> And continually tear their cheeks.
> Keep it from entering my herds:
> Even in calving, let it calve in the veld,
> Let it calve at Qoaling and Korokoro.
> To these cattle of our village it brings distress,
> It has come with a dirge, a cause of sadness.
> Thesele, the other one, where have you left him?
>
> (Moshoeshoe I, ii. 25–35)

In struggles against outsiders restraint and reconciliation are not commended, even in the praises of those chiefs who were most noted for these qualities, although there is a striking exception to this in the praises of Moshoeshoe:

> Lay down the stick, son of Mokhachane,
> Sit down:
> The village of the stick isn't built,
> 'What can you do to me?' doesn't build a village;

> The village that is built is the suppliant's, Thesele,
> Great ancestor, child of Napo Motlomelo,
> Protective charm of the Beoana's land.
>   (Moshoeshoe I, iii. 18–24)

In other words, Moshoeshoe should not take up a stick against his
enemies, and ask them contemptuously: 'What can you do to me?'
Instead he should beg them for peace, and in this way his village
will prosper. But the reference to the chief as 'Great ancestor'
almost certainly indicates that this stanza was not composed in the
aftermath of war, but was added to the chief's praises some time
after his death—almost the only instance in which such an addition
is known to have been made.

Such pacific sentiments, however, are by no means uncommon
in poems which relate to civil wars and internal chieftainship disputes, for on such occasions the *seroki*, like most men, is often
torn by conflicting emotions. He champions the cause of his chief
and delights in his victories, but at the same time he is distressed
by the suffering of his kinsmen on the opposing side, and may
even advocate a reconciliation. Joel's *seroki*, for example, stands
fully behind his chief in his struggle against Jonathan, but begs
him to be merciful and magnanimous:

> You've scolded, it's enough, Mighty Warrior,
> People aren't beasts, Mighty Warrior,
> They're Tickets[1] from the village of your father:
> Speak with them a little, and leave them alone.
>   (Joel, i. 271–4)

And similarly, when the dispute between Lerotholi Mojela and
his brother Molapo has been settled in Lerotholi's favour, his
seroki points out that his people, the Makaota, have returned to
their allegiance, and begs the chief not to be angry with them any
more:

> Go slowly, tortoise of the land:
> They're here, the Makaota have returned!
> Speak with your heart, Nkoebe's kinsman,
> Let your heart return to its home, Chief!
>   (Lerotholi Mojela, lines 148–51)

Of a chief's virtues in times of peace—of his justice, industry
and humour, for example—almost nothing is heard. True, there

---

[1] For this term, see the praises of Lerotholi, v. 32, p. 150 below.

are many allusions to his generosity, but in effect these are allusions to his prowess in war, since he could not afford to be generous unless he had successfully guarded his own stock and plundered that of others. Even when cattle-raiding ceases the ideas of wealth and generosity continue to be coloured by those of military success and bravery. It is only in the later *lithoko* that one may catch glimpses—though no more—of what the Sotho expect of their chiefs in the everyday conduct of affairs. Seeiso, for example, is warned that he must be gentle and even-tempered with his followers;[1] and Moshoeshoe II is asked not to appropriate lands for his own use, but to leave them for commoners to plough.[2]

Today, as the traditional patterns of Sotho life are being steadily broken down, and as the powers and prestige of the chieftainship are being inexorably whittled away, the *lithoko*'s importance for the ordinary Sotho is rapidly declining. They are neither composed nor chanted as commonly as in the past. Very few men can remember more than a few lines, and fewer still can chant them effectively in public. Even at Matsieng, the home of the King, there is not a single *seroki*.

But while the *lithoko* are being forgotten by the ordinary villagers, the rise of nationalism and the advent of independence have given them a new significance for the more educated Sotho. Formerly these people tended to look to the cultural heritage of their colonizers for their inspiration: now they are looking more to their own. Living within the framework of southern Africa's racial conflict, they are intensely proud of their history, and in particular of their resistance to European pressures during the lifetime of Moshoeshoe and during the Gun War, and they see in the *lithoko* a vivid and dramatic record of these struggles, a record, moreover, which still has a powerful message for them today. The titles of the newspapers of the three main political parties tell their own story. One, that of the governing party, is *Nketu*, a praise-name of Moshoeshoe. Another is *Makatolle*, a praise-name of Masopha. The third is *Mohlabani*, 'The Warrior', and on its cover page are two lines from the praises of Lerotholi:

> Take your shield, hold it firm, son of RaSenate,
> You see that your fatherland is going.
>
> (Lerotholi, i. 5–6)

---

[1] See, e.g., iii. 130–41, 153–7.   [2] Line 60.

IV

AN ANALYSIS OF THE PRAISE-POEMS

1. *Theme and Structure*

THE subject of every poem is the hero, whether he be a chief or a warrior, and the aim of the poet is to praise him for what he is and for what he has done. To this end apostrophe and exclamation are interwoven with narrative, and the resultant composition is intermediate between the ode and the epic.[1]

The *lithoko* may be divided into stanzas. In the absence of rhyme and consistent metre, these are no more than units of meaning, which, although varying considerably in length, normally contain between four and six lines. In almost every stanza the focus is upon the hero, who dominates the foreground, while supporting and sustaining him in the background are his kinsmen and comrades. In some his physical qualities are displayed: in others he is seen in action. In some he appears in his own person: in others he is transformed by metaphor or simile. In some he is encouraged: in others entreated. In some he is congratulated: in others cautioned. In most we see him as if present ourselves: in a few we see him through the eyes of others. Occasionally he moves into the background, and we are shown instead the consequences of his actions —the discomfiture of his enemies, perhaps, or the rejoicing of his followers. The poet may even address these people, jeering at the former, or reminding the latter of their good fortune. But the allusion to the hero's excellence, whether direct or indirect, is almost invariably clear and unmistakable.

Initially, when chanting *lithoko* after a campaign, the *seroki* would consistently present his stanzas in a particular order. Since he would be telling his audience what the chief had done, this order would be determined, in part at least, by the requirements of the narrative. Indeed many of his stanzas would be merely fragments of a story, and would only become fully meaningful when com-

---

[1] Cp. the comments of G. P. Lestrade in his chapter on 'Traditional Literature' in I. Schapera (ed.), *The Bantu-Speaking Tribes of South Africa* (1937), pp. 295–6.

bined with other such fragments to form a coherent sequence. Many other stanzas, however, while alluding to what had happened, would be complete and satisfying units on their own. Moreover the *seroki*'s dominant concern would be to praise the chief, not to recount a story, and so he would often turn aside from his hero's exploits and expatiate instead on his beauty, for example, or his ancestry; and most stanzas of this type too would need no introduction or continuation. No doubt the position in the poem of all these independent stanzas, as they may be termed, would in some measure depend on the *seroki*'s aesthetic preferences, but it is not always easy to see how these were determined.

The poem with the clearest and most logical over-all structure is that which was composed for Letsie II after he had fought in the campaign against Masopha in 1898. The *seroki* begins by introducing his subject, rather like a composer stating his theme, and Letsie is fulsomely praised with reference to his character, his home, his parentage and his beauty (lines 1–25). Then comes the narrative. News is brought to the chief's village of Masopha's rebellion (26–9). He sets out (30–1) and attacks (32), but suffers a humiliating reverse (33–44). He passes a watchful night (45–7), and complains of the insolence of Masopha's followers (48–9). On the following morning he speaks with his counsellors, and his men awake heavy-eyed (50–3). He attacks once again, and this time inflicts terrible losses on Masopha's warriors (54–67), who flee, and then come in to beg for peace (68–76). Letsie is still angry (77–80), but the poet begs him to be merciful (81–2). Before he has time to reply, Masopha surrenders Moeketsi, the man who has been largely responsible for the disturbance (83–6). Letsie remains to bury Masopha's dead, for they had been his own subjects (87–90), and he had come, not to wage war, but to punish (91–4). Now the poet is triumphant. The people from Matsieng are like a cloud of dust rising in every pass (95–7): Masopha's followers have been rendered impotent (98–9): Letsie has gained his revenge (100–1). Finally, on a quieter note, he advises the chief to refresh himself and to return home (102–3).

There were many campaigns which, like that against Masopha, consisted of a single expedition, and there are many poems which, like that of Letsie II, relate solely to such a campaign. The fourth poem of Masopha, for example, describes his raid on the Mpondomise in 1861; the second poem of Jonathan relates to his attack on the San of Soai in 1871 or 1872; and the first poem of Griffith tells of the part which he played against Masopha in 1898. None of these poems is as logical and straightforward, or as balanced and well-rounded, as Letsie II's, but they all present a fairly coherent and intelligible narrative.

Many wars, however, were more protracted than that against Masopha and consisted of many different engagements scattered over a very wide area. Such, for example, were the wars with the Free State in 1858 and in 1865–8; such was the Gun War in 1880–1; and such was the civil war between Jonathan and Joel, which began as part of the Gun War and continued spasmodically for several years afterwards. In poems inspired by these wars the *seroki* does not dwell exclusively on any particular encounter, but moves rapidly from one aspect of the conflict to another. And much the same is true of the more recent *lithoko* which have been inspired mainly by protracted chieftainship disputes. Consequently, although there may be an occasional passage of narrative, there is no complete story that runs its full course from beginning to end. Indeed many of these poems consist almost entirely of independent stanzas.

In some poems the ordering of these stanzas appears to be mainly arbitrary. In others, with a little imaginative effort, it can be seen to follow a definite train of thought. In the fifth poem of Lerotholi, for example, the *seroki* opens with the bold statement that the chief is the father of unending debts, i.e. he is the cause of endless troubles, for he has refused to allow the surrender of the Sotho's guns to the Cape authorities (lines 1–3). In the following stanza he says that these debts will eventually be paid by Lerotholi's ancestors, i.e. that these troubles will eventually be settled with their assistance, and in this context he refers specifically to Moshoeshoe (4–8). This leads him to the consideration that Lerotholi is very similar to Moshoeshoe in both his courage and his kindness (9–13); and, with this in mind, he begs the chief to make peace for the sake of those whose fathers have been killed in the war (14–16). Still longing for peace, he warns the 'Boers' (i.e. the Cape forces) that they should leave Lesotho (17–19), for, as he relates in the following stanzas, Lerotholi is a water-snake that has devoured a Boer, he is a cliff from which a Boer has fallen (20–8). Indeed Lerotholi has killed so many of his enemies that the poet fears to name them all lest the chief's kinsmen become jealous, for they would then go and cause more trouble for the Sotho with Sprigg, the Cape's Prime Minister (29–36). Then, in a steadier mood, he compares Lerotholi with his great-uncle, Posholi, and alludes to the support which he expects from his relatives, Lesaoana and Masopha (37–41). Finally, in a most effective exclamatory conclusion, he refers to him as the tongs of the chiefs, i.e. as the warrior who can always be sent into the heat of battle, when the spears are bouncing up and down like maize-cobs on the boil (42–3).

Unlike Letsie II, Lerotholi took part in several wars, and praise-poems were composed for him, perhaps by several different *liroki*, on each occasion. Towards the end of his life some of these were no doubt being chanted in uninterrupted succession, though not necessarily in the correct chronological order, and it would be impossible to tell from the manner of the performance alone where one poem ended and another began. Certainly this is the way in which they are sometimes chanted today, and so too are the praises of other chiefs, such as Maama, Jonathan and Griffith. Nevertheless by the time Mangoaela recorded seven of them in or shortly before 1919 their stanzas had not been confused together, and each poem could still be distinguished and set apart. In this particular case—and perhaps the same is true in other cases too—the division of the *lithoko* into the original poems is not to be attributed to Mangoaela's judgement alone, for it is known that he collected these praises from more than one individual. But it is most unlikely that he consulted seven different individuals and that they each gave him a single different poem.

In the praises of Lerotholi's contemporaries, however, Mangoaela found that the original poems were in some cases beginning to lose their separate identities as their stanzas became intermingled. The first three poems of Maama, for example, as Mangoaela recorded them, relate exclusively to the Gun War; but the fourth, which begins as a simple narrative account of the Moorosi War, is interrupted by stanzas which relate, apparently, to the Gun War (38–40, 55–66), and is rounded off by a passage relating to an incident in the second war with the Free State (67–81). Similarly Jonathan's first poem is concerned mainly with his protracted struggle with Joel, but contains one stanza relating to the capture of Langalibalele in 1873 (209–13), and three which

relate to the second Free State war (218–31). His second poem
describes his attack on the San of Soai, and so does his third,
although its first stanza relates to his dispute with Joel. This dispute forms the sole topic of his fourth and final poem. In Joel's
lithoko the first poem relates mainly to his prolonged conflict with
Jonathan, but also contains references to his capture of Langalibalele's cattle (116–58, 223–50)[1] and the attacks on the San of
Soai (191–205). The second poem, too, relates mainly to the conflict with Jonathan, but also contains references to the second Free
State war (12–16, 48–50); the raids on the San (22–35, 51–60); the
capture of Langalibalele's cattle (67–70); and finally, it seems, a
dispute with the Khoakhoa (71–6). The third poem relates solely
to the attacks on the San.

The poems of Lerotholi and his contemporaries were all
recorded by Mangoaela within fifty years of their composition.
Not surprisingly he found that, on the whole, the praises of earlier
generations were even more confused. Indeed some of them, as
they appear in his collection, may fairly be described as *mélanges*
in which the narrative element has almost disappeared, and in
which it is often impossible to see any connecting link between one
stanza and the next. When a chief's *lithoko* consist of several such
mélanges one can only assume that each poem was recorded on a
separate occasion, for it is difficult to see why a continuous recitation should have been divided up in such a way.

One of the best examples of a *mélange* is the only surviving poem
of Lerotholi's father, Letsie I. In this the *seroki* alludes in turn to a
victory over Gert Taaibosch's Kora during the disturbances of the
Orange River Sovereignty (1–5); to an unknown incident involving Moroka's Rolong (6–9); to the Tlokoa's attack on Thaba
Bosiu in 1829 (10–13); to the Sotho's revenge in 1853 (14–17); to
an encounter in which a young Kora had a narrow escape (18–19);
to battles with certain Nguni groups in 1835 and 1836 (20–4);
to an obscure incident involving the Hlubi chief Mhlambiso
(25–6); to Letsie's superiority over some of his kinsmen in battle
(27–31); to the Sotho's victory over the Tlokoa in 1853, when
Letsie spared the life of Sekonyela's ally, Letlala, the chief of the
Siea, because some of his own followers were also Siea (32–8); to a
complaint, or so it seems, about the way in which the plundered

---

[1] The significance of some of these lines is obscure, but the most likely interpretation appears to be that which relates them to Langalibalele.

cattle were distributed after this battle (39–41); to Letsie's conduct in the fight itself (42–6); and finally, for the second time, to what appears to be a complaint about the sharing of the booty (47–9). Another good example of this type of *mélange* is the first poem of Moshoeshoe I.

Clearly these *mélanges* are made up of stanzas which originally formed part of several different poems, which have survived because they are particularly memorable, and which have finally been strung together in sequences that owe nothing either to considerations of chronology or to a coherent train of thought. The arbitrariness of these sequences may be indicated by their variability. For example, the praises of Mopeli, Moshoeshoe's brother, were published both in *Leselinyana* on 9 April 1915 and in Mangoaela's collection in 1921. In content the two versions are very similar, but in the ordering of their stanzas they are entirely different. Similarly at the present day one can hear many different versions of the praises of Moshoeshoe I. In November 1968 we recorded two of these. One was seventeen stanzas long, the other thirteen. Only five and a half stanzas were common to both. The fourth stanza in one poem appeared as the twelfth in the other; the eighth as the third; the eleventh as the tenth; the fifteenth as the ninth; the sixteenth as the fourth; and the first half of the seventeenth as the eighth.[1]

Some *liroki* have excellent memories, and one may still hear men chanting passages of 200 lines and more with only minor departures from the texts recorded by Mangoaela. Nor can they have learnt them from his collection, for some of them are completely illiterate, and only a few are even aware of his name. But the *liroki* hold no official positions in the courts of their chiefs, and there are no sanctions for accuracy. Lapses of memory are to be expected. What is significant, however, is that the consequent shortening and confusion of the *lithoko* appear to make no difference to the Sotho's enjoyment of them. They are not required to tell a straightforward story, but to praise a chief in beautiful and impressive language, and in this the *mélanges* of Moshoeshoe I and Letsie I are just as effective as the well-ordered poems of Lerotholi and Letsie II. We have asked many people which *lithoko* they like best, and why. The most popular appear to be those of Moshoeshoe, 'because he was our greatest chief and his praises are full of

---

[1] The first version is published as Moshoeshoe I's third poem in this volume.

history'; Masopha, 'because the *lithoko* are the poetry of war, and Masopha was a great warrior'; and Maama, 'because the language of his *lithoko* is so beautiful'. Some favoured Lerotholi's *lithoko* for similar reasons. No one mentioned the name of Letsie II, and no one, with the exception of one highly educated civil servant, suggested that the coherent development of a poem might be a reason for liking it.

2. *The Eulogue*

Among the Sotho the same man may be referred to by several names, but usually he is best known by that given to him at birth. This is not always the case, as is shown by the following examples from the family of Moshoeshoe I. His grandfather, who was called Motšoane by his parents, became better known by a nickname, Peete; his eldest son, Mohato, became better known by his initiation name, Letsie; and his nephew, Lesaoana, became better known by his teknonym, RaManella (or RaManehella), 'Father of Manella'. Indeed the name Moshoeshoe itself is a praise-name which the chief adopted as a young man: at birth he had been called Lepoqo.

In the *lithoko*, such familiar appellations are commonly replaced by other references, some of which are used so often with regard to certain chiefs that they are known as their praise-names. Kunene, who applies the term 'eulogue' to all these references, including the praise-names, has provided a very detailed study of their nature and their formation. The classification of them which follows is based very largely upon his, and in general we use the same terminology.

(1) Descriptive eulogues. These are simple descriptions of the chief's character, condition or physique, unadorned by any figures of speech. Makhabane, for example, is 'the young man of Kali'; Masopha is 'the warrior of great cunning'; Maama is a 'wild man with a stallion'; Seeiso is 'The new chief of the youth'; and Moshoeshoe II is 'The tall chief of Thakhane and her kin'.

(2) Metaphorical eulogues. In these the chief is identified with something or somebody else, usually an animal, a bird, a reptile or a plant; a part of the body, an inanimate object or a natural phenomenon; or a character or monster from a folk-tale. Moshoeshoe I, for example, is a lion, a hyaena and an enormous cleft in the rocks in which cattle and people disappear; Mopeli is a tawny cow,

a crocodile and a watery abyss in which his enemies are drowned; Lerotholi is a koodoo, a bull and a serpent of the waters; Maama is a vulture, a whirlwind and the black bird of lightning; Jonathan is a buffalo and the right eye of Lerotholi; Lerotholi Mojela is a tree with ample branches providing shade for his followers; and Griffith is *Kholumolumo*, a fabulous monster which devoured almost every living creature.

Normally a metaphor is sustained throughout the stanza in which a eulogue of this type appears, but sometimes the *seroki* is content merely to indicate that his hero possesses the qualities which the eulogue suggests, and is unconcerned with problems of consistency. This may be illustrated by the following two stanzas, the first of which is taken from the praises of Masopha, and the second from the praises of Jonathan:

(a)   The prop of the village of Mohato, Masopha,
            Stood up and looked out for Sekonyela,
            He, the warrior of great cunning.
                                    (Masopha, i. 56–8)

(b)   Cow of great villages, white-faced cow,
            Don't make light of the dispute:
            You see that we people have gone.
                                    (Jonathan, i. 151–3)

Mixed metaphors also abound, as in the following remarkable stanza from Griffith's praises:

        Peete's nephew is just like a wildebeest,
    He's just like a lion, the Binder, he roars,
    When he jumps you might think him a leopard, the Koena!
    For the Crocodile in the face is his parents indeed,
    He resembles Peete and Mokhachane,
    The blacksmith of Mokhachane, the Binder,
    The painted hyaena of Moshoeshoe!
                                    (Griffith, ii. 79–85)

With even less regard for consistency the same chief is described as hail which rides on horseback,[1] while Mopeli appears as a crocodile with piercing horns[2] and Masopha, in lines already quoted, as a bird of prey which bares its teeth as it swoops in to attack.[3]

---

[1] The praises of Griffith, i. 11.   [2] The praises of Mopeli, iv. 9.
[3] The praises of Masopha, iv. 45–54.

Moreover some eulogues are so common, or are applied so frequently to a particular chief, that their metaphorical nature is forgotten. For example, Lerotholi is referred to as *Tholo*, Koodoo, with such familiarity that sometimes this eulogue has no more force than the name Lerotholi itself, and it may even be used with pronouns and concords of the first, or personal, class of nouns, instead of those of the ninth, to which it belongs. For example, the very first stanza of Lerotholi's *lithoko* reads as follows:

> *Mor'a Masututsane'a Mokhachane,*
> *Tholo ha a hlabane, oa sututsa,*
> *O qhoba ntoa ka mangole*
> *Lekena la RaNneko'a Bakoena.*

> The son of the Pusher of Mokhachane,
> The Koodoo doesn't fight, he pushes,
> He drives on the army with his knees,
> Lekena of RaNneko of the Koena.
>   (Lerotholi, i. 1–4)

In the second and third lines one would have expected:

> *Tholo ha e hlabane, ea sututsa,*
> *E qhoba ntoa ka mangole,*
> . . .

and this would have been translated:

> The Koodoo doesn't fight, it pushes,
> It drives on the army with its knees,
> . . .

(3) Deverbative eulogues. These are formed from verbs in ways which are unusual in the vocabulary of everyday speech. Most of them are narrative in effect, telling of what the chief has done, or of what has been done to him. Letsie, for example, is 'the repeller', because he once repelled the Kora of Gert Taaibosch, and 'the extinguisher of fire', because he once drove the Tlokoa from their capital village; Molapo is 'the Agitator', because he once caused an agitation among his enemies, and 'the weakener', because he weakened one of them. A few, however, allude to what the chief does habitually. Lerotholi, for example, is 'the people's provider', because he always provided them with food and drink.

(4) Associative eulogues. These link the chief with his relatives, his friends and the places of his home, and, as noted above, are

classified by Kunene as 'eulogues of associative reference'. Moshoeshoe I, for example, is 'the comrade of Shakhane and Makoanyane'; Letsie is RaLerotholi, 'Father of Lerotholi'; Molapo is 'the comrade of the child of Mokhachane'; Masopha is 'the brother of Mpinane'; and many a chief is referred to as *Mokoena*, i.e. as a member of the Koena (Crocodile) clan. It is more common, however, for an association to be established through a qualifying phrase added to one of the other types of eulogue. Thus Moshoeshoe is 'the Binders' tawny lion'; Posholi is 'the young chief of Makhabane and his people'; Letsie II is 'The lightning of Likhoele'; and Griffith is 'The deluge of Mokhachane... The hail of the little daughter of Nkoebe'. Moreover the other types of eulogue may in themselves be associative in function. Thus, when Mopeli is called *Koena* (Crocodile) he is being linked with all the other members of the Koena group; and when Maama is called *Nong* (Vulture), he is being linked with all the other members of his regiment, the *Manong* (Vultures).

The importance of eulogues may be indicated by statistics alone. In Letsie I's *lithoko*, for example, there are 16 different eulogues in 49 lines; in Letsie II's 23 in 103 lines; and in Lerotholi Mojela's 65 in 177 lines. In many passages two, three or even more eulogues are chanted in succession in apposition to each other, while occasionally they appear to be used as exclamations which have no syntactical relationship whatsoever with the words around them.

3. *The Stanza*

It has already been noted that stanzas vary considerably in length. While roughly half of them begin with a eulogue or a group of eulogues (including some which are made up of nothing else), about a third have eulogues only in the middle or at the end, and about a sixth have no eulogues at all. Clearly the stanza is flexible in form, and there are no prescribed rules which it must invariably obey.

Yet there is one particular structure which is discernible, either complete or in part, in roughly one fifth of the stanzas in the nineteenth-century *lithoko*, and which is of special interest in that it is very similar to that analysed by Cope in the Zulu praises.[1] It consists of a statement, a development and a conclusion, and

---

[1] T. Cope, *Izibongo: Zulu Praise-Poems*, pp. 50 et seq. Cope's analysis is based partly on the work of Raymond Kunene.

normally it is based on a deverbative or a metaphorical eulogue. Stanzas of this type may be termed 'structured stanzas', the word 'structured' being used here to indicate conformity, to a greater or lesser degree, to a readily discernible common pattern.

It is easy to see how the deverbative eulogue provides the foundation for such a stanza. It is usually introduced into a poem, almost invariably with other names, in the opening line or lines of a stanza. This initial presentation of the eulogue may be referred to as the statement. Although in most cases it relates to one of the chief's exploits, in itself it tells us very little of what happened. For example, from the description of Moshoeshoe I as the Shaver one may conjecture that he once swept off someone's cattle, but no more. In the following line or lines, therefore, it is normal for the incident to be described in greater detail, with the chief being the subject of the cognate verb, i.e. the verb from which the eulogue has been formed. Thus Moshoeshoe, to use the same example, is described as the Shaver 'Who's shaved off RaMonaheng's beard', i.e. as the warrior who has captured RaMonaheng's cattle. This amplification of the narrative may be termed the development, and its link with the statement through the cognate verb may be described as morphological. In the conclusion one is told of the consequences of the chief's action. RaMonaheng's beard

> '... hasn't yet grown,
> It will go on growing for years!'

i.e. he is still poor, and it will be a long time before he fully recovers. The whole stanza may therefore be presented in the following way:

Statement: The Chooser of the people from Kali's, the Shaver,
Development: Who's shaved off RaMonaheng's beard,
Conclusion: And as for growing, it hasn't yet grown,
                          It will go on growing for years!

(Moshoeshoe I, i. 38–41)

The following three examples of structured stanzas are taken from the praises of Makhabane, Posholi and Letsie I respectively.

(a)

Statement: Motlou is the Milkers' warrior whom the
                                                    enemy can never observe:
Development: The unobserved warrior makes RaLeotoana
                                                    unobservant,

Conclusion: He made him unobservant, he abandoned his ox,
                 He left it with a gash on its shoulders!
                                (Makhabane, lines 27–30)

(In this stanza the conclusion really begins halfway through the third line.)

(b)

Statement: The shooter at the rabbit, Sekhonyana's kinsman,
Development: Shot at the rabbit in the midst of the Thembu,
                 He shot as he jealously guarded his ox.
Conclusion: When he shoots, the country becomes his!
                                (Posholi, iv. 94–7)

(c)

Statement: Father of Lerotholi, the Locusts' repeller,
Development: Repeller, repel, please, the wretched little Bushmen,
                 Repel Gert's Bushmen, and make them return.
Conclusion: The Bushmen ran, they left their round buttocks,
                 Their tortoise-like buttocks they left behind!
                                (Letsie I, lines 1–5)

In this last example the development, although an injunction in form, is narrative in effect, for, as the conclusion makes clear, Letsie has already done that which is being required of him. This is not uncommon. The following stanza, for example, is taken from the praises of Maama:

Statement: Son of Letsie, stopper of the oxen,
Development: Stop the oxen as they run below Qeme:
               I stopped those with down-bent horns in the veld,
Conclusion: They were taken to the Frog, to Moshoeshoe.
                           (Maama, iv. 73–6)

Usually, as in the quotations given above, the structured stanza is four or five lines long, and each element is one or two lines long. There are, however, many exceptions to this. For example, the following stanza from Molapo's praises consists of six lines, and its development consists of three:

Statement: Crocodile of the Senders,
               Crocodile, 'MaSekhonyana's refuser,
Development: You refused when the nation was being assembled,
               When your nation of the Beoana was being gathered
                                   together,
               When Monyeke and RaQethoane were being gathered
                                     together:

Conclusion: Then Nkakole and his people crossed the Caledon.
(Molapo, ii. 5–10)

And in the following stanza from Lerotholi Mojela's *lithoko* the whole structure is compressed into two lines, the first providing the statement, and the second the development, such as it is, and the conclusion:

Statement: Mohato's defender, Lekena,
Development and Conclusion: The Koena defended: we were saved.
(Lerotholi Mojela, lines 37–8)

As indicated above, it is common for deverbative eulogues to be followed by structured stanzas, for they provide a natural foundation for them. In this, however, they are not unique, for similar foundations may be provided by metaphorical eulogues, especially those which appear to require amplification, either because they are so bold and unusual, or else because they allude to a particular exploit, but only vaguely. Mopeli, for example, is described as a watery abyss that is full and a green lake in which people plunge. From this one may conjecture that some of his enemies have been killed in battle, but no more. In the following lines, therefore, the *seroki* is more explicit:

> The lake once made the Élite fall,
> It's made a hundred people fall:
> . . .

The Élite were a regiment of the Rolong chief, Moroka, and so clearly the reference is to the battle of Viervoet (or Kononyana) in which more than 100 of Moroka's warriors met their deaths, many of them by jumping in terror from the precipices of Viervoet mountain. In the final line of the stanza one is told of the outcome:

> There wasn't one who rose alive!

Once again, therefore, the stanza is made up of a statement, a development and a conclusion, but this time the link between the first two elements is not morphological, through the cognate verb, but metaphorical, through the sustaining of the metaphor.

Statement: The watery abyss is full, RaNtsubise,
He's a lake that's green, where people plunge;

Development:	The lake once made the Élite fall,
	It's made a hundred people fall:
Conclusion:	There wasn't one who rose alive!

(Mopeli, iv. 1–5)

Another example may be taken from the praises of Maama:

Statement:	The boom of Mokhachane, Maama,
Development:	When it thundered it scared the Ndebele:
Conclusion:	The hyaenas departed from the mountains,
	And the rabbits migrated in their hundreds.

(Maama, iii. 66–9)

Another from the praises of Jonathan:

Statement:	The extraordinary lightning of the Camp
Development:	Struck Qalo, it struck Sebothoane;
	It was everywhere suddenly, it struck Mathokoane.
Conclusion:	Burnt was the mountain, it was turned into ashes,
	Burnt were the pegs at the back of the house,
	Burnt were Hoatane and Kolojane!

(Jonathan, i. 50–5)

And another from the praises of Griffith:

Statement:	The Khomphoro bird of the Binders of
	Mokhachane
Development:	Flew and settled at the shop,
	Close to the village of Senekane:
Conclusion:	There it's been seen by the red-skinned Bushman.

(Griffith, i. 77–80)

Although the structure of these stanzas is essentially the same as that of those based on deverbative eulogues, there are two ways in which it has become slightly looser. First, in the examples quoted from the praises of Jonathan and Griffith the narrative flows smoothly from the eulogue, as the subject, to the verb, and so there is no pause between the statement and the development. Indeed the eulogue can hardly be said to be 'stated' or presented at all. This is common in stanzas based on metaphorical eulogues, but rare in those based on deverbative eulogues. Second, the metaphorical link is clearly less restrictive than the morphological, and so the development is more free.

There are many variations in the pattern, both with deverbative and with metaphorical eulogues. For example, in the following stanza from the praises of Masopha, the morphological link

between the statement and the development is maintained through
a pun on the verb *ho hlomella*, which can mean either 'to give arms
to' or 'to implant on':

> *Hlomellane oa Lioli, Masopha,*
> *Hlomella ba ha Senekane lehlaka,*
> *E tle ere ha ba ea mose,*
> *Ba ee ba le pepile!*

Statement: Imparter of arms to the Hawks, Masopha,
Development: Implant a reed on the people from Senekal's,
Conclusion: That when they go across the river
                          They go with it on their backs!

(Masopha, vii. 1–4)

Moreover when a deverbative eulogue indicates not only the
action, but also the object of the action, then the link with the
development may be formed by the repetition of this object
rather than by the cognate verb. There is an excellent example of
such a link in the praises of Moshoeshoe I:

Statement: The yellow cow of the regiments,
                                          the comrade of Shakhane
                          And Makoanyane, the one who set fire to the dust,
Development: The dust came out from the bowels of the earth
                          At the village of RaTšooanyane:
Conclusion: It was seen by RaTjotjose, the son of Mokhethi.

(Moshoeshoe I, i. 42–6)

The conclusion too may vary. In some instances it does not
indicate the results of the chief's action, but the reasons for it,
as in the following stanza from Lerotholi's praises:

Statement: Peete's warrior, Deliverer,
Development: Deliver the commoners and chiefs,
Conclusion: We commoners and chiefs are distressed:
                          . . .

(Lerotholi, iv. 18–20)

In others it may point to a contrast with the chief's action, as in
this celebrated stanza from Masopha's praises:

Statement: The one who digs open the passes that were closed,
Development: That had even been closed with Gert's little Bushmen!
Conclusion: Most, they've ascended those at the sides,
                          They ascended by the women's little passes,
                          They ascended at the 'push-me-up' pass.

(Masopha, v. 1–5)

In all these examples the variations are only slight, and the structure remains firmly intact; but as the variations become more drastic and extreme, so the structure becomes weaker, until eventually it is so loose that it is hardly discernible. The various stages in this progressive relaxation (which is not an historical process, of course, but merely a concept of analysis) may easily be illustrated.

It is very common, for example, for the conclusion to be completely omitted, as in the following extracts from the praises of Makhabane and Joel respectively:

Statement: The builder of the Great Chief's kraal, Clever Ones,
Development: He's built it with an ox, Motlou.
                                      (Makhabane, lines 38–9)

Statement: The son of Kholu, the mighty flood,
Development: The flood may overthrow the Khoakhoa,
                     It's overthrown Matela Tselanyane.
                                      (Joel, i. 61–3)

And in the opening stanza of Jonathan's *lithoko* the development is omitted, with striking effect:

Statement: The binder of the young cow for the Glarers,
Conclusion: Today as they milk it it stands!
                                      (Jonathan, i. 1–2)

Admittedly such omissions may occasionally be due to lapses of memory, but there can be little doubt that most of them reflect the poets' original intentions.

In the next stanza, which is taken from Masopha's praises, all three elements are present, but the conclusion, which gives reasons rather than results, appears in the middle of the development:

Statement: Defender of the family of Makhabane,
Development
   and Conclusion: Defend on the pass, for people are flying,
Development: Defend on the ridge at Rafutho's.
                                      (Masopha, vii. 15–17)

And the structure is even weaker in the following stanza, which is taken from Moshoeshoe I's *lithoko*:

Ram, butt, Kali of the Beoana,
Butt, the cowards are afraid,
They see when the darkness spreads.
                  (Moshoeshoe I, ii. 5–7)

It may be argued that the eulogues, 'Ram' and 'Kali of the Beoana', form the statement; that the repeated verb 'butt' forms the development; and that the rest of the stanza forms a variant conclusion in which reasons rather than results are indicated. But clearly the structure is beginning to break down, and the supporting argument is somewhat strained. Such arguments are even more open to objection in stanzas like the following, which is taken from Jonathan's *lithoko*:

> The lion, my men, has three lairs:
> It lies down at Tsikoane, it lies down at Leribe,
> It would also return and climb Qoqolosing.
> (Jonathan, i. 75–7)

Here it might be contended that the simple metaphor, 'The lion', forms the statement, that the rest of the stanza forms the development, and that the conclusion, as so often happens, has been left out; in which case one would be virtually committed to finding a structured stanza wherever a metaphorical eulogue is followed by any development in which the metaphor is sustained. But such an analysis would be misleading, for the structure has become so vestigial as to be irrelevant.

There are also a few stanzas which conform to the pattern of statement, development and conclusion, but which are not based on eulogues at all. Some of them, for example, open with a statement which merely indicates the chief's action, and which therefore provides the same sort of foundation as a deverbative eulogue. Thus, in one stanza in Masopha's praises, we are told that the chief 'listened'. The development is more informative, for it tells us what he heard:

> He heard the Koena's refusal
> When the cattle were being taken from Botha-Bothe,
> The cattle of the orphan of Mohato and his kin.

i.e. while still a child at Botha-Bothe he witnessed the Tlokoa's seizure of some of his family's herds. Finally the Tlokoa are warned that when Masopha becomes a man he will come and look for these cattle. The whole stanza may therefore be presented in the following way:

Statement: The heifer of the woman with light complexion,
                The child of the woman of Khoele listened,

Development: He heard the Koena's refusal
When the cattle were being taken from Botha-Bothe,
The cattle of the orphan of Mohato and his kin.
Conclusion: You should eat them and leave the bones,
When he grows up he will seek them.
(Masopha, i. 14–20)

There is a similar stanza in the praises of Posholi:

Statement: The brown lightning has just been called,
Development: It's just been called by the child of its master:
Conclusion: We saw it had come
When we saw that the places of meeting were blocked.
(Posholi, iii. 26–9)

In some instances the subject is not the chief himself, but someone else. In the following stanza, for example, which is also an
extract from Posholi's *lithoko*, the subject is one of the chief's
enemies. In the opening statement we are told that he 'wouldn't
listen', i.e. that he was stubborn; in the development we see the
form which this stubbornness took; and in the conclusion we see
its results:

Statement: A wretched Ndebele, Peeka's little son,
wouldn't listen,
Someone who hadn't even donned a penis sheath,
Development: Saying that the herds should cross the Orange,
and go over:
Conclusion: Yet they cross into the mouths of Those Who
Pull Out Spears!
(Posholi, iii. 13–16)

Stanzas of other types too can occasionally be fitted into the
pattern. The following quotations, for example, are from the
praises of Lerotholi and Jonathan respectively:

Statement: On the plain at Sepechele's a certain young man
raised the alarm and told others to raise it:
'Let the horses charge at the men from Sprigg's!'
Development: They ran, they trampled beneath their feet the men
of the Sparkling Soldier.
Conclusion: Your people you can recognize on the ground,
You can choose them from the corpses, for
they're dead!
(Lerotholi, iv. 32–6)

Statement: Look in the hollow and see,
Development: Look in the hollow at Lipohoana's,
                   Look at Pitsi's and RaMpai's:
Conclusion: A Nguni has died, a Sotho has died!
                           (Jonathan, i. 40–3)

Clearly the elements which make up the structured stanza vary considerably in length, content and form; they do not always appear in the same order; and the development and the conclusion may sometimes be omitted. Clearly, too, the weakening of the structure is a very gradual process, and it would be both difficult and unprofitable to try to determine the point at which it may be said to break down completely. No doubt certain broad criteria could be indicated, but in order to be fully comprehensive they would have to be hedged around with so many qualifications that they would cease to be useful as tools of analysis. For these reasons we merely indicate the nature of the structure, and draw attention to some at least of the many variations which may occur.

Stanzas of this type, especially those based on deverbative eulogues, become progressively less common after the Gun War praises—a development which is difficult to explain, but which is probably to be attributed to a change in aesthetic taste rather than to the general shift in subject matter from wars to internal chieftainship disputes.

4. *The Line and the Rhythm*

Lines, like stanzas, are units of meaning. Although there is no strict metre to which they must conform, most of them are of roughly the same length and contain either three or four stressed syllables. Some, however, contain two or five, and a few even contain one or six.

The fact that each line is a unit of meaning is naturally reflected in the *seroki*'s chanting, for either he pauses between one line and the next, or else he conveys the sense of division through his intonation or emphasis. The way in which he does this varies considerably, and depends mainly on the meaning of the passage rather than on any artistic conventions. In some lines, for example, he lengthens the last stressed syllable: in others he places a particular emphasis upon the first as he raises his tone.

Although normally the meaning is such that the division between lines is fixed and inviolable, this is not always so. For example, in the following passages from the praises of Maama two methods of division are possible. In both cases the first is that given by Mangoaela, and the second is that indicated in the chanting of Mr. Kolobe Moerane in November 1968:

(1) (a) From these wild beasts he took the heads,
          He took the skin of the lion and the leopard, and he said:
          'Today there is born a warrior!'

    (b) From these wild beasts he took the heads,
          He took the skin of the lion and the leopard,
          And he said: 'Today there is born a warrior!'
                                             (Maama, ii. 48–50)

(2) (a)   I've killed the florid redskin, the wretched little white man;
              I threw him to the ground.

    (b)   I've killed the florid redskin,
              The wretched little white man, I threw him to the ground.
                                             (Maama, ii. 54–5)

Moreover a marked caesura in the middle of a line may occasionally be so lengthened that it becomes in effect a division between lines. For example, the following passage from Jonathan's *lithoko* may be presented as three lines (as in Mangoaela's text, which is the first version given below), or as two (as commonly chanted today):

(a)   The Buffaloes' Buffalo flashed,
              The mouths of the mountains quivered,
              The plain thundered,
                    . . .

(b)   The Buffaloes' Buffalo flashed,
       The mouths of the mountains quivered, the plain thundered,
           . . .
                                             (Jonathan, i. 119–21)

The rhythm of the *lithoko* is irregular but magnificently effective. Unfortunately it is obscured for the English reader by Sotho's disjunctive orthography. Broadly speaking, the stress falls on the penultimate syllable of each word, but in the Sotho for 'Don't say', for example, '*U se ke ua re*', it is far from obvious that there is only one stress and that it is on *ua*. Presented conjunctively, this would be *Usekeuare* (the last *u* being pronounced as *w*), and the position of the accent would be apparent at once. In our English translations we have kept as close as possible to the rhythm of the Sotho, and, when recited at great speed, this will give the reader at least some idea, however pale and distorted, of the effect of the original.

5. *Poetic Qualities*

Two of the qualities most common in English poetry, namely rhyme and metre, are entirely lacking in the *lithoko*, and essentially, like free verse, they may be distinguished from ordinary speech by their rhythm. Without this it would be impossible for them to be chanted. Other distinctive features are their frequent use of eulogues, which has already been discussed, and their many and varied images, which have been illustrated in almost every quotation made.

Parallelism too is common, and is almost invariably effected through the repetition of words and phrases, or through the repetition of ideas through synonyms. Parallelism through the repetition of syntactical forms is no more common than in ordinary speech, except in so far as it is the concomitant of the other types of parallelism. Since this subject has been analysed in considerable detail by Kunene, our own treatment of it is very brief.

Parallelism through the repetition of words and phrases may be illustrated by the following lines from the praises of Griffith and Seeiso respectively:

> In every direction fled all the Koena:
> Some went down by Mokoallong,
> Some went down by Sefikeng.
> (Griffith, i. 55–7)

> He refused to listen when the letter was read,
> When the letter was read at the Meja-Metalana,
> . . .
> (Seeiso, i. 52–3)

Parallelism through the repetition of ideas by synonyms is exemplified in the following lines from Seeiso's praises, in which he is addressed as:

> Lover of Sempe's girl,
> Of the mother of Ntšebo, Seeiso,
> I mean, above all, of the woman, of Moipone.
> (Seeiso, i. 173–5)

In these lines 'Sempe's girl', 'the mother of Ntšebo', 'the woman' and 'Moipone' all refer to the same person, Seeiso's senior wife.

Both types of parallelism are often found together, as in the following passages from the praises of Griffith and Seeiso respectively:

> The Binders' comrade was enraged and said:
> 'Lying, deceitful runaway,
> Hurry, go and report,
> Put questions for me to the Chief to no purpose,
> Put questions for me to the father of 'MaNeo,
> Put questions for me to Lerotholi with care.'
>
> (Griffith, i. 24–9)

In these lines 'the Chief', 'the father of 'MaNeo' and 'Lerotholi' are all the same person.

> 'I opposed the placing of your junior brother,
> I opposed the placing of Chief Bereng,
> It was said that Bereng, though junior, should rule you.'
>
> (Seeiso, ii. 40–2)

There are many different patterns of repetition which occur, but the most common are those which are exemplified in the first two quotations in this section. In the first the repeated words appear at the beginning of each line:

> Some went down by Mokoallong,
> Some went down by Sefikeng.

In the second they appear at the end of one line and at the beginning of the next:

> He refused to listen when the letter was read,
> When the letter was read at the Meja-Metalana.

This second pattern is generally referred to as 'linking'. Both patterns occur frequently in structured stanzas based on deverbative eulogues, for in these the cognate verb may appear in the eulogue at the beginning or at the end of one line and then in the indicative or imperative mood at the beginning of the next.

Although less common than parallelism, alliteration and assonance are also used to good effect. In most instances, it is true, they may be attributed to the system of grammatical agreement in the Sotho language, whereby the concords which are used with a noun are often phonetically similar to its prefix. Thus, for example, Jonathan is described as '*Leihlo le letona la Lerotholi*' (The right eye of Lerotholi); and Joel is described as '*sekhohola se seholo*' (The mighty flood). In some instances, however, they are clearly contrived, as in the following lines from the *lithoko* of Moshoeshoe I and Lerotholi respectively:

> *Khomo e tšoana ea matsoai, ea matsoai, tšoanyane,*
> *Tšoanyane, tsoo u tsamaea, kea tla,*
> *Kea tla, ke u fihlele tseleng, ka mona ha Phokotsa.*

> Black cow of the salt, of the salt, black cow,
> Black cow, go on, I am coming,
> I am coming to catch you up on the way,
> > right here at the home of Phokotsa.
> > (Moshoeshoe I, i. 32–4)

> *Ngoan'a rangoane, Letlatsa, u tiee:*
> *U tiise thari, masoto a tiee.*

> Child of my uncle, Letlatsa, stand firm:
> Make firm the skin cradle with straps that are firm.
> > (Lerotholi, iv. 71–2)

In some passages natural and contrived alliteration and assonance are combined, as in the following lines from Mopeli's praises, which have already been quoted as a structured stanza:

> *Koekoelete e tletse, RaNtsubise,*
> *Ke letša le letala lea oela;*
> *Letša le kile la lihela Mangana,*
> *Le lihetse batho ba le lekholo:*
> *Ha hloka le ho tsoha ope a rula!*

> The watery abyss is full, RaNtsubise,
> He's a lake that's green, where people plunge;
> The lake once made the Élite fall,
> It's made a hundred people fall:
> There wasn't one who rose alive!
> > (Mopeli, iv. 1–5)

In other respects too the *lithoko* are poetic rather than prosaic. Normal word orders, for example, are often varied, with the inversion of the subject and the verb being particularly common. Furthermore the general style tends to be terse and compressed, with the long and complicated tenses in which Sotho abounds being used only rarely. Although this latter quality is due mainly to aesthetic considerations, in part it is determined by the nature of the line, which tends to be a short but self-contained unit of meaning, so that it is unusual for one line to flow smoothly into the next. Indeed most lines could stand as complete sentences in themselves, for the relations between them are seldom made explicit by the use of conjunctions. For example, in the following passage from Mopeli's *lithoko*, in which the chief is described as a crocodile that is not easily provoked, one would have expected an adversative conjunction like *empa* (but) at the beginning of the second line:

> It's unwilling to be provoked by foreigners:
> When they brandish their sticks, they call it.
> (Mopeli, ii. 24–5)

And in the following extract from Griffith's praises, in which the chief is described as a bull which drove away 'the bull of the Leopards', i.e. Moeketsi, the son of Masopha, the sense would seem to demand an adversative conjunction at the beginning of the fourth line, in which an allusion is made to Moeketsi's initial victory over Griffith's elder brother, Letsie:

> The bull stabs others in just the right spot,
> It's stabbed the bull of the Leopards in the shoulder,
> That of the Leopards has even fled:
> Still it is said that it's very courageous,
> That it hurled the other one over the rocks!
> (Griffith, ii. 273–7)

Two of the most common conjunctions in everyday speech, *'me* (and) and *empa* (but), hardly appear in the *lithoko* at all. (In some passages, including that quoted from Griffith's praises above, we have felt it necessary to add conjunctions to the English translations in order to make the meaning clear.)

Another aspect of each line's independence is the degree to which it may be inconsistent with the lines around it, for, just as the *liroki* rarely look at their subject from the same angle from one stanza to the next, so they may boldly alter their approach from one line to the next. Changes in person or in tense are extremely common. For example, in the following extract from Lerotholi's praises, the third person plural in the first line, which is a straight-forward statement, is followed by the second person singular in the second, which is addressed to the enemy:

> Now the aggressors have drawn in their claws:
> You provoke it, and from it you flee!
>
> (Lerotholi, iv. 65–6)

And in the following lines from Masopha's praises the perfect tense is followed by the past:

> The eagle has entered the cattle-posts of the Kora,
> It entered the Kora's and the Ropoli's,
> . . .
>
> (Masopha, i. 23–4)

Both types of change may be found in the following lines from Joel's praises:

> The crocodile fought against things that were mighty,
> The lion fights against regiments that are strange,
> Against Griffith and the Sparkling Soldier.
> You fought against Major Bell,
> The mighty champion from the Cape!
>
> (Joel, i. 17–21)

More striking still is the following stanza, which is taken from Masopha's *lithoko*:

> Son of 'MaMathe, you're a scorching hollow,
> You're a fire that burns those who light it:
> If the people from Jumba's were to sit in its warmth,
> The one who sat near it might get sore from burns!
> Jumba conveys his burns to the chief's,
> To the presence of Letsika and Seloanyana.
>
> (Masopha, iv. 73–8)

After referring to those who might sit by the fire, the poet tells us that Jumba, one man alone, has actually sat by the fire and has suffered accordingly.

Indeed *liroki* may often convey an account of what has happened by combining straightforward statements with hypotheses, questions, and, most commonly of all, exhortations and commands. In Posholi's praises, for example, one of his opponents is asked: 'How can you say we can fight in the hollow?'—but, as the next line indicates very clearly, they had already fought in the hollow, and Posholi had been victorious.[1] And in the opening stanzas of

---

[1] The praises of Posholi, i. 29–31.

Jonathan's second poem his expedition against the San of Soai is described mainly through a series of injunctions:

> Broad-nosed man from the Agitator's, go up,
> Hartebeest, go up the slope which we're climbing:
> Now things are different, you can't graze without clothing!
>   Crocodile, bow down as you go, servant of Josefa and Lerotholi:
> Go across streams that are full,
> Go across the Orange, go across the Seate,
> . . .

(Jonathan, ii. 1–6)

6. *The Praise-Poems and the Historian*

As a source of detailed historical evidence the *lithoko* are disappointing. They provide very little information which cannot be found in other sources—and these are copious for the period which they cover—and such information as they do provide is often incoherent and distorted. Nor is this surprising, for their primary aim is not to give a lucid factual account of what the chief has done, but to extol and praise him. They are not historical narratives, but poetry with historical allusions. In general, accuracy and clarity have been sacrificed for the sake of eulogy and aesthetic excellence.

The chief's role in events is often exaggerated. For example, the praises of Letsie II give the impression that his were the only forces that took part in the attack on Masopha, whereas in fact they were merely one contingent among several; and they also indicate that after the final battle Masopha entered into negotiations with him and begged for mercy, whereas in fact he dealt mainly with the Paramount Chief, Lerotholi. Similarly there are several chiefs today who are fulsomely praised in their *lithoko* for having killed countless Germans and Italians in the Second World War, but who readily admit that they never turned a gun against the enemy. Furthermore a chief may occasionally be credited with the achievements of his allies. In the praises of Maama, for example, it is clearly implied that he drove the Mfengu, Tokonya, from his home,[1] whereas in fact it was Masopha who did this. And Lerotholi is said to have burnt down 'Major Bell's', i.e. the camp at Hlotse Heights,[2] although it was Joel and other chiefs in the north who attacked the camp.

---

[1] The praises of Maama, iii. 66–76.   [2] The praises of Lerotholi, iv. 116.

Even when the facts are not distorted by praise they are often obscured by imagery. In 1873, for example, Jonathan secured the capture of the Hlubi chief, Langalibalele, and delivered him into the hands of the Cape authorities. This is how the incident is related in his *lithoko*:

> The Buffaloes' defiant one slaughtered the wildebeest,
> He chopped off its head and sent it to the chief's;
> He gave it to the Roan One and the Magistrate,
> To men who don't reward warriors:
> They might also have rewarded him even in Natal.
>
> (Jonathan, i. 209–13)

This stanza appears in the middle of a poem which deals mainly with Jonathan's dispute with Joel, and it is only the reference to 'the Roan One', i.e. to Captain Allison, the leader of the troops from Natal, which enables one to identify the allusion with any certainty. There are many other passages which cannot be elucidated at all. There are still *liroki* who can chant them magnificently, but when asked to explain them they simply shrug their shoulders and say: '*Ke lithoko feela*' ('They're just praises'), as if this were an explanation in itself!

For all this, however, the *lithoko* do occasionally cast a new light upon an incident, or provide valuable confirmation of other evidence. The stanza quoted above, for example, clearly indicates Jonathan's dissatisfaction with his share of the Hlubi's cattle, and is one of many in which disputes over plunder are made known. And the Moorosi War praises of Lerotholi and Maama clearly reveal, not only by their content, but also by their dull and almost prosaic style, the reluctance with which those chiefs fought on that occasion.

More valuable still, the *lithoko* are an extraordinarily faithful expression of Sotho attitudes and ways of thought in general. Much of our evidence about Sotho history is of Sotho origin, but in almost every case it has been produced with European susceptibilities in mind. Letters, for example, have been written to Europeans, and speeches have been made in their presence. The *lithoko*, however, have been composed for a Sotho audience alone, and this gives them a certain spontaneity and freedom. In reading them the European enjoys the rare privilege of being an unseen observer. Accuracy may have been sacrificed for the sake of eulogy, and clarity may have been sacrificed for the sake of aesthetic excellence, but at least nothing has been altered to satisfy the requirements of outsiders.

Notes on the Sotho Texts and the English Translations

The only eulogues with initial capital letters are praise-names. All such names are translated, except those which are used so often that they may be regarded as common and usual names for the chiefs concerned, and those for which it is difficult to find aesthetically pleasing translations which fit the *lithoko*'s rhythm. Thus we make no attempt, for example, to translate Jonathan's praise-name of Seoehla (a cow with down-hanging horns), a name which was given to him because his bow legs seemed to curve and hang downwards like the horns of such a cow; or Seeiso's praise-name of Tšoana-Mantata (I who fetch the black cow for myself).

Teknonyms are usually left untranslated, with the initial letters of both the prefix and the child's name being in capitals. Thus Moshoeshoe may be referred to as RaMohato (Father of Mohato), and Seeiso's senior wife may be referred to as 'MaNtšebo (Mother of Ntšebo).

Half-brothers and half-sisters are referred to as brothers and sisters respectively.

Unless the context indicates otherwise, references to Moshoeshoe and Letsie are references to Moshoeshoe I and Letsie I.

The word *Mokoena* (pl. *Bakoena*), which means 'a member of the Koena (Crocodile) people', is translated as 'Koena'. The praise-name *Koena* (Crocodile) is translated as 'Crocodile'.

Genealogical Table

The table on p. 62 is far from complete, and is designed merely to indicate the family relationships between the chiefs whose *lithoko* appear in this volume. The names of such chiefs are given in capital letters. The names of Paramount Chiefs are italicized.

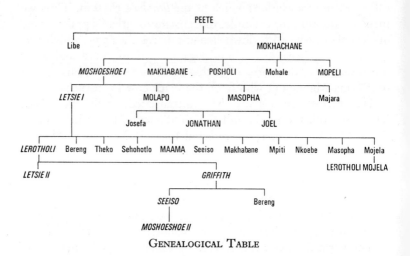

GENEALOGICAL TABLE

THE PRAISE-POEMS

1. *Peete*

Peete (*c.* 1734–1824) was the father of Libe and Mokhachane, and was the grandfather of Moshoeshoe. His family called him Motšoane, but because of the circumstances of his birth he was more generally known as Peete. His mother was the wife of Motloang, a junior Koena chief who was killed in battle while still young. According to custom she should then have gone to live with Motloang's younger brother, Mokoteli, and the children of their union would have been regarded as Motloang's. Instead she went to live with a Hlubi called 'Mualle. Their son, Motšoane, was still regarded as Motloang's, and in due course he was brought up at the village of Mokoteli and his followers. These people gave him the name of Peete to show their amusement at 'Mualle's attempts to speak Sotho, for to them his speech was an unintelligible stuttering, like 'peetepeetepeete'. (The ideophonic verb, *ho re petepete*, means 'to speak indistinctly'.) Subsequently he established his village at 'Mate in the valley of the Hlotse river. He never attained any prominence, and in 1824, when he must have been about ninety years old, he was captured and eaten by cannibals as Moshoeshoe and his followers were migrating from Botha-Bothe to Thaba Bosiu.

Only one stanza of his *lithoko* survives, and this has been recorded by Mangoaela. It relates to his dispute with a neighbouring Fokeng chiefdom, the Maotoana.

The hare's one which lives in a tough spot,[1] Motšoane,
It belongs to the school of 'Mate:[2]
It's the hare which the Little Feet[3] are always surrounding,
Dancing for its benefit the dance of men![4]

[1] i.e. Peete, like the hare, lives in a place which is difficult to attack.

[2] 'Mate was Peete's village, where, presumably, he lived with his regiment, the men who had gone through the initiation school with him.

[3] There is a play here on the name of his enemies, the *Maotoana*, which means 'Little Feet'.

[4] i.e. the Maotoana are always attacking him. Cp. Moshoeshoe's words to President Boshof in May 1858, when the Free State President had sent his commandos against the Sotho but had then been compelled to sue for peace: 'It is the custom in our country that when the people of a town go to dance in another town, the compliment is returned by the people of the visited town to

2. *Mokhachane*

Mokhachane (*c.* 1760–1855) was Moshoeshoe's father, and his home was Menkhoaneng, not far from 'Mate. He rapidly eclipsed his elder brother, Libe, and, by bringing the adherents of Mokoteli's descendants under his own control, he became known as *Morena oa Bamokoteli*, Chief of the Mokoteli. Thus he rescued his family from the obscurity into which it had fallen under his father, Peete. Although a shrewd and capable man, he yielded his authority to Moshoeshoe during the early years of the *lifaqane*, and thereafter lived under his son's rule until his death in 1855.

Parts of his *lithoko* have been recorded by Casalis in his *Études* (pp. 53–58), where he gives a French translation of a poem commemorating the chief's earliest exploits; by Tlali Moshoeshoe, who has recorded a *mélange* thirty-four lines long in his 'Litaba';[1] and by Mangoaela, who has recorded fifteen lines. Since Casalis does not provide the original Sotho, and since the 'Litaba' will be published elsewhere in due course, only Mangoaela's text is given here.

These lines relate to the time when Mokhachane returned to his village after a disastrous attack on his neighbours, the Qhoai Fokeng, in which several of his men had been killed and in which he himself had been wounded and taken prisoner. After some delay Moshoeshoe had ransomed him with thirty head of cattle, but by that time many of his followers had despaired of his life and were preparing to migrate.

The consistent use of the first person singular indicates that the author was almost certainly the chief himself.

> My mother-in-law 'MaQhoai[2] doesn't shave me,
> She's left me with blood on my head:
> Here is the blood, it clings to my forehead.[3]
> So let it be, I brought it on myself!
> 5   At the time when I first came out of the grave,[4]
> Coming from Molise's, the son of RaNkhoana's,[5]

---

the town of the visitors, and agreeably to this usage, we were going to invade the Free State in every direction, and to burn everything before us.' (G. M. Theal, ed., *Basutoland Records* (1883), ii. 364.)

[1] See p. viii, fn. 1, above.

[2] Mokhachane's elder brother, Libe, had married a Qhoai wife, and he could refer to Libe's mother-in-law as his own.

[3] The chief's head had been cut in the fight, but 'MaQhoai had not tended the wound. Line 3 has been added to Mangoaela's text from a variant of the same passage given by the historian Sekese in an early edition of a school reading book. The Sotho is:

Mali ke ana, a ntiisa phatla.

[4] He had been away from his people so long that they had believed him dead.

[5] Molise was a man of the Qhoai chiefdom.

I arrived when my people were about to leave
And were already destroying the walls of the huts:
I arrived when they were putting the necklace of the orphan on my
                                        child Ntsieli.[1]
They said: 'Greetings, you who have come from the spirits!   10
Why did you go and tarry among the spirits so long that now we
                                        are leaving?'
    The sorcerers, RaMorakane and Peo,[2]
Said: 'Why was he captured?
Indeed his head should have been cut off
And so become medicine for initiates,[3] Conqueror,[4]   15
And so be Sekhaba 'Mapule's.'[5]

3. *Moshoeshoe I*

Moshoeshoe I (*c.* 1786–1870) may justly be regarded as the founder of the
Sotho chiefdom, and so closely were his fortunes bound up with his
people's that the details of his life may be gathered from the brief account
of Sotho history which is given in the Introduction. Although the last of
the many wars in which he was involved ended only in 1868, just two
years before his death, the last incident to which his *lithoko* allude is his
successful attack on the Riet River Kora in 1836, for this, apparently,
was the last occasion on which he fought personally.

    There are three main sources for these *lithoko*.

    (1) In his *Études* (pp. 63–7) Casalis has given a French translation of
what he calls a *Chant de Guerre de Moshesh, en mémoire d'une victoire
remportée sur les Griquois*. It is forty-nine lines long, and probably refers to
the victory over the Riet River Kora mentioned above. Although Casalis
translated this poem within a few years of its composition, and although

---

[1] Ntsieli was Moshoeshoe's elder sister. After her marriage and the birth
of her son, Tšoeunyane, she became better known as 'MaTšoeunyane.
[2] Casalis has recorded a passage which is very similar to this final stanza.
According to him 'Ramokané et Péo' were wise old men who shook their heads
over Mokhachane's rashness in his first exploit, for they feared that he would be
killed and decapitated. It seems that this idea has been distorted a little in being
related to this subsequent incident. The word *baloi* (sorcerers) need not be taken
literally, but may refer merely to persons who were not well disposed towards
Mokhachane.
[3] i.e. his head should have been used in the preparation of medicines for boys
in the initiation school.
[4] One of Mokhachane's praise-names.
[5] According to information given personally by Mangoaela to Damane,
Sekhaba was the Qhoai's leading doctor, and as such would have been responsible for preparing the initiates' medicines.

his title suggests that it is concerned with one incident alone, in fact it has already been confused with some stanzas relating to Moshoeshoe's campaign against the Thembu in 1835. Unfortunately the original Sotho has not been recorded, and very little of it can now be recovered.

(2) Mangoaela has recorded two poems, and these appear as poems (i) and (ii) below. The first is a *mélange* of stanzas drawn from several different poems, and the various incidents to which it relates are described in the footnotes. The occasional use of the first person suggests that at least some of the original poems were composed by the chief himself. The second relates solely to the raid on the Thembu in 1835. It seems almost certain that Moshoeshoe was not its author, for it contains no reference to him in the first person, and there is a veiled criticism of him in the closing stanza. Moreover Casalis has recorded a few lines which are very similar to the penultimate stanza, and in his annotation he refers to *le poète* in such a way as to suggest that he does not mean Moshoeshoe.

(3) Moshoeshoe's praises are commonly chanted today, and there are as many different versions as there are *liroki*. One of the best versions is that chanted by Chief Lishobana Mpaki Molapo, a great-grandson of Moshoeshoe, who was born in 1895, and who lives at Sekubu in the Botha-Bothe District. In November 1968 he committed this to writing, and it appears below as poem (iii). It is a *mélange*, and contains a few stanzas and lines which also appear in poems (i) and (ii), although for the most part they are in variant forms. It is an interesting poem in that its first and fourth stanzas have clearly been added after Moshoeshoe's death, for they refer to him, either directly or indirectly, as an ancestor; and it is quite possible that the second and third stanzas are later additions too. Moreover the fourth stanza is unusual in that it stresses the value of conciliating one's enemies. In this it does not reflect the passions of the immediate aftermath of war, but Moshoeshoe's mature political wisdom as remembered by later generations.

(i)

The child of 'MaMokhachane,[1] Thesele,[2]
Thesele, the enormous cleft:
The cattle have entered it, they've gone for ever,
And the people have entered it, they've gone for ever![3]
5 You who have cattle killed for the Koena,
Please have cattle killed for your grandmother,
Please have cattle killed for 'MaSetenane,[4] that she may be adorned

[1] A man may be referred to as the child of any of his ancestors. Here Moshoeshoe is described as the child of Mokhachane's mother.
[2] The praise-name Thesele is formed from the verb *ho thesela* (to thump, butt, smash)—an indication of the way in which he dealt with his enemies in battle.
[3] i.e. Moshoeshoe has captured his enemies' cattle and killed their warriors.
[4] The wife of Libe. In the previous line she is referred to as Moshoeshoe's *nkhono*, a kinship term which is normally given to a man's grandmother, but may also be given, as here, to the wife of his father's elder brother.

And wear to the full the fat of cattle and of people.[1]
The Frog[2] of the armies, the comrade of Shakhane[3] and
                                                     RaMakoane,[4]
The one who set fire to the dust,[5] which came from the bowels of 10
                                    the land of RaTšooanyane:
The child of the chief of Qhoai saw it,
It was seen by RaTjotjose, the son of Mokhethi,[6]
The cloud, the gleaner of shields.[7]
   When the Frog isn't present in the armies of men,
The lords of the armies continually cry: 15
'Frog and RaMakoane, where are you?'
The armies of men have turned back on the way,

---

[1] It was customary for female relatives of rank to wear the hard fat or suet of slaughtered animals around their necks as signs of their importance and prosperity. The idea of wearing the fat of slaughtered enemies is probably a touch of savage humour. In line 8 Mangoaela's '*A re ke*' ('That she may say that it is') has been altered to '*A re khi*' ('That she may wear to the full').

[2] The frog always croaks when there is rain, and may therefore be regarded as a symbol of prosperity.

[3] One of Moshoeshoe's warriors.

[4] RaMakoane, i.e. Makoanyane, was the commander of Moshoeshoe's regiment, and the most famous of all his comrades-in-arms.

[5] Because clouds of dust were thrown up by his warriors as they moved along.

[6] According to the French missionary Arbousset, 'Ratoutouse' (i.e. RaTjotjose) was a counsellor of 'Selolou', chief of the Qhoai Fokeng, and was captured and ransomed by Moshoeshoe in retaliation for the capture of Mokhachane. See 'Excursion Missionnaire' (1840: an MS. in the P.E.M.S. Archives, Paris), pp. 42–3. According to the missionary historian Ellenberger, however, Moshoeshoe attacked 'Ratjotjosane' in order to defy the Sekake group of Mpiti, a more senior chief who was exercising authority over the Mokoteli during Moshoeshoe's youth. The Sekake had planned to raid Ratjotjosane, a Fokeng chief, and summoned Moshoeshoe to join them, but when he pretended to be ill they decided to stay at home. He then attacked Ratjotjosane on his own account. The Sekake demanded the spoil, and Mokhachane dutifully handed it over. But then Moshoeshoe and his friends recovered the animals by force, and Mpiti's authority was destroyed. See *History of the Basuto* (1912), pp. 109–10. Ellenberger's account is based on that given by Moshoeshoe's counsellor, RaMatšeatsana, in *Leselinyana*, 15 April 1891, although RaMatšeatsana refers to 'Ratjotjose', not 'Ratjotjosane'. In view of the following stanza, which clearly relates to Moshoeshoe's defiance of the Sekake, it is probably the incident recounted by Ellenberger which is referred to here. Perhaps RaTjotjose ruled over a section of the Qhoai Fokeng, in which case it would be correct both for Arbousset to describe him as a counsellor of 'Selolou', and for Ellenberger to imply that he was a chief. RaTšooanyane was no doubt one of the Qhoai Fokeng: indeed he may even have been 'Selolou' himself.

[7] Moshoeshoe is 'the cloud', probably because he is like a cloud of dust advancing on his enemies; and 'the gleaner of shields' because he gathers up the shields which they have thrown away in flight.

Seeking the Frog and RaMakoane.

Moshoashoaile,[1] Maphule's cow with white-streaked back,

20 Moshoashoaile, the white-streaked cow, the white-streaked cow of
                                                            Maphule,

The cow of the man of Maphule has a white-streaked back.[2]

It hasn't yet grown, it's still lean,

Its hair is still rough, the milk-cow,[3]

The milk-cow of Setenane[4] and his friends,

25 Of Setenane and his friends, of RaPolile[5] and his friends.

The spear of the child of Khoana, Thamae,[6]

The spear was damaging:

The razor-sharp spear has just come from Mahiseng,

It's just come from the home of Khoabane of the Tramplers:[7]

30 The spear was damaging to the bowels of a man,

It damaged the bowels of the child of Mphaphang.[8]

---

[1] A variant form of Moshoeshoe.

[2] It is common for chiefs to be referred to as cattle, i.e. as the sources of their people's prosperity. The various colours by which they are described merely indicate their beauty. Maphule cannot be identified, but was probably one of Moshoeshoe's ancestors.

[3] i.e. Moshoeshoe's power is not yet at its height: his people have not yet seen him in his full glory. Mangoaela's '*Ha eso ho hole*' ('Its home is far away') has been altered to '*Ha e e-s'o hole*' ('It hasn't yet grown').

[4] Setenane, son of Libe, was Moshoeshoe's cousin.

[5] Presumably another of Moshoeshoe's relatives.

[6] The spear, apparently, is Moshoeshoe himself. Thamae was the son of Mokoteli. The phrase 'child of Khoana' appears to stand in apposition to Thamae, and so Khoana may be identified as Mokoteli. There is a play on words here, for *khoana* can also mean 'a cow with a white-streaked back', as in line 21 above.

[7] The name Mahiseng may be given to any place where the Marabeng people are living, and in 1824 or 1825 they had sought refuge with Moshoeshoe at Thaba Bosiu. Khoabane was their chief, and the Tramplers were his regiment. Perhaps Moshoeshoe set out for the battle from Khoabane's village; or perhaps Khoabane had actually presented him with a spear, and this idea has been linked with the metaphor in which the spear is Moshoeshoe himself. Mangoaela's '*Khoabane le Makata*' ('Khoabane and the Tramplers') has been changed to '*Khoabane'a Makata*' ('Khoabane of the Tramplers').

[8] The reference to Mphaphang makes it clear that this stanza relates to Moshoeshoe's victory over the Ngwane of Matiwane at Thaba Bosiu in 1828. In his *Relation d'un Voyage d'Exploration* (Paris, 1842), p. 590, Arbousset records the following passage in a composition which he describes as the Sotho song of victory on this occasion, but which in fact seems to be Moshoeshoe's praise-poem: 'La sagaie a dévoré le fils de Kabékoé, elle a déchiré les chairs du fier 'Mpépang.'

Black cow of the salt, of the salt, black cow,[1]
Black cow, go on, I am coming,
I am coming to catch you up on the way, right here at the home
of Phokotsa.[2]

Thesele of the Binders[3] of Mokhachane,   35
The wiper of dirt from his shields,
From his shields while they're still in the huts.[4]

The Chooser[5] of the people from Kali's,[6] the Shaver,
Who's shaved off RaMonaheng's beard,
And as for growing, it hasn't yet grown,   40
It will go on growing for years![7]

The yellow cow of the regiments, the comrade of Shakhane
And Makoanyane, the one who set fire to the dust,
The dust came out from the bowels of the earth
At the villages of RaTšooanyane: 45
It was seen by RaTjotjose, the son of Mokhethi.

Cloud, gleaner of shields,
Strike a blow at Nanne and Mosala.[8]

The wild beast[9] roared, it trampled on Qhoaebane,[10]
Who was still in the hut at his wife's,   50
At 'MaLihlahleng's, at someone's aunt's.[11]

[1] The black cow, it seems, is Moshoeshoe himself, for a cow that consumes plenty of salt is believed to give excellent milk.

[2] The historical allusion is not known.

[3] In the initiation school Moshoeshoe gave himself the name of 'the Binder', and his regiment was therefore known as 'the Binders'. The origin of the name is unknown, but it may well signify the way in which Moshoeshoe brought his enemies under control. (Cp. Jonathan, i. 1, p. 170 below.)

[4] i.e. Moshoeshoe is always ready for battle.

[5] The significance of this praise-name is not known: some authorities today suggest that Moshoeshoe 'chose' the best cattle for himself when the spoil was being distributed.

[6] Kali is Monaheng, one of Moshoeshoe's most famous ancestors.

[7] One of Moshoeshoe's first exploits was to sweep off the cattle of RaMonaheng, a Marabeng chief who was then living at Khololong (which is now better known as Commando Nek in the Free State). It was on this occasion that he gave himself the onomatopaeic name Moshoeshoe, the sound '*shoeshoe*' (pronounced '*shweshwe*') representing the sound made by a razor in shaving. For variants of the first two lines of this stanza, see p. 21 above.

[8] Presumably men of the Qhoai Fokeng, among whom these names are common today.

[9] The word *Selalome*, 'wild beast', has been added to Mangoaela's text.

[10] Evidently one of the Qhoai Fokeng.

[11] The phrases 'at his wife's', 'at 'MaLihlahleng's', and 'at someone's aunt's' all stand in apposition to each other. The identity of 'MaLihlahleng's nephew or niece is not known.

The one who goes stripped to his in-laws', Lepoqo,[1]
To his in-laws', to the home of Lesaoana and his kin.[2]
RaMohato[3] may stab with his spear in his hand:[4]
55   Wildfire approaches Mohato's household.[5]
Leave me alone, Mokhitli of the Black Cows,[6]
For indeed I'm with child, I, RaMolapo,[7]
I'm pregnant: in March I shall be confined.[8]
The flashing shield of RaMasopha[9]
60   Is bright with fire,
So the shield gives the warning itself,[10]
It gives it for the left-handed Tyopho to hear,
To hear when his son-in-law's attacked.[11]
Tyopho's son-in-law was devoured by a hyaena,
65   He was devoured by the Binders' tawny lion:
It comes from the undergrowth, fawn,
And its three cubs keep it company.[12]

---

[1] Lepoqo (Dispute) was the name given to Moshoeshoe at birth, for at that time there was a dispute about witchcraft in the village.

[2] To appear naked before one's in-laws was taboo. Moshoeshoe, however, went 'stripped' for battle. Presumably the Qhoai Fokeng could be referred to as his in-laws, the connection being established through Libe's wife; and presumably Lesaoana was one of their number. (Certainly the Lesaoana mentioned here is not Moshoeshoe's nephew of that name.)

[3] i.e. Moshoeshoe himself: his eldest son, Letsie, was named Mohato at birth.

[4] i.e. he may fight at close quarters.

[5] i.e. Mohato's household is threatened by war.

[6] *Nkemolohe* (Leave me alone) is what a woman says to a man when he is forcing his attentions on her against her will. Mokhitli was a relative of the Marabeng chief, Khoabane, and had been resisting Moshoeshoe's policies. The *Litšoane*, the 'Black Cows', were his regiment. There is a play on words here, for *mokhitli* can also refer to a man who is having sexual intercourse with a woman; and *tšoana* can refer to a woman's private parts.

[7] i.e. Moshoeshoe himself: Molapo was the second son in his senior house.

[8] i.e. Moshoeshoe is planning to execute a raid in March. (For the image of pregnancy, cp. Posholi, iii. 127–31, p. 90 below.)

[9] Masopha was the third son in Moshoeshoe's senior house.

[10] According to Casalis, 'Le bouclier du chef est couvert de plaques de cuivre fort luisantes, qui réfléchissent les rayons du soleil'. (*Études*, p. 66.) In this way Moshoeshoe's enemies were warned of his approach.

[11] The reference to Tyopho makes it clear that this stanza relates to Moshoeshoe's expedition in 1835 against the Thembu of Vusani, alias Ngubencuka, whom the Sotho call Kobo-e-Ngoka. Tyopho was chief of the Gcina, who, although of Xhosa origin, lived among the Thembu, and had evidently inter-married with them. (See J. H. Soga, *The South-Eastern Bantu*, p. 286.)

[12] Moshoeshoe's three 'cubs' on this occasion were his sons, Letsie, Molapo and 'Neko (the eldest son in his second house).

The husband of Mokali and RaNtheosi[1]
Is no longer a lion, the husband of women,
It's a little terror, it's the spotted hyaena of those
                                    from RaMatlole's,[2] 70
Which devours the udders of the cows as they run:
As for the people, I only nibble them!

(ii)

You've been saying there's no one at Kholu's:[3]
The spear of someone from Kholu's is stabbing,
It stabbed a man's leg, he couldn't stand![4]
He supported himself by a tree, Binders.
    Ram, butt, Kali of the Beoana,[5]   5
Butt, the cowards are afraid,
They see when the darkness spreads.[6]
    It has no teeth, the Binders' lion,[7]
As for the people, it only nibbles them!
    Tyopho was devoured by the Binders' hyaena,   10
When its three cubs kept it company,
The spotted hyaena of the people from RaMatlole's.
He tried with a thorn tree to block the door,
He defended with a baby's cradle-skin![8]
    The husband of Mokali, the aged leopard,   15

---

[1] These are masculine names. It was the custom for women in the initiation school to give themselves such names, and evidently two of Moshoeshoe's wives—it is not known which two—called themselves Mokali and RaNtheosi.

[2] Matlole was Motloang, Peete's father. His father's identity is disputed, but he was either Sekake or Monaheng (Kali).

[3] Kholu was Moshoeshoe's mother. This line is addressed to the Thembu, who had been saying that there were no warriors among the Sotho.

[4] In an article in *Leselinyana*, 15 March 1893, the historian Sekese tells how Moshoeshoe stabbed an opponent in the leg, and how that opponent then dropped his weapons and fled.

[5] Moshoeshoe is here referred to as his ancestor, Kali. The Beoana were Kali's regiment, and the term is often used in the *lithoko* to refer either to the royal family or to the Sotho in general.

[6] The 'darkness' is the darkness of war.

[7] i.e. Moshoeshoe is past his prime as a warrior. In fact he was about fifty years old.

[8] i.e. Tyopho tried to defend his home in every way possible, and was so desperate that he even made use of a *thari*, the soft skin in which a baby is carried on its mother's back.

The husband of Mokali and RaNtheosi,
The flashing shield of RaNtheosi,
The flashing shield of RaMasopha,
Which is bright with fire.
20   The waistcoat of cloth,
The one who clings fast to the black and white cow!
The black white-spotted ox once flexed its muscles,
And Kobo's kaross was left on the branches,
Was left in the bushes, on the ridge.[1]
25   Black white-spotted ox, though you've come with gladness,
Yet you have come with grief,
You have come with cries of lamentation,
You have come as the women hold their heads
And continually tear their cheeks.[2]
30   Keep it from entering my herds:[3]
Even in calving, let it calve in the veld,
Let it calve at Qoaling and Korokoro.[4]
To these cattle of our village it brings distress,
It has come with a dirge, a cause of sadness.
35   Thesele, the other one, where have you left him?[5]

---

[1] The meaning of this stanza is uncertain, but clearly the poet is playing on the fact that Kobo (i.e. Kobo-e-Ngoka, Ngubencuka) means 'kaross' in Sotho. He jocularly refers to Moshoeshoe as *'Norobaki*, the Sotho form of the Dutch *onderbaadjie*, 'waistcoat'; for just as a waistcoat grips a man round the chest, so, apparently, Moshoeshoe fastens on Kobo's cattle. The black white-spotted ox is Moshoeshoe himself. Perhaps in the battle Moshoeshoe and his men put an opponent to flight, and that opponent, who would not have been Kobo himself, but one of Kobo's warriors, flung his clothes on a bush as he fled. In line 24 Mangoaela's *letateng* ('on a kaross', which seems inexplicable) has been changed to *letsatseng* ('on the ridge').

[2] Moshoeshoe has returned to Thaba Bosiu with gladness, since he has brought back some plundered cattle; but he has returned with grief, since his brother Makhabane has been killed. Line 29 means literally: 'And continually support their necks'. A Sotho woman, when stricken with grief, clasps her hands together and places them on her neck, now on the right, now on the left, as she inclines her head from side to side.

[3] 'it' here refers to the plundered cattle. On the way home the Sotho found a snake in their path, and it was believed that this had defiled the cattle. According to Casalis, the poet took advantage of this circumstance to express the people's grief at the death of Makhabane: the Thembu's cattle should be kept apart from the Sotho's, for they had been defiled by the serpent of death. (*Études*, pp. 66–7.)

[4] Qoaling is a mountain and Korokoro a stream several miles west of Thaba Bosiu.

[5] Thesele is Moshoeshoe: 'the other one' is Makhabane. Makhabane and some of his men had been cut off and surrounded in a wood. For the veiled criticism in these lines, see p. 31 above.

(iii)

You who are fond of praising the ancestors,
Your praises are poor when you leave out the warrior,
When you leave out Thesele, the son of Mokhachane;
For it's he who's the warrior of the wars,
Thesele is brave and strong,   5
That is Moshoeshoe-Moshaila.[1]
    When Moshoeshoe started to govern the Sotho
He started at Botha-Bothe[2]
Thesele, the cloud departed from the east,
It left a trail and alighted in the west,   10
At Thaba Bosiu,[3] at the hut that's a court.[4]
    Every nation heard,
And the Pedi heard him too.[5]
Moshoeshoe, clear the road of rubbish,
That the Maaooa[6] may travel with pleasure,   15
And travel with ease.[7]
The Ndebele from Zulu's heard too.[8]
    Lay down the stick, son of Mokhachane,
Sit down:
The village of the stick isn't built,[9]   20
'What can you do to me?' doesn't build a village;[10]
The village that is built is the suppliant's, Thesele,[11]

---

[1] A variant form of Moshoeshoe.
[2] When Moshoeshoe left his father's home of Menkhoaneng *c.* 1820, he established his village at Botha-Bothe.
[3] Moshoeshoe led his followers from Botha-Bothe to Thaba Bosiu in 1824.
[4] At almost every chief's court there is a hut in which the food for his men is kept. The description of the court at Thaba Bosiu as a hut probably indicates that the chief nourished and sustained his followers there.
[5] i.e. they heard that he was chief, and went to join him.
[6] i.e. the Pedi, who for 'No', instead of saying 'E-e', like the Sotho, say 'Aooa'.
[7] i.e. Moshoeshoe should make it easy for the Pedi to join him.
[8] The term 'Ndebele' may be used by the Sotho to refer to anyone of Nguni origin. In fact many people came from Zululand to join Moshoeshoe.
[9] i.e. one cannot build up one's power through war.
[10] i.e. one cannot build up one's power by a contemptuous attitude towards others.
[11] i.e. the chief who begs for peace will prosper. With the exception of the last word, lines 20-2 are all said to be quotations from Moshoeshoe's political maxims.

Great ancestor, child of Napo Motlomelo,[1]
Protective charm of the Beoana's land.[2]

25   The cave of the poor and the chiefs,[3]
Peete's descendant, the brave warrior,
He's loved when the shields have been grasped,
When the young men's sticks have been grasped.[4]
He's taken the hide of the ox[5] of the Mafatle,[6]

30   He's made it a guard,
By a guard I mean a shield,
And with it he'll parry in the midst of war.

The children of Napo are stubborn indeed,
They want him to rescue the nation,

35   Saying that government is of cattle and people.[7]
He's the yellow cow of the regiments,
He's the comrade of Shakhane and Makoanyane,
The one who set fire to the dust:
The dust came out from the bowels of the land,

40   It was seen by RaTjotjose, the son of Mokhethi.[8]

The spotted hyaena of the children of Matlole,
The one whose hair is all shaved but the top,[9]
It devours the udders of the lively cattle.[10]
The cow of 'MaMmui,[11] the tawny cow,

45   With downhanging horns, Moshoeshoe.

Swarthy child of 'MaSetenane,
You who have cattle killed for the Choosers,[12]
Please have cattle killed for your grandmother,
Have cattle killed for 'MaSetenane,

---

[1] A Koena ancestor.   [2] i.e. of Lesotho.

[3] The cave is a symbol of protection.   [4] i.e. when there is war.

[5] 'the hide of the ox', i.e. the shield.

[6] The Mafatle were probably Mokhachane's regiment. (Cp. Posholi, iii. 127, p. 90 below.) The origin of the name is obscure.

[7] i.e. it is the duty of those who rule to protect cattle and people.

[8] Cp. i. 42–6, p. 69 above.

[9] Presumably Moshoeshoe once had his hair cut in this way, although there is no other evidence for this.

[10] Lit. 'of the cattle as they live', i.e. 'as they move'. Cp. i. 68–72, p. 71 above.

[11] 'MaMmui cannot be identified. However the name may still be found among the Fokeng today, and so possibly she was related to Moshoeshoe through his mother, Kholu, or his senior wife, 'MaMohato, both of whom were of Fokeng origin.

[12] 'The Chooser' was Moshoeshoe himself: see i. 38 above. His followers could therefore be referred to as 'the Choosers'.

That she may be adorned, and wear to the full the fat   50
Of cattle and of people.[1]
    Thesele, the enormous cleft of the place of protruding rocks,
The cattle go in by it, they've gone for ever,
In go the long-bearded people,
In go the great-horned cattle.[2]   55
    He's the swarthy child of 'MaSetenane,
A man with a broad-bridged nose,
The bridge of his nose is like a bird's, the Chooser,
Because he's descended from the father of Khokhoba.[3]
    The women are trilling for Moshoeshoe: 60
The men have lengthy spears.
He's loved when the shields have been taken.
    RaMohato is dancing with a person who's young,
He's dancing with a child who can't yet dance:
While dancing he says: 'What a terrible dancer!'[4]   65
    Leave me alone, Mokhitli of the Black Cows,
For indeed I'm with child,
For I'm pregnant.[5]
    The flashing shield of RaMasopha,
When struck it is bright with fire:[6]   70
The loudmouths' villages were burnt.[7]
Moshoeshoe-Moshaila is RaKali's,[8] the Shaver.

4. *Makhabane*

Makhabane (*c.* 1790–1835) was a younger brother of Moshoeshoe. Soon after the migration to Thaba Bosiu in 1824 he established his village a few miles away on the slopes of Ntlo-Kholo mountain. Throughout the *lifaqane* he was a tower of strength to his elder brother, and there are at least two references to his loyalty in his *lithoko*. Firstly he is described as 'the support of the pot in the fire', i.e. as a warrior who supports Moshoeshoe in the heat of battle; and secondly he is referred to as 'The builder of the Great Chief's kraal', i.e. as one who builds up Moshoeshoe's power through the cattle which he plunders. At the same time he wanted more cattle for himself, and this too may be reflected in the *lithoko*. In his anger

[1] Cp. i. 5–8, pp. 66–7 above.   [2] Cp. i. 1–4, p. 66 above.
[3] Khokhoba's identity is unknown, and so is his father's.
[4] The allusion is not known.   [5] Cp. i. 56–8, p. 70 above.
[6] Cp. i. 59–60, p. 70 above.   [7] The allusion is not known.
[8] For Kali, see i. 38, p. 69 above. His father was Tšoloane.

he is personified as flared nostrils which stab people for nothing at all,
i.e. which fight hard but gain no reward; and he is also described as a
hoe which breaks up new ground but brings in only a small harvest.
For all his loyalty, therefore, he frequently acted on his own initiative in
plundering communities which Moshoeshoe was trying to win over
through kindness and generosity. It was partly because of this that
Moshoeshoe led his third expedition against the Thembu in 1835, for
these were people whom he could not possibly regard as potential
adherents, but whose herds might satisfy the demands of his subordinates.
On this occasion Makhabane insisted on separating his warriors from the
main Sotho army, probably in the hope of retaining for his own exclusive
use all the cattle which he might capture. In the event his regiment was
cut off and surrounded in a wood, and he and many of his men were
killed. It is still widely believed that Moshoeshoe had despaired of
controlling him; that he may even have feared him as a rival; and that for
these reasons he deliberately abandoned him.

The poem which is given below is taken from Mangoaela's collection.
It is a *mélange*, and the incidents to which it alludes are described in
footnotes wherever possible. The consistent use of the second or third
person to refer to Makhabane suggests that the poet was someone other
than the chief himself.

(There is also a shorter version of the same poem, with very little that
is new, in the first chapter of *Raphepheng* (Morija, 1915), E. Segoete's
brief account of Sotho life in the early years of the nineteenth century.)

Go outside and get arms, Motlou[1] of the Clever Ones,[2]
of the people of Tšolo.[3]
The child of the chief has commanded his people,
Once he's commanded he doesn't keep commanding,[4]
The great giver of shade, the young man of Kali.[5]
5   You've said there's no buffalo at Peete's,[6]
Yet the furious conqueror breaks down the doors
At the homes of Kakatsa and RaMosala.[7]
The child of the chief, the turner of Makhetha,[8]

[1] The meaning of this praise-name is not known. Perhaps it is derived from the word *tlou*, 'elephant'.
[2] One of Makhabane's regiments.
[3] A Koena ancestor, the elder brother of Monaheng's father Tšoloane.
[4] i.e. he expects to be obeyed at once.   [5] Kali, i.e. Monaheng.
[6] This line is addressed to Makhabane's enemies. Cp. Moshoeshoe, ii. 1, p. 71 above.
[7] It is not known who these men were.
[8] Makhetha was a brother of the celebrated Mohlomi (see p. 1 above), and during the late 1820s he was the leading chief among the Monaheng. His followers were constantly skirmishing with Moshoeshoe's, and Makhabane himself attacked them on many occasions. Makhetha was killed by one of Posholi's followers *c.* 1830, when he was a very old man.

He's turned the people from Tšele's on their beds,[1]
That they turn, and their hearts love Lesotho.   10
  The nostrils that are flared,[2] the comrade of Taoma,[3]
                    they're stabbing people with violence,
But they stab them for nothing at all.[4]
  Chief, arise, uncle of Mohato,
Uncle of the Slayer and Molapo.[5]
  The mother of doves, the mother of crows,[6] hasn't he plucked   15
                              the black cow's tail,
The cow of Ntisane Sekhoane and his people![7]
  The red and white hartebeest, the hoe of the Milkers,[8]
Which breaks no new ground by breaking new ground,[9]
It's broken new ground at Popa, in a sandy, gravelly place.[10]
This year the hard workers are digging a plot,   20
RaKhoalite and his friends have dug only a plot.[11]
  Isn't this cow like a beast that is wild, Motlou of the Clever
                        Ones and the Scatterers![12]

---

[1] Tšele's people were a section of the Hlakoana. In later years they were closely connected with the Monaheng, and this link may have existed as early as Makhabane's lifetime. To turn on one's bed means to change one's mind. Evidently Makhabane made them alter their attitude towards Moshoeshoe.

[2] The flared nostrils symbolize the chief when he is angry.

[3] Evidently one of Makhabane's warriors.

[4] i.e. either there is no plunder or else Makhabane does not receive his fair share of the spoil. The latter interpretation is probably correct. Cp. lines 17–21 below.

[5] Mohato (i.e. Letsie), the Slayer (i.e. Masopha) and Molapo were the first three sons in Moshoeshoe's senior house.

[6] The significance of these names is not known.

[7] Ntisane was a Tloung chief, and evidently Makhabane once plundered some of his cattle.

[8] The regiment formed at Makhabane's initiation school. Makhabane had no doubt called himself the Milker in the hope that he would capture cattle and so provide milk for his followers.

[9] He breaks new ground, but not with the usual results, for the harvest is very small: i.e. he has fought hard, but either the plunder is small or else he has been stinted in its distribution. Cp. lines 11–12 above.

[10] i.e. he has fought at Popa (a mountain in the present district of Maseru, not far from Roma), but has gained only a few cattle. There were several encounters with Makhetha's Monaheng in this area, and perhaps the reference is to one of these.

[11] It would appear from the context that RaKhoalite was Makhabane himself, but otherwise the name is unknown.

[12] The Scatterers, i.e. those who scatter their enemies, were another of Makhabane's regiments.

There's a man over there among those of Monyane[1]
Whose name, they say, is the Testicled He-Goat:
25 He continually calls for the death of the shields,[2]
He thinks he can call the Whites and they'll come![3]
Motlou is the Milkers' warrior whom the enemy can never
observe:[4]
The unobserved warrior makes RaLeotoana unobservant,
He made him unobservant, he abandoned his ox,
30 He left it with a gash on its shoulders![5]
Motlou's the support of the pot in the fire,[6] the one who cuts
large hunks of meat.[7]
The lion is standing on the Tsatsa-le-'Meno,[8]
It's standing and scolding the Makaota,[9]
Saying that the commoners should acknowledge the government.[10]
35 Single-spotted cow, swim and come here,
You should cross to the other side of Pahong,[11]
You should cross to the other side of Lentsoaneng.[12]

[1] 'those of Monyane', i.e. the Monaheng. Monyane was Makhetha's father. The man referred to is presumably Makhetha or one of his sons.

[2] i.e. he is continually provoking war.

[3] The Monaheng called in some Kora to help them against Moshoeshoe. The poet is apparently joking that they think that they can call in Europeans too.

[4] He has charms which cause his enemies not to notice him.

[5] RaLeotoana, 'Father of the Little Leg', was the name given to a Kora cripple who was killed when plundering Makhabane's herds in 1830. (See Arbousset, *Relation*, p. 601, and an article by Sekese in *Leselinyana*, 1 Jan. 1900.) Evidently he, or one of his companions, was riding an ox, and this was wounded and fell into Makhabane's hands.

[6] In the past, when a pot was placed on a fire, a stone was used to support it. The poet here implies that, in a similar way, Makhabane supported Moshoeshoe in the heat of war.

[7] We have changed Mangoaela's *lelikila* (for which no one can provide a translation) to *lelukula*, 'one who cuts large hunks of meat'. The idea is that Makhabane feeds his followers well.

[8] The whereabouts of Tsatsa-le-'Meno are not known. There is a ridge of this name in the mountainous country around Qacha's Nek, but it is most unlikely that this is referred to here.

[9] The Makaota, 'the Lean Ones', were Sotho who had been impoverished during the *lifaqane* and who eked out a precarious living by hunting and gathering. Eventually most of them settled down under Moshoeshoe's rule after he had given them cattle under the *mafisa* system.

[10] i.e. they should recognize Moshoeshoe (or possibly Makhabane) as their chief.

[11] This name is no longer known.

[12] There is a rock called Lentsoaneng near Menkhoaneng, where Moshoeshoe, and presumably Makhabane too, was born. But the significance of this stanza is unknown.

The builder of the Great Chief's kraal, Clever Ones,
He's built it with an ox, Motlou.[1]

5. *Posholi*

Posholi (*c.* 1795–1868) was the younger brother of Moshoeshoe and
Makhabane. Like Makhabane, he loyally supported the chief during the
lifaqane, but often defied him by attacking other communities. It was one
of his warriors, for example, who finally killed Makhetha, the Monaheng
chief, *c.* 1830.

A few years later he established his village at Thaba Tšoeu in what is
now the Mafeteng District of Lesotho. In 1846, after a dispute with
Moshoeshoe's eldest son, Letsie, he migrated south-westwards to the
area of Mayaphuthi, close to the Orange. In the vicinity of his new home
were several Afrikaner immigrants, who were soon complaining of what
they described as his people's 'encroachments' on their farms; and he also
become involved in petty skirmishing with the various Nguni groups
which were living just south of the Orange, in what later became the
Wittebergen Native Reserve.

During the disturbances of the Orange River Sovereignty he migrated
for greater security to the summit of the nearby mountain of Bolokoe
(Vechtkop). There the boundary laid down by Major Warden cut him
off from the main body of the Sotho, and for a while he was treated and
even behaved as a British subject. In February 1851, for example, he
assisted Warden against Moshoeshoe's vassal, Moorosi, and some allied
Thembu chiefs in the battle of Dulcies Nek. He soon tired of this discipline, however, and became notorious for his persistent cattle-raiding
and for his forcible occupation of Afrikaner farms, for these were the
methods by which he chose to assert the Sotho's territorial claims in the
south-west.

He continued in this policy after the abandonment of the Sovereignty
by the British and the establishment of the Orange Free State. While
Moshoeshoe was endeavouring to recover his land through negotiation
with the Afrikaners, Posholi was steadily goading them into war by his
depredations. When hostilities finally broke out in 1858 his village at
Bolokoe was burnt, and he retreated towards Thaba Bosiu. Then, as the
Afrikaners camped below the mountain, he and other chiefs swept
round behind them, raided deep into the Free State, and brought back to
Lesotho an enormous booty in captured livestock. It was partly because
of this that Boshof begged so swiftly for peace.

After the war Posholi withdrew a little towards the centre of Lesotho,
and apparently established his village near the junction of the Orange and

[1] i.e. Makhabane builds up Moshoeshoe's power by giving him the cattle
which he has plundered. The ox which is mentioned may well be that which he
captured from RaLeotoana.

the Makhaleng. Unfortunately his immediate neighbours in the south-west were the Monaheng, whose leading chief at this time was Jan Letele. These were the very people whom he had antagonized during the *lifaqane*, and in the war of 1858 they had deserted Moshoeshoe and had thrown in their lot with the Afrikaners. They were now regarded as Free State subjects, and between them and Posholi's followers there was constant raiding and counter-raiding.

In the second Free State war Posholi's regiments were again pro-minent. At the very outset he joined forces with Moorosi in a raid on the southern Free State, but was not as successful as in 1858. Towards the end of 1867 he was ordered by Moshoeshoe to hold the mountain fortress of Mathebe (Tandjesberg), and it was there that he was killed by the invad-ing commandos in January 1868, just two months before Wodehouse intervened and declared the Sotho to be British subjects.

Today Posholi is popularly remembered as a reckless and insubordinate chief, who lacked Moshoeshoe's wisdom and foresight, and who brought endless troubles on the Sotho by his constant cattle-raiding. Even in his *lithoko* (iv. 81) he is described as

> The youth who lives on the property of others.

But he is also greatly admired for his personal courage and his deter-mined opposition to the Afrikaners, and on these subjects too his *lithoko* have much to say.

Mangoaela has recorded four poems. The first is concentrated on Posholi's struggles with the Monaheng rebels: the other three are *mélanges*. In the first poem the repeated use of the first person singular to refer to the chief indicates almost beyond doubt that the poet was Posholi himself. In the second and third poems, however, the first person singular is not used to refer to the chief at all (except perhaps in iii. 99) and the way in which the first person plural is used in iii. 44–6 indicates very clearly that the author of this stanza at least was someone else. The fourth poem is interesting in that lines 1–57 are in part a variation of the first poem, and the first person singular is often used; whereas lines 58–97 are almost entirely original, and only the second and third persons are used. It seems unlikely, therefore, that this second part was composed by the chief.

(i)

> The lion of Mangolo, Mokhachane's son,
> Of Mangolo and Mangolonyane,[1]
> Mangolo's lion is standing in the plain,
> It's standing in the hollow, at Marajaneng,[2]
> It complains of the name of hare.

5

[1] Mangolo and Mangolonyane are hills near the present town of Zastron in the Orange Free State. Posholi's villages were in their vicinity.
[2] i.e. Spitz Kop, in the same area.

Who is the chief who calls me a hare,
Me, the young chief of Makhabane and his people,
The lion, the devourer of RaMokeretla[1] on the slope?
    Let the rebels remain in tribulation!
Shao,[2] remain with that evil,[3]   10
Remain and tell Manamolela;[4]
Report to Letele[5] and RaMoiketsi,[6]
And also report to RaMokoena-Seqha.[7]
    We fired at the rabbits, they entered a shelter,
By rabbits we mean Manganane and his men,   15
The nephew of Thaane Sehlabaka and his men.[8]
    Someone ruined the fort[9] with excrement[10]
When he saw the Leche[11] of RaMathalea[12]
Appear with curving claws:
He said to the Claws,[13] 'Devour them!'   20
    White shield of the husband of Nkopi and 'MaBotle![14]
    What have you plundered to give to your wives?

---

[1] RaMokeretla was a Monaheng chief: his father was Mokoena, his grand-father the celebrated Mohlomi. The incident alluded to is not known, but no doubt occurred during the prolonged skirmishing between Posholi and the Monaheng chiefs in the late 1850s and early 1860s.

[2] RaMokeretla's brother.

[3] i.e. 'I have just defeated you, and there is nothing that you can do about it'.

[4] Another Monaheng chief.

[5] There were two Monaheng chiefs of this name. One, often referred to as 'old Letele', was a son of Mohlomi. The other, alias Qoane or Jan Letele, was a son of Mokhoaetsi and a grandson of Mohlomi. Since RaMokoena-Seqha in the following line is probably to be identified as Jan Letele, the reference here is probably to 'old Letele'.

[6] RaMoiketsi, alias Lebenya, was a son of Mohlomi's son, Mojakisane.

[7] RaMokoena-Seqha is probably to be identified as Jan Letele (see fn. 5 above), whose son was Mokoena. *Seqha* means 'bow', and its addition to Letele's teknonym may be a contemptuous insinuation that there were San connections in the family. Jan Letele was the most restless and turbulent of all the Monaheng rebels.

[8] The phrases 'Manganane and his men' and 'The nephew of Thaane Sehla-baka and his men' stand in apposition to each other. Manganane was another Monaheng chief, being the son of Mohanoe, the son of Makhetha, Mohlomi's brother.

[9] i.e. a fortified position on a mountain.   [10] i.e. in fear.

[11] The Leche (meaning unknown) were one of Posholi's regiments.

[12] i.e. Posholi himself, Mathalea being his daughter.

[13] One of Posholi's regiments. The man who addressed them was Posholi himself.

[14] Two of Posholi's wives. Further identification has not been possible.

I've plundered for Qampu and Ntjahali.[1]
You Boers beyond the river, in the town,[2]
25 Don't attempt to be tempted,[3]
For you're Bushmen, and I don't respect you:
Even to Smithfield we went across,
We tore down your shelters of rush![4]
Mofephe, seeing that I once took you up,[5]
30 How can you say we can fight in the hollow?[6]
Your people you can choose from the corpses, for they're dead![7]

(ii)

Lightning, brown one of 'MaMakhabane,
Lightning, brown one of the water, turn round,
Return to the corpses of yesterday.[8]
The lightning with black and white wings is striking:
5 The white-winged one doesn't normally strike,[9]
It allows Mofephe[10] to cover the veld
And finally strikes him in the plain.
The warrior from there at the Cape is fighting,

---

[1] Qampu and Ntjahali, both wives of Posholi, were daughters of the Taung chief, Hlalele.

[2] The river is the Orange: the town is Aliwal North. Cp. iv. 17 below.

[3] This probably means: 'Don't be tempted to help the rebels against me'. The Monaheng chiefs received considerable assistance from the Afrikaners, to whom they sold the livestock which they plundered.

[4] In April 1858 Posholi's forces, in conjunction with others, overran the south-eastern portions of the Free State and passed quite close to the town of Smithfield.

[5] As this stanza makes clear, Mofephe had once been Posholi's subject, but had turned against him and had been defeated. He was the son of a certain Komane (see iii. 61 below), who is otherwise unknown. It is just possible that Mofephe was the same person as Bele (see iv. 13 below), and if this is the case then he was a Nguni and Komane would be the Sotho form of Ngomane. There is a village known as Bele's near Dulcies Nek in the Cape Province, and it is possible that the Thembu who lived there had once been under Posholi, but had later become involved in hostilities with him.

[6] As the following line makes clear, Mofephe and Posholi had already fought in the hollow.

[7] Cp. Lerotholi, iv. 35–6, p. 145 below.

[8] i.e. Posholi should attack again the people whom he has already defeated.

[9] The two types of lightning probably represent two of Posholi's regiments. Cp. Joel, i. 223–5, pp. 197–8 below.

[10] For Mofephe, see i. 29 above.

No longer does he look for crowds.[1]
The black cow with white spots is like the guinea-fowl of the   10
                     Claws:
The cow of RaMothele[2] is black with white spots,
The black one with white spots is like the guinea-fowl of the
                     Claws.[3]
The cow is taking all the cream,
It took it at the chief's, at Makaula's.[4]
Greetings, war, which makes men weary,   15
It's made Molulela and Lehana weary.[5]
The lion of Bolokoe and Marajaneng,[6]
The lion of Bolokoe, its claws are black,
Its claws are black with the blood of the Thembu.[7]
Here is the lion that's hidden its twins,   20
It's hidden Maluke and Selete.[8]

(iii)

RaMathalea, the hungry one[9] of the Claws,
The swimmer in the waters of the sea,[10]

[1] 'The warrior from there at the Cape' is almost certainly Posholi. The description is not meant to be taken literally, but merely signifies the chief's excellence in battle, since warriors from the Cape were thought to be particularly courageous and effective. 'No longer does he look for crowds': i.e. he needs no more followers, for he is strong enough as he is.

[2] RaMothele is almost certainly Posholi himself, but the name Mothele is unknown among his descendants. Possibly RaMothele is a variant form of RaMathalea (see i. 18 above).

[3] Lines 10–12 merely indicate the chief's beauty. The bright and variegated colours of the guinea-fowl are much admired among the Sotho.

[4] Makaula, alias Silonyana, was chief of the Baca, and co-operated with the Sotho in an attack on the Mpondomise of Mbale in June 1861. Perhaps that incident is referred to here and perhaps Posholi took the lion's share of the spoil on that occasion.

[5] Molulela was almost certainly a Tlokoa, among whom this name is common today. Lehana was a son of Sekonyela, the Tlokoa chief. Posholi took part in Moshoeshoe's expeditions against the Tlokoa in May 1852 and October 1853.

[6] i.e. Vechtkop (his mountain stronghold) and Spitz Kop.

[7] The Sotho may use the word Thembu to refer to any of the Cape Nguni chiefdoms, and with these Posholi was involved in many encounters. The reference to Bolokoe, which was Posholi's home during the disturbances of the Orange River Sovereignty, suggests that the allusion is to one of his many skirmishes at that time with the various Nguni groups in the Orange valley.

[8] Two of his sons, but not twins.

[9] He is hungry for the cattle of other chiefs.

[10] i.e., probably, a warrior who fights well against Europeans, whose home was popularly believed to be on the seas: see, e.g., Maama, i. 32–4, p. 156 below.

Who no longer swears by Mlanjeni,
For he says there's an Mlanjeni even at Setori's;[1]
5 But he doesn't eat the cattle that are yellow,
If he eats them it's like eating the *kaalo* mouse,
It's like eating the *kaalo* mouse of the Ndebele.[2]
The Thembu, people with stubborn hearts,[3]
RaSheqa has long been telling them of Government,
10 At the time when they still gave help to the Magistrate:
He said that the cattle shouldn't go beyond the school,
They should graze by the Kraai, and turn back.[4]
A wretched Ndebele, Peeka's little son, wouldn't listen,[5]
Someone who hadn't even donned a penis sheath,[6]
15 Saying that the herds should cross the Orange, and go over:
Yet they cross into the mouths of Those Who Pull Out Spears![7]
The canons exchanged fire at the ford:[8]

[1] Mlanjeni was the Xhosa prophet who became famous in 1850 when he began to predict that, if the Xhosa killed all their yellow cattle, then their ancestors would reappear and drive the Europeans into the sea. Many Sotho, including Posholi, believed in his teaching. However, as these lines make clear, Posholi became disillusioned, and declared contemptuously that he could find an Mlanjeni at the home of Setori, who is said to have been one of his relatives.

[2] The Sotho eat almost every type of mouse, but not the *kaalo*, which is one of the smallest.

[3] Lit. 'with hard heads'.

[4] The allusions in this stanza are not clear. RaSheqa (meaning unknown) appears to have been a European (see iv. 57 below), and it is possible that he was John Ayliff, the Superintendent of the Wittebergen Native Reserve, which was established in 1850. It is possible too that he was the same person as the Magistrate mentioned in line 10. The Thembu referred to here appear to have been at least of the inhabitants of the Reserve: cp. ii. 19 above. Evidently RaSheqa wanted these people to submit themselves to British authority, and for some time they followed his advice. He also warned them that their cattle's grazing should be confined to the area around the Wesleyan Mission Station of Kamastone, 'the school', and the valley of the Kraai River: otherwise Posholi might plunder them.

[5] The term Ndebele may be used by the Sotho to refer to anyone of Nguni origin. The identity of Peeka's son, and the incident referred to, are not known.

[6] The penis sheath worn by the adult males of many Nguni communities was a never-failing source of amusement to the Sotho, and there are several references to it in the *lithoko*.

[7] There is a play on words here which cannot be adequately reproduced in the English translation. In Xhosa, the language used by Peeka's son in line 15, *uku wela* means 'to cross': in Sotho, the language used by the poet in line 16, *ho oela* means 'to fall into'. Those Who Pull Out Spears (i.e. after stabbing) were evidently one of Posholi's regiments.

[8] The incident referred to may well be the indecisive battle at Dulcies Nek in February 1851, when British forces came into collision with Moshoeshoe's vassal, Moorosi, and with certain Thembu chiefs. Posholi assisted the British.

One roared, and its roar could be heard,
It went, it could be heard at the Cape and the Bay:[1]
Another could be heard at Mokoteli's.[2]   20
    RaMohato[3] condemned, and so did the Depriver,[4]
Saying: 'Get away from there, hungry one of the Claws:
You're badly placed near the mouths of the monsters,
You're badly placed near the mouths of the guns,
For it's there that the canons exchange fire continually.'   25
    The brown lightning has just been called,
It's just been called by the child of its master:[5]
We saw it had come
When we saw that the places of meeting were blocked.[6]
    The child of Nkejane[7] quickly evaded,   30
He's taken the horn of a goat and tasted.[8]
Son of Matlake,[9] look out, it's crushing you![10]
He too has taken a goat's horn and tasted;
But the lightning was turned aside a little,
It was turned aside, it fell at Hlojoaneng.[11]   35
    Great warrior, elephant of the Claws!
The chief is speaking on the shelves:[12]

Strictly speaking, the canons did not exchange fire, since only one side, the British, possessed them. The ford referred to may be one across the Dulcies Spruit. As a result of this incident, Dulcies Nek became known to the Sotho as Lekhalo la Likanono, 'The Pass of the Canons'.

[1] i.e. Cape Town and Port Elizabeth ('the Bay' being Algoa Bay).

[2] i.e. it was audible in Lesotho. For Mokoteli, see the introductory notes to Peete's praises, p. 63 above.

[3] RaMohato, i.e. Moshoeshoe.   [4] 'the Depriver', i.e. Letsie.

[5] i.e. Posholi has just been summoned to war by Letsie. It was common for Moshoeshoe's orders to Posholi to be transmitted through Letsie.

[6] Posholi's warriors were so many that they filled the places where the army was to assemble.

[7] Nkejane is probably the Sotho form of Ngiyane, the name of a Hlubi who lived in the Wittebergen Native Reserve.

[8] A warrior would sometimes take into battle a goat's horn containing medicines which were believed to give protection when tasted.

[9] Identity not known.

[10] 'it' here is the lightning, i.e. Posholi himself.

[11] Clearly the protective medicines have been successful, for instead of attacking Nkejane and the son of Matlake, Posholi has fought at Hlojoaneng. This area cannot now be identified.

[12] *Mehaoloana* are the raised platforms at the edge of a hut which serve as shelves for pots, etc. Here, apparently, they represent a mountain on the outskirts of a battle. The following lines make it clear that the chief is Sekonyela; that the mountain is Marabeng; and that the occasion is the Sotho attack of May 1852.

He summoned 'Mota[1] and Lenono[2] to himself,
He summoned Makoti and RaMahlaela;[3]
40   It was said: 'Drive the cow, it's there, RaMahlaela.
Go and calm down the lightning's flash.'[4]
Brown lightning of the water, turn round,
Return to yesterday's tracks.
    When the lightning was at Tsatsi's,[5] it stopped,
45   And we saw its rays
Clothing the mountain of Sekonyela and his men.
    The cattle are shared at Sefikeng,[6]
Posholi of the family of 'MaTšoeunyane,[7]
They were shared, they were given to Mashabatela[8] and his men,
50   They were given to Nqaele, the child of Bungane,
                who comes from the land of the Hlubi.[9]
    The dark woman's child is loved at Mokhachane's:
He was given a horse, he was given a gun,
He was given a horn of gunpowder too,
That the nations should call him, for he's brave.[10]
55   Strike the lizard,[11] RaMathalea, you who swear by the
                                        crocodile:[12]
The lizard has gone with the spear,[13]
It's gone with the spearshafts of RaMathalea.
    The brown lightning of 'MaMakhabane,
The lightning with black and white wings is crackling:

---

[1] Sekonyela's brother.   [2] A Tlokoa.   [3] Two of Sekonyela's followers.
[4] Sekonyela's forces were being overwhelmed by the Sotho, and so he sent RaMahlaela with two head of cattle to beg for peace, which Moshoeshoe granted. Posholi's part in all this is obviously exaggerated here.
[5] It is impossible to identify this village.
[6] A mountain mainly in what is now the Berea District of Lesotho. The cattle being shared out were those plundered from the Tlokoa.
[7] Posholi's elder sister.   [8] Identity unknown.
[9] The Hlubi chief Bungane was the father of Mthimkhulu and Mpangazitha: Nqaele too was evidently descended from him, but cannot otherwise be identified. Many Hlubi had found refuge with Moshoeshoe, and no doubt Nqaele was one of them. The poet is hinting that Posholi should have received a greater share of the spoil, since cattle were given out to such insignificant men as Mashabatela and Nqaele.
[10] i.e. he was given these things so that he should be ready when summoned to war.
[11] It is not known whom the lizard represents.
[12] The Koena, of whom Posholi was one, had the crocodile as their totem and swore by it.
[13] i.e. it had been stabbed and ran away with the spear still in its body.

The white-winged one doesn't normally strike, 60
It allows Mofephe, the child of Komane, to run all over the veld,
It finally strikes him in the plain, right in the heart of the veld.[1]
  We saw Bolokoe, 'Mamothibisi,[2]
There went around an Ndebele of Sele's Mthimkhulu.[3]
  The insects laughed, they fell on their backs, 65
They looked at their tiny feet above and thanked the chief:
'The lion of the Piercers has killed us meat!'[4]
  A vulture may come from there at Moletsane's,[5]
Another came from there at Mokoteli's,[6]
Another came from the Magistrate's:[7] 70
On arriving they met in a hollow,
And said: 'The man of the Piercers has killed us meat!'
  A vulture runs with someone's shoulder,
It left with someone's carcase:
They were telling each other rumours, 75
Saying: 'Why is the Yellow One[8] thin this year?'
The Yellow One becomes thin through the mouths of people,
Of Take And Bring Here and his friends.[9]
  The chief, the tree[10] of Semethe[11] and his kin,
Of the time when the millet is sprouting ears, 80
Of the time when the millet has formed its feather,

---

[1] For lines 58–62, cp. ii. 1–7, p. 82 above.

[2] An alternative name for Bolokoe.

[3] Sele, chief of the Hlubi, was the father of Bungane. Mthimkhulu was Bungane's son, and was killed *c.* 1822. Posholi had several Hlubi neighbours and was often in conflict with them. Perhaps these lines refer to an occasion when some Hlubi were chased round Bolokoe. For the use of the term Ndebele to refer to anyone of Nguni origin, cp. line 13 above.

[4] i.e. 'Posholi has killed many warriors and we can devour their bodies'. The Piercers were one of Posholi's regiments.

[5] Moletsane, the Taung chief, lived at Mekoatleng in the north.

[6] 'Mokoteli's', i.e. Lesotho. See line 20 above.

[7] The Magistrate was probably the Superintendent of the Wittebergen Native Reserve.

[8] Posholi himself.

[9] Take And Bring Here is almost certainly Moshoeshoe, who demanded that Posholi should surrender to him all the cattle which he plundered. Cp. iv. 42–3, p. 93 below.

[10] The dictionary definition of *senokonoko* is 'the tree Royena hirsuta: bark of the sorghum plant'. Either of these could 'burst' in a fire and put out a man's eye. Lines 80 and 81 merely indicate the time of the year when the incident occurred.

[11] One of Posholi's sons.

It burst, it burned Peeka's child,[1]
It finished his last remaining eye.
    A vagabond comes from the Ndebele there,
85 A lunatic came from Matekoane's:
He's just been spying on the herds at the Leqholoqha.[2]
    Matimokanye's beer was bubbling,[3]
The beer was bubbling through the night, Claws,
As it bubbled it stirred up the dregs:
90 It was heard by Qhoaempe,[4] in the school of initiation,
Then Mbale[5] heard it from afar,
It was heard by the uninitiated boy from the land of the Ndebele![6]
RaMothele's cow is black with white spots,
It's black with white spots, like the guinea-fowl of the Claws,[7]
95 The cow's like the black one from the waters of the Lethena,
From the waters of the Lethena and the Leqholoqha.[8]
    His cow's like an eagle, Claws,
It's white on its head and its shoulders:
It's the cow of my children's share of the spoil,
100 Of Maluke and Mapeshoane,
Of Sekoati and Maphakela,
Of Chopho and Selete.[9]
    The vagabond of the Shatterer's Molomo and his men,[10]
The leader of the armies which go to fetch the cow that is red and
                                white-spotted![11]
105   The Piercer from there at the Orange, at the Caledon,
The Piercer is breaking new ground for the pumpkins and gourds,

---

[1] For 'Peeka's child', see line 13 above.
[2] The poet now turns to the campaign in June 1861 in which Posholi and other chiefs crossed the Drakensberg to attack the Mpondomise of Mbale, who are the Ndebele referred to in line 84. Matekoane was perhaps one of the Mpondomise's chiefs: the Leqholoqha is a river. Posholi is a 'vagabond' because of his wanderings, and a 'lunatic' because of his fury. There is probably a play on words here, for Matekoane, apart from being a man's name, can also mean cannabis, or dagga: hence, Posholi's fury.
[3] The image of fermenting beer conveys the idea of someone's anger, probably Posholi's, although the name Matimokanye is now unknown.
[4] Identity unknown.   [5] The chief of the Mpondomise.
[6] i.e. Mbale himself.   [7] For lines 93–4, cp. ii. 10–12, p. 83 above.
[8] Rivers below the Drakensberg.
[9] All these men were Posholi's sons.
[10] 'the Shatterer' was Posholi's brother, Mohale. Molomo was Mohale's son.
[11] No doubt such a cow formed part of Posholi's booty.

But the nations are stopping his rain.[1]
The owner of cattle, the boy of Lefatle,[2] is making a cut for
                      the medicine of defence:[3]
Hasn't he defended against the Bosses![4]
The Bellowers' hide,[5] the chewer of beans,[6] great cow!   110
What have you plundered to give to your wives?
As for him, he's plundered for his wives,
He's plundered for Qampu and Ntjahali,
He's plundered for Hlalele's little girls.[7]
These roan ones are those of Mathalea[8] and her house,   115
The black ones are those of the house of Ntjahali,
But they've come with hooves that are red.[9]
The red and white cow is from the voice of the chief,
It has come from the voice of the Magistrate.[10]
    Men, you shouldn't exaggerate things: 120
That's something of old, of long, long ago,[11]
Of Mohlomi of the Locusts and his men,[12]
Of Nkopane of the Shooters and his men.[13]

[1] i.e. Posholi wishes to occupy new land between the Orange and the Caledon, but the people of other nations, mainly the Afrikaners, will not allow him to do so.

[2] Lefatle (meaning unknown) was a praise-name of Mokhachane.

[3] *Moretele* ('the medicine of defence') is a medicine used to ward off evil: it is applied by being rubbed into incisions in the skin.

[4] A translation of *Mabasa*, which is derived from the Afrikaans *baas*. The reference, of course, is to the Afrikaners.

[5] The 'Bellowers' were presumably one of Posholi's regiments. Posholi himself was their 'hide', i.e. their shield.

[6] The 'beans' referred to here are probably medicines which were thought to give various kinds of assistance to a warrior.

[7] For lines 111–14, cp. i. 22–3, pp. 81–2 above.   [8] Posholi's daughter.

[9] Their hooves are red with blood because, after being captured, they have been driven hard to Posholi's home.

[10] Apparently Posholi has been rewarded by 'the Magistrate'. If this is so, then the occasion referred to is the battle at Dulcies Nek (see line 17 above), and the Magistrate is probably Major Warden, the British Resident in the Orange River Sovereignty.

[11] i.e. exaggeration is something which should belong to the past. Why the poet should say this is not clear: perhaps he is indicating that in praising Posholi he speaks only the truth.

[12] Mohlomi was the famous Monaheng chief who died *c.* 1815. The Locusts (an uncertain translation of Matsie) were his regiment.

[13] Nkopane was Mohlomi's elder brother. The Shooters, i.e. those who throw up new shoots, those who thrive, were his regiment. (By an odd coincidence Mathunya may also mean those who shoot with guns, but firearms, of course, were unknown to Nkopane.) For this use of the names of Mohlomi and Nkopane to denote the distant past, cp. Maama, ii. 86, p. 161 below.

Young oxen have come from the belly of the chief,
125 They've come from a man, from RaMathalea,
Out came the kids and the lambs.[1]
The udder of Lefatle's son's cow is swelling,[2]
It's swelling and shaking, Stealthy Approachers,[3]
Its navel is swelling, it reaches its knees:
130 When it calves down men will hear of it,
The nations will hear it's a marvel.[4]
Swamp, tremble, RaMathalea, RaMathalea of Thesele[5] and his
house,
That the wretched little herds of the Whites should fall,
That the herds should fall, that the goats should fall,
135 That also the sheep of the Boers should fall,
That the herds of the Ndebele should fall,
And those of your family from Mokoteli's![6]
Chief, scatter the people with a wind, that it leaves,
That the people of your family from Monaheng's
140 Should be startled and go to the Makhaleng![7]
The men from Mohale's went up the Makhaleng,[8]
And Sepere built his village on the Ketane:[9]
Even long ago he didn't know him![10]

[1] i.e. Posholi has provided well for his followers.

[2] Lefatle, i.e. Mokhachane: see line 108 above.

[3] Evidently one of Posholi's regiments.

[4] i.e. Posholi is about to perform some military exploit. For this use of the image of pregnancy, cp. Moshoeshoe, i. 56–8, p. 70 above.

[5] Thesele, i.e. Moshoeshoe.

[6] This stanza is a variation of a famous stanza from the praises of the Taung chief, Moletsane. The family 'from Mokoteli's' can only mean the royal house. Most Sotho authorities, when asked to explain why Posholi should plunder the herds of his relatives, refer vaguely to his disputes with Moshoeshoe and Letsie but cannot be more specific.

[7] 'your family from Monaheng's', i.e. the Monaheng rebels. The Makhaleng is a tributary of the Orange, and its valley was closer to the centre of Lesotho than the Monaheng's villages. Perhaps Posholi wanted the Monaheng to migrate there so that they could be controlled more easily; or perhaps it was because he wanted his own followers to occupy their homes.

[8] Mohale was Posholi's brother, and his followers did in fact settle in the Makhaleng valley.

[9] Sepere was a relative of the Phuthi chief, Moorosi. The Ketane is another tributary of the Orange.

[10] The significance of this line is obscure. Perhaps Posholi was complaining that Sepere was encroaching on his land. 'Even long ago he didn't know him!': i.e. Posholi had controlled this area for a long time and had never seen Sepere there before.

The alarm is fine which rings out at Liphiring:[1]
At Mohale's it was heard by Selala Lengotsoana,[2]   145
Who said: 'Mohale, listen, the alarm!'
At Sepere's it was heard by the child of 'MaMaqampu,[3]
Who said: 'Sepere, listen, the alarm!'
It is said that over there, at the home of the man who belongs to
                         the Leche,[4] a fight is going on,
At the home of the man who belongs to the Leche the bodyguard 150
                         of the chief is fighting.
He goes on taking, he goes on pouring.[5]
He unleashed Leluma[6] and the Helper,[7]
He unleashed the last ones, the Helpers,
He poured in the brave young warriors:
Then the fighting went well at the place of swimming.[8]   155
    The lion of Bolokoe and Marajaneng,
Bolokoe's lion has claws that are black,
Its claws are black with the blood of the Thembu![9]
    He's simply sitting with his claws;
He put out his claws, long and pointed,   160
They struck out at Hlasoa,[10] they laid him low;
Then, as for Makoloane,[11] they poured on him their smell.[12]
It hasn't eaten Hlasoa, it's spat on him, that's all,[13]
It went on toying with him in the hollow,
In the heart of the veld, at Bolokoe, 'Mamothibisi.[14]   165
    The elephant is fighting with twins on its back,
With Maluke and Selete on its back.[15]

[1] Liphiring is a mountain not far from the junction of the Makhaleng and the Orange. No doubt it was the scene of fighting at some time between Posholi and the Monaheng.
[2] Apparently one of Mohale's followers.
[3] Apparently one of Sepere's followers.
[4] The Leche (meaning unknown) were one of Posholi's regiments. Cp. i. 18, p. 81 above.
[5] i.e. he continually pours his warriors into the battle.
[6] One of his sons.
[7] Probably a praise-name of one of his sons, but it is not known which. The Helpers mentioned in the following line were clearly his regiment.
[8] 'at the place of swimming', i.e. at the river, which was no doubt the Orange.
[9] For lines 156-8, cp. ii. 17-19 above.
[10] Identity unknown.   [11] Identity unknown.
[12] i.e. they simply made him aware of their presence.
[13] To spit on someone means to deal with him leniently. Cp. Letsie II, line 82, p. 213 below.
[14] Cp. line 63 above.   [15] Cp. ii. 20-1 above.

(iv)

The lion of Mangolo, Mokhachane's son,
The lion of Mangolo and Mangolonyane,
Mangolo's lion is standing on the height,
It stood on the hill, at Marajaneng,[1]
5 It's standing on the cliff of Matlakeng,[2]
It's standing thus with its lungs beating.[3]
    As it stood it glared at Qethoane,[4]
Complaining of the name of hare.
It says: 'Who is it who calls me a hare,
10 Me, the wearer of the leopard-skin,[5]
Me, the young chief of Makhabane and his people,
Surpassing even the Major[6] in height?'[7]
    Bele, seeing that I once took you up,
How do you think we can fight in the hollow?
15 I say that your men you can choose from the dead,
You can choose them from people's corpses![8]
    You Boers beyond the river, at Aliwal town,[9]
Don't try to stretch out your hands,
Seeing that you're Bushmen, and I don't respect you.
20 Even into Smithfield I went,
I trampled underfoot your shelters of rush:
You fled in a hurry, you abandoned your shelters![10]
    Shao, tell those rebels that they may know,
Tell Letele and Manamolela,

[1] For lines 1–4, cp. i. 1–4, p. 80 above.

[2] Matlakeng (Aasvoëlberg) is a mountain close to the present town of Zastron.

[3] The Sotho used to talk of the lungs beating rather than the heart.

[4] Another mountain close to the present town of Zastron. It was the site of several Monaheng villages.

[5] A warrior distinguished for bravery was entitled to wear a leopard-skin. Cp. Maama, iii. 18, p. 162 below.

[6] i.e. Major Warden, the British Resident in the Orange River Sovereignty. Posholi was in fact a tall, powerful man.

[7] For lines 8–12, cp. i. 5–8, pp. 80–1 above.

[8] For the identification of Bele and the interpretation of this stanza, see i. 29–31 and relevant footnotes, p. 82 above.

[9] 'Aliwal town', i.e. Aliwal North, on the southern bank of the Orange, was known to the Sotho as RaLetsoai's. RaLetsoai was the name which they gave to Piet de Wet, the first European to reside on the site. It means 'Father of Salt', and was given to him because he used to sell this commodity.

[10] For this stanza, cp. i. 24–8, p. 82 above.

Then inform RaMoiketsi too[1]   25
For him to tell for Korotsoane[2] to know:
Tell also the Boers at Litšoeneng,[3]
And tell RaMokoena-Seqha too[4]
That the two-faced creature today they've bound,
This wretched little man they've bound,   30
They've bound old RaMokeretla.[5]
    In the year before last you saw,
At the hills of the children of Monyane,
Of the children of Monyane Monaheng,[6]
At sunrise a Boer was lying flat,   35
A red-skinned Boer was lying flat,
The child of the Boer was dead indeed![7]
    He shone a light on the cattle, he took them,[8]
He sent them into the hands of Moshoeshoe.
He gave thanks, did the Paramount Chief,   40
He gave thanks, as he nodded his head:
'Thus fights a subject, RaMathalea,
He fights in plundering for the house of the Chief'.
    You Whites, you haven't any friendship,
For you're lacking the spirit of alliance, Bosses: 45
Otherwise I wouldn't have fired at Qethoane.[9]
    I fired at a rabbit, it jumped from its shelter,
The rabbit of that place they say is Manganane:[10]
The nephew of Thaane, son of Sehlabaka, defiled the fortified cave,
Someone bespattered the fort with diarrhoea,   50
For he saw the Leche of RaMathalea,[11]

---

[1] For Shao, Letele, Manamolela and RaMoiketsi, see i. 10–12, p. 81 above.
[2] No doubt another Monaheng chief.
[3] Litšoeneng is a hill west of the present town of Zastron.
[4] For RaMokoena-Seqha, see i. 13, p. 81 above.
[5] For RaMokeretla, see i. 8, p. 81 above. The men who have bound him are almost certainly Posholi's regiment, the Claws.
[6] Monyane, a son of Monaheng, was the father of Makhetha, whose sons once occupied the site now known to Europeans as Beeste Kraal, but still known to the Sotho as Thabana tsa Bara ba Makhetha, 'The Little Hills of the Sons of Makhetha'. These are the hills referred to here.
[7] It is impossible to identify this incident.
[8] Evidently Posholi captured some cattle at night.
[9] The allusions in this stanza are obscure.
[10] For Manganane, who is also Thaane's nephew in the following line, see i. 15–16, p. 81 above.
[11] For lines 47–51, cp. i. 14–18, p. 81 above.

The biter belonging to the Leche of young men,
The champion with powerful sinews,
The champion who's come with a cow from the Boers,
55 Who said: 'The heifer's not come stepping quickly,[1]
The heifer from the centre, from a line of men,
From RaSheqa's, from the pick of the warriors'.[2]
  Hey, Moletsane[3] and Seeker,[4] you're amazed:
There's something coming and covering you,
60 It comes in great numbers, it comes through the plain.[5]
  Hasn't it jumped, the leopard of the steep,
Of the steep, of the sloping hill!
It exploded and landed on Tlhoane's buttock![6]
  The black and white shield of the husband of Nkopi
65 Has coped with the stick made of iron.[7]
  Young man, you who wash for the people,
Wash for the people of RaSenate[8] that they may put on clothes,
For this is the time when first they kill.[9]
  Men went back to yesterday's corpses,
70 Men have gone back to the corpses to count.[10]

---

[1] 'The heifer's not come stepping quickly', because its owners have not given chase.

[2] For RaSheqa, see iii. 9, p. 84 above. The idea may well be that the heifer has been captured from a well-guarded position that was difficult to reach.

[3] The chief of the Taung at Mekoatleng.

[4] 'Seeker', i.e. Posholi's brother, Mopeli, who lived at Mabolela, not far from Moletsane.

[5] i.e. Posholi's great army is coming to protect you. As far as is known, only twice did Posholi's warriors go north to help Moletsane and Mopeli—in May 1852 and October 1853, on both occasions against Sekonyela.

[6] Tlhoane's identity is not known.

[7] Lit. 'Has met with the stick made of iron', i.e. with a gun. There is a play on words here with Nkopi, the name of one of Posholi's wives, and *kopane*, 'has met', which is reproduced by the translation of *kopane* as 'has coped with'.

[8] i.e. Letsie, Senate being his daughter.

[9] The significance of this stanza is not clear. It is known that Posholi helped Letsie in some of his earliest expeditions. It has been suggested by Chief 'Mako Moliboea Molapo that washing for Letsie's people means preparing oneself to help them, and that putting on clothes denotes getting ready for war. According to Mr. Stephen Pinda, however, men who had killed for the first time were often troubled by dreams, and were given medicines to drive these dreams away and to restore their confidence and fighting spirit. *Ho solisetsa batho*, he argues, means, not to wash oneself for people, but to give them these medicines; while to put on clothes, he agrees, means to prepare oneself for fighting again.

[10] The incident alluded to cannot be specified.

The heaven of the people of Libe of Matlole,[1]
Of the family of Libe and the Giraffe,[2] Koena,
He's eaten tobacco on the mountain, at Qethoane,
He finished the tobacco among those who provoked him.[3]
The trouble-maker who longs for meat, the belly of the eater of   75
                                  castrated goats:
The goats were stepping on the rocks at Qethoane,
They were plump, they wound all over the fortress.[4]
The giver of drink[5] knows hail very well,[6]
He's taken the horn, he's taken the caller,
He took the little horn of the springbok too.[7]   80
The youth who lives on the property of others,
Today it is finished. What shall he eat,
RaSeabeng[8] of the mother of Motšoane?[9]
The warrior from there at the Cape is fighting,
No longer does he look for crowds,[10]   85
He helps himself with his hair:
These are the crowds, his hair![11]
The stick of the walker of the youths
Walks and disappears at Tolomaneng.[12]
RaMathalea wears the skin of a leopard,   90
The young chief of the family of Makhabane.[13]
RaMathalea has no fear of the hunt:[14]
How will he fear it when it's he who invites it?

[1] Libe, Mokhachane's elder brother, was Posholi's paternal uncle. Matlole, alias Motloang, was the father of Peete, and was therefore Libe's grandfather.

[2] Mokhachane was known as 'the Giraffe' because of his speed.

[3] In this context to eat tobacco means to fight and destroy. Those attacked were no doubt the Monaheng at Qethoane.

[4] Posholi himself is referred to in the first line of this stanza. The castrated goats were the Monaheng rebels on the mountain fortress of Qethoane.

[5] 'The giver of drink', because he provides milk for his people.

[6] i.e. he can bring hail on his enemies and can ward it off from his own followers.

[7] i.e. he has taken the horns which contain the medicines which can attract hail.

[8] Seabeng is believed to have been one of Posholi's daughters.

[9] Motšoane, i.e. Peete, Posholi's grandfather.

[10] For lines 84–5, see ii. 8–9, pp. 82–3 above.

[11] i.e. his own resources are adequate.

[12] Significance unknown. Tolomaneng is a mountain in the area now known as Palmietfontein, in the Herschel District. There is evidence which suggests that Posholi lived there for a short time in the early 1830s.

[13] For lines 90–1, see lines 10–11 above.

[14] 'a hunt', i.e. a group of men, an army coming to attack him.

The shooter at the rabbit, Sekhonyana's kinsman,[1]
95   Shot at the rabbit in the midst of the Thembu,
He shot as he jealously guarded his ox.
When he shoots, the country becomes his!

6. *Mopeli*

Mopeli (*c.* 1810–97) was a son of Mokhachane by one of his junior wives, and grew into manhood, probably at Thaba Bosiu, during the last years of the *lifaqane*. In 1831 he had a finger shot off by the Kora of Piet Witvoet when they attacked Makhabane's village at Ntlo-Kholo, and in 1835 he took part in the raid on the Thembu of Ngubencuka.

After the *lifaqane* he continued to live at Thaba Bosiu, where he was one of the first Sotho to be influenced by Christianity. By 1843 he had been baptized into the Church with the name of Paulus and at the end of 1844, together with four other members of Moshoeshoe's family, he accompanied the missionary Arbousset to Cape Town, where he stayed for a year for educational purposes.

On his return early in 1846 he again took up residence at Thaba Bosiu, mainly, it seems, out of respect for the wishes of the missionaries. For several years, however, many of his adherents had been living north of the Caledon, and in 1848 he went to join them, ultimately establishing his village at Mabolela, close to the present town of Clocolan. He soon abandoned the Church, and became one of the most fiery participants in the Sotho's struggles with the Tlokoa. He also played an important part in the battle of Viervoet in June 1851, when Warden's mixed force sustained a sharp defeat, and when more than 100 of Moroka's Rolong were killed.

In the war of 1858 he was a leading figure in the Sotho's resistance in the north, and in subsequent years his adherents were continually exasperating the Free Staters by moving onto their farms in disputed areas. In 1865 his village was totally destroyed in one of the first major engagements of the second war; and in 1867, at his own request, he and his followers were received as subjects by the Free State and were allocated a reserve in the Witzies Hoek area. Separated from the rest of the Sotho, he remained there until his death in 1897.

He was highly respected for his intelligence and his natural dignity. According to oral tradition today, Moshoeshoe valued him as a counsellor, but became estranged from him after his desertion in 1867.

[1] Sekhonyana, alias Nehemiah, was a son of Moshoeshoe who migrated to the area now known as East Griqualand after the war with the Free State in 1858. There he ran into difficulties with the Mpondomise of Mbale, and this stanza probably refers to the expedition in June 1861, when Posholi and other chiefs went to his assistance. The Sotho may use the word Thembu to refer to any Cape Nguni group.

Mangoaela has recorded six of his praise-poems, of which only the first four are reproduced here. The first relates to his skirmishing with the Tlokoa during the Orange River Sovereignty. The second relates mainly to the first war with the Free State in 1858. The third, according to Mangoaela, relates to the second war with the Free State, and conveys not a hint of the disasters and humiliations which Mopeli suffered. The fourth relates mainly to the battle of Viervoet, but also refers to hostilities with the Tlokoa. The fifth and sixth are *mélanges*, and contain many lines which may also be found in the first four poems. It is partly because of this, and partly because of the obscurity of so many of their allusions, that they have been omitted from this volume. Apart from Mangoaela's collection, four poems were published in *Leselinyana*, 9 April 1915. These too have been omitted, since they are mainly variations of the poems published by Mangoaela, and contain very few lines that are entirely different.

In the poems printed in this volume the first person singular is never used in such a way as to refer clearly to the chief. In Mangoaela's fifth and sixth poems, however, it is so used in several passages which are variations of passages in these poems. The question of authorship must therefore remain open.

(i)

The tawny cow of the Makaota !¹
The cow of Gert's comrade is here,²
Maketekete's father's³
Is here, the tawny one from the home of fierce battle.⁴
Speak to me, black and white cow of the north,   5
Cow of the hill of Moliko,⁵ regard me.
Don't shun me as you come by my side,
As if you'd been fetched at night,
Whereas you've come at high noon,

¹ i.e. Mopeli himself. The Makaota, or 'Lean Ones', were people who had been impoverished during the *lifaqane* and had been compelled to live by hunting and gathering. Many of them later settled under Mopeli.
² Gert is Gert Taaibosch, the Kora chief. His comrade is Sekonyela. Evidently Mopeli had captured one of Sekonyela's cows.
³ This phrase stands in apposition to 'Gert's comrade', for Maketekete's father was Sekonyela.
⁴ 'the tawny one' here seems to be the cow captured from Sekonyela, and not, as in line 1, Mopeli himself. The reference to it in the following line as a black and white cow is no obstacle to this interpretation, for there is very little consistency in the *lithoko* on such matters. In line 12 below, for example, Mopeli himself is called 'Little black cow'.
⁵ Moliko (Britsberg) is a hill near the present town of Senekal in the Orange Free State.

10 You come in full view of your masters.[1]
Come down, come here to be herded.
   Little black cow of the people from Mokhachane's,
Black, treading firm when the shields have been taken,[2]
When the death of young men has been taken:
15 He's a coward to you, young men.[3]
   The old men watched from the mountain, they saw with their
                                                            eyes

On the very first day, on the day when it started,
When the bulls were kicking up dust at each other.
There, the sun became dark, it was black,
20 It was darkened by the smoke of the guns,
By the smoke of the guns and the canons![4]
   The Closer[5] of the village of Mohale,[6] the Tripper,[7]
The Closer closed with a shield from a tree,[8]
He closed with a gun, RaMachakela,[9]
25 He closed with a gun, and the people lived!

   [1] i.e. the cow had not been captured by stealth, but in a fair fight.
   [2] For this phrase denoting the outbreak of war, cp. the praises of Moshoeshoe,
iii. 27, p. 74 above.
   [3] In the Sotho: *O boi ho lona, bahlankana.* In another of Mopeli's poems the
following lines appear:

> *Ke boi, kea tšaba, RaNtsubise'a Matsie,*
> *Ke Lekoala la motse oa Mohale, Mokhopi,*
> *Ka koala ka sethunya, RaMachakela,*
>   . . .

> I'm a coward, I'm afraid, RaNtsubise of the Locusts,
> I'm the Closer of the village of Mohale, the Tripper,
> I closed with a gun, RaMachakela,
>   . . .

The word *lekoala* in the second line normally means 'a coward'. Here, however,
it is treated as a deverbative eulogue from the verb *ho koala*, 'to close', i.e. to
defend. The effect is one of surprise. In the present passage line 15 has clearly
become detached from the other lines which give it its full significance, which
appear as lines 22 et seq. In isolation, however, it may be understood to imply
that in battle Mopeli will show that he is not a coward, and that the young men
are wrong.
   [4] In fact canons were never used in the hostilities between the Sotho and the
Tlokoa, and they are probably mentioned here for poetic effect. They were used
by Warden's forces at Viervoet in 1851, but it seems unlikely that there would
be a reference to this battle, in which the Tlokoa did not take part, in a poem
which otherwise refers solely to the Tlokoa.
   [5] i.e. the Defender. See fn. 3 above.   [6] Mopeli's brother.
   [7] 'the Tripper', because he tripped up his enemies.
   [8] Presumably a shield made of wood, although this would be most unusual.
   [9] i.e. Father of Machakela, Machakela being his eldest son.

Let the cowards be castrated, that they breed no children,
For they'll only be breeding other poltroons.
They spoil the country with their dung,[1] the shits,
They disappear at the Leopard-That-Roars![2]
The stopper of the red white-spotted cattle as they graze in the   30
                        areas reserved,[3]
As they graze at Khalise and Mpharane,[4]
On the way to the ruins of Tšoeu Matekase.[5]
When they said he was the husband of Seara,
He arose and swept off all their herds![6]
When they said he was the husband of Sebina,   35
He demeaned the prince of Tlokoeng underfoot![7]
They said to him: 'You're from the Kalahari':[8]
He harried RaMmuso to defeat![9]
They said to him: 'You're a pot for the shit':
He shattered the pate of Lesaoana![10]   40
  The tawny cow of the Makaota!
  The cow of Gert's comrade is here,
It's come to be marked with a crocodile.[11]

---

[1] i.e. their bowels are loosened by fear. Cp. Posholi, i. 17, p. 81 above.

[2] This area is said to be on or near the Berea Plateau.

[3] i.e. areas reserved for winter grazing, or for the growing of thatching grass, reeds, etc. It seems that the Tlokoa had captured some of the Sotho's cattle, but that Mopeli had recovered them as they were being driven away. (The verb *ho thiba*, 'to stop', is commonly used with the sense of 'to recover': see, e.g. Maama, iv. 73–5, p. 168 below.

[4] Hills close to Sekonyela's stronghold of Marabeng.

[5] Tšoeu, son of Matekase, was a Tlokoa, and it is known that at some time he fled to Lesotho and transferred his allegiance to Moshoeshoe. Clearly he had already done so when the incident alluded to here took place. The site of his former village is not known.

[6] 'Seara' and 'arose' reflect a play in the Sotho on *Seara* and *arella*. Literally line 34 means: 'He rounded up (*arella*) all the herds, finishing them!'

[7] 'Sebina' and 'demeaned' reflect a play in the Sotho on *Sebina* and *binakella*. Literally line 36 means: 'He trampled (*binakella*) on the prince of Tlokoeng!' Tlokoeng, a locative formed from Tlokoa, means 'the land where the Tlokoa live'.

[8] The Tlokoa referred contemptuously to the Sotho as *Bakhalahali*, 'people of the Kalahari desert', with the implication that they were San.

[9] 'Kalahari' and 'harried' reflect a play in the Sotho on *Mokhalahali* and *khala*. Literally line 38 means: 'He defeated (*khala*) RaMmuso!' RaMmuso was Sekonyela, 'Muso being one of his daughters.

[10] The Lesaoana referred to here is not Moshoeshoe's nephew, but a Tlokoa. 'Pot for the shit' and 'shattered the pate' reflect a play in the Sotho on *thuoana* and *thua*. Literally line 40 means: 'He broke Lesaoana's head!'

[11] Moshoeshoe and his brothers, being Koena, 'People of the Crocodile', used to earmark their cattle with a crocodile-shaped cut.

When we said war was a difficult matter,
45 Someone wouldn't listen, he swore by Mokotjo.[1]
He sat at Seqaobe, and then he was crying![2]
Had he not called in the Whites,
With their sabres coming rattling from every side,
With the canons booming and the plain thundering,
50 What would he now still see? Would it be even a goat?[3]

(ii)

Chief, command us, RaMoeletsi,[4]
Command us, roan cow that gives much milk,[5]
For they've always been stirring up quarrels.
When they were going to cross the Lithane[6]
5 The shields' scraggy animal was limping from the hip:
Mopeli sang for it the war-song.[7]
      The cow from Mabula,[8] white-spotted round the eyes,
The spearman of Mabula is
A rock-rabbit, a spy,[9] the comrade of Lelaka RaSenate.[10]
10 He sits on a summit, deceiving the fools,
Saying to Senekal:[11] 'There is the moon':

[1] Mokotjo was Sekonyela's father, and it was Sekonyela who was swearing by him.

[2] Serious hostilities broke out between the Sotho and the Tlokoa in September 1848. The Sotho quickly gained the upper hand, and Warden summoned the disputants to a meeting at Seqaobe, about 12 miles from Sekonyela's home, in November that year. Hostilities continued, however, and a further meeting was held at Seqaobe in June 1849. At both meetings Sekonyela complained bitterly about his losses.

[3] Subsequently Warden intervened actively against the Sotho and their allies, the Taung, and the poet claims that Sekonyela had the Europeans to thank for any stock which he had managed to retain.

[4] i.e. Moletsane, the Taung chief, Moeletsi being one of his sons.

[5] A praise-name of Moletsane.

[6] The Lithane (Molen Spruit) is a tributary of the Caledon.

[7] According to Mangoaela, this poem relates exclusively to the first Free State war in 1858. However the sixth of Mopeli's poems in his collection (which is not printed here) contains a stanza which is similar to this opening stanza, and which makes it clear that the people who had been stirring up quarrels were the Tlokoa. 'The shields' scraggy animal' may well refer to the Taung's hard-pressed warriors, whom Mopeli encouraged by singing the war-song.

[8] A mountain about 25 miles south-west of Mopeli's village of Mabolela.

[9] Rock-rabbits may often be seen looking out from the hills as if they were spies.

[10] RaSenate was Letsie, Senate being his daughter, but nothing is known of a son called Lelaka.

[11] The Commandant-General of the Free State forces in 1858.

While he regarded it
He set fire to his buttocks with burning fuel!
   Please feel the point, creator of wars,
It's the first time your cattle have been plundered by the Sotho!   15
By devouring Oetsi's you formed a habit![1]
   Do you think a cannibal can stop making progress
Once he's devoured those of Manamolela?[2]
   The crocodile of Mabula,
The crocodile of the monitors,[3] the Father of Machakela,   20
The crocodile makes no distinction between people,
It will go on saying that people are people.[4]
It has no fault, it's unwilling to be provoked,
It's unwilling to be provoked by foreigners:
When they brandish their sticks, they call it.[5]   25

(iii)

   In that year of the onslaught of war,
When Makate and Khoalipana were disputed,[6]
When Thaba-Tšoeu was taken, and Linokong too,[7]
Then he stood firm and took an oath, did the Seeker,[8]
Saying: 'By Peete and Mokhachane,   5
The Frog will hear on the plateau[9]
That the red bull's kicking up the soil!'[10]

[1] Oetsi was chief of the Kholokhoe, and until 1856 he and his people lived in the area which is still known as Witzies Hoek. In 1856 the Free Staters swept off much of their stock and drove Oetsi and many of his followers into Lesotho.

[2] The persons addressed are probably the Free Staters: the cannibal probably represents the Sotho. Manamolela may well be the Monaheng chief with whom Posholi was fighting in the south-west: see Posholi, i. 11, above. There is no evidence, however, that Mopeli was involved personally in these hostilities.

[3] The idea seems to be that Mopeli is superior to those around him just as a crocodile is superior to monitor lizards.

[4] i.e. Mopeli will not fight others simply because they are not Sotho: he respects the humanity of all men.

[5] i.e. although he wants peace he will fight if he is seriously threatened.

[6] Makate is a mountain six miles east of Mabolela. Khoalipana is some high land about 23 miles to the north.

[7] There are several mountains called Thaba Tšoeu ('White Mountain'). The one referred to here is otherwise known as Wonder Kop, and is about 27 miles north-north-west of Mabolela. Linokong is an area close to the Thaba Tšoeu. This territory quickly fell under Free State control in 1865.

[8] In 1831 Mopeli had a finger shot off by the Kora of Piet Witvoet when they attacked Makhabane's village of Ntlo-Kholo. In the praises composed on that occasion he was called the Seeker because he was seeking his lost finger.

[9] The Frog was Moshoeshoe: the plateau was Thaba Bosiu.

[10] i.e. that Mopeli is preparing to fight.

The wretched little white one's a despicable thing,
It stands in the marsh, at the Lebabalasi,[1]
10   It exchanges fierce looks with the bull of Peete.
The bull from the land of the Whites has been stabbed in a
                                                    dangerous spot:
It crossed the Tikoe, it went to Maphororong:[2]
We've heard that they now point it out at 'Makhoana's![3]
It has no voice, it fears to speak:
15   The voice that rings out is Mokhachane's son's:
It rang out, it was heard among the Ndebele,
Shepstone heard in the company of Mpande[4]
That the crocodile was furious, it was fighting,
It was no longer on friendly terms with people.

(iv)

The watery abyss is full, RaNtsubise,[5]
He's a lake that's green, where people plunge;
The lake once made the Élite[6] fall,
It's made a hundred people fall:
5   There wasn't one who rose alive![7]
A Rolong was hurrying along the road,
When going to the Major's and Gert's.[8]
He said: 'Chake's sitting on the crocodile's face,[9]
He's sitting on the crocodile's piercing horns,

---

[1] A tributary of the Tikoe, or Sand, River.

[2] The Tikoe is the Sand River down to its junction with the Vet, and is thereafter the Vet. Maphororong is Doornberg.

[3] The village of the Taung chief 'Makhoana (who was no longer alive in 1865) was probably on or near the site of the modern Makkawaan's Bank in the Orange Free State.

[4] Theophilus Shepstone was Secretary for Native Affairs in Natal. Mpande (Panda) was chief of the Zulu. Their names are mentioned merely to indicate the extent of Mopeli's fame as a warrior.

[5] i.e. Mopeli himself, Ntsubise being a daughter.

[6] One of the regiments of the Rolong chief, Moroka.

[7] The reference is to the battle of Viervoet in 1851, in which more than a hundred Rolong met their deaths, many of them by jumping in desperation from the heights of Viervoet mountain. In line 5 the poet makes fun of the Rolong by using their dialect.

[8] The Major was the British Resident in the Orange River Sovereignty, Major Warden: Gert was the Kora chief, Gert Taaibosch.

[9] Chake was Moroka's brother. To sit on the crocodile's face means to provoke Mopeli. It is known that Chake had killed a Sotho, presumably a follower of Mopeli, and that later he was killed at Viervoet. (See S. M. Molema, *Chief Moroka*, p. 76.)

He's sitting on trees with countless branches.   10
While he's alive we'll continue to speak of him,
We'll say that good fortune however is God:
It's God however who's helped him!'[1]
   The driver of the enormous monster
Which comes with its mouth agape,   15
It bellowed as it came to Mpharane,
The ruins of Mosi, the child of 'Moi.[2]
   The raven cawed and said: 'Where are you going?'
The crow cawed and said: 'Where are you going?
The land beyond the river is a land of wars,   20
The land of RaMokhele Montoeli,[3]
It's been spoilt since the time of its masters.[4]
Mighty men, men who were chiefs,
Were always stripping and fighting,
When they cut off men's heads   25
Right up to the Tuke,[5] where the pools are deep.'
   Crocodile, Seeker, close the fords,
That of RaMatobo and that of Mokhotsako.[6]
Tooane[7] says: 'And close over here!
There are two of us, I'm staying with Masoenyane,   30
With Masoenyane, with the child of Tšiame.[8]
   Confine the ogre to the veld, Seeker,

[1] i.e. if Chake survives this danger it will be the work of God. This speech is partly in the Rolong dialect.

[2] Another passage of Mopeli's praises (not printed in this volume) makes it clear that 'the enormous monster' was trying to capture the Sotho's cattle, and that Mopeli drove it away. No doubt the monster represents Warden's mixed force, which was driven away at the battle of Viervoet. The Mpharane referred to here is a mountain a few miles north of the present town of Marseilles. Mosi was a chief who once lived there. Warden's force no doubt passed close to this mountain on its way to Viervoet.

[3] RaMokhele Montoeli was one of the ancestors of the Taung, who were occupying the area of Viervoet. Apparently the raven and the crow were advising Warden that in going to this area he was running into trouble. The reference to the river in line 20, however, cannot be explained.

[4] i.e. there had been much fighting in that land ever since the time of its original owners.

[5] A stream near Mabolela, now known as Mopeli Spruit.

[6] Presumably these are fords across the Caledon, since Mopeli is being exhorted to keep the enemy out from the heartlands of Lesotho. Their positions are not known.

[7] Identity unknown.

[8] Masoenyane was a Kholokhoe. Evidently his father was Tšiame, but nothing more is known of him.

If it crosses[1] it'll kill us,
It may kill us and our children,
35 RaKhosi[2] and Mokhachane,
Children who can't flee:[3]
If we leave here they'll stay.'
   Cutter of the bull's sharp horn:
It's wicked, even the calves it gores,
40 Even the calves and females it gores.[4]
   Cutter of the king's bull's fury,
Cut the flame from the heart of the chief:
Chief, you should know us, that we're people.[5]
   The cattle with backs that are streaked with white, the cattle of
                      the husband of Moroesi,
45 Of the husband of Moroesi Moletsane,[6]
The white-streaked cattle are two, they are three:
One white-streaked cow has pointed at Moroka,
One white-streaked cow was pointing at Sekonyela.[7]
   How, when you eat from the horn of a goat,
50 Do you think you can fight with the father of Masopha,[8]
The Frog[9] who's the saviour of people?
He saved the people of Motonosi.[10]
   Swelling Udder[11] fetched them at a time of plenty,

---

[1] i.e. if it crosses the Caledon.   [2] Identity unknown.
[3] They cannot flee because they are too old.
[4] Several Sotho women and children were killed in the disturbances of the Orange River Sovereignty.
[5] This line is apparently addressed to Warden.
[6] Moroesi, daughter of the Taung chief, Moletsane, was one of Mopeli's wives.
[7] The significance of this stanza is not known.
[8] i.e.: 'When you have very little food and so cannot support a large following, how do you think you can fight Moshoeshoe?' The lines that follow suggest that the chief being addressed is Sekonyela. This passage is reminiscent of some well known lines in the praises of Moletsane:

> 'Seeing that you eat in a hut, Rolong,
> Against whom do you think you can turn your shield,
> . . .?'

[9] A praise-name of Moshoeshoe.
[10] i.e. the Tlokoa, Motonosi being Sekonyela's great-grandfather. Between 1840 and 1842 they were involved in hostilities with the Kora of Gert Taaibosch and others. Many of them sought refuge with Moshoeshoe, and most of these people returned to Sekonyela when the war was over.
[11] i.e. Sekonyela. Literally *sepholo* ('Swelling Udder') means 'a cow's teat full of milk': as a praise-name it implies both wealth and generosity.

When they came to his home he spoiled them,
He gave them a gift of powdered tobacco,   55
Like snuff intermingled with dagga.[1]
We'll smoke them, devouring and ending them,
We of the family of Libe, of Mokhachane,
People of the family of Qhoqholoane of the Crushers.[2]
We're not to be attacked with a little black dog,   60
By someone who is tricky and dishonest.[3]
The cow of 'MaLibe, with horns bent forward,
With horns bent forward it beautifies the Locusts[4]
Of our family, of RaLibe of the Striped Ones.[5]
Roan cow with back that is streaked with white, cow of the 65
                                        Maoa-Mafubelu,
Cow of the Hlotse stream, cow that is black with white spots![6]
As the cattle were going to ascend the mountain
The cow that was black became the stopper
For the comrade of Mosheshe and RaBohoko.[7]
The one who goes round from 'MaNtšebo's[8] went round,   70
Round he went behind 'Mota,[9]
Round he went behind the village of the louse:[10]
He fetched the cattle from Kubu-se-'Mele.[11]
RaNtsubise, the Locusts' fetcher,

[1] i.e. he imbued them with the spirit of contention.
[2] Identity unknown.   [3] The precise reference is not known.
[4] i.e. Letsie's regiment. (The translation of Matsie as Locusts is uncertain.)
[5] The father of Libe was Peete. The Striped Ones were evidently his regiment.
[6] The Maoa-Mafubelu is a tributary of the Hlotse. Before the *lifaqane* the Mokoteli's villages were close to their junction, and no doubt Mopeli was born in this area.
[7] Mosheshe and RaBohoko were both Taung: their comrade was probably Moletsane. Evidently some of the Taung's cattle had been captured—probably by the Tlokoa—and Mopeli had cut them off as they were being driven away and had recovered them.
[8] Identity unknown. It is most unlikely that the reference here is to Lerotholi's senior wife, for she would have been only a girl at this time.
[9] Sekonyela's younger brother, whose village was at Makosane, just below the Leribe plateau. It was attacked and burnt by Sotho forces in May 1852, and it is no doubt to this campaign that the poet alludes here.
[10] The dictionary definition of *tšoele* ('louse') is: 'clothes moth, in the larval stage; museum beetle in the larval stage; evil-doer'.
[11] i.e. Sekubu, an area in the present Botha-Bothe District of Lesotho. In 1852 it was still under Tlokoa control, and no doubt 'Mota had tried to secrete some of his cattle there. Mopeli had gone round his village at Makosane and had captured them.

75   Fetches the cattle from Boribeng,[1] far away,
        The cattle at Qoing, at Moojane's.[2]
            The crocodile went begging for meat-scraps, the Seeker,
        He goes to crave bits that have fallen from the axe.[3]
        You commoners are merely crying:[4]
80   Indeed even he, the master's adherent,
        The adherent of RaLesaoana,[5] Koena,
        When he's captured cattle he's denied them:
        He's not even given a milk-cow!
            Even when he's drawn off an animal's blood,
85   When he's drawn off the blood and filled his little pot,
        The cow's owner's child would simply pour it out,
        He would drain it off into his own little pot![6]
            Sharp-eared one of the Mapeli,[7]
        You hear, you understand fully:
90   Moshoeshoe, the king, gives orders with authority,
        He gave orders to the Locusts and the Hawks,[8]
        Some being the Takers of Peka-Motse,[9]
        And others being the Thieves.[10]

7. *Letsie I*

Letsie I (*c.* 1811–91) was the eldest son of Moshoeshoe by his senior wife. At birth he had been called Mohato, but was given the name of Letsie at the initiation school as a tribute to the celebrated Monaheng chief, Mohlomi, who was also called Letsie. The meaning of the name is obscure, but it may be connected with the word *tsie*, meaning 'locust': if so, then it no doubt conveyed the idea that Letsie destroyed his enemies as a locust destroyed crops.

In 1833 he was sent to live at Morija, where Casalis and Arbousset had founded their first station. There, like his uncles, he sometimes embarrassed Moshoeshoe by his unauthorized raids on Sotho and other

---

[1] A flat rock on the Leribe plateau near Pitsi's Nek.

[2] Whereabouts unknown.

[3] i.e. in the distribution of the spoil after the campaign Mopeli does not make excessive demands.

[4] Commoners have no reason to complain that they receive nothing when, as the following lines reveal, Mopeli himself is so shabbily treated.

[5] i.e. of Makhabane, Lesaoana being his son.

[6] i.e. even when he was given something it was taken away by one of Moshoeshoe's sons.

[7] One of his regiments.   [8] Masopha's regiment.

[9] Molapo's regiment. Peka-Motse, i.e. Peka, was one of Molapo's villages.

[10] The regiment of Jobo Lelosa, Moshoeshoe's brother.

communities. In 1835 and 1836, however, his zeal for plunder was harnessed to expeditions against certain Nguni and Kora groups, and an allusion to this may no doubt be detected in his praises:

> Letsie devours no Sotho's cattle,
> Letsie devoured the Ndebele's,
> . . .

Though living at Morija he never became a Christian. On the contrary, he was critical of his father's trust in the missionaries and in the British, and at the time of the Sotho's general disillusionment with Europeans during the Orange River Sovereignty his criticisms appeared to have been justified. He was a leading figure in several campaigns during that period, and was generally regarded by the British authorities as one of the most hostile and intransigent of the Sotho chiefs.

In the war of 1858 his forces harried the Free State commandos in the south before falling back on Thaba Bosiu, and his village at Morija was then razed to the ground. In the second war with the Free State his role in the fighting was small, and indeed at one stage he was reported to have taken refuge in the Maloti. By the end of the war he had moved his village to Matsieng, about seven miles east of Morija.

When Moshoeshoe died in 1870 he became Paramount Chief in his stead, but continued to live at Matsieng. He had very little control over his brothers, Molapo and Masopha, and but for the presence of European administrators the chiefdom might well have fallen part. During the Gun War he professed loyalty to the administration, but his sincerity was often doubted, and in any event he was unable to enforce obedience. It was characteristic of his rule that when he sent in his own guns to Maseru they were captured on the way by his son, Lerotholi. He died in 1891, and was buried on Thaba Bosiu.

Of all the chiefs whose praises appear in this volume Letsie alone had a reputation for cowardice—a reputation which was so firmly established that it was reflected even in the eulogies at his funeral. There is no hint of it, however, in his *lithoko*. These, as recorded by Mangoaela, consist of a single poem, which is a *mélange*, and which is remarkable for the high proportion of structured stanzas which it contains. The chief is referred to in the first, second and third persons singular, and it seems probable that he composed at least some of the poems from which the stanzas of the *mélange* have been taken.

> Father of Lerotholi, the Locusts'[1] repeller,
> Repeller, repel, please, the wretched little Bushmen,
> Repel Gert's Bushmen, and make them return.[2]
> The Bushmen ran, they left their round buttocks,

[1] Letsie's regiment: see introductory notes.
[2] The 'Bushmen' were the Kora of Gert Taaibosch. The incident alluded to no doubt occurred during the Orange River Sovereignty.

5   Their tortoise-like buttocks[1] they left behind![2]
      Father of Lerotholi, the Locusts' thief,
      The thief is a robber, father of Lerotholi,
      When Moroka[3] came he stinted him,
      He stinted him, he gave him no people at all![4]
10   They came, did the people of 'MaNthatisi,
      They tried to extinguish the fires in our hearths;
      The old men stripped off their karosses to fight them,
      The cattle came back, we people lived![5]
      The extinguisher of fire of the people from Mokhachane's
15   Extinguished the fire of the Likonyela,[6]
      And, even as to lighting it, they no longer light it,
      They go away weeping to the land of the Whites.[7]
      What a narrow escape it was, Kora youngster,
      When you got away from us Man-Eaters![8]
20   The devourer of the cattle of Mjaluza,[9] the man who is full of
                                                              invention,
      Letsie devours no Sotho's cattle,
      Letsie devoured the Ndebele's,[10]

---

[1] i.e. their buttocks which were shaped like two tortoises.
[2] Their buttocks were conspicuous as they fled, and it almost seemed as if they were being left behind.   [3] The Rolong chief at Thaba Nchu.
[4] The significance of this stanza is obscure. Perhaps the reference is to the combined Sotho/Rolong attack in 1836 on the Kora of Riet River and their Xhosa allies. There was much bad feeling between Moroka and the Sotho chiefs on this occasion, and it is just possible that Moroka begged for assistance in the battle and that Letsie refused to grant it. Or perhaps some of Moroka's followers had deserted him for Letsie, and Letsie refused to send them back. This certainly happened later in the 1850s.
[5] The people of 'MaNthatisi, Sekonyela's mother, were the Tlokoa, who attacked Thaba Bosiu in 1829 while the main Sotho forces under Moshoeshoe were raiding the Thembu below the Drakensberg. Only the old men and the youngsters remained, including Letsie and his comrades, who were then in the initiation school. Nevertheless they succeeded in driving the Tlokoa away.
[6] Sekonyela's regiment.
[7] This stanza refers, not to the Tlokoa attack of 1829, but to the Sotho's final and decisive victory over the Tlokoa in October 1853, when Sekonyela's stronghold at Marabeng was taken, and when he himself sought refuge with British officials.
[8] Another of Letsie's regiments. It is impossible to specify the incident alluded to here.
[9] A Xhosa chief who fled from his home in 1835 and settled at Qethoane (Koesberg) between the Orange and the Caledon. There his people began to waylay Sotho travelling to and from the Colony, and so in August 1836 Letsie and Molapo attacked and destroyed his village, killed him and many of his followers, and swept off most of their cattle.   [10] i.e. the Nguni's.

He's devoured those of Tyopho[1] and Mjaluza,
Mashapha's[2] have been devoured with their baggage.
    The cattle of the millet have slipped away, 25
They slipped away, they returned to Mhlambiso's.[3]
    The surpasser of those who surpass the peoples,[4]
Mafa, I can surpass both you and your uncle,
And your uncle, your father's brother:[5]
You brandish your mighty sticks 30
That have just been cut at Masite,[6] at the rapids.
    The lizard, the serpent of the waters, Letsie,
He licked, he blew away the villages at Hlatsing:[7]
Letlala he was afraid to lick,[8]
He's afraid, because he's old, this Siea, 35
He's afraid of the wailing at home,
He's afraid of the crying from the depths of the hut,
He's afraid of the crying of Letuka Tlhabeli.[9]
    It hasn't any milk, any thick milk, the roan cow,
It belongs to those who fight battles: 40

---

[1] For Tyopho, chief of the Gcina, see Moshoeshoe, i. 62 et seq., p. 70 above.
[2] Mashapha was another chief of Nguni origin, but beyond this it is impossible to identify him.
[3] Mhlambiso, son of Mthimkhulu, was a Hlubi chief who went in the early 1840s to settle near the newly established Wesleyan mission station of Kamastone. The incident alluded to cannot be identified. It is known that in 1849, during the disturbances of the Orange River Sovereignty, some Hlubi under Letsie, who wanted to slip away from him, sent some of their cattle in advance to Mhlambiso. Perhaps the allusion is to this. The reference to 'cattle of the millet' is not understood.
[4] i.e. the surpasser *par excellence*. Cp. line 42 below: 'Stamper of the stampers.'
[5] Mafa was the son of Moshoeshoe's sister, 'MaTšoeunyane, whose husband, Mahao, was the brother of Letsie's mother, 'MaMohato. Mahao had several brothers, but the most prominent among them was Paulus Matete, who lived in Morija and was for many years Letsie's most important adviser. Matete is almost certainly the uncle referred to here.
[6] A mountain not far from Morija. There is still a small forest there where sticks may be cut.
[7] Hlatsing, i.e. the country of the Siea, the Tlokoa's kinsmen and allies. This stanza refers to Moshoeshoe's attack on Sekonyela in October 1853.
[8] Letlala was chief of the Siea, and was also the brother of 'MaNthatisi, Sekonyela's mother. He was captured, but his life was spared on Moshoeshoe's instructions.
[9] Letuka, son of Tlhabeli, was another Siea chief. He had taken refuge with the Sotho, probably during the Tlokoa's war with the Kora and others during the early 1840s. In 1853 he was living under Letsie at Morija. According to the poet, Letlala's life was spared out of consideration for Letuka's feelings.

It doesn't produce any milk for 'MaSenate.[1]

Stamper of the stampers,[2] husband of Mokhali,[3]

Stamp the ground, the sorcerers are asleep,

Maqatela and 'Mota are asleep.[4]

45   The mantis is smeared with white clay,[5] the Hound,

I, the girl from the school[6] at Kholu's,[7] I've entered the pass![8]

The complainer as he eats of the people of Mokhachane's,

The complainer as he eats lacks food for the journey,

They say that the food is enough for the warriors![9]

8. *Molapo*

Molapo (*c.* 1814–80) was the second son of Moshoeshoe by his senior
wife. In many ways his early career was similar to Letsie's. Like him, he
was sent to Morija in 1833; he was eager to acquire cattle, and sometimes
disobeyed Moshoeshoe by plundering others; and he was at least partly
satisfied by the raids on various Nguni and Kora communities in 1835 and
1836. Unlike Letsie, however, he distinguished himself brilliantly in these
encounters and thus gained a reputation for daring and bravery; and, so
far from remaining impervious to the Gospel, he was baptized into the
Church in 1840 with the name of Jeremiah.

Meanwhile his relations with Letsie had been steadily deteriorating, for
it was most unusual for two important chiefs to remain in such close
proximity. In 1843 he began making arrangements to leave Morija, and
in due course he migrated to Peka, north of the Phuthiatsana, on territory
which was claimed by Sekonyela. At the end of 1846 the mission station
of Cana was founded a few miles south of the river, but, although he himself went to live there, many of his people remained where they were.

---

[1] i.e. although Letsie was a warrior, he was not given enough cattle, and so was
unable to maintain his senior wife, 'MaSenate, as he should have done.

[2] i.e. the stamper *par excellence*.

[3] Mokhali, i.e. 'MaSenate, Letsie's senior wife.

[4] Maqatela's identity is unknown, but he was probably a Tlokoa. 'Mota was
Sekonyela's younger brother.

[5] At the battle of Viervoet a few Sotho warriors had been inadvertently killed
by their own comrades. To avoid this in the attack on Sekonyela, Moshoeshoe
ordered his men to smear their faces with white clay.

[6] It is the custom for girls at the initiation school to smear their faces and
bodies with white clay, and so Letsie likens himself to such a girl.

[7] Kholu was Moshoeshoe's mother.

[8] 'the pass', i.e. of Sekonyela's stronghold of Marabeng.

[9] As in lines 39–41, there is a complaint that, although Letsie is a warrior, he
is not given his fair share of the spoil.

In 1848 hostilities broke out between the Tlokoa and the Sotho when Sekonyela determined to put an end to what he regarded as Moshoeshoe's encroachment on his land. Molapo was at the centre of this struggle, but when, with the assistance of Gert Taaibosch's Kora, and with the tacit support of Major Warden, Sekonyela temporarily gained the upper hand, he withdrew for a short while to Tšoanamakhulo. After the final defeat of the Tlokoa in 1853, he was sent to occupy their country, and established his village at Leribe. By this time he had become thoroughly disillusioned with the British and their religion, and had reverted to the Sotho's traditional beliefs.

His role in the war of 1858 was not conspicuous, but in the years that followed his people were among those who most irritated the Free Staters by moving onto their farms. When war broke out again in 1865 he retired to the mountain fortress of Thaba Phatšoa, but never had occasion to defend it. In the early months of 1866 a Free State commando raided deep into the Maloti and swept off the enormous herds of cattle which he had secreted there; and in the lowlands his crops were being steadily and ruthlessly destroyed. In March that year, therefore, he made his own separate peace with the Afrikaners in the Treaty of Mpharane, whereby he agreed that he and his people should become Free State subjects and that they should take no further part in the war. When peace was finally restored, however, they were reunited with the rest of the Sotho under Moshoeshoe.

In 1873 he assisted the Cape authorities in the capture of Langalibalele, the Hlubi chief who had fled into Lesotho from Natal; and in 1880, shortly before the outbreak of the Gun War, it was generally believed that he would be willing to surrender his firearms if required to do so. These speculations were ended by his death.

During his lifetime he was respected both for his exceptional intelligence and for the bravery which he had displayed in his youth. He was on excellent terms with his father, even after the Treaty of Mpharane. Today, however, he is widely regarded as a traitor to the Sotho in particular, because of the Treaty of Mpharane, and to the Africans of southern Africa in general, because of his betrayal of Langalibalele.

Four of his praise-poems have been recorded by Mangoaela, all of them very short. The first was inspired by the campaign against the Thembu in 1835; the second and fourth relate to the fighting with the Tlokoa during the Orange River Sovereignty; and the third is a single stanza which alludes to hostilities with Major Warden and Gert Taaibosch. In none of them is Molapo referred to in the first person singular, but they are all so short that their authorship must remain an open question.

(i)

The Brave Warrior wears charms, he's thinking at night,
He's thought of things evil, he's thought of things dark,

He's thought of splashes of blood in their hundreds.[1]
The comrade of the child of Mokhachane[2]
5   Cut off the cattle, but desisted from plunder
While the other cutters-off were taking their pick,
While Kompi and Moorosi were taking their pick,[3]
Going around to every group of cattle.
They went among the cattle of his men, the Recoverer's:[4]
10   Yes, 'Neko too was quarrelling![5]
Wouldn't you give the runner's cow for running,[6]
While the other cutters-off were taking their pick?
They went among the cattle of his men, the Recoverer's,
And even there they meant to take their pick!
15   When the cattle were facing the Mokoallong,[7]
And were about to cross the river to go home—

[1] The text translated is that given by A. M. Sekese, Chief Jonathan Molapo's secretary, in *Leselinyana*, 15 March 1893, and is as follows:

> *Sekoere se roetse, se ja bosiu,*
> *Se jele limpe, se jele lintšo,*
> *Se jele tse makholo liqaphatsi.*

This text is accepted by leading authorities among Molapo's descendants today. The translation given is that suggested by Chief 'Mako Moliboea Molapo, except that in line one he would translate *Sekoere se roetse* as: 'The great warrior is clothed in fury.' The verb *ho ja* normally means 'to devour', and is often used to refer to the seizure of cattle. Its use to signify thinking, or 'devouring in the mind', is original, but acceptable. To think of splashes of blood means to think of the bloodshed of war. In line 2 Mangoaela gives *linepe* (milk-cows) instead of *limpe* (evil things), and if this is correct then the translation which most naturally suggests itself is the following:

> The Brave Warrior wears charms, he's eating at night,
> He's eaten the milk-cows, he's eaten the black ones,
> He's eaten splashes of blood in their hundreds.

Here eating splashes of blood would signify killing the enemy as one captures his cattle.
[2] i.e. of Moshoeshoe's brother, Tšiame. When in later years Molapo went to live at Leribe, Tšiame went to live close by in the area of Tsikoane.
[3] Kompi was Adam Krotz, a hunter from Philippolis who had guided the French missionaries to Thaba Bosiu in 1833 and who had subsequently settled among the Sotho. Moorosi, chief of the Phuthi, was one of Moshoeshoe's subordinates. Evidently Molapo was annoyed when they were allowed to take the pick of the plundered cattle.
[4] i.e. Letsie's.
[5] 'Neko was the eldest son in Moshoeshoe's second house. Clearly he too was complaining that others were being granted the pick of the booty.
[6] Molapo gives up all hope of receiving a decent reward and asks, half in despair, half in jest: 'Won't you give me a cow for running so fast?'
[7] The Mokoallong is said to be a river which flows between Elliot and Barkly East.

Allow your horse to run, Light-Footed Warrior,
To cut off the oxen at their head.[1]
Famous one of those who are famed for hunting elands,
When cattle must be captured you hold back your horses![2]   20

(ii)

Runner-to-help of the Takers whenever the alarm is sounded,[3]
Runner to the help of the cow that is black,[4]
Run, for the Famous Chief's house is burning,
The house of Sefafe's child, Kali, is burning![5]
Crocodile of the Senders,[6]   5
Crocodile, 'MaSekhonyana's[7] refuser,
You refused when the nation was being assembled,
When your nation of the Beoana[8] was being gathered together,
When Monyeke and RaQethoane[9] were being gathered together:
Then Nkakole and his people[10] crossed the Caledon.[11]   10

[1] Evidently the cattle which the Sotho had captured slipped away and began to return to their homes: Molapo turned back and rounded them up again.

[2] This stanza is probably addressed to Moorosi and his followers, who were renowned for their skill in hunting elands. According to the poet, they were less proficient and enthusiastic in cattle raiding.

[3] Lit. 'The Takers' alarm which runs to help'. The Takers were one of Molapo's regiments.

[4] According to Chief 'Mako, 'the cow that is black' was a Molibeli chieftainess whom the Tlokoa had captured and whom Molapo's men rescued. However, there is no mention of any such incident in the contemporary evidence.

[5] In 1846 Kali, a Molibeli chief who was subject to Moshoeshoe, went to live in the area of 'Male, about ten miles from Sekonyela's residence. Two years later Sekonyela ordered him to move, but Moshoeshoe and Molapo advised him to stay where he was. In September 1848 the Tlokoa burned down his village. In retaliation Molapo and his cousin, Lesaoana, swept off about 800 head of the Tlokoa's cattle, killing two men as they did so. 'Famous Chief' was evidently one of Kali's praise-names.

[6] Lit. 'Those Who Send Out', or 'Those Who Bring Out'. They were another of Molapo's regiments. The origin of the name is unknown.

[7] 'MaSekhonyana was Moshoeshoe's third wife. Molapo was brought up in her house.

[8] i.e. the Sotho. See Moshoeshoe, ii. 5, p. 71 above.

[9] Identities unknown.   [10] Identities unknown.

[11] The most natural interpretation of this stanza is that Sekonyela was trying to gather some of Moshoeshoe's followers to himself, and that Molapo resisted this. If this is correct, then Nkakole and his people crossed the Caledon from the right bank to the left, moving towards the more central parts of Lesotho. But at the time of the burning of Kali's house, Molapo, so far from concentrating the Sotho, was pushing them outwards, and Sekonyela was complaining of their

Cut off the curling-horned cattle, Sender:
The cow at one time we tended,
Tending it at Senyotong and Tlapaneng.[1]

(iii)

Agitator's comrade, Tlhakanelo, you're malicious,[2]
You ought to have told the Major[3] and Gert,[4]
Saying: 'As for going, we go there to Mokoteli's:[5]
There's someone there who's stubborn, the Agitator,
5 He doesn't avoid by retreating.
He's obstinate, when thrown at he resists,
When thrown at he avoids by leaping forward, the Brave Warrior,
In the place where the spears are still coming with fury.'

(iv)

The Agitator, the Brave Warrior, the comrade of the Breaker[6]
and Sekujoane,[7]
He caused an agitation among the regiments,
He devoured the child of Letlala,
He devoured a man who was close to the chief,
5 Who was close to his cousin,

---

encroachment on his land. It is possible, however, that this stanza refers to a later time—1850, 1851, or 1852—when the Sotho were more under pressure, and when Molapo would have been more concerned with attracting as many followers to his own area as possible.

[1] Senyotong (a stream and an area) and Tlapaneng (a mountain) are in what is now the Berea District of Lesotho. The cow referred to is possibly a chief who once lived under Moshoeshoe at those places; then, in the general expansion of the Sotho, went to live near the Tlokoa; was subjected to pressure by Sekonyela to join him; and ultimately went back to the more central parts of Lesotho to live near Molapo. The chief in question cannot be identified, but may well be Nkakole. To 'cut off' cattle means to recover them as they are being driven away by the enemy.

[2] The Agitator was Molapo himself. His comrade, Tlhakanelo, was a son of the Rolong chief, Moroka, and was of roughly the same age as himself. He was 'malicious' because, although he knew of Molapo's bravery, he nevertheless allowed the British and the Kora to become involved in hostilities with him.

[3] i.e. Major Warden.

[4] Gert Taaibosch, the Kora chief.

[5] 'to Mokoteli's', i.e. to Lesotho. For Mokoteli, see p. 63 above.

[6] The Breaker was Molapo's cousin, Lesaoana, the son of Makhabane.

[7] Sekujoane (meaning unknown) is said to have been a praise-name of the Molibeli chief, Ntsane.

Who was close to the Chief Sekonyela.[1]
The Enterer[2] is squatting in a group of men,
He goes on sipping coffee with the son of Mokhachane.[3]
Shield, Thesele's[4] weakener,
Weaken Letsosa while he's still making love,   10
Having gone to make love in the land of the Phuthi,
At the village of Kamolase Mahasa.[5]

9. *Masopha*

Masopha (*c.* 1822–98) was the third son of Moshoeshoe in his senior
house. He was named after the Ngwane chief Masumpa, the father of
Matiwane, since he was born at Botha-Bothe at the time of a Ngwane
attack. He was too young, either to take part in the wars of the *lifaqane*, or
to migrate with Letsie and Molapo to Morija. Instead he remained with
his father at Thaba Bosiu, where he was converted to Christianity and
took the name of David.

In common with many other Sotho he turned against his new religion
during the disturbances of the Orange River Sovereignty, and it was at
this time too that he first won renown as a warrior. His most celebrated
exploit was his assault on Sekonyela's mountain stronghold of Marabeng
in 1853, when, with extraordinary courage, he forced his way to the
summit up a narrow and heavily guarded pass. In 1854 he migrated to
Thaba Phatšoa in what is now the Leribe District of Lesotho. This move
was opposed, apparently, by his brother, Molapo, and by his cousin,
Lesaoana, both of whom had territorial interests in the north-east, and it
was no doubt in deference to their wishes that in 1855 he withdrew to live
on the Berea plateau.

In the first Free State war in 1858 he was one of the Sotho's leading
commanders in the north; and in 1861 he led his regiments below the

[1] Letlala, the Siea chief, was the brother of Sekonyela's mother, 'MaNthatisi,
and so his son was Sekonyela's cousin. The incident alluded to is not known.
[2] 'The Enterer', presumably because Molapo was not afraid to go in among
his enemies.
[3] The son of Mokhachane referred to here is probably Tšiame: see i. 4,
p. 112 above. The significance of this stanza is uncertain. Perhaps it is merely an
indication of Molapo's coolness in battle.
[4] Thesele, i.e. Moshoeshoe.
[5] Letsosa was probably a Fokeng, for the name is common among the Fokeng
today. Presumably he was one of Sekonyela's subjects. There is still a village
called Mahasa's in the territory which was once controlled by the Phuthi chief,
Moorosi. Presumably the home of Letsosa's wife was in this area. The incident
alluded to is no longer remembered, although one may conjecture that Letsosa
was injured by Molapo's men as he returned to Sekonyela's country after visiting
his wife's village.

Drakensberg to help his brother, Sekhonyana, in an abortive attack on the Mpondomise of Mbale and the Thembu of Jumba. As soon as the second war with the Afrikaners broke out in 1865 he raided the Free State in the general directions of Winburg and Bloemfontein, and captured large numbers of cattle, sheep and goats. As he was returning he was intercepted by a Free State commando near Verkeerdevlei and most of his booty was lost. Shortly afterwards his village was destroyed, and he then joined his father on the summit of Thaba Bosiu. When Louw Wepener and his men tried to force their way up the Rafutho pass in August 1865 Masopha and his warriors were among those who repelled them. Indeed throughout this war he remained close to Moshoeshoe, and in this way firmly established his reputation as the most courageous of the chief's many sons.

After his father's death in 1870 he conducted himself almost as if he were independent of Letsie and of the Cape administration. For example, in defiance of the Governor's Agent, he refused to move his village, which was now at the foot of Thaba Bosiu; and in the Gun War, although he did not take a very active part in the fighting itself, he was the leading spirit among the rebels in the north. However, the establishment of direct imperial rule in 1884 and the accession of Lerotholi to the paramountcy in 1891 led to a gradual strengthening of the central authorities, and in January 1898, after a particularly flagrant act of disobedience, Masopha's power was broken by Lerotholi's forces in the battle of Khamolane. A few months later he died.

Today he is remembered as one of the greatest champions of Sotho independence in the last century, and his praises are among the most popular. Nine poems have been recorded by Mangoaela. The first relates almost exclusively to Masopha's conflicts with the Tlokoa and their allies during the Orange River Sovereignty. The second is a short *mélange*, and contains some interesting references to his dispute with Molapo and Lesaoana. The third, according to Mangoaela, relates to the first Free State War in 1858. The fourth describes the campaign against the Mpondomise in 1861, and is particularly interesting in that it is the earliest poem in this volume to bear any resemblance to a constructed narrative. Broadly speaking, it tells of Masopha's departure from home; his journey across the Drakensberg; his battle with the Mpondomise; and his return home. The fifth, a single stanza, relates to the attack on Marabeng in 1853. The sixth is mainly a variant of the fourth. The seventh relates both to the first and to the second war with the Free State. The eighth is a short *mélange*, and contains variants of stanzas from the first two poems. The ninth relates to an occasion during the Sovereignty when Masopha put an end to the troublesome raids of Jacob the Griqua.

There is only one clear reference to Masopha in the first person singular (see vi. 26–7, p. 134 below), which suggests—though no more— that most if not all of these poems were composed by someone other than the chief himself.

(i)

The cow of the house of spears,[1] the Hawk,[2]
The black and white cow that's rebellious!
Weave it a rope, it's broken it,
Its milkers are still lamenting,
Both Letlala and his men and Maketekete and his men.[3]   5
   The black and white cow dropped mud in the milk,
It kicked it up with its foot at the back,
It said that the axe-heads should part from their handles,[4]
That a cow should run with a calf on its back,
That a person should run with a child on her back.[5]   10
   Who is the Motlejoa among you Hawks,[6]
Motlejoa, the one who goes round the kraal,
Who rounds up the ox that is black with white spots, the ox that is
                        black and white-spotted?[7]
   The heifer of the woman with light complexion,
The child of the woman of Khoele[8] listened,   15
He heard the Koena's refusal
When the cattle were being taken from Botha-Bothe,[9]
The cattle of the orphan of Mohato[10] and his kin.

[1] i.e. the man who comes from a family of warriors. Cp. Moshoeshoe II, line 3, p. 267 below.

[2] Lit. 'African lammergeyer, lammervanger'.

[3] Just as a cow refuses to be milked, and breaks the rope with which its milkers attempt to control it, so Masopha refuses to be brought under control by the Siea of Letlala and the Tlokoa of Maketekete, Sekonyela's son.

[4] i.e. that the axes should be wielded in battle until their heads fell away from their handles.

[5] This stanza depicts the confusion and alarm which Masopha causes.

[6] Motlejoa was a notorious cannibal during the *lifaqane*. The Hawks were Masopha's regiment. This line may be taken to signify: 'Who is the most fearful warrior among you Hawks?'—the unexpressed answer, of course, being Masopha.

[7] This translation of lines 12–13 is extremely uncertain. (It is based on the tentative suggestion of Mr. Xavier Sekhomo and Mr. Casimir Sekhomo of Mapoteng that the word *terea*, which is not Sotho, is derived from the Afrikaans *draai*, 'corner', and that as a verb it signifies 'going round corners', or merely 'going around' in a protective way.)

[8] i.e. either his grandmother, Kholu, or his mother, 'MaMohato, both of whom came from the Khoele branch of the Fokeng.

[9] Masopha was born at Botha-Bothe *c.* 1822. While he was still a child the cattle of Moshoeshoe and his followers were plundered by the Tlokoa, among others, in spite of their resistance, or 'refusal'.

[10] Mohato, i.e. Letsie.

You should eat them and leave the bones,
20 When he grows up he will seek them.[1]
It appeared with anger in its heart,
The Hawk of Nthe and Mahlape.[2]
The eagle has entered the cattle-posts of the Kora,
It entered the Kora's and the Ropoli's,
25 It said that the Bushman should come to be killed here.[3]
Your hider, the hider of you Steadfasts,[4]
Has hidden while the old people speak of him,
Saying: 'Today the Joiner's appeared:
He joined the bachelors together,
30 He stabbed them with a single spear!'
The spear of Posholi's child is of iron,
Another of Posholi's child's spears cuts clean,
It's made a clean cut on Mojapo's head!'[5]
As for him, he doesn't give things to himself, nor does he speak
of himself,
35 Steadfast's not generous to himself with his mouth:
The *seboku* grass even may speak of him,
It spoke of him, saying he was a warrior.[6]
The child of the chief, the thundering shot,[7]

[1] The Tlokoa are warned that they should not consume these animals completely, for when Masopha becomes a man he will come and look for them.
[2] Nthe and Mahlape were his sisters.
[3] The Kora of Gert Taaibosch were Sekonyela's allies, the Ropoli his subjects. The 'Bushman' referred to in line 25 is almost certainly a Griqua called Jacob, whose raids caused considerable distress among the Makaota, some of Moshoeshoe's subjects living north of the Caledon. In 1852 or 1853 Masopha swept off his cattle, and then invited him to come and be killed, i.e. to try to recover them. In the ensuing skirmish Jacob was wounded and his son was killed.
[4] Another of Masopha's regiments.
[5] Mojapo may possibly be a variant form of Jakobo, i.e. Jacob. See fn. 3 above.
[6] The *seboku* grass can speak of his bravery, because it is there that the enemies whom he has killed come to rest. Cp. the following line from the *mokorotlo*, or war-song:
'The grave of the warrior—the *seboku* grass.'
[7] The translation of *sekete se molumo* as 'thundering shot' is extremely uncertain. It is based on the suggestion of Mr. Stephen Pinda of Mafeteng that *sekete* is derived from the Afrikaans *skiet*, meaning 'shoot', and that *sekete se molumo* (a thundering *sekete*) means 'one who shoots with a thundering noise'. However, Chief Lebihan Masopha points out that today the word is most commonly used to denote the number 1,000. He suggests that it has been adopted for this use because it originally meant an enormous multitude; and that *sekete se molumo* means a man who comes thundering against his enemies as if he were an army in

That strikes the eland with a thud,
That strikes the brown ambler with a thud: 40
Even that eland they didn't skin.[1]
    Being with 'Nau, the son of Ntšeke,[2]
He went through the pass of Mahlatsa and Lipetu
As the snow fell hard on their shoulders:[3]
They were going to enter the valley of Maqhaoe.[4] 45
    Then after a while, a very short while,
The sun rose, and threw out its rays:
The chief[5] too threw out his regiments.
He summoned the Tufts,[6] he summoned the Hawks,
He told the Hounds to go and devour them.[7] 50
    After his ears had heard,
He pricked up his ears like a jackal,
He heard it said that the watchman of the Steadfasts,
The watcher who watches for alarms,
Had watched for Kabai and Setloboko.[8] 55
    The prop of the village of Mohato,[9] Masopha,
Stood up and looked out for Sekonyela,
He, the warrior of great cunning.
    He's driven out Ntsane of the land of the Siea,

---

himself. Chief 'Mako points out that *sekete* can also mean 'mercury'. He suggests that it has been adopted for this use because it originally meant something silvery and shining, and that in this context it means a bullet.

[1] The eland here no doubt signifies an enemy warrior. 'Even that eland they didn't skin': i.e. they were in such a hurry that they did not cut away parts of his body for use as medicines, or, alternatively, they did not plunder his cattle. If this stanza is to be taken with the stanza that follows, then the incident referred to occurred when the Sotho forces were going to attack the Tlokoa in May 1852.

[2] i.e. Makoanyane, Moshoeshoe's most celebrated warrior.

[3] The Sotho regiments evidently passed by these mountains as they went to attack the Tlokoa in May 1852, and it is known from another source that snow did indeed fall on this occasion.

[4] A small stream and valley in the Leribe District.

[5] i.e. Moshoeshoe.

[6] Another of Masopha's regiments, so named because each man shaved off his hair, leaving only a single tuft.

[7] i.e. the Hounds, one of Letsie's regiments, were to seize the enemy's cattle.

[8] Kabai, a brother of Sekonyela, lived near the Wesleyan mission station of Mpharane. Setloboko cannot be identified, but was evidently one of Sekonyela's followers.

[9] Mohato, i.e. Letsie.

60 He's driven out Ntsane from his cleft in the rock.[1]
He went to report in the presence of Moshoeshoe,
Saying that the plunderer of his cattle
Was yonder, having disappeared in war.
   The fierce monster,[2] the devourer of the enormous cow,
65 The devourer of the cow of Maethe's family![3]
   You're so many, you people of Mokoteli,
You're so many, you people of Mokhachane,
And it's you who beget the Young Wildebeest![4]
Moshoeshoe's begotten him, RaMahlolela,[5]
70 He begat a new young warrior,
He's begotten a new one, an opener of the fords.[6]
To the Hawks what word has he spoken?
   His comrades mock and insult him,
They say: 'Little Buttocks, tiny behind!'[7]
75 The small villages, when they see him, despise him.
Mohato's family's young initiate there
Is brown, with muscles that are tough:
His thigh is like an oribi's, Steadfast,
The brother of Mpinane.[8]
80   If it were the case that men could be bought,
Then the Young Wildebeest would be bought![9]
   The one who digs open of the Repeater[10] and Moshoeshoe
Dug open the passes that were closed,
That had even been stamped and made firm:
85 They were even to be closed with the wretched little Bushmen,

[1] No doubt this was an incident in the campaign of May 1852, but the details are not known.

[2] The translation of *Kulubutu* as 'The fierce monster' is uncertain. Some authorities think that it means 'one who appears suddenly', or 'one who throws in all his forces as soon as battle begins'.

[3] Maethe cannot be identified. The incident alluded to is not known.

[4] Lines 66–8 have been liberally translated to convey the underlying meaning that Masopha must indeed be a powerful chief, since he has sprung from such a large community. Literally they mean:

      Since you are so many, people of Mokoteli,
      Since you are so many, people of Mokhachane,
      Wouldn't you beget the Young Wildebeest!

[5] Mahlolela, alias Tholoana, was Masopha's daughter.

[6] i.e. one who takes the lead in overcoming difficulties.

[7] Masopha was in fact a small, wiry man.

[8] Mpinane, Masopha's sister, was otherwise known as Nthe.

[9] i.e. Masopha would be popular and in great demand.

[10] i.e. Mohale, Moshoeshoe's brother.

To be closed with Gert's little Bushmen themselves!¹
He darted out, did the kite, and he snatched,
When he snatched he snatched the crane
That was white, pure white, and that came from the land of the
Griqua.²
Most have climbed up by the passes of the women, 90
But *he's* climbed up by the passes of the men,³
He's climbed into the centre, where the warriors are thronging,
Where the spear that goes astray stabs the horse!⁴
Someone died, his mother missed him,
He fell head first, as if he'd rise:⁵ 95
He pointed his head towards the land of the Griqua,
Foreboding now the killing of his people.⁶

(ii)

The excreter at the cattle-posts, the child of Thesele,⁷
The one who excretes at the posts for herding cattle,
The excreter excretes in the great cattle-kraals,
He excreted in the kraal at Motsetseli's:
The girls are afraid to take out the dung, 5
They say that the head herdboy's excrement is there!⁸

---

¹ A more popular version of this stanza may be found in v. 1–5, p. 133 below. The allusion is to the Sotho's victory over the Tlokoa in October 1853, when Masopha led an attack up the only pass at Sekonyela's stronghold of Marabeng. Across this pass was a wall, and below the wall some of Gert Taaibosch's Kora had drawn up their wagons and were ensconced behind them. Nevertheless Masopha fought his way to the summit. Here Taaibosch's Kora are contemptuously referred to as 'Bushmen'.

² Although sandwiched between two stanzas relating to the victory over the Tlokoa, this stanza refers to Masopha's attack on Jacob the Griqua. See line 25 above, and cp. ix. 1–6, below.

³ Other Sotho forces went round to the other side of Marabeng and climbed up the steep cliffs there. The poet implies that, compared with Masopha's frontal assault, this was women's work.

⁴ i.e. the warriors are so crowded together that if a spear misses a man it is bound to hit a horse.

⁵ i.e. it was difficult to believe that he was dead. Cp. Maama, i. 28, p. 156 below.

⁶ This stanza probably refers to the attack on Jacob the Griqua and to the death of Jacob's son.

⁷ Thesele, i.e. Moshoeshoe.

⁸ It is an insult to excrete in another man's kraal. No doubt in this case the insult would be added to the injury of plundering his cattle. Motsetseli was probably a Tlokoa, and according to some authorities today he was the son of

Since they were striving to go ahead
People took the path of the travellers.[1]
Meat is prepared in the fire for the Hawk,
10   The spears it prepares in the fire for itself.[2]
Lion cub, don't cry for bravery:
Bravery belongs to the mighty lions,
The Agitator's bravery and the Depriver's.[3]
Yellow Wildebeest, Young Wildebeest,
15   Yellow, very yellow, you left your parents' village
When you went away from home, from RaMohato,[4]
Preferring to remain to one side,
Having left to go outside, to rocky wilds.[5]
As for you, Agitator, Father of Little Vultures,[6] are you willing?
20   As for you, Breaker of Makhabane,[7] are you willing
That the Hawk should cut a share?
If he doesn't cut a share, he simply grabs a handful:
He begs you for a share, his masters.[8]
Lion, give help to Phakathao Bungane:
25   In the eyes of Phakathao you're a saviour.[9]
In the eyes of Thesele, of the son of Mokhachane,
You're an emigrant.[10]
Stabber, what chased the hartebeests away?

Nkhahle, a chief who was senior to Sekonyela in status, but inferior to him in authority. It is known that a few months after the Sotho's expedition against the Tlokoa in May 1852 Masopha attacked some Tlokoa cattle-posts, and this may well be the exploit alluded to here.

[1] i.e. they were so eager for war that they did not bother to conceal their approach.

[2] i.e. he allows others to cook for him, but he does his own fighting.

[3] The Agitator was Molapo, the Depriver Letsie.

[4] RaMohato, i.e. Moshoeshoe.

[5] This stanza no doubt relates to Masopha's migration to Thaba Phatšoa in 1854.

[6] i.e. Molapo, because he fed the little vultures on the bodies of his enemies.

[7] i.e. Lesaoana, Masopha's cousin.

[8] Both Molapo and Lesaoana lived in the north-east, and it would appear from these lines that they objected to Masopha's intrusion into this area.

[9] Phakathao is the Sotho form of a Nguni name which it would now be difficult to form with any certainty. Moreover the man himself cannot be identified, although the reference to Bungane suggests that he was a Hlubi. The incident alluded to is no longer remembered, but one may tentatively conjecture that Phakathao was living in the Thaba Phatšoa area, and that Masopha afforded him some kind of protection.

[10] Perhaps Moshoeshoe was opposed to Masopha's migration.

They feared the Young Bull Wildebeest.[1]
   Assist him to look, you Koena, for he's looking,   30
If you don't give him something he'll depart,
He'll go to see Monyake, and he'll stay:
It may be that they will give him something.[2]
   Indeed, in truth, they've made him a gift,
They gave him the Griqua's ox, the ox that is black with a white- 35
                                     streaked back.[3]
   The roan cattle have come with the herdsman,
They've come with the Bushman from the Griqua;
As they come, they pull him and shake him,
Making him look for the fords.[4]
   Send Seholoba, the child of Peane,   40
To go to report them, to ride a yellow horse and report them.[5]

(iii)

   The blower of the horses of the Whites![6]
Blower, kill the Whites at the river
And leave the people from 'MaLehlasoana's:
Don't pay any heed to those of Mokhalong,
They're wretched little Bushmen, they're Gert's little Bushmen, 5
They're little Bushmen, they have no use.[7]

[1] Perhaps Masopha chased some of Sekonyela's adherents away from the area of Thaba Phatšoa.

[2] Once again there appears to be a complaint that Molapo and Lesaoana, and perhaps Moshoeshoe too, were reluctant to grant Masopha any land. Monyake was a son of the Taung chief, Moletsane, whose headquarters were at Mekoatleng in the north.

[3] The significance of this stanza is obscure. Perhaps Monyake had given Masopha some assistance in plundering the cattle of Jacob the Griqua.

[4] This stanza no doubt refers to the attack on Jacob the Griqua, but its precise significance is not clear. Perhaps Masopha brought back the body of Jacob's son, 'the Bushman from the Griqua', together with some of his cattle.

[5] Presumably Seholoba was one of Masopha's men, and was sent to report the capture of Jacob's cattle to Moshoeshoe.

[6] i.e. the one who captures the horses of the Whites, for he 'blows' them to his home; or, possibly, the one who repels the Free State commandos, for he 'blows' them away.

[7] According to Mangoaela, the whole of this poem relates to the first war against the Free State in 1858. If this is so, then these lines clearly refer to the events of 12, 13, and 14 April. A commando under Senekal crossed the Caledon and advanced towards the Berea plateau. It was driven back to its lager near Cathcart's Drift, where there was heavy fighting for three days. Eventually the Sotho withdrew. The people from 'MaLehlasoana's cannot be identified,

They're just like the son of What's-His-Name, of So-And-So.
If I say it's So-And-So he'll hate me![1]
10   Blower, you're a warsong that's beginning to be sung,
You're a song that's begun at Mokhethoaneng,[2]
You were sung at 'MaMohale's,[3] at home.
You're a song which is sung when the sun is fierce,
When it scorches the fallow and unploughed fields
Below the house of Kuku, the doctor,
15   At the homes of Ntharetsane, Leputla, and their people.[4]
    Imparter of arms to the Hawks, Masopha,
Implant a reed on the people from Senekal's,
That when they go to the river they go crying![5]
    When speaking they say they've been driven from the land
20   By herdsmen of whom they have no knowledge.
It may be they're Mokhachane's herdsmen:
In their midst was a light-skinned child:
If it hadn't been he who returned,
With his head bent low among the regiments,
25   Over there, yonder, at Lithamahaneng,[6]
And here among the cattle at Lepoqo's,[7]
The passes they'd have climbed on every side.[8]
    The child of 'MaMokoteli,[9] the stirrer,[10]
    The stirrer's the spear that is barbed: when he stabs

---

although they may well be the same people as 'those of Mokhalong'. These were a Tlokoa group, who, as the allies of the Kora chief, Gert Taaibosch, during the time of Orange River Sovereignty, could still be referred to contemptuously as his 'little Bushmen'. It is known that Senekal's force was assisted by non-European contingents.

[1] The object of this jibe cannot be identified. Cp. Lerotholi Mojela, lines 96–7, p. 239 below.
[2] A mountain area on the left bank of the Caledon, close to Cathcart's Drift.
[3] 'MaMohale was one of Masopha's wives.
[4] Evidently there was fighting in this area. The identities of Kuku, Ntharetsane and Leputla are not known.
[5] Masopha is exhorted to stab Senekal's men with a spear, 'a reed', and so to drive them back across the Caledon. 'Imparter of arms' and 'Implant' reflect the pun in the Sotho on *Hlomellane*, 'one who gives arms', and *Hlomella*, 'plant on'.
[6] This name is no longer known.
[7] i.e. at Moshoeshoe's, at Thaba Bosiu. Lepoqo was the name given to Moshoeshoe at birth.
[8] i.e. but for Masopha the Free Staters would have gained access to the summit of Thaba Bosiu.
[9] For Mokoteli, see p. 63 above.
[10] Lit. 'the kneader', i.e. one who stirs up trouble and causes confusion.

He stabs with the thin sharp spear. 30
    There, you see, Moletsane's people,[1]
And you, RaMokhele Montoeli's people![2]
Taung beyond the river, pay heed,
When you burn the dry grass you then fear it,
And so it's put out by the Hawk at the river,[3] 35
The Hawk, the charmer away of the hail:
The hail was humming, it went along the hills.[4]
    We regiments at the river, crowds and crowds,
Those of us with sabres, and those with little bridles,
Those with little bridles with straps all over, 40
We were watched as if we were dancing,
People kept placing their hands on their foreheads:
Hawk, the battle was made a shade for the eyes![5]
    The black and white cow of the thieves,
The cow of the rebellion of Masakale, 45
The cattle were pastured all over the veld.[6]
    The Hawk of the family of Nthe and Mahlape,[7]
The village was built on the slope, Steadfast.[8]
    Iron is plucked from the fire still hot:
Hawk, when it cools it can shatter the hammers.[9] 50
    RaMahlolela,[10] the tongs of the shields,
The tongs of the village of Mohato, the Hawk,
A court without tongs isn't fitting,

---

[1] i.e. the Taung of Moletsane.

[2] RaMokhele Montoeli was an ancestor of the Taung chiefs. Cp. Mopeli, iv. 21, p. 103 above.

[3] i.e. the Taung provoke their enemies to fight, but are then afraid, and so these enemies have to be held in check by Masopha at the Caledon.

[4] i.e. Masopha diverted the enemy away from Lesotho.

[5] This stanza probably refers to the Sotho attack on the Afrikaners at Cathcart's Drift on the evening of 14 April 1858. According to a report made by the Free State Commandants (see *Basutoland Records*, ii. 344–5), the battle was watched by 'a great number of women and children on the ridges of the hills'.

[6] The significance of this stanza is not known. Masakale is a common name among the Fokeng, but there is no other clue to the identity of the man.

[7] Masopha's sisters: see i. 22, p. 118 above.

[8] Probably Masopha's own village.

[9] i.e. Masopha acts swiftly when passions are high, especially in battle, and in this way he is most effective. When passions have cooled it is impossible to get anything done.

[10] i.e. Masopha, Mahlolela being his daughter.

It would seem to be a court without youth.[1]

55   Regiments from home, you're shedders of karosses,
As you returned you shed your karosses,
You shirkers from the home of the chief,
Regiments without any wounded![2]
He wouldn't gallop, he wouldn't trot,

60 He wouldn't pretend to walk fast.[3]
You're brave, and no one denies it:[4]
A young warrior indeed is Masopha,
It's he who gives strength to the chiefs,
Who gives strength to the side of RaMosa[5] and Letsie.

65   Young men with whistles that summon,
Those whistles of yours don't amuse us:
They belong to them alone, and to the people of RaSenate.[6]
They're noisy: so toss them away, far away,
Those of yours.[7]

(iv)

The striker of rock,[8] the digger of the mountain,[9] the chief of
                             those who make a trail above,
The mighty chief, RaMahlolela,[10]
He's as big as the mountains, the hairy one.

[1] Just as tongs pull irons out of a fire, so Masopha can be effective in the heat of battle. Without a man of this calibre a village would appear to be destitute of warriors.

[2] The 'Regiments from home' are almost certainly Letsie's warriors, who are here derided for cowardice. Shedding one's kaross enables one to run faster. According to Sotho tradition Letsie was a coward both in the Battle of the Berea in 1852 and in the war against the Free State in 1858.

[3] This no doubt implies that he always moved with dignity.

[4] The reference is probably to Masopha's regiment, the Hawks, for 'You' here is plural.

[5] i.e. Molapo, Mosa being his daughter.

[6] i.e. Letsie, Senate being his daughter.

[7] This stanza suggests that another chief had been summoning Masopha to help him in war, but that Masopha had refused to go, saying that only Letsie had the right to summon him. The incident concerned is now forgotten.

[8] Lit. 'One who strikes something hard', i.e. who attempts something difficult.

[9] i.e. one who digs a path over a mountain. In 1861 Masopha crossed over the Drakensberg range to assist his brother, Sekhonyana, alias Nehemiah, against the Mpondomise of Mbale. The name 'digger of the mountain' also conveys the general idea of one who undertakes a difficult and hazardous task.

[10] i.e. Masopha, Mahlolela being his daughter.

The armies departed from Nyaba-Nyaba,[1] Masopha,
They departed from Nyaba-Nyaba by the pass,   5
The armies slipped away with their spear-bags on their backs.
    The widow-bird took the finches in a group[2]
To spend with them the night at Pitsaneng.[3]
At daybreak he ascended the mountains,
The husband of Maluke[4] crossed over the passes.   10
He saw the mountains with their shadows, and he stopped:
He stopped there and then looked around,
He looked around carefully to examine the paths:
The paths he saw that went to the Leqholoqha,[5]
That went to Letsika's[6] and Silonyana's.[7]   15
    Crocodile of the crocodiles,
Crocodile, sender, uncle of Josefa,
Uncle of Josefa and Lerotholi![8]
    The herds slipped away, the herds of Jumba and Mbale[9] slipped
                                                                away,
They slipped away and disappeared among the trees.   20
    The scarer who scares among the Thembu,[10]
This year he can scare no longer:
He scared away the cattle, he forgot the people:
He scares away the cattle but leaves behind the herdsmen,

    [1] There is a small mountain called Nyaba-Nyaba near Thaba Phatšoa, but it is most unlikely that this is the place referred to here, for Masopha had long since left the area in 1861. According to Captain Webb, the compiler of the Basutoland Gazetteer, Nyaba-Nyaba may have been an earlier name of Machache, a mountain which dominates much of the western Sotho lowlands, including Masopha's ward. Possibly, therefore, the reference is to Machache.
    [2] i.e. Masopha led his warriors in a group. It is common for a widow-bird to be seen at the head of a group of finches.
    [3] There are many places with this name. Possibly the Pitsaneng referred to here is a mountain close to Mount Fletcher.
    [4] Masopha's senior wife.
    [5] A river below the Drakensberg, in the Mount Fletcher district.
    [6] Letsika (meaning uncertain) was a praise-name of Sekhonyana, alias Nehemiah. After the first war with the Free State in 1858 he had crossed the Drakensberg and settled in the Matatiele area.
    [7] Silonyana was chief of the Baca. Although not on good terms with Sekhonyana at this time he nevertheless took advantage of the Sotho's expedition to attack his old enemy Mbale.
    [8] Josefa was the son of Molapo, Lerotholi the son of Letsie.
    [9] Jumba and Mbale were the two chiefs whom the Sotho attacked. Mbale was chief of the Mpondomise. Jumba was a neighbouring Thembu chief.
    [10] The Sotho could use the word Thembu to refer to any Cape Nguni chiefdom, and here it may well refer to Mbale's people as well as Jumba's.

25 The herdsmen remain at the cliffs,
They fell from the cliffs, from RaTholoana.[1]
The black crocodile of those who strike the ship,[2]
The black crocodile with assagais and shield,
The young warrior of the Inviters,[3] the Helper,
30 The lord of the great armies is called at dusk and dawn.
Perhaps the young lad has gone to the Leqholoqha,
The zealous, energetic young lad, the crocodile![4]
The great warrior has gone out from Matsieng,[5]
He's slipped away from home by himself.
35 When he came among the foreigners he won fame:
The tumult could be heard even far, far away,
At last it could be heard in the land of the Ndebele.
The Helper of the regiments,
Masopha of Mokhachane,
40 The name of 'The Helper', RaMahlolela, suits you well,
That name suits you well, it likes you,
For indeed, for in truth, you're helpful to people.
The hurrier who eats food that's still hot,
Who eats food while the fire is still blazing![6]
45 As the battle caught light and burned,
And became almost a fiery blaze,
In went the falcon of Mokhachane,
In went the falcon, the bird of prey,
This bird of prey of my master.[7]
50 As it went in its eyes were glaring,

---

[1] i.e. Masopha, Tholoana being his daughter. There is a touch of sarcasm in this stanza. Masopha is no longer as frightening as he was, for he could only drive away the cattle and had to leave the herdsmen behind—dead on the field of battle.

[2] 'those who strike the ship', i.e. those who perform exploits of daring and bravery.

[3] Another of Masopha's regiments.

[4] Once again there is a touch of sarcasm and surprise. Line 30 suggests that Masopha was always being called upon to help his kinsmen in war. In fact, however, as lines 31–2 indicate, he was being called because he was being sought, for Letsie disapproved of his expedition against Mbale and even tried to recall him after he had set out.

[5] i.e. from Letsie's village.

[6] For Masopha's impetuosity, cp. iii. 49–50, p. 125 above.

[7] i.e. of Moshoeshoe.

Its teeth were bared in its open mouth,
Its teeth were bared in its gaping mouth;[1]
As it entered it spoke to the Hawks,
Saying to the dogs: 'Devour them, they're there!'   55
    Then the Hawks clambered into them with sticks,
And the Plumes[2] clambered into them with sticks to destroy them,
They devoured them and divided them among the birds,
That the vultures should eat them and be filled,
That the evening should find that we'd finished them,   60
That the sun should set on a quarrel that was ended.
    The vultures rejoiced in that land of the Nguni,
The birds of that land of the Ndebele,
Black, and sitting in the trees.
    The son of 'MaMathe,[3] the lion of men,   65
The lion that once spoke in fury to the people
Turned about, and the Nguni disappeared,[4]
Mbale's little Nguni were missing!
    Helper, speak with and gladden the regiments,
Speak with Letsika and Silonyana.   70
    'MaSekhonyana's[5] conciliator
Reconciled the chiefs who rejected each other,
Letsika and Silonyana.[6]
    Son of 'MaMathe, you're a scorching hollow,
You're a fire that burns those who light it: 75
If the people from Jumba's were to sit in its warmth,
The one who sat near it might get sore from burns!
Jumba conveys his burns to the chief's,
To the presence of Letsika and Silonyana.[7]

---

[1] Lit.:
> '. . . in an open space,
> . . . in a desert space.'

[2] Another of Masopha's regiments. More precisely, *Liqokofa* are aigrettes of ostrich feathers.

[3] Mathe, alias Nthe, was his sister. 'MaMathe, his mother, was more commonly known as 'MaMohato.

[4] i.e. they fled.   [5] 'MaSekhonyana was Moshoeshoe's third wife.

[6] Silonyana, chief of the Baca, had claimed that Sekhonyana (alias Letsika) was living on his land, and, shortly before this expedition, Sekhonyana had felt obliged to burn his village and retreat towards the Drakensberg. According to the poet, Masopha effected a reconciliation between the two, and this may be true. Certainly Silonyana assisted the Sotho by attacking Mbale on this occasion.

[7] In spite of the hypothetical nature of lines 75–6, lines 77–8 indicate that Jumba had actually suffered at Masopha's hands.

When the regiments of us people of Moshoeshoe galloped,
80   Including the Plumes of my master,
Then Jumba's kinsman, Mbale, was scared,
He was scared when the First Fruits[1] appeared,
When they appeared there at Jumba's, in the pass.
    Chopho's kinsman is driving as he returns,
85   Chopho was driving a Thembu maiden
Who had sparkling studs and buttons
And, above all, bright, glittering ornaments.[2]
    Hold up your head, you Thembu maiden,
Hold up your head and look me in the eye,
90   That you may know when you tell the men
That the tracks of the lion aren't followed
On the occasion of the Young Wildebeest's departure.[3]
    The girl is fortunate, Thembu!
    Men, if you scorn the divining bones' warning
95   And refuse to hear what a woman has to say,
Refusing to hear when a woman advises you,
Remember:[4] stubbornness devoured the lords,
It devoured the people from Jumba's and Mbale's.
The devourer of Jumba's herdsmen destroyed them:
100   The cattle at Jumba's will be herded by whom?[5]
    The black cow[6] has appeared round a corner,
It's appeared at Popa, at Majoe-a-Litšoene,[7]

---

[1] Posholi too assisted Sekhonyana on this occasion, and the First Fruits were one of his regiments. They were so named probably because they were said to appear first in battle.

[2] Chopho was one of Posholi's sons. His 'kinsman' in line 84 was evidently Masopha. Why the poet should refer to Chopho's brother in line 84 but to Chopho himself in line 85 cannot be explained. As the following lines make clear almost beyond doubt, it was Masopha who was bringing home the Thembu maiden.

[3] i.e. when they arrive home the girl must tell the Sotho that Masopha is not being pursued by his enemies.

[4] The word 'Remember' has not been translated from the Sotho, but has been added to make the sense clear. Cp. Griffith, ii. 348, p. 230 below.

[5] i.e., apparently, the Mpondomise had ignored the warning of a female diviner, and had suffered accordingly.

[6] i.e. the cattle which Masopha has plundered, or possibly the Thembu maiden.

[7] Popa is a mountain in the western foothills of the Maloti. The Majoe-a-Litšoene, 'The Baboons' Stones', are certain rocks on the mountain.

It's appeared at Popa, still piping its anger,[1]
As it piped it gave joy to the old:
Mafata rejoiced, and so did RaPapali.   105
RaKotoanyana also rejoiced,
Rejoicing he went over to Likolonyama.[2]
   The black cow sent the chant of war:
Black cow, send a shriek of joy to the Chief's!
Send a paean to RaFobokoane,[3]   110
To the father, to the Chief, to Moshoeshoe.
Bear witness that you've come with gladness,
That you've come without fear, without flight,
Without any following alarms.
   This black cow's a reward, which we bear,   115
It's a reward, we bear it, we stagger along
And with it we'll make our report to Letsie,
With it we'll make our report to the Recoverer.[4]
   Don't worry yourself, Letsie Moshoeshoe,
It's the string of a dog, it's not usually despised: 120
Tomorrow it'll kill an eland.[5]
   Great cow of the sloping path, red cow,
Uninitiated girl, the Thembu's cow,[6]
As you came home you were initiated
By Molomo of the Resounding Kerrie and his friends.[7]   125
   The black cow is 'With whom I shall eat?'[8]

[1] In the Sotho: *E hlahile Popa, e ntse e popa.* The meaning of the verb *ho popa* is unknown to most Sotho today. According to Mr. Stephen Pinda, however, it means 'to bellow with rage'. The pun on the name of the mountain, Popa, is maintained through the translation 'piping its anger'.

[2] Mafata, RaPapali and RaKotoanyana were presumably some of Masopha's older followers. Likolonyama is a mountain close to the confluence of the Caledon and Phuthiatsana rivers.

[3] RaFobokoane, i.e. Moshoeshoe. Fobokoane was a warrior who was brought up in the house of his senior wife, 'MaMohato, and who was killed in the early years of the *lifaqane*.

[4] i.e. Letsie.

[5] The string is Masopha himself. Today he has brought only a little booty, 'a dog', but in future he will be more successful.

[6] i.e. the captured girl mentioned in lines 84–93 above. She was a cow 'of the sloping path' because she had just been brought over the Drakensberg.

[7] Molomo was the son of Mohale, Moshoeshoe's brother. The Resounding Kerrie was one of Mohale's praise-names. The reference to the girl's initiation is not understood. Clearly it is not meant to be taken literally.

[8] Normally *k'o-mo-ja-le-mang*, 'I shall eat with whom?', is an animal which has died of starvation. The owner is reluctant to throw away the meat, but no

Stabber of the enemy, comrade of Lejaha, the son of Makhabane,[1]
With whom shall I eat this cow?
When he was returning, coming from the Lethena,[2]
130 In his heart he would think of his masters:
He would think of Mpiti Sekake and his men,
He would think of RaLibe of the Striped Ones and his men.[3]
The black cow had horns turning over,
The black cow had horns overturning the Mpondo![4]
135 We'll continue to overturn them,
The people of Jumba, from the land of the Ndebele.
Scrape off a little for me, black cow from the herds of the Let-
hena,
Cow from the herds of the Lethena and the Leqholoqha.
We heard you when still far away,
140 When we were still at home, at Tšoanamakhulo,[5]
We heard indeed that you were scraping a little.[6]
Great cow, with extended teats,
Its teats are too much for the herdsmen,
They were too much for Nkhehle and Mpilo.[7]

---

one will eat it with him. In this case, however, *k'o-mo-ja-le-mang* is evidently
booty of which the other chiefs will not take a share, since they disapproved of
the expedition.

[1] Lejaha, son of Makhabane, was Masopha's cousin.

[2] A river below the Drakensberg.

[3] Mpiti's people were known as the Sekake, being named after his father.
They were senior relatives of the Mokoteli, and exercised chieftainship rights
over them until Moshoeshoe threw off their yoke while still a young man.
RaLibe was Peete, whose regiment was called the Striped Ones. Masopha
thought of his ancestors, probably because this gave him comfort as he prepared
to face the opposition of Letsie and others; also, perhaps, because he wanted to
sacrifice to them.

[4] In fact the people whom Masopha had attacked were the Mpondomise,
but the Sotho were rarely concerned with accuracy when referring to Nguni
communities.

[5] A stream and valley just to the south of Teyateyaneng. This area was under
Masopha's control.

[6] The significance of this stanza can only be conjectured. *Ho kutlola* means
'to remove the roughness of, to polish, to file; to scrape; to shuffle'. The translation 'to scrape off a little' is based on the tentative suggestion of Mr. Stephen
Pinda, who believes that 'Scrape off a little for me' in line 137 means 'Give me a
little of your booty'; and that 'We heard indeed that you were scraping a little'
in line 141 means 'We heard indeed that you were sharing out a few plundered
cattle'.

[7] i.e. the cow has so much milk that it exhausts its herdsmen. The cow is
possibly Masopha himself. Nkhehle and Mpilo were evidently two of his
followers.

He summoned his men from the east, 145
He summoned Makibile and Matata,[1]
Saying: 'Destroy Tlake's cow! It's there!'
Tlake's cow we divide among the vultures,
Birds that are fond of being fed.[2]
Who is it who despises Masopha, 150
Saying he's not a man, but a little man?
Who is it who despises Masopha,
Saying he's not a hyaena, but a little hyaena,
Saying he's not a doctor, but a little doctor?

(v)

The one who digs open the passes that were closed,
That had even been closed with Gert's little Bushmen!
Most, they've ascended those at the sides,
They ascended by the women's little passes,
They ascended at the 'push-me-up' pass.[3] 5

(vi)

The young warrior[4] went yesterday to the chief's, to Moshoe-
shoe,
He went to beg cattle from the plateau.[4]
They gave him the cowards', he refused them,
The cowards' he made food for the journey.[5]
He went to see the valleys in the shadows,[6] and he rested; 5

[1] Evidently two of Masopha's followers.
[2] Tlake cannot be identified, and the incident alluded to is now forgotten.
There is a play on words here, for Tlake, apart from being a man's name, can
also mean a kind of vulture, and the vulture's cow is a man's corpse.
[3] For this stanza, see i. 82–6, 90–3, pp. 120-1 above. The 'push-me-up'
pass denotes the cliffs which the Sotho climbed by pushing each other up.
[4] 'the plateau', i.e. the summit of Thaba Bosiu.
[5] Masopha went to Moshoeshoe to ask his permission to raid the Mpondomise
and Thembu. Moshoeshoe refused, but instead offered him some cattle of his
own. These were the cowards' cattle, not because Moshoeshoe was a coward,
but because they had not been captured in war. Masopha was far from satisfied
with them, but took them as food for his journey over the Drakensberg. There
is also a pun here. The word *makoala*, 'cowards', was also the name of a man
whom Masopha had just 'eaten up' on Moshoeshoe's orders for killing a man
accused of witchcraft or adultery.
[6] 'in the shadows', i.e. of the Drakensberg mountains.

He saw the paths that went to the Leqholoqha,
That went to Letsika's and Silonyana's.[1]
  The herdsman who spies among the Thembu
Spied on the cattle, ignoring the herdsmen.
10   The hurrier who eats food that's still hot,
As the battle caught light and burned,
And became almost a fiery blaze,
In went the falcon of my master;
The dog went in with glaring eyes,
15 Baring its teeth in its open mouth;
As it entered it spoke to the Hawks,
It spoke to the Plumes of RaTholoana,
Saying: 'Young warriors, stab them with spears,
Stab them, and divide them among the birds.
20 The vultures will rejoice in that land of the Nguni,
The black vultures that sit in the trees.'[2]
  Swarthy avenger, you who are Steadfast, brother of Mpinane,
Fight and avenge the head of your uncle,
Avenge Makhabane's head.[3]
25 So, you have seen, you Koena:
I've avenged Makhabane's head!
I've killed the chief of the Thembu![4]

(vii)

  Imparter of arms to the Hawks, Masopha,
Implant a reed on the people from Senekal's,
That when they go across the river
They go with it on their backs![5]
5   The crocodile of the crocodiles,
Of Peete and Mokhachane,
Has just captured drove upon drove of cattle
In between Winburg and Bloemfontein.
When at Verkeerdevlei they made him abandon them,

---

[1] For this stanza, see iv. 11, 14–15, p. 127 above.
[2] For this stanza, see iv. 43–63, pp. 128-9 above.
[3] Makhabane, Moshoeshoe's brother, was killed in the raid on the Thembu of Ngubencuka in 1835.
[4] Possibly one of the Mpondomise or Thembu chiefs was killed in this campaign in 1861, but there is no other evidence for this.
[5] For this stanza, see iii. 16–18, p. 124 above.

They came down upon him like a downpour of rain !¹   10
   The puller, the comrade of RaLinkeng,
Pulls the fight with his hind legs,
Bringing it in to Moshoeshoe.²
   He's kind, he's the Hawks' grass hat.³
   Defender of the family of Makhabane,   15
Defend on the pass, for people are flying,
Defend on the ridge at Rafutho's.⁴

(viii)

   Yellow Wildebeest, Young Wildebeest,
You left your parents' village when you went away from home,
From RaMohato.⁵
   Little Wildebeests, who are you to make a speech?
Won't you allow that the Wildebeest should speak, from the family 5
                                 of the Agitator
And the Depriver;⁶
That Mpinane's⁷ family's Old Wildebeest should speak,
That we, the people, should be lost in wonder?
   The cow of the house of spears, the Hawk,
The black and white cow that's rebellious,   10
Weave for its benefit a rope, it's broken it,
Its herdsmen are still lamenting,
Letlala and his men and RaMaketekete and his men.⁸
   The husband of Maluke seized a multi-coloured cow,
He seized a little beauty, a cow of the shields;⁹   15

¹ The poet now turns from the war of 1858 to the war which began in 1865. In June that year Masopha and other chiefs raided the Free State and swept off large numbers of cattle, sheep and goats. On their return they were intercepted near Verkeerdevlei and were forced to abandon most of them. Cp. Lerotholi, ii. 36–42, p. 142 below.
² i.e. as Masopha returns to Lesotho from the Free State he draws the Free State commandos after him.
³ Just as a grass hat protects its wearer against the sun, so Masopha protects his warriors.
⁴ In August 1865 the Free Staters under Louw Wepener tried unsuccessfully to force their way up the Rafutho pass and on to the summit of Thaba Bosiu. Masopha was one of the defenders at the top of the pass.
⁵ For this stanza, see ii. 14–16, p. 112 above.
⁶ The Agitator was Molapo, the Depriver Letsie.
⁷ Mpinane, i.e. Nthe, Masopha's sister.
⁸ For this stanza, see i. 1–5, p. 117 above.
⁹ 'a cow of the shields', i.e. a cow captured in war.

Some say that it's reddish white,
Others that it's white with long, black stripes.
    The cow that is black with white-striped back has dipped mud
                                        in the thick sour milk,
It kicked it up with its feet at the back;
20 It said that the axe-heads should fall from their handles.
A dog raised a howl in the village,
A sheep ran away with a lamb,
A woman ran away with a child on her back, . . .[1]

                              (ix)

    Indeed, by my father, I saw it![2]
There's a man who's wiped out the red herdsman,
Who's just devoured Jacob the Griqua![3]
    The kite of the people from Mokhachane's
5 Darted out and struck the crane,
It struck the crane that was blue, pure blue, and that came from
                                        the land of the Makaota.[4]
    The Hawk that is truly a Hawk,
Which wouldn't be remembered with happy memories,[5]
When a child remembers it there among the Griqua,
10 The person with the child would pinch it with his nails,
Its father would strike it with a switch,
They'd say: 'You remind us of a mighty sorcerer
Who once threw down something that was mighty and enormous!'

                        10. *Lerotholi*

Lerotholi (1836–1905) was the eldest son in Letsie's second house and, in the absence of any male children in the first house, was his father's heir. His military career began in earnest in 1865 with the second war against the

---

[1] For this stanza, see i. 6–10, p. 117 above. The dots at the end (which are taken from Mangoaela's text) probably signify that the poem continues after this stanza in the same way as the first poem.
[2] 'it' is a translation of *le* in the Sotho, which here signifies *letsatsi*, 'day'. 'I saw the day', i.e. the day on which something extraordinary happened.
[3] For Jacob the Griqua, see i. 25, p. 118 above.
[4] For this stanza, cp. i. 87–9, p. 121 above.
[5] Lit. 'Which wouldn't be remembered with memories'.

Free State, in the course of which he fought well in many engagements, and was badly wounded in at least one of them. His praises allude specifically to the battle at Mopeli's village in June 1865; to a raid into the Free State in the same month; to the defence of Thaba Bosiu in August 1865; and, apparently, to an incident at Kolo in November 1868.

After the war he was placed at Likhoele, in what is now the Mafeteng District of Lesotho. Although he assisted the Cape authorities to suppress Moorosi's rebellion in 1879, he did so reluctantly, as his praises make clear; and in the following year, in the Gun War, he emerged as the dominant figure in the Sotho's resistance in the south. This time he gained wide respect not only for his courage as a warrior—once again he was wounded—but also for his skill as a tactician.

On the death of his father in 1891 he became Paramount Chief, and moved his village from Likhoele to Makeneng, a small hill opposite Matsieng. During his reign the authority of the paramountcy was greatly strengthened, especially in 1898, when Masopha, who had been flouting his orders almost with impunity, was decisively beaten in the battle of Khamolane. Lerotholi was present on this occasion, but did not take an active part in the fighting. He died in 1905.

He was an outstandingly popular chief, perhaps even more so than Moshoeshoe, for, compared with his grandfather, he was relatively simple and straightforward, and his people understood him better.

Mangoaela has recorded seven of his praise-poems, and he informed Damane personally that he did not collect them from one man alone, but from several individuals in and around Makeneng, including Pelepele and Mahe, two of Lerotholi's warriors. The first and second poems relate to the war with the Free State; the third, fourth, fifth and sixth to the Gun War; and the seventh to the war with Moorosi. Only in the last is there a strong narrative element.

It is commonly said that Lerotholi composed his own *lithoko*. However he appears in the first person singular in only two poems, the fourth and the seventh, and even in these not consistently so; and the author of the sixth was obviously one of his Taung adherents, for it is in the Taung dialect. Clearly, although he composed some of these poems, he did not compose them all.

(i)

The son of the Pusher[1] of Mokhachane,
The Koodoo doesn't fight, he pushes,
He drives on the army with his knees,[2]

---

[1] The Pusher is said to have been a praise-name of Moshoeshoe.
[2] i.e. Lerotholi does not fight like other warriors, but forces the battle to go in the way that he wants.

Lekena[1] of RaNneko[2] of the Koena.

5   Take your shield, hold it firm, son of RaSenate,[3]
You see that your fatherland is going.
    Forge lightning, warrior of RaMakhobalo,[4]
Forge it, and sharpen its keenness.
Won't you go away, you people of the Major,[5]
10   Since the lightning has just struck people?
The sweeping bird of lightning has gone there,
It swept along its wings and it burned.
There were flashes of lightning and blazing fires,
It seemed as if the lightning had nested in the mountain,[6]
15   Coming from the favourite[7] of the chiefs and all the people,
Lekena of the father of Senate.
    The one who trudges on with the spears,
With the spears, Lekena, the son of Thesele,[8]
The witness of affairs,[9] Kholu's[10] reverser,
20   He reversed some affairs that were difficult.[11]
    It is Brand[12] and his men who have come as if in anger,
They have come as if in anger to the father of Mohato.[13]
    The hail that is sent by a sorcerer is strong.[14]
    There were flashes of lightning and fires were seen.

---

[1] The praise-name *Lekena*, 'Enterer', alludes to the way in which Lerotholi used to enter the ranks of his enemies in battle. It is used so often to refer to him that it is left untranslated.

[2] i.e. of Moshoeshoe, 'Neko being the senior son in his second house.

[3] RaSenate, i.e. Letsie, Senate being his daughter.

[4] i.e. Moshoeshoe, Makhobalo being a son who was attached to his second house.

[5] i.e. Major Warden, British Resident in the Orange River Sovereignty until 1852. Apparently Europeans in general could be referred to as his people.

[6] The Sotho believed that lightning was a bird, and that if it struck the same place many times it had a nest there.

[7] Lit. 'the daughter-in-law'. A daughter-in-law is a favourite because, as soon as she arrives at her husband's home, she assists her new relatives in every way that she can.

[8] Thesele, i.e. Moshoeshoe.

[9] 'The witness of affairs', probably because he was always present at crises.

[10] Kholu was Moshoeshoe's mother.   [11] The allusion is not known.

[12] J. H. Brand was President of the Free State from 1864 to 1888.

[13] Mohato, i.e. Letsie, whose father was Moshoeshoe.

[14] Taken on its own, as it appears here, this line refers to Lerotholi. In fact, however, it is merely a fragment of a stanza, which is given in full in ii. 24–30, p. 141 below. There it is clear that the reference is to the Afrikaners, whom Lerotholi drives away.

The Koodoo digs the anthill,[1] its horns become sharp,   25
It has horns that are sharp, the bull of Peete.
It has no horns, it butts with its forehead:[2]
Does it think it can struggle with the bull of Thesele?
It always pulls a yoke, and its neck is tired,
Its neck is tired by heavy loads.   30
You people at Ntšohi's,[3] and you at Matabohe's,[4]
Didn't you hear when it trembled,
When the earth was ashake and trembling?
RaMakholo[5] is one who has heard it,
A noise resounding near the mountain.[6]   35
They said: 'Take the chance to deal with them thus,
RaLetšabisa,[7] descendant of Kholu, son of a man who is somebody,
For they're always destroying our seed,
They're destroying our seed in the fields.'[8]
The Koodoo, the belt of feathers of Moshoeshoe,   40
The belt of feathers that's dear to the hearts of Peete and
                        Mokhachane![9]
The servant of God,
God has let them fight,
Saying: 'This nation isn't just sitting,
It's sitting with a bull that goes on resisting.'   45
As he resisted we nations were saved.
He resisted with a ramrod
That the Nguni[10] should live, that the Sotho should live,

[1] It is thought to dig the anthill in order to sharpen its horns.
[2] 'It' here is not Peete's bull, but Brand's: cp. ii. 11–15, p. 141 below.
[3] Ntšohi was a Fokeng living on the south-western side of Masite mountain: his village is still known as Ntšohi's.
[4] Matabohe, another Fokeng, lived close to Ntšohi, and his village is still known as Matabohe's.
[5] A Tlokoa living east of Kolo mountain, at Likhakeng.
[6] The allusion is almost certainly to an incident which occurred in November 1868. Some Afrikaners, who had apparently been stealing horses, were detected in a gully. Lerotholi and about fifty of his men gave chase, and pursued them as far as Kolo mountain. Lerotholi was wounded and fell from his horse; two of his men were killed; and one of the Afrikaners was killed.
[7] RaLetšabisa, i.e. Lerotholi, Letšabisa being his daughter.
[8] During the 1865–8 war the Afrikaners tried to reduce the Sotho to submission by a scorched earth policy.
[9] Just as a warrior was proud of his belt of feathers, so Lerotholi's ancestors were proud of him.
[10] There were many Nguni among Moshoeshoe's followers.

That even the people from Kwelela's[1] should live!
50   You too from Aliwal North are here.
What made us say you had come
Was seeing that Shepstone was giving us trouble.
Shepstone is seeking a public appeal:
Cattle have been paid but they don't suffice,
55   And even those cattle embroiled men in quarrels.
The cattle can embroil the children of this land,
They'd embroil the lion of the Hounds of Makhoarane,
They embroiled him with the child of his uncle.[2]

(ii)

The one who trudges on with the spears, Lekena,
The son of Thesele, the witness of affairs,
The reverser of Kholu and Moshoeshoe![3]
    Koodoo, speak nicely with Brand,
5   Tell him how things are at home,
Say: 'Here at 'MaLibe's, as for leaving, we're leaving.'[4]
    It's black, it's tawny, the bull of Peete,
    Its bellowing enters the heart!

[1] Kwelela was a Nguni chief who lived under Lerotholi.

[2] In line 57 the lion is Letsie, the Hounds are one of his regiments, and Makhoarane is a mountain near his home. In line 58 'the child of his uncle' is Lesaoana, the son of Makhabane. At the outbreak of war Lesaoana invaded Natal and captured a large number of cattle. The British High Commissioner, Sir Philip Wodehouse, demanded the payment of a fine, and sent John Burnet, the Magistrate at Aliwal North, to Thaba Bosiu to collect it. Burnet met with little success. MacFarlane, the Magistrate from Weenen in Natal, also visited Thaba Bosiu, but he too was disappointed. Theophilus Shepstone, who was Secretary for Native Affairs in Natal, did not visit Lesotho in person on this matter, but dealt with it from Natal. Moshoeshoe, instead of compelling Lesaoana to surrender his booty, tried to raise the fine by a public appeal. This caused much bad feeling among the Sotho, and in particular between Letsie and Lesaoana.

[3] For this stanza, see i. 17–20, p. 138 above.

[4] 'Here at 'MaLibe's', i.e. in Lesotho. The significance of this stanza can only be surmized. In the Treaty of Thaba Bosiu, which Moshoeshoe was compelled to accept in April 1866, a large area of land was ceded to the Free State, but subsequently the Sotho refused to vacate it. The Afrikaners therefore renewed hostilities, and the Sotho suffered heavy losses. In May 1867 Letsie formally became a Free State subject, and was granted a small location in the conquered territory; but still the Sotho continued to occupy areas which they had agreed to vacate. Once again therefore the Afrikaners went to war, and once again the Sotho were hard pressed. Perhaps in this stanza the poet is advising Lerotholi to yield to the Free State's demands.

Crocodile, adder of the family of Tlalinyane,[1]
Adder of the father of Motloang![2]   10
    The Koodoo digs the anthill, its horns become sharp;
The bull from Brand's[3] is digging too.
Does it think it can struggle with Thesele's?
Doesn't that from Brand's have a neck that's tired,
A neck that's tired by heavy loads?[4]   15
    The Koodoo fights the fight like a rhino.
He's a crab, he protects his young:[5]
He says that Moshoeshoe shouldn't come down from his platform,
                      but should stay,[6]
For brave warriors have been defeated, Wepener and his men,[7]
Fighters who fight on the ships.[8]   20
    Young man, running to give help on every side,
Run to give help at Mopeli's, at Mabolela,[9]
When the home of Ntsubise[10] and her family is burnt.
    The hail that is sent by a sorcerer is strong:
In vain we tried to avert the hail.   25
It hummed, it swept off the soil from the fields!
Kofa, the son of Marebele, and his friends,
The know-alls of our village, were missing:
Nowadays the doctors are the Koodoo and RaMahlolela,
We've warded it off: it departed from Moshoeshoe.[11]   30

---

[1] A junior son of Moshoeshoe.

[2] The father of Motloang was Moshoeshoe's brother, Mopeli.

[3] Lit. 'The one from Brand's'. The word 'bull' has been used to make the meaning clear.

[4] For this stanza, cp. i. 25–30, p. 139 above.

[5] The crab is regarded by the Sotho as being particularly protective towards its young.

[6] Moshoeshoe sometimes addressed meetings from a platform. The idea is that Lerotholi is such a powerful warrior that Moshoeshoe can remain secure on Thaba Bosiu.

[7] Louw Wepener, a Commandant in the Free State forces, was killed when trying to storm Thaba Bosiu in August 1865. Evidently Lerotholi was present on this occasion.

[8] The finest Europeans were believed to live on ships. Cp. Maama, i. 32–4, p. 156 below.

[9] In June 1865 Free State forces attacked and destroyed Mopeli's village at Mabolela. Lerotholi took part in this battle.

[10] One of Mopeli's daughters.

[11] In this stanza the hail is the advancing Free State army. The doctors, the 'know-alls' (lit. the 'I know's') could do nothing to avert it, but Lerotholi, 'The Koodoo', and Masopha, RaMahlolela, were more successful.

The lightning flashed, it gave birth in the mountain,
Coming from everyone's favourite, Lekena.[1]
It is he who was placed by Kholu and Suping,[2]
Who said: 'Moshoeshoe, this hoe's like a hammer.[3]
35   The sun is ignored even when it's still!'[4]
The diviners and the visionaries have spoken:
'Where's the crocodile going as it swims the deep waters?'
He crossed because his heart was full.[5]
When at Verkeerdevlei he abandoned the cattle,
40   Some came before him, and some came behind.[6]
The great snake of the waters crossed over with plenty,[7]
The great snake of the waters of the Axes and the Glarers.[8]
The bulldog of Mokhachane, Lekena,
Keeps driving the leopards round the mountain—
45   By leopards we mean those from Brand's—
Turning their faces westwards,
There where the sun goes down.[9]
The lightning has burnt the veld below,
It swept along with karosses, burning,
50   It's burnt the crow and the vulture.[10]
Raise the alarm for those at Kolo to hear,
And those at Ntšohi's and those at Matabohe's.
As for the din, they've heard it,
When they appeared, they shouted:

[1] See i. 13–16, p. 138 above.

[2] Although they did not in fact do so, Kholu (Moshoeshoe's mother) and Suping (i.e. Mokhachane, Moshoeshoe's father) are here said to have placed Lerotholi in his first village. As far as is known, this was at Likhoele. Suping means 'one who remains at a deserted village', i.e. one who stays behind when others leave.

[3] It is like a hammer because it is so hard.

[4] Lit.: 'It has no sun although it (i.e. the sun) is standing.' At times of drought the sun is said to stand still: the earth is hard and cannot be worked. This hoe, however, is so tough that it can be used even during droughts.

[5] i.e. he crossed the Caledon because his heart was full of anger.

[6] Soon after the outbreak of war in 1865 Lerotholi joined Masopha in raiding the Free State. They captured many cattle, sheep and goats, but were forced to abandon most of them when they were intercepted by a Free State commando at Verkeerdevlei. Cp. Masopha, vii. 5–10, pp. 134–5 above.

[7] Even so his booty was still considerable.   [8] Two of his regiments.

[9] This stanza probably alludes to the incident at Kolo, which is in the west of Lesotho. See i. 31–5, p. 139 above.

[10] The crow, a dark bird of carrion, and the vulture, a light bird of carrion, perhaps signify the Free Staters' African allies and the Free Staters themselves.

'Take your chance to act thus, RaLetšabisa,   55
For they're always destroying our seed.'[1]

(iii)

Mohato's[2] gripper, Lekena,
You who grip fast the people,
Grip fast the people from Sprigg's![3]
   Strike the people with the buffalo of shields,[4]
That the white clay dust should blind them.[5]   5
   The crocodile looked through the depths of the water,
It looked with eyes that were red:
The boys of the Whites fell in![6]
The boys have fallen into the mouth of a snake.
The black snake, the serpent of the waters of the Chief   10
Vomited a flash of lightning!
   The rainbow of Moshoeshoe's country
Leaned against the clouds and the earth
When the earth was ashake.
   The rhino of RaNtolo[7] and the Ripper[8]   15
Went to meet the war which was still far away.
It carried the war on its wings, Koena,
It said to its dogs:[9] 'Devour them! There they are!
Dispatch them with spears Sotho-fashion, destroy them,
Destroy them in thousands and thousands,   20
For the vultures that are white to alight on them!'
   Burn the *mosukutsoane* bush, RaLetšabisa,
That your shields become strong.[10]
   The cliff of the chiefs, with moons,

---

   [1] For this stanza, see i. 31–9, p. 139 above.   [2] Mohato, i.e. Letsie.
   [3] Gordon Sprigg was Prime Minister at the Cape during the Gun War.
   [4] 'the buffalo of shields', i.e. a spear, which can pierce a shield like a buffalo's horn.
   [5] The Sotho used to smear their shields with white clay, and this would come off as powder when a shield was struck.
   [6] It was believed that a crocodile could draw people into its pool by fixing them with a hypnotic stare.
   [7] i.e. Moshoeshoe's brother, Mohale, Ntolo being his daughter.
   [8] i.e. Moshoeshoe's brother, Tšiame.
   [9] 'to its dogs', i.e. to its warriors.
   [10] The Sotho believed that their shields would be strengthened if they were held in the smoke given off by the *mosukutsoane* bush when burning.

25   With the Pleiades,[1] Koena,
      He's the rainbow of Molapo's country.

                              (iv)

        The cow doesn't pass all its dung:
        Eat me up, you men!
        How do you think you can eat me up?[2]
        The young warrior of spears, Lekena,
5   He's a bitter herb, he's not eaten,
        Even the birds don't eat him, he's bitter,
        He's bitter like bitterwort, the Lion of the Axes![3]
        The child of RaLibe[4] set light to a fire,
        He burned the house of his friend,[5]
10   He started a row with the Sparkling Soldier.[6]
        It was then that he said: 'Stop cattle-raiding, Sprigg,
        You'll see me stop raiding yours.'
        Since you eat in your house, you miser,
        Against whom do you think you can turn your shield?
15   Do you think you can turn it against the people's provider?[7]
        Haha!
        You've eaten a dog, while I ate a cow![8]

[1] Lerotholi is a cliff, because the chiefs can use him for their defence. Moons and the Pleiades convey the idea of sparkling decorations.

[2] This stanza does not belong exclusively to the praises of Lerotholi, but forms an interlude which a *seroki* can use whenever he needs a little respite. 'The cow doesn't pass all its dung': i.e. the *seroki* does not wish to exhaust the chief's praises. When he calls on the men to eat him up, they reply: *Re ka u ja*, 'We can eat you up'. He retorts, 'How do you think you can eat me up?'— literally, 'You can eat me doing what to me?'—and then proceeds with his chanting.

[3] i.e. he cannot be defeated by his enemies.   [4] RaLibe, i.e. Peete.

[5] 'his friend', as the following line makes clear, is a sarcastic reference to Sir Bartle Frere, the High Commissioner, who was largely responsible for the policy of disarmament.

[6] Literally *Mabekebeke* means glittering ornaments, and it was given as a name to the High Commissioner, Sir Bartle Frere, because of his highly deco-rated uniform. Frere never visited Lesotho, but was seen by a Sotho delegation in Cape Town shortly before the Gun War.

[7] Lines 13–15 are reminiscent of some famous lines from the praises of the Taung chief, Moletsane: see Mopeli, iv. 49–50, p. 104 above. A chief who eats alone in his house, instead of with his warriors in his court, is obviously either poor or stingy or both.

[8] i.e. you have failed and I have succeeded.

Peete's warrior, Deliverer,
Deliver the commoners and chiefs,
We commoners and chiefs are distressed: 20
Whom shall we see and call our friend?
Our uncles behave like Ndebele.[1]
Those who sit on the fence[2] we've seen.
We'll be helped by strangers,
People from various nations,   25
In truth, by the Tlokoa and Ndebele.[3]
    Crocodile, fight, Ntšebo's father,[4]
Crocodile, fight, the country's going,
The country for which you were born is going:
When the Repeater[5] died he gave you a spear,   30
He's given you a spear for cattle and men.[6]
    On the plain at Sepechele's[7] a certain young man raised the
                  alarm and told others to raise it:
'Let the horses charge at the men from Sprigg's!'
They ran, they trampled beneath their feet the men of the Spark-
                  ling Soldier.
Your people you can recognize on the ground,   35
You can choose them from the corpses, for they're dead![8]
    Your people's little shield breaks easily on the branches:[9]
The child of RaLibe[10] brandished his shield.
    In this war the spirits have fought:
Those of the house of our father are fighting, and those of the house 40
                  of our mother.

---

[1] The uncles referred to are men like Tlali (George) and Sofonia, who supported the Cape administration during the Gun War. To behave like Ndebele probably means to behave in a despicable way; but there may possibly be a reference to the Gcaleka and Mfengu, who had surrendered their firearms shortly beforehand.

[2] Lit. 'Those who watch the defeated', i.e. those who wait to see which side is defeated and who then join the victors.

[3] The Tlokoa of Lelingoana joined the Sotho in their defiance of the Cape administration, and the Mpondomise of Mhlonhlo were also in rebellion.

[4] Ntšebo was Lerotholi's daughter by his senior wife.

[5] i.e. Moshoeshoe's brother, Mohale.

[6] i.e. to capture cattle and to kill men.

[7] The Sepechele plain is in the Mafeteng District, and there was a fierce but inconclusive battle there in January 1881.

[8] Lines 35-6 are addressed to Lerotholi's enemies. Cp. Posholi, i. 31, p. 82 above.

[9] This line is also addressed to Lerotholi's enemies.

[10] RaLibe, i.e. Peete.

RaMakha[1] and his friends are commending the struggle,
And they say: 'Take your chance to act thus, Deliverer!'
The guardians of the old and of the lame praise too,
And they say: 'Take your chance to act thus, Deliverer,
45 That our old men die at home,
That they die at home, and we bury them ourselves.'[2]
    Those foreigners almost made fools of us,
The men there at Cape Town and Bay.[3]
Aren't the Englishmen liars!
50 By the men at the Cape it was said we were helped:
We saw help being given to Sprigg![4]
    Also to us the Boers will give help:
This Brand is now Peete,
For he forges weapons to give us.[5]
55   The warrior who's famous on every side,
There on the ocean the Koena is famous.
Even Mojela[6] and Malebanye[7] are known there,
The Kindler of Fires[8] is a kaross,[9] without question![10]
    The Ambushers' battle at Manyareleng
60 Is a battle which is fought with a letter:
It's been printed, it's even been written.[11]

---

[1] RaMakha, i.e. Setenane, a son of Mokhachane's elder brother, Libe.

[2] i.e. Lerotholi must fight to prevent the dispersal of his people.

[3] Bay (i.e. Algoa Bay) was Port Elizabeth.

[4] There are two possible interpretations of this stanza. Firstly it may refer to the expectation of many Sotho that Frere would support them against the Cape Government and to their disappointment when he supported Sprigg instead. Secondly it may refer to their disappointment with the Award made by Frere's successor, Sir Hercules Robinson, at the close of the Gun War. The first interpretation is probably correct.

[5] There were several Afrikaners who smuggled firearms and ammunition to the Sotho during the Gun War, and although their activities had no official backing, President Brand was widely credited with them. 'This Brand is now Peete': i.e. 'Brand is now concerned for our welfare in the same way as our ancestor Peete'.

[6] Lerotholi's brother.

[7] The husband of Lerotholi's daughter, Letšabisa.

[8] i.e. Lerotholi's brother, Maama.   [9] i.e. his fame is widespread.

[10] Lit. 'he is not asked': i.e. he is so famous that there is no need to ask him who he is.

[11] The Ambushers were a regiment of Lerotholi's brother, Bereng. According to the poet, their battle with the Cape forces at Manyareleng, near Boleka mountain, was so important that it became the subject of much correspondence. There was much fighting in that area, especially in April 1881.

The Beoana[1] had formed a group,
And had said: 'Let the people from Sprigg's be beaten!'
And indeed they were beaten at Manyareleng.
   Now the aggressors have drawn in their claws: 65
You provoke it, and from it you flee![2]
   He keeps on wandering from town to town:[3]
Some say that he's left his chieftainship;
Some believe he's in the Rolong's land;[4]
Even in the Transvaal he's thought to be!   70
   Child of my uncle, Letlatsa,[5] stand firm:
Make firm the skin cradle with straps that are firm.[6]
Our uncles behave like Ndebele.
   The war is fought on the outskirts,[7] Koena:
It's fought at Likhoele, there's fighting at Leribe.   75
   The spearman of the people from Mokhachane's
Fires with a gun and holds a spear.
With the spear he stabs among those who are here,
He stabs the cowards who've stayed behind.
   Desist from taking my cattle, Sprigg,   80
You'll see me desist from taking yours.
   The big baboon has made me a small one:
It forced me to vomit the root I'd eaten.[8]
   Heavens above, I'll not eat anyone,
I can only eat him if he's sent against me.   85
   Sprigg too has started against me,

---

[1] The Beoana, i.e. the Sotho. See Moshoeshoe, ii. 5, p. 71 above.

[2] 'it', i.e. war.

[3] The subject of this stanza is probably Sprigg, who was replaced by Scanlen as Prime Minister at the Cape in May 1881. However, it may possibly be Frere, who ceased to be High Commissioner in September 1880. The idea is that he has been forced to leave home, and that he is wandering far and wide.

[4] 'the Rolong's land', i.e. Thaba Nchu.

[5] The son of Samuel Matsoso, a junior son of Moshoeshoe.

[6] The idea is that a chief should look after his people as a mother looks after her baby when she straps it to her back in a kaross.

[7] Literally *liqola* are the holes made at the edge of a skin when it is pegged to the ground for tanning. In fact most of the fighting during the Gun War took place on the outskirts of Lesotho.

[8] When a small baboon eats something that is wanted by a larger baboon, then the latter may seize it, turn it upside down, and then shake it until the food comes out. It is not clear what Lerotholi surrendered, or to whom. Certainly he never gave up his guns, although he may have contributed to the partial payment of the fine when the war was over.

He continually asked me for guns.
Often the lightning strikes at the tree,
Often it struck at the home of the chief,[1]
90   It struck among the Boers and the policemen.
As for me, I haven't seen my uncles,
Ntsane and Tlali I haven't seen.
I've seen Sekhonyana and Sofonia.[2]
At RaMohoere's there was only Sekoai:
95   At Moletsane's there was only Bohosi.[3]
The bitter aloes of Mohato,[4] Lekena,
He's a bitter herb, he isn't eaten,
Even the dogs don't eat him, he's bitter:
It's bitter like bitterwort, the Lion of the Axes.
100   Mohato's constrictor, Lekena,
The python with a stomach of holes made by bones,[5]
Like the belly of a lion and a hyaena.
The lightning comes from Letsie, at Makhoarane,[6]
The lightning comes from the home of Senate:[7]
105   It came and it climbed to the top of Mathebe,[8]
It was seen far and wide, the lightning of Letsie.
It has climbed up Likhoele,[9] it looks all around,
It says: 'There's nothing, not a sign of a man.'
Hurry and shoot them first,

---

[1] i.e. the magistrate at Mafeteng, or possibly the Governor's Agent at Maseru.

[2] Ntsane, Tlali (or George), Sekhonyana (or Nehemiah) and Sofonia were all sons of Moshoeshoe who threw in their lot with the Cape administration. The significance of these lines is not clear. Perhaps Sekhonyana and Sekoai had actually fought against Lerotholi; or perhaps they had come to him on some private intrigue.

[3] Sekoai, son of RaMohoere, was a Tloung in the Mafeteng District, and was loyal to the Cape authorities. Alfred Bohosi was the most prominent 'Loyalist' among the Taung of Moletsane, most of whom joined in the rebellion. He was killed in the area of Sepechele's. The significance of Sekoai and Bohosi being alone is not known.

[4] Mohato, i.e. Letsie.

[5] The python has swallowed so many animals that their bones have made holes in its stomach.

[6] Makhoarane mountain is only a few miles from Matsieng, which was Letsie's home.

[7] Letsie's daughter.

[8] A mountain in the Mafeteng District, where there was much fighting during the Gun War.

[9] The mountain where Lerotholi's village was situated.

Confound the drawing of their swords!   110
  The lightning has finished the white vultures:[1]
Somebody's people all died
In everybody's view.
  The heaven that rises high, Lekena,
That rises high above the nations!   115
  He's just entered Major Bell's and burnt it;[2]
He's just entered Maseru and set it aflame;[3]
The constrictor has entered Mafeteng.[4]
The camps[5] are almost ruins, Koena,
They're just like the gates of initiation schools![6]   120

(v)

  Lekena's the father of unending debts:[7]
He's just refused that the guns should go,
That the guns should be loaded and taken to the Cape.[8]
  Lekena's the father of unending debts:
They'll eventually be paid by those who begat him,[9]   5
By his parents, the Frog[10] and Mokhachane.
Those who've begotten the Lion of the Axes
Begat it, and for it erected a reed.[11]
  Moshoeshoe has sired himself in Lerotholi,
His courage is like that of the Binders'[12] Lion,   10

---

[1] i.e. the Europeans.
[2] Major Bell was the Magistrate at Hlotse Heights, which was partially burnt by the rebels, though not by the forces of Lerotholi himself.
[3] Maseru, like Hlotse Heights, was partially burnt by the rebels, though not by the forces of Lerotholi.
[4] Lerotholi attacked Mafeteng in September 1880, but was easily driven off.
[5] It was during the Gun War that the magistracies became known as camps.
[6] When boys finally leave an initiation school they set fire to it, and it is left in ruins.
[7] i.e. Lerotholi has caused endless trouble.
[8] This stanza probably refers to an incident in July 1880, a few months before the outbreak of war, when Letsie's guns, which had been loaded onto a cart and sent from Matsieng towards Maseru, were captured on the way by men acting on Lerotholi's instructions.
[9] i.e. the Sotho will survive these troubles with the help of Lerotholi's ancestors.
[10] i.e. Moshoeshoe.
[11] When a child is born a reed is planted on the roof of the house or is raised on the fence surrounding the courtyard.
[12] Moshoeshoe's regiment.

He bites and he heals like him.[1]
The lion's claws are hid, Lekena of Mokhachane,
It walks on its pads, the Lion of the Axes.
    Establish peace, Lekena of Mokhachane,
15 Make it for the orphans of Thesele,[2]
Of the people who've remained among the spears.[3]
    Boers, don't try to try:
You should cross over there to Colesberg,[4]
You should go around below Bloemfontein.
20   This year the water-snake throws people down,
The water-snake, the python of the family of Seeiso.[5]
It swallowed a Boer, he ended in its stomach,
In vain did his kinsmen seek him.
Frantically searching the regiments they missed him.
25 The white man keeps saying: 'Baas Willem!'[6]
This Willem he's calling, where is he?
Willem has fallen from a precipice,
He's fallen from a cliff, from Lerotholi.
    All these people he's brought to an end:
30 The coloured slave's[7] in the stomach of Lerotholi,
The Bushman's in the stomach of Lerotholi,
The Ticket's[8] in the stomach of Lerotholi.
But we're afraid to expound in full,
For our kinsmen, *they*'d become jealous,
35 They'd go to report to that rascal Sprigg,
And he'd go on causing gunsmoke for us.
    The child resembles Chief Posholi,

---

[1] i.e., like Moshoeshoe, he defeats his enemies and then deals mercifully with them.

[2] Thesele, i.e. Moshoeshoe.

[3] i.e. of the people who have been killed in battle.

[4] i.e. the Cape soldiers should leave Lesotho and should go across the Orange to Colesberg.

[5] One of Lerotholi's brothers.

[6] Baas Willem's identity is not known for certain, but he may be the same person as Willem Erasmus, an Afrikaner soldier who is said to have been killed by Maama. See Maama, i. 13, p. 155 below.

[7] Among the Tswana San were used as slaves, and were referred to as *makhoba*. The Sotho, who had no slaves, used the same word to refer contemptuously to people of mixed breed, who were similar to the San in colour.

[8] The Rebels in the Gun War called the Loyalists *Mateketa* or *Mateketoa*, lit. 'The Ticketed Ones', because their guns, when surrendered, were labelled.

By his voice you'd say he was RaMathalea,[1] even when giving com-
mands,
When saying that RaNneela[2] should give medicines for binding,
That with them he should bind the various peoples,[3]   40
And that RaMahlolela[4] should give him medicines for making his
enemies blind.
    Tongs of the chiefs, of the pluckers of iron,[5]
When the spears are bouncing like cobs on the boil!

(vi)[6]

    The fat is burning, RaLetšabisa,
The Koena's rousing the war with the savour of roasted meat,[7]
The bull of the family of Maama and Seeiso.
    The Government hurls stones at the pool of the crocodile:
But how still and how quiet is the pool,   5
And its waters are undisturbed![8]
The bull can entice red people,[9]
The snake of the waters can smother them with dust,
That they fall in the lake,
In the deep, dark, watery abyss, Koena.   10
    The jumping of the spears in battle,
Some are striking even with axes:
He's continually wiping away his sweat.
    The lion can help the crocodile in trouble:[10]

----

[1] i.e. Posholi, Mathalea being his daughter.

[2] i.e. RaManehella, alias Lesaoana, the son of Makhabane. He was one of the
leading rebels in the north.

[3] i.e. he should bind them to himself as their chief.

[4] RaMahlolela, i.e. Masopha, Mahlolela being his daughter.

[5] For the metaphor of the tongs, cp. the praises of Masopha, iii, 51–4,
pp. 125–6 above.

[6] This poem is in the Taung dialect, and the references to the Taung in
lines 14 and 24 make it clear almost beyond doubt that the poet was of Taung
origin.

[7] The burning fat is the fury of war. Just as a man's appetite is roused when
he smells roasted meat, so his valour is roused when he hears of fighting.

[8] For the hypnotic effect of the crocodile's gaze, see iii. 6–8, p. 143 above.
The Government had tried to break the spell by disturbing the pool, but had
failed.

[9] 'red people', i.e. people with light complexions, Europeans.

[10] i.e. the Taung, whose totem was the lion, can help the Koena, whose totem
was the crocodile; as indeed they did in the Gun War.

15 They're alarmed by the voice of the rain when it roars:
The black clouds fell on them with hail,
The white ones came on them with snow,[1]
The wind may come upon them from the east,
It fanned the flames of the regiments to a blaze,
20 The fire set light to the pool of the crocodile
That's green, that's Mokhachane's, that's the crocodiles' pioneer.[2]
    Watchman of the household of Senate, roar,
The nation's allowed you to fight,
For Katiba's allowed you, the son of Moletsane.[3]
25   The voice of the crocodile clothed the nation.[4]
    Then a young man who'd stayed a year slipped away.[5]
Those who've stayed for six months should just stay,
They'll come home when people are just staying,
When the old men are scraping their karosses,
30 And the women are going happily to the lands.[6]

(vii)

    Meet the women, RaLetšabisa,
Two women with baskets on their heads,
Who say: 'Since you're holding a shield by its handle,
Crocodile, what bad news have you heard?'
5 For myself, I've heard no bad news from anyone:
Only the voice of Mohato have I heard
When he told us to take our horses and go there.[7]
    When at Phatlalla[8] we pitched our camp:
Two days we stayed there
10 While the chief[9] was still reckoning with the pen,

[1] Lines 15–17 no doubt indicate the hardships of war.
[2] i.e. Lerotholi was provoked to fight.
[3] Katiba was one of the leading rebels among the Taung.
[4] i.e. the nation listened to Lerotholi as its leader.
[5] i.e. a young man who had been working for a year, probably at the diamond mines in Kimberley, but possibly on a European's farm, returned to Lesotho.
[6] i.e. they will come home at a time of peace and contentment, when people are pursuing their normal occupations, for Lerotholi will have won the war.
[7] Mohato, i.e. Letsie, had instructed Lerotholi to go and assist the Cape authorities against the Phuthi of Moorosi.
[8] It had been arranged that the Sotho should cross the Orange at Phatlalla.
[9] The chief was probably Griffith, the Governor's Agent.

Picking out those who should enter the boat.
   Oh, Mokeke's son's an amazing rogue:
He spoiled our relations with Maseru,
He spoiled them and made them disgusting.
He'd throw the Koena into waters that were deep.[1]   15
   Lekena drew back
Saying: 'I'm not a hippo, or a fish, but a man:
I can't jump into these deeps that I see!'
   The child of the family of RaSenate,[2] the one who turns aside,
He turned aside and went along the mountains,   20
Saying: 'I'm afraid when Moorosi is fought.
Beyond the river only paupers should fight,
Ntho, the son of Mokeke and his friends,
Those who flatter for sugar among the Whites!'
   The milk-cow which nourishes birds,[3]   25
Which nourishes orphans, the child of Thesele,[4]
Let all these children multiply,
And the cattle give birth and multiply for us.
   The protector of the son of Mokhachane,
Who protects against the sun and makes it as dusk,   30
Saying that the orphans should walk in the shade,
That those should live whose fathers have died.
   The father of Ntšebo[5] has come with cattle,[6]
The cattle that are black are mixed with the red:
The red when they're counted are six,   35
The black were as few as the fingers of a hand.[7]
   Its colour has changed, it's now white,
It's now like the ashes of a ruined village,
The cow of our alliance with Maseru.

---

[1] Mokeke's son, Ntho, was one of Letsie's senior advisers, and, unlike Lerotholi, was in favour of giving the Government at Maseru full and enthusiastic support against Moorosi. The waters referred to are those of the Orange, but they also symbolize the troubles of war.
[2] RaSenate, i.e. Letsie, Senate being his daughter.
[3] Probably the birds are the tick-birds, or cattle-egrets, which are often seen around cattle in summer.
[4] Thesele, i.e. Moshoeshoe.   [5] Ntšebo was Lerotholi's daughter.
[6] The cattle are no doubt those with which Lerotholi was rewarded by the Government for his help against Moorosi.
[7] Lit.: 'The black ones finished only a hand.' Obviously Lerotholi was dissatisfied with his reward.

40   We don't know what colour it'll turn this year
       When it carries back the millet to the home of Letšabisa.[1]

11. *Maama*

Although only the eldest son in Letsie's fourth house, Maama (*c.* 1848–
1924) was second only to Lerotholi in importance. There was no male
issue in the first house; the third house was in disgrace; and, although
there were two younger brothers in Lerotholi's house, namely Bereng and
Theko, Maama probably took precedence over them by Sotho custom.
Furthermore he was Letsie's favourite, and it is known that his father
would have wished him, rather than Lerotholi, to be his successor.

His role in the final struggle against the Free State appears to have been
very limited. After the war he went to the Cape to be educated at Zonnebloem College, and on his return he was placed in the area which is still
known as Maama's in what is now the Maseru District. In 1879 he fought
in the war against Moorosi, though with many misgivings, and in the Gun
War he committed himself wholeheartedly to the side of the rebels. He
served first on the Maseru front, but then, at Lerotholi's request, he
moved down to the Mafeteng front. After the Gun War he was constantly
involved in disputes about land, and by 1924, the year of his death, the
area under his control had been considerably diminished.

Four of his poems are to be found in Mangoaela's collection. His son,
Chief Molapo Maama, who is still alive today, states that he himself
recorded these poems at Mangoaela's request and at his father's dictation.
He also states that Maama was the poet. This statement is clearly true of
the first, second and fourth poems, in which the first person singular is
used very frequently. In the third poem, however, the first person
singular is not used at all with reference to the chief. When the *seroki*
Kolobe Moerane chanted Maama's praises at Molapo's village in November 1968, he recited the first two poems almost in their entirety, and then
went straight on to the fourth. It is possible, therefore, in spite of Chief
Molapo's assertion, that Mangoaela collected the third poem from
another source, and that its composer was not Maama himself.

The first three poems all relate to the Gun War, and refer time and
time again to Maama's great exploit, the killing of a European soldier at
Sepechele's. The fourth relates mainly to the war with Moorosi. It
begins as a quiet and almost prosaic narrative, with very few eulogies and
very little parallelism. The story is then interrupted by stanzas which
appear to have been inspired by the Gun War, and the concluding
stanzas refer almost certainly to an incident in the second Free State war.

---

[1] The poet complains that the war with Moorosi has spoilt the Sotho's relationship with the Government, and he wonders what this relationship will be in the
following winter, at the time when the millet is harvested and brought back to
the village.

All four poems are well liked today, but the first in particular is greatly admired for the beauty of its language.

(i)

Maama, Lekena's[1] evader,
RaLetšabisa's[2] evader, Vulture!
When Lerotholi's Vulture is fired at, it ducks.
The enormous Vulture crouched down into cover,
Its head it put under its wings.   5
The black lightning bird of Seeiso's[3] home
Burned Maseru as the sun was declining.
And so Trower left, out he was thrown
In mid-afternoon.[4]
There, you see, you Sparkling Soldier![5]   10
When you have seen you have seen, Sparkling Soldier,[6]
As the guns point their mouths at each other.
The owner of the grey horse was sleeping.[7]
Why are you sleeping, European child,
While the steady rains are falling?   15
A man's been devoured by Letsie's Vulture,
He's been devoured by RaSenate's[8] Young Vulture,
The Vulture of Sekhobe and Makhabane,[9]
The child of the heavenly lightning, Maama the Kindler of Fires.

[1] Lekena, i.e. Lerotholi.
[2] RaLetšabisa, i.e. Lerotholi, Letšabisa being his daughter.
[3] Seeiso was Maama's brother.
[4] Maama and other chiefs led several attacks against the Government's headquarters at Maseru during the Gun War. In fact, however, the Camp was never taken; its main buildings were not burnt; and Richard Trower, a trader whose store in Maseru had been fortified, was not expelled.
[5] The Sparkling Soldier was the High Commissioner at the Cape, Sir Bartle Frere: see Lerotholi, iv. 10, p. 144 above.
[6] i.e. 'Remember what you have seen and act accordingly'.
[7] i.e. the owner of the grey horse was dead. Maama personally killed a European in the Gun War, and he refers to this exploit repeatedly in his *lithoko*. According to Chief Lekete Letsie (1856–1946), who witnessed this event, and who later passed on this information to Damane, the occasion was the *Ntoa ea Lisabole*, 'the Battle of the Swords', at Sepechele's; the man killed was an Afrikaner called Willem Erasmus, who was riding a grey horse; and Maama shot him dead as he and his men charged into the enemy ranks. This battle may probably be identified as one which was fought on 14 January 1881.
[8] RaSenate, i.e. Letsie, Senate being his daughter.
[9] Maama's brothers.

20   The wethers butted against each other,
The ram butted against that from Sprigg's.[1]
I struck the European, I threw him down:
Someone fell before the face of the horse,
He fell before the face of my horse, Koloboi.[2]
25 His friends gathered up a nonentity,
They took up a corpse but the spirit was gone:
They collected it up, they dumped it in a wagon,
They acted as if he would wake!
The dark blood of the Cape European, the blood from the veins
of his head
30 Slipped away, and we hadn't yet written,
And, as for telling them, we hadn't yet told them.
It went to tell his people on the ships,
It told his people where the fish swim to and fro,
Where the waters are continually stirred.[3]
35 They[4] said: 'It is thus, we've just come from battle,
We've come from the blaze at RaMabilikoe's,[5]
Here at Mafa's[6] and RaMabilikoe's,
Here at the Dancer's[7] and the father of Mpoi's,[8]
At the nek between Boleka and Mathebe.[9]
40 As we were playing, someone fell.
Your child has been eaten by Koeeoko,[10]
He's been eaten by Koeeoko of Letsie,
Kooeeko, which eats the Whites' children.'
I, the offspring of 'MaMojela, have sprung on people,[11]

[1] Gordon Sprigg was Prime Minister at the Cape during the Gun War.
[2] Koloboi was Maama's horse.
[3] For the Sotho's belief that Europeans lived on ships, cp. Lerotholi, ii. 20, p. 141 above.
[4] In talking of 'They' the poet forgets that it is the blood that goes to report. In a similar passage in iii. 38, p. 163 below, he is more consistent.
[5] RaMabilikoe, a Fokeng chief, lived at Mathebe, only a few miles away from Sepechele's.
[6] Mafa, another Fokeng chief, lived at Thaba Tšoeu, which was also in the vicinity of Sepechele's.
[7] i.e. at Mafa's.   [8] i.e. at RaMabilikoe's.
[9] One would have expected the poet to say: 'between Thaba Tšoeu and Mathebe', for these two mountains were the homes of Mafa and RaMabilikoe. Instead he speaks of Boleka, another mountain in that area, and Mathebe.
[10] A river monster in a Sotho folk-tale. It devoured a little boy who was constantly provoking it.
[11] Lit.: 'I, the son of 'MaMojela, have eaten people.' In fact Maama was not 'MaMojela's son, for Mojela was only a half-brother. The pun on 'MaMojela

I've sprung on people with my left hand. 45
It may be because I'm left-handed,
Perhaps I can sicken their stomachs.[1]
   I, the buffalo of Nkoebe's family, buffet people with my horns,[2]
I buffet them with a ramrod on the plain,
At Mathebe, at the plain of provocation,[3] 50
At Mohlanapeng,[4] where White anger was roused.
   Mohato's[5] aggressive wild boar, Maama,
I, the warthog of Seeiso's[6] family, I'm launching attacks on people.
   For myself, with a stick I'm not content,
With a stick I don't feel at ease: 55
I'm happy when I strike with the truncheon, with the pistol,
The stick of the hand from the palms of Letsie.[7]
   Where are RaSenate's[8] Young Vultures?
The bulldogs of Mohato, where are they?
   Don't hide my actions, young men of my country! 60
Will you not say it was I who struck him?
Will you not say it was I who killed first?
   The grey horse came without being bought,
It came without being bought or sold,
But it draws towards me the head of a man, 65
It is brought by me,[9] the kicker of the shields,[10]
The son of Letsie, with wide-nostrilled nose,

---

and *ke jele* ('I have eaten') cannot be reproduced in the relevant English words, but is reflected in 'offspring' and 'sprung'.

[1] There is a belief among the Sotho that one will be sick if one eats food given to one by a left-handed man. Maama was left-handed, and he suggests that this is why he was able to cause his enemies so much discomfort.

[2] Lit.: 'I, the buffalo of Nkoebe's family, fight people' (as bulls fight each other, fencing with their horns). Nkoebe was another of Letsie's sons. The pun on Nkoebe and *koeba* cannot be reproduced in the relevant English words, but is reflected in 'buffalo' and 'buffet'.

[3] i.e., almost certainly, the Sepechele Plain. The reference is probably to the battle which was fought there on 14 January 1881: see line 13 above.

[4] Mohlanapeng, otherwise known as RaLiemere's, is a village on the plain.

[5] Mohato, i.e. Letsie.   [6] Seeiso was Maama's brother.

[7] i.e. Maama is not content to fight with a gun ('a stick'), but prefers to fight at close quarters with the pistol ('the truncheon', 'the stick of the hand') given to him by Letsie.

[8] RaSenate, i.e. Letsie, Senate being his daughter.

[9] The idea is that Maama entices the horse towards him and so is able to shoot its rider.

[10] 'the kicker of the shields', i.e. the performer of the *mohobelo* dance, in which shields are kicked.

With nostrils that are flared,[1] Maama.
I bit a man, he didn't rise,
70   He lay down, and the undergrowth rose above him
Till at last he vanished on the ground!

(ii)

Maama, the favourite[2] of the family of Senate,[3]
The favourite in amid the rocks,
In amid the rocks, at the home of Letšabisa,[4]
Behind the hut of Letšabisa's mother!
5   When I was fighting, as a man of Lerotholi,
I fought like a bull of mixed breed:
As I fought I raised clouds of dust.
I've stabbed the white bull from Sprigg's.
Stab the European, that he tires, Senate's man:
10   Let me kill him, I'll never be afraid of him.
I see him, the Chief,[5]
Lerotholi RaLetšabisa's watching to see
A wild man with a stallion![6]
You saw me, young men, when we left the plain,
15   Being fired at with a smoking canon.
They had groundless fears, did the children of Mojela,
Mojela and Sariele fled![7]
When I reached them I spurred them on,
I gave them the war-song, the chant of men,
20   The mountains of home gave the alarm for me:
There were echoes at the high mountain of Likhoele.[8]
The bitter herb,[9] Mokhachane's returner,[10]

---

[1] Maama's nostrils were flared in anger. Cp. Makhabane, lines 11–12, p. 77 above.

[2] Lit. 'the son-in-law'. A son-in-law was usually a popular figure at his wife's home.

[3] Letsie's daughter.   [4] Lerotholi's daughter.

[5] The Chief here is Lerotholi.

[6] 'A wild man with a stallion', i.e. Maama, in a frenzy of rage, riding a stallion.

[7] Mojela was Maama's brother. Sariele (i.e. Azariel) was a greatgrandson of Libe, Mokhachane's elder brother. Both men had homes in the Mafeteng area, and took part in the fighting there.

[8] Lerotholi's home.

[9] For the metaphor of the bitter herb, cp. Lerotholi, iv. 5–7, p. 144 above.

[10] No matter how fierce the battle, Maama will always return to the fray. Cp. Jonathan, i. 65, p. 174 below.

The chief who returns when men are dying,
When the bullets are splitting men's heads,
When the swords are striking men's necks, 25
When the grenades are bursting, and the fires blazing,
Blazing, and showing their darting flames,
When many are saying: 'It's the last day!'[1]
There returned the Crocodile of the son of Mokhachane,
The little Crocodile of the family of Seeiso. 30
    Put back your stick, Mohato's son, and take out your gun.
I struck a man from his horse with a gun,
The white-horsed European died indeed!
The grey-horsed European[2] fell among the staves with the ostrich
                              plumes on the shields,[3]
He fell among the Young Vultures' spearshafts.[4] 35
    You're always saying that you're brave, you Vultures, Young
                              Vultures of Maama,
In courage you're surpassed by the great one:
The first to fall was the Vulture's man,
The Young Vulture's man has fallen first.
In surpassing 'Matšoana you've excelled, 40
You've surpassed Sethobane and RaPontšo![5]
    Good fortune has come from the ancestors,
It's come from Peete and Mokhachane,
It's arisen from Letsie[6] and Moshoeshoe.
    My men have told me in person 45
That when I was born Letsie rejoiced:
RaLerotholi, it is said, was enraptured:
From these wild beasts he took the heads,[7]
He took the skin of the lion and the leopard, and he said:
'Today there is born a warrior!' 50

[1] The idea of the last day comes from Christianity.
[2] The white-horsed European and the grey-horsed European are clearly one and the same man.
[3] A Sotho's shield was supported by a stick surmounted by ostrich feathers.
[4] The Young Vultures were one of Maama's regiments.
[5] 'Matšoana, Sethobane and RaPontšo were all Maama's warriors.
[6] Letsie was still alive, but since, because of his age, he took no part in the fighting, he could be thought of as being concerned with his people's welfare in much the same way as the ancestors.
[7] The reference here is to the ritual of *lelomolo* in which a baby was treated with certain medicines. In Maama's case these medicines had been prepared from animals noted for their strength and ferocity, and it was believed that they had conveyed these qualities to the young child.

And this indeed was the truth:
The bull stabs some in the flanks,
Others it stabs in the ribs.
    I've killed the florid redskin, the wretched little white man;
55 I threw him to the ground.
The wailing of that man reached far away,
In the end it could be heard at the Cape and the Bay,[1]
And Smithfield town heard too![2]
    I, the young cub, have been sired by the strong,
60 And so I'm a mighty warrior:
I was sired by bulls that were strong,
I've been sired by Peete and Mokhachane;
I was sired by Libe, the child of Matlole,[3]
And Mohato, Thesele's boy.[4]
65   RaMatiea,[5] go and report,
You who like taking news,
Go and inform Letsie,
That he may make known to my mother's family that they may
                                   know,
That he may make known to the folk from Molibeli's:[6]
70 I, their dog, bite when I'm sent to attack,
I bit Sprigg's man.
    The whirlwind of Senate, Maama,
Thundered, it took the young man from his horse,[7]
It deprived him of his bridle and bit,
75 It devoured him to the ground with the insects.[8]
    A white man left home and was swearing,
Thumping and beating on his chest;
One day he took off his hat,
He stamped on it with his boots,

[1] The Bay, i.e. Algoa Bay, was Port Elizabeth.

[2] A town in the southern Free State.

[3] Matlole, i.e. Motloang, was Peete's father, and was therefore Libe's grandfather.

[4] 'Mohato, Thesele's boy'; i.e. Letsie, Moshoeshoe's son.

[5] RaMatiea, a Hlakoana chief, was one of Maama's counsellors.

[6] The Molibeli, like the Mokoteli, were Koena. 'MaMotena, Maama's mother, was of Molibeli origin.

[7] Lit. 'it took the herdsmen from his horse'. Most herdsmen were young, and so the word *molisa*, 'herdsman', could be used simply to denote a young man.

[8] Three ideas are compressed together in this line. (i) It threw him to the ground. (ii) It devoured him. (iii) The insects devoured him too. Once again the reference is to the killing of the European at Sepechele's.

Indeed with his feet he trampled it: 80
'Bring the guns here, you Kaffirs!'[1]
 Ours we refused to give,
Our spears are our dangerous weapons of old.[2]
Even when RaTlali left them they were fighting;[3]
They continued to cut off men's heads; 85
They've devoured Nkopane and Mohlomi.[4]
 Child of Mohato's[5] wife, Maama,
Warthog of the family of Seeiso,[6] elephant of the Searchers,[7]
Maama, strike, that the Young Vultures may strike,
That Sethobane and RaPontšo[8] may strike, 90
That the Dog-eaters[9] may stab them with spears!
 Letsie, give us cattle, we're yours:
We're dogs, bulldogs of yours:
You'll strike with us at the nations!

(iii)

 Vulture, Young Vulture, Kindler of Fires,
Kindler of dry grass at the Tsoaing![10]
Since you're a Vulture, Maama,
Won't you take the war[11] on your wings, and trudge on,
Won't you then take it with all your strength? 5

---

[1] For this stanza, cp. iii. 46–50, p. 163 below, where it is clear that the European referred to is Sprigg, the Cape Prime Minister.
[2] Under the terms of the Disarmament Proclamation the Sotho were to be deprived of their spears as well as their guns.
[3] i.e. these spears were being used as long ago as the early years of the eighteenth century, when RaTlali, alias Mokheseng, a son of Monaheng, the Koena chief, was killed in battle.
[4] Mohlomi was the Monaheng chief who was renowned for his wisdom and for his skill as a doctor: Nkopane was his elder brother. Mohlomi died in the early years of the nineteenth century, and Nkopane probably died in the same period. Neither of them died by the spear, but their names are used merely to denote antiquity. Cp. Posholi, iii. 120–3, p. 89 above.
[5] Mohato, i.e. Letsie.   [6] Maama's brother.
[7] One of Maama's regiments.
[8] Two of his warriors: see line 41 above.
[9] Any regiment may be referred to as Dog-eaters: the name simply implies ferocity.
[10] The Tsoaing river forms part of the boundary between the present Maseru and Mafeteng Districts, and its valley was the scene of much fighting.
[11] There is no object in the Sotho, but it appears from the context that 'the war' is to be understood.

The burning grass comes from Thaba-Chitja,[1] the striker,
It arrived and it covered the little villages.
RaPakeng and his people[2] were burnt by the embers,
They were burnt by the scorching of war !
10   Someone's coming from Ulu-ulu,[3] Maama,
He's coming from a mountain that's tall, very tall,
He's coming from Thaba-Mautse,[4]
With 'Ho !' and 'Just try to stop me !' together ![5]
The feeder of the animals, Maama,
15   He feeds the dogs, he feeds the people,
He feeds the crows too till they're full:
They sat in full view on the bushes ![6]
You're always saying you're leopard-skin wearers:
You've worn a young leopard today,
20   You wore it, it didn't defeat you.[7]
A mighty uninitiated man with a stallion,
Mohato's uninitiated man with a stallion ![8]
Maama, the evader of spears,
RaLetšabisa's[9] evader !
25   He was at Maseru, at the Meja-Metalana,[10]
He heard the voice of Lekena[11] speaking:
'The war over there at Meeling[12] has become too much for me !'
You're always saying the Makena[13] are brave,

---

[1] Maama's village was near Thaba-Chitja mountain.

[2] Mangoaela's text, *Ba lipakeng*, 'Those in between', has been altered to *Bo-RaPakeng*, 'RaPakeng and his people'. RaPakeng, a Siea, lived in what is now the Maseru District, near the village of Leutsoa's. Evidently he was loyal to the Cape authorities.

[3] Another mountain in Maama's area. The person coming from it is Maama himself.

[4] Another mountain in Maama's area.

[5] Lit.: 'Having joined "Ho !" and "Seize me !"' These cries showed a warrior's enthusiasm as he rushed out to fight.

[6] He feeds the dogs and crows on the bodies of his enemies: he feeds the people on the cattle which he plunders.

[7] Wearing a leopard-skin is a sign of bravery (cp. Posholi, iv. 10, p. 92 above); but wearing a leopard means coming to grips with a fierce adversary.

[8] Maama was in fact uninitiated.   [9] RaLetšabisa, i.e. Lerotholi.

[10] The Meja-Metalana is a small stream near Maseru.

[11] Lekena, i.e. Lerotholi.

[12] Meeling, which means 'On the borders', is an area on the Free State boundary a few miles south-west of Mafeteng.

[13] The Makena, 'the Enterers', were one of Lerotholi's regiments.

You forget they've just called the Vultures, the Young Vultures of
the father of Lineo.[1]

The whirlwind of Senate, Maama,   30
Took hold of a man and dashed him from his horse:[2]
It shied from the body, did the European's horse,
It shied from the body with the spirit now ended.
The Whites gathered up a nonentity:
They supposed he would wake.[3]   35
The dark blood from the veins of his head
Spurted out and formed a rainbow;
It went to cause alarm over there among the ships,
It went to tell his kinsmen news that was amazing,
And, as for writing, they hadn't yet written: 40
It said: 'Just now we've come from the war
In the nek between Mafa and RaMabilikoe.
As we were playing, someone fell:
We thought he was merely lying flat,
But in fact he's devoured by the Vulture of Letsie.'[4]   45
Above all it's reported to Sprigg,
The man who made a resolve, leaving home,
Seizing his white helmet hat,
And crushing it under his feet,
Saying he could enter with ease at Lerotholi's![5]   50
But he didn't know that
Here at RaLibe's[6] there'd been born
A little black bull, displeasing in appearance,[7]
A blesbok, a he-goat, Letšabisa's uncle,[8]
The Young Vulture that returns from afar.[9]   55
A grievous plight, as the lightning flashed,
As the mist crept over the earth,

[1] One of Maama's daughters. In the first part of the war Maama fought on the Maseru front, but was later summoned by Lerotholi to assist him on the Mafeteng front.
[2] The poet now returns to the killing of the European. For lines 30–1, cp. ii. 72–3, p. 160 above.
[3] For lines 32–5, cp. i. 23–8, p. 156 above.
[4] For lines 36–45, cp. i. 29–43, p. 156 above.
[5] For this stanza, cp. ii. 76–81, pp. 160–1 above.
[6] Libe's father was Peete. 'at RaLibe's', i.e. in Lesotho.
[7] The implication is that, in spite of his displeasing appearance, Maama was extremely powerful.
[8] Letšabisa was the daughter of his brother, Lerotholi.
[9] For the significance of returning, see ii. 22, p. 158 above.

As the grenades exploded,
As the bullets split asunder the heads of men,
60 As the swords cut clean through the necks of men,
And the young men swore and said:
'Chief, today, this day is the last!'[1]
    The Vultures that are small are those that leave first:
The big ones are those that leave after an effort,
65 Men such as Khoabe and Mosaeea.[2]
    The boom of Mokhachane, Maama,
When it thundered it scared the Ndebele:[3]
The hyaenas departed from the mountains,
And the rabbits migrated in their hundreds.[4]
70   You men from Mokhachane's, what do you think
Drove Tokonya from his home,
When he went to Maseru with ears that were closed?[5]
At the time of his departure he left behind
An enormous calabash for drinking:
75 When he dies you should keep it,
And the handle should be turned into a penis-sheath![6]
        Maama, the uninitiated comrade of Sethobane and Phafane![7]
        The Chief called out to the Young Vultures' man:[8]
The horses he's fetched at night.[9]
80 He came upon a rock and sat down,

---

[1] For this stanza, cp. ii. 22–8, pp. 158–9 above.

[2] The young warriors are sent into battle first, and the older men follow later. On the advice of Chief Molapo Maama, Khoale in Mangoaela's text has been changed to Khoabe.

[3] Ndebele, i.e. Nguni. During the Gun War many of the Nguni who lived among the Sotho remained loyal to the Cape authorities. These were the men whom Maama 'scared'.

[4] i.e. the Nguni fled in terror from their homes.

[5] Tokonya was a petty Hlubi chief who had been living in Masopha's area. He surrendered his guns to the Government, and so Masopha drove him away into the Free State. Subsequently he took refuge in Maseru. Maama himself was not directly involved in this incident. Tokonya's ears were closed because he was obstinate; or because he was deafened by Maama's thundering; or both.

[6] For the Nguni's penis-sheath, cp. the praises of Posholi, iii. 14, p. 84 above.

[7] *Thobane le Sephafane* in Mangoaela's text has been changed to *Sethobane le Phafane*. For Sethobane, see ii. 41 and 90, pp. 159 and 161 above. For Phafane, see iv. 5, p. 165 below.

[8] i.e. Lerotholi summoned Maama to his assistance.

[9] Maama was so enthusiastic that he began making his preparations during the night. Cp. Griffith, i. 7–10, p. 215 below.

Looking for the Pleiades to appear.[1]
 The aggressive wild boar of your family, Mohato,[2]
Maama, the warthog of the family of Seeiso,[3] the one who thumps
          people around,
He's left-handed too, is Maama:[4]
He's a telegram, he sends the news.   85
 The pursuer from the people of Mokhachane's,
The glaring flame, the light of the Chief;
The Chief, the blaze of the son of Libenyane![5]

(iv)

 I left my home on horseback,
I left the Korokoro[6] at a gallop,
I departed from Popa, from Majoe-a-Litšoene,[7]
In the company of Mohatla among the Young Vultures,
Galloping with Phafane and Lechakola,[8]   5
Going to Letsie for my orders.[9]
 When I came to the home of the chief of the Hounds[10]
Even my father asked me no questions:
I saw that his eyes were full of tears,[11]
He told Setha[12] to tell me to pass on.   10
 I left my home, but it wasn't pleasant:
My heart stayed behind at the village of the Chief,
It stayed behind for Letsie's orders.
 We Vultures swept along as we went;
The Tsoaing we passed at night.   15
We came to the Orange, we camped a long time.
 At dawn I was instructed about my regiment,

[1] i.e. for the approach of dawn.   [2] Mohato, i.e. Letsie.
[3] Seeiso was Maama's brother.   [4] Cp. i, 46–7, p. 157 above.
[5] The Chief in line 87 is probably either Letsie or Lerotholi. In line 88 the
Chief is Maama himself. Libenyane, 'Little Libe', was Mokhachane, and his
son, of course, was Moshoeshoe.
[6] A stream near Maama's home.
[7] Popa was a mountain near Maama's home: the Majoe-a-Litšoene, 'The
Baboons' Stones', were certain rocks on the mountain. Cp. Masopha, iv. 102,
p. 130 above.
[8] Mohatla, Phafane and Lechakola were three of Maama's warriors.
[9] i.e. for orders about the war with Moorosi.
[10] The Hounds were Letsie's regiment.
[11] Evidently Letsie was unhappy about sending the Sotho to fight Moorosi.
[12] Setha Matete was one of Letsie's most influential counsellors.

I was instructed by Letsie's Fierce Warrior,[1]
Bereng gave me orders and encouragement,
20 Saying, 'Maama and Koali,[2] we're in the veld,
With these our friends, Moletsane's people,[3]
Our friends from the family of Mophethe, of the brother of Thulo.'[4]
    It was then that I felt my body stiffen,
Then too I felt my hands grow cold:
25 I was almost unable to take my gun.
    Beyond the Orange, I, brother of Seeiso,
Here at the Sebapala river,[5]
At the rocks, at the home of Moorosi's son,[6]
I, from Mokabai's,[7] I've eaten men,
30 I, the servant of Senate, have killed.[8]
    Matlole,[9] Mokhachane and Peete's father rejoiced:
The Repeater,[10] the son of Mokhachane, rejoiced;
The Agitator and the Hawk rejoiced:[11]
'That's the way to act, son of Letsie,
35 White-eyed son of Mohato:
When you have killed, return home,
Return to the Chief, to Letsie.'
    I'm no longer Maama, the Kindler of Fires:
I, the servant of Senate, am a sweeper,

---

[1] i.e. by Bereng, son of Letsie.

[2] Koali was a son of Makhobalo, a son of Moshoeshoe's second house. His home was in the Korokoro valley.

[3] i.e. the Taung of Moletsane, who were then living in the Mohale's Hoek District.

[4] Mophethe, brother of Thulo, was the chief of a group of Taung living around Masite in the Maseru District.

[5] The Sebapala joins the Orange about six miles from Moorosi's Mountain.

[6] It is not known which son of Moorosi is referred to here.

[7] Mokabai, i.e. Senate, Letsie's daughter.

[8] Lit. 'I, Senate's Nguni, have killed.' The Nguni who lived among the Sotho were rarely men of any importance, and many of them attached themselves to chiefs as their personal servants. In March 1879 there was a clash with Phuthi at the Sebapala as the Cape forces and the Sotho were moving towards Moorosi's Mountain. Evidently Maama and his men killed one or more of the enemy on this occasion.

[9] Matlole was Motloang, Peete's father. It would seem from the second reference to Peete's father further on in this line that Maama was unaware of this fact.

[10] i.e. Mohale, Moshoeshoe's brother.

[11] i.e. Molapo and Masopha rejoiced.

I've swept off his herdsmen from Fako.[1]   40
   I'm the wandering dog of the Lord of the Hounds,[2] the croco-
                                             dile's wether,
The ram that butts at the break of dawn.
   The young men see my face,[3]
They see, the Young Vultures of the household of Senate:
We accompanied Jonathan, the Agitator's son,[4]   45
In the far-off land of the Sebapala.
   You too who are fond of telling,
And you who speak much, be quiet:
For my part, nothing is done for me, the Kindler of Fires of the
                                 family of 'MaLoela,[5]
I do things for myself.   50
   At the time when the warriors are riding,
I never restrain my horse and hold back:
I go ahead, I, Lebakae's comrade,
I, comrade of Leuta's child, am like a leopard.[6]
   I'm the son of the Chief and I'm strong indeed,   55
You've seen me break a man's back:
A certain Thembu remained on the ground,
When his people passed by he was speechless![7]
   Someone was devoured by Letsie's Vulture,
He was devoured by RaSenate's Young Vulture: 60
The Young Vulture flapped at him his wings,
It singed the lashes of his eyes and he died:
Someone's child did indeed pass away,
Causing distress to his family.
Here at Fako's they're still lamenting, they're still lamenting the 65
                                             Ndebele:[8]
It's said that a lion has devoured a man with a penis-sheath![9]

[1] Fako was the name which the Sotho gave to Griffith, the Governor's Agent.
It seems probable, therefore, that this stanza does not relate to the war with
Moorosi, but to the Gun War.
[2] i.e. of Letsie.
[3] This probably means that Maama was conspicuous when there was fighting
to be done.
[4] i.e. with Jonathan Molapo.   [5] One of Maama's sisters.
[6] Lebakae, the son of Leuta, was one of Maama's warriors.
[7] The incident alluded to is not known. The reference to Fako, i.e. Griffith,
in line 61 below suggests that it occurred in the Gun War.
[8] i.e. at Griffith's they are still lamenting the death of a Nguni.
[9] As in the preceding stanza, the incident alluded to is not known, but the
mention of Griffith suggests that it occurred during the Gun War.

Why are you famous when you're not a tough warrior, when
you're not a fearsome tough warrior,
When you're not a brandisher of guns, Maama?[1]
Brother of 'MaBoi,[2] diminisher,
70 Run and diminish the veld, wild beast![3]
Since I'm a Bushman, when I look at myself,
Being a Bushman, I ignore my loads![4]
Son of Letsie, stopper of the oxen,
Stop the oxen as they run below Qeme:[5]
75 I stopped those with down-bent horns in the veld,
They were taken to the Frog, to Moshoeshoe.[6]
If Moshoeshoe weren't lord of the people,
If Letsie too weren't lord,
People would say that the oxen should be returned to their owners.
80 As for me, they now stand with my father,
They stand with enormous horns.[7]

12. *Jonathan*

Jonathan (*c.* 1844–1928) was the second son in Molapo's senior house.
His elder brother, Josefa, was insane, and so he was nominated by his
father as his heir and successor. Thus he was given precedence over Joel,
who claimed that as the eldest son in Molapo's second house he was
senior to Jonathan, and who also happened to be several years older.

[1] According to Chief Theko Maama, the words *makoa* ('tough warrior') and
makoakoali ('fearsome tough warrior') in line 67 are derived from the word
koakoariri, which means 'hard hide or skin; strong person or animal'. Maama
was never initiated, and the poet asks how it is that, with this unmilitary background, he has become so famous.

[2] One of Maama's sisters.

[3] The idea is that by running fast over the veld Maama will make it seem
smaller.

[4] 'I ignore my loads', i.e. I am completely confident that I can do what I
have to do. Cp. Griffith, ii. 406, p. 223 below. The San's 'loads' were his prominent buttocks, which, of course, he carried without difficulty.

[5] An extensive plateau in what is now the Maseru District.

[6] The reference to Moshoeshoe, the Frog, makes it clear that this incident
took place during the second Free State War. Presumably the Afrikaners had
captured some of the Sotho's cattle and Maama had cut them off near the
Qeme plateau and recaptured them.

[7] The only interpretation of this stanza which can be suggested is far from certain
—that Moshoeshoe and Letsie refused to return the cattle to the people from
whom they had been captured, but retained possession themselves. They would
perhaps be tempted to do this when the Free Staters had taken so much of their
own livestock during the war. In the last line Maama appears to express his
agreement with their action.

Jonathan insisted on his chieftainship rights over Joel; Joel would never recognize them; and between the two men there soon developed the most implacable hatred. It was for this reason that Molapo placed Jonathan at Fobane, in the south-west of his district, and Joel at Qalo, in the north-east, as far away from each other as could conveniently be arranged.

In the second Free State war Jonathan no doubt fought alongside the other Sotho chiefs in the north, and it is known that he assisted in the defence of Thaba Bosiu in August 1865. But after the Treaty of Mpharane in March 1866, when Molapo made his own separate peace with the Free State, he took no further part in the fighting.

In 1871 he led an expedition into the Maloti against the San of Soai, who had been plundering stock in the Leribe District. Several chiefs, including Joel, had already tried to exterminate them, but without success. Now Jonathan inflicted heavy losses on them and took some of their women and children captive. Shortly afterwards, in 1873, Langalibalele, the Hlubi chief, after a dispute with the authorities in Natal about the registration of firearms, fled with his followers and herds over the Drakensberg and into Basutoland. The nearest chief of any importance was Molapo, and Griffith, the Governor's Agent at Maseru, offered him a share in Langalibalele's herds if he would help to capture him. Molapo was agreeable and sent out a force under Jonathan, who lulled the Hlubi chief into a false sense of security and then brought him down to Leribe, where he was immediately placed under arrest. Jonathan also proved his loyalty to the Cape authorities in the war against Moorosi in 1879, although there is no reference to this in his *lithoko*.

When Molapo died in 1880 he duly succeeded him. At first there was no trouble, but when in the Gun War he sided with the Cape Government he was supported by only a few of his brothers, and the rest of them, headed by Joel, turned against him. Moreover at Fobane he was uncomfortably close to his uncle, Masopha, and to RaManella, the son of Makhabane, both of whom had committed themselves wholeheartedly to the rebel cause. He therefore moved eastwards to the mountain fortress of Tsikoane, but in November 1880 this was captured by a combined rebel force and he and his men were compelled to take refuge at the nearby Magistracy of Hlotse Heights. There, on several occasions, they assisted the Cape soldiers in beating off fierce rebel attacks, but beyond this they were powerless.

Outside the Magistracy Joel was in firm control, and at first his position was unaffected by the cessation of hostilities. After a while, however, small groups of warriors began to desert him and to go over to the man whom they still regarded as their lawful chief. Eventually, in November 1882, after a dispute over Molapo's herds, Jonathan took the initiative, defeated Joel on the Leribe plateau, and then followed him up and set fire to his village. The fighting which then began lasted intermittently until November 1885, and in almost every encounter, whether with Joel, with his allies, or with both, Jonathan was victorious, finally emerging as master of his own district, and being strong enough to establish his residence at his father's old village of Leribe. Petty skirmishing still occurred from time to time, but it was never very serious, and by the turn of the century Jonathan was probably the second most powerful chief in the country after the Paramount. In his old age he was constantly troubled by disputes between his sons, and most of these were still unresolved when he died in 1928.

Four of his praise-poems have been recorded by Mangoaela. The first relates mainly to his struggles with Joel and his allies between 1880 and 1885, but contains one stanza which relates to the capture of Langali-balele (lines 209–13), and three which relate to the second Free State war (lines 218–31). The second is a fairly straightforward narrative of the attack on the San of Soai. The third is mainly a variant of the second, but the elements of the narrative have become confused and are no longer in any coherent order, and the first stanza is completely out of place in that it refers to the dispute with Joel. This dispute is the sole topic in the fourth and last poem.

In our endeavours to interpret these poems we have been fortunate in having the assistance of Chief 'Mako Moliboea Molapo, a son of Moli-boea, Jonathan's brother and ally. Chief 'Mako, who was born in 1895, was brought up under Jonathan's supervision, came to know him very well, and gathered much information from him about Sotho history in general and about his *lithoko* in particular. According to Chief 'Mako, Jonathan did not compose his own praises, but occasionally chanted them, though never at great length. The names of the poets were given, not only by 'Mako, but also by other descendants of Molapo, as Mahasele Matekane, Mokhethi Moshoeshoe, Morallana Tsotetsi and others. This information is supported by the evidence of the *lithoko* themselves, for in only one line (ii. 38) is the first person singular used to refer to the chief.

It seems almost certain that these poems were recorded for Mangoaela by A. M. Sekese, Jonathan's secretary, whose help he acknowledges in his preface.

(i)

The binder of the young cow for the Glarers,
Today as they milk it it stands ![1]
'Ox that is black with white spots, had you not come with sad-
ness—'[2]

[1] The Glarers were one of Jonathan's regiments. The young cow signifies Joel, whom Jonathan has brought under control.

[2] This line, although not an exact quotation, is nevertheless reminiscent of Moshoeshoe's praises, ii. 25–6: see p. 72 above. Grammatically it does not fit in with what goes before or after, and is even incomplete in itself. Its function may be simply to indicate the connection between Jonathan and Moshoeshoe, but it is just possible that it has a deeper significance. It relates to Moshoeshoe's return from the expedition against the Thembu, in which, according to many Sotho, he had deliberately allowed his brother Makhabane to be killed. The poet may therefore be hinting at the idea of hostility between brothers.

He is black with white spots, black and white, Seoehla,[1]
His black shield is white-streaked, Mokhachane's man,   5
Who keeps on thrusting his shield against stones.[2]
    The young man of Tebang,[3]
The splitter of Napo Motlomela,[4]
The right eye of Lerotholi,
The second hand of RaLetšabisa.[5]   10
    Listen to me: Seeiso's[6] kinsman
Is usually praised without being known.[7]
    The black white-spotted ox, the great fighter, grabbed the ox
                     that is red with white spots,
The black white-spotted ox has seized the red, white-spotted ox
                             with a cord
As it fights rejecting the rope.[8]   15
    The striker attacked it and threw it to the ground,
The fearsome giant of Kali Tšolo,[9]
The powerful ogre of Peete Motloheloa.[10]
    Mohatanya's son died with his hands and nails shuddering:
He's just spoken badly at the meeting,   20
At the assembly of Maama and Seeiso,
For he's a man who almost makes trouble.[11]

---

[1] Seoehla means, literally, a cow with down-hanging horns. This name was given to Jonathan because he was bow-legged, i.e., because his legs seemed to curve and hang downwards like the horns of such a cow.

[2] i.e. he continues to meet difficulties with angry determination.

[3] Tebang, an area north of the Vaal, was the home of the Koena in the late seventeenth century.

[4] A distant ancestor of the Koena.   [5] RaLetšabisa, i.e. Lerotholi.

[6] Seeiso was a son of Letsie.

[7] The poet implies that, unlike most poets, he knows Jonathan well, and can therefore praise him properly.

[8] i.e. Jonathan brought Joel under control. For the 'black white-spotted ox', cp. line 3 above.

[9] Kali, i.e. Monaheng, was one of Jonathan's ancestors. He was not in fact the son of Tšolo, but of Tšoloane, Tšolo's younger brother.

[10] Motloheloa's position in the royal genealogy is much disputed, but he was certainly a descendant of Monaheng, and he was certainly not Peete's father.

[11] After the Gun War Letsie sent his sons, Maama and Seeiso, to hold a *pitso*, or assembly, in the Leribe District to explain to Jonathan and Joel that hostilities were at an end. According to Chief 'Mako, one of Joel's men, Mosoansoanyane, son of Mohatanya, insulted Jonathan's followers at this *pitso*, and so almost caused a disturbance. In subsequent hostilities between Jonathan and Joel, he was captured, and, because of his conduct at the *pitso*, Jonathan ordered that he should be killed.

The splitter, the blesbok, the kinsman of Mphaphathi,[1]
The great blesbok, the blesbok,[2] the leader of the blesboks,
25 It's going to cross, that the blesboks may cross—
By blesboks we mean the people of Maiseng,[3]
We mean Ntsoakele and his men[4]—
In the evening the springboks will cross.[5]
    He broke off a group, did the chief,
30 He came with it, the Buffaloes'[6] Lion,
He migrated with it among foreigners.[7]
    The crocodile stood in the light of the plain,[8]
It stood with its horn which was sharp already:
Its eye was fixed on the mountains.[9]
35 Tšupane, if you spread lies abroad
As you go to and fro through the country,
You'll eventually step on the Buffaloes in a hollow at Qoqolosing,
Being with their calves and suckling them,
With prominent udders and breasts![10]
40 Look in the hollow and see,

---

[1] Jonathan's sister.
[2] The significance of this name is not known. Lines 26–7 have been added to Mangoaela's text. The Sotho is as follows:

> *Linone re bolela ba Maiseng,*
> *Re bolela bo-Ntsoakele—*

[3] Josefa, Jonathan's elder brother, received the name of *Leisa*, 'the Sender', at his initiation, and his followers were therefore known as the *Maisa*, 'the Senders'. *Maiseng* is a locative formed from *Maisa*.
[4] Ntsoakele was the military commander of the Senders.
[5] The springboks no doubt signify one of Jonathan's regiments.
[6] Another of Jonathan's regiments.
[7] In November 1880 a combined rebel force, including the regiments of RaManella and Joel, drove Jonathan from his village at Tsikoane and forced him to take refuge with Major Bell, the Magistrate at Hlotse Heights.
[8] 'in the light of the plain', i.e. in a conspicuous position on the plain.
[9] As Jonathan looked towards the villages of his enemies—his brothers Joel, Hlasoa and Khethisa as well as RaManella—he looked towards the mountains. The poet is obviously mixing his metaphors when he talks of a crocodile with a horn.
[10] Tšupane, according to Chief 'Mako, was one of Joel's most famous warriors, and he used to go around boasting that he would drive the Buffaloes out of the country: these were the 'lies' that he was spreading abroad. Qoqolosing is a mountain which rises from the Leribe plateau, where Jonathan's forces routed Joel's in November 1882. Perhaps Tšupane was either killed or wounded on this occasion. The statement that the Buffaloes were suckling their calves indicates their ferocity, for animals are particularly dangerous when protecting their young.

Look in the hollow at Lipohoana's,
Look at Pitsi's and RaMpai's:
A Nguni has died, a Sotho has died !¹
  At that time the Glarers rejoiced,
They stood above the village: 45
In the houses the babies' cradle-skins were burnt !²
  White-faced cow with down-pointing horns, father of 'Neheng,³
                               rejector of the path,
We've just stopped you crossing the Caledon
As you went towards RaChaka's, at Sekameng.⁴
  The extraordinary lightning of the Camp⁵   50
Struck Qalo,⁶ it struck Sebothoane;⁷
It was everywhere suddenly, it struck Mathokoane.⁸
Burnt was the mountain, it was turned into ashes,
Burnt were the pegs at the back of the house,⁹
Burnt were Hoatane and Kolojane !¹⁰   55
  The men from Masopha's tried vainly to quench it,

---

¹ The poet continues to describe the events of November 1882. Lipohoana's is a village on the Leribe plateau. After the battle many of Joel's men were pursued homewards through Pitsi's Nek and RaMpai's Nek. Joel had a large number of Nguni under him. No doubt several of their warriors were killed on this occasion, as well as some of the chief's Sotho adherents.

² After the battle Jonathan's warriors entered Joel's village of Phomolong, at Qalo, and set fire to it. The burning of the skins in which the babies were carried on their mothers' backs symbolizes the total destruction of everything in the village.

³ One of Jonathan's daughters.

⁴ It was common during the war between Jonathan and Joel for their followers to flee across the Caledon into the Free State at times of crisis. Evidently Joel had been hoping that Jonathan too would cross, but Jonathan 'rejected the path', i.e. held on to his position, and in this he was fully supported by his warriors. Sekameng is a mountain on the right bank of the Caledon, close to de Villiers Drift. RaChaka's identity is not known.

⁵ i.e. of Hlotse Heights.   ⁶ i.e. it struck Joel's village at Qalo.

⁷ Sebothoane is that part of the Leribe plateau which overlooks Hlotse Heights. The poet may still be referring to the events of November 1882, but more probably he has turned to those of 3 May 1883, when Joel moved against the Camp from the north-east, while Hlasoa, Khethisa and RaManella moved against it from the south. In the morning Jonathan drove off the attackers in the south, pursued them, and set fire to many of their villages; in the afternoon he returned to the Camp; and in the evening and during the night he attacked and defeated Joel at Sebothoane.

⁸ Hlasoa's village at Mathokoane was among those burnt in May 1883.

⁹ i.e. the medicated pegs which were believed to protect the house against misfortune. Clearly they had been ineffective on this occasion.

¹⁰ RaManella's villages at Hoatane and Kolojane, close to Mathokoane, were also burnt in May 1883.

To calm down the blaze, to calm down the flames,
The sorcery of burning grass in the winter:[1]
Burnt were the people, burnt too were the horses,
60 Ablaze were the straps on the saddles too!
    It's not that the Buffaloes drive off, they weaken,[2]
People's villages will come to an end.
    The Crocodile, the entangler of Molapo,
The entangler of the Crocodile of Mphaphathi's[3] family,
65 The warrior who returns,[4] kinsman of Josefa,[5]
The warrior who returns when the milk cow is fighting,
When thick milk is flowing from the young cow, the milk cow,[6]
When the spirit of death overhangs us,
When we even see shadows above.[7]
70   It was stubborn and roared angrily, the wild beast from the fam-
                ily of Moliboea and Seetsa:[8]
It saw the people from Matela Tselanyane's,[9]
It beat them off, it left them in the plain.[10]
    Stealthily it walked, hiding its colours,
Fearful of the white-spotted black on its shoulders.[11]

---

[1] Masopha's forces, under his son Lepoqo, also moved against the Camp in May 1883, but took no part in the fighting. There was a clash between Jonathan and Masopha's sons in March 1884, but it seems improbable that this would be referred to here. The ferocity of Jonathan's warriors is likened to that of a veld fire started by lightning that had been induced by sorcery.

[2] Perhaps the idea is that Jonathan does not wish to drive Joel's people away, but to bring them back to their allegiance to him.

[3] Mphaphathi was Jonathan's sister.

[4] i.e. no matter how badly things are going, Jonathan always returns to the fray. Cp. Maama, ii. 22, p. 158 above.

[5] Jonathan's elder brother.

[6] The milk cow is Joel. Cows are particularly difficult to handle when their milk is thick, i.e. when they have just calved.

[7] The 'shadows' are probably vultures which, as they circle expectantly over the battle, come between the warriors and the sun. It is possible, however, that they are the spirits of the dead, whom the warriors see in their imagination; in which case 'shades' would be a better translation.

[8] Jonathan's brothers.

[9] i.e. the Khoakhoa, who were Joel's neighbours in the east, and who supported him against Jonathan. Matela was their chief, Tselanyane one of their ancestors.

[10] The stanzas that follow suggest that the incident alluded to is Jonathan's victory over Joel in the Sekubu area in March 1884.

[11] i.e. as it moved it tried to camouflage itself. The only occasion on which Jonathan could be said to have acted with stealth was when he went northwards in March 1884 and defeated Joel in the area of Sekubu.

The lion, my men, has three lairs: 75
It lies down at Tsikoane, it lies down at Leribe,
It would also return and climb Qoqolosing.[1]
 Isn't it the same beast as yesterday's, my friend?
Isn't it that beast which has just inflicted harm?[2]
It continued walking stealthily, coming along the plain: 80
When it came to Maloloja's
It offsaddled the horses, letting them pass water.[3]
 The Buffalo doesn't strike at night, the Splitter,
It strikes when the sun is already high.
 The lioness of the Buffaloes, the Splitter,   85
The leopard that chops down the wild olive trees,
That keeps chopping down the standing trees.[4]
 'MaLimapane, the consort of RaPolo, gave trouble to Limo.[5]
 The lightning shone, it held bundles of flashes,
One was hurled out, it went along the plain: 90
Hlasoa was unable to speak,
He's been left babbling Ndebele!
He goes to tell Joel:
'Here are the troubles of your villages, Mighty Warrior:[6]

[1] Jonathan had villages at Tsikoane and Leribe. He had no village at Qoqo-losing, but it was below that mountain that he had defeated Joel in November 1882 and May 1883.

[2] i.e. for all his stealth and his camouflage, he is still the same man as the one who defeated Joel in November 1882 and May 1883.

[3] On his way to Joel's area he rested at RaMpai's Nek, where Maloloja, RaMpai's son, had his village.

[4] Wild olive trees are noted for the toughness of their wood. Chopping them down signifies a victory over powerful enemies.

[5] In a well-known Sotho story, Limo, a cannibal, captures a girl called Tselane, and puts her in a bag with the intention of taking her home to his wife. On the way he stops at the home of RaPolo, and is given so much beer that he becomes drunk. 'MaLimapane, RaPolo's wife, then opens the bag, takes out Tselane, and inserts instead some poisonous snakes and insects. In due course Limo goes on his way. When he arrives home he opens the bag, and is immediately killed by the snakes and the insects. In this line Jonathan is likened to 'MaLimapane, a name which means 'the tricky one'; and Joel is likened to Limo, a name which means 'the cannibal'. Moreover RaPolo was the name given in the initiation-school to one of Jonathan's wives, 'MaMotsarapane, and so he was, literally, 'the consort of RaPolo'. This line therefore has two meanings:
 (a) 'MaLimapane, the consort of RaPolo, gave trouble to Limo.
 (b) The tricky one, the consort of RaPolo, gave trouble to the cannibal.
It is just possible that the allegory is meant to be taken one step further. Jonathan and Joel were both claiming the guardianship of Motšoene, Josefa's son, whose role in life may therefore be compared to that of Tselane in the story.

[6] i.e. Joel.

95   You're always denying the Buffalo its grazing.'[1]
        Hlasoa's returned, and now he is crying:
        'Although you're brave, Binders[2] and Takers,[3]
        You'll never be able to emulate the Glarers:
        They pierce through a house at the back and enter.'
100   Agitator's[4] son, the stick devours people,
        It devoured the children of its junior brother's family,[5]
        It devoured those of Joel and Hlasoa.
        Ah, you're a lion, a leopard that eats noisily!
        Do you bite dogs, that your paws become red?
105   The owners of the dogs are still wailing![6]
        At that time the mountains resounded,
        Fothane resounded, and Botha-Bothe,
        And Qoqolosing, on top of the plateau:
        Eventually there were echoes at Mathokoane,
110   There were echoes at Hleoheng and Molumong.[7]
        You men who live at Fobane,[8]
        Do you still provoke the Buffalo that's calved?[9]
        When it strikes, the Buffalo from the Agitator's,
        It sends the Buffaloes to the veld:
115   The people are unable to speak,
        Among them are Hlasoa and RaFobokoane[10] and his men.
        Men are stiffening their little necks,
        Intending to attack this fearless warrior.
        The Buffaloes' Buffalo flashed,
120   The mouths of the mountains quivered,
        The plain thundered,
        The hollows became misty,

---

[1] After the Gun War Jonathan's people were constantly harassed by Joel's when they tried to cultivate their lands and graze their cattle.
[2] One of Moshoeshoe's regiments.   [3] One of Molapo's regiments.
[4] The Agitator was Molapo.   [5] i.e. of Joel's family.
[6] The dogs are the warriors whom his enemies send against him.
[7] All these are mountains in or around the Districts of Leribe and Botha-Bothe, and all were the scenes of fighting at one time or another between 1880 and 1885.
[8] There were followers of both RaManella and Masopha at Fobane, a mountain just north of the Phuthiatsana River.
[9] Once again there is the idea that an animal is particularly dangerous when protecting its young: cp. lines 37-9 above.
[10] RaFobokoane, i.e. Lepoqo, the son of Masopha.

They behaved as they would in the month of September.[1]
    The moon, the beginning of June,
The waylayer's July, the son of the Agitator: 125
Travellers in that month no longer go forward,
They remain in fear of entering on the road![2]
    Mokhachane's widow-bird has grown its tail:[3]
Let the breakers who break new ground break new ground![4]
    Ambusher, sun, the Agitator's son,   130
The one who warms us when cold,
When the cattle have bare patches of skin, Seoehla,[5]
When their skins are patchy from moulting.[6]
    The fawn cow, the sturdy cow of the Agitator's Takers[7]
Swept along with its wings, Crocodile,[8]   135
The sharpness of the family of Mphaphathi.[9]
    Your tree, Manama,[10] entangles,
It goes on entangling as its roots are growing.
    The last grain that stays in the court, Buffaloes,
People who are fit to be set apart as seed: 140
You could be set apart as seed, Buffaloes,
To continue being sown in the valleys, Seoehla![11]
    The little fawn milk-cow, Seoehla,

---

[1] The significance of this line is obscure, but, taken in conjunction with the following stanza, it suggests that, although in fact it was summer, Jonathan's opponents were so chilled with fear that they behaved as if it were winter.

[2] People are averse to travelling in the cold months of the year. Jonathan is likened to these months since, because of his ambushes, his enemies are afraid to move around freely.

[3] The widow-bird loses its tail in winter and grows it again in spring. 'Mokhachane's widow-bird has grown its tail': i.e. Jonathan has gained his revenge, he has recovered his former position. However, *tjotjo* ('widow-bird') can also mean a type of weasel; *ho hloma* ('to grow again') can also mean 'to place erect'; and according to Chief 'Mako these are the meanings which these words bear here. He would therefore translate this line: 'Mokhachane's weasel holds its tail erect', i.e. it is excited and ready for action.

[4] i.e. let those who want to fight do so, for Jonathan is now ready for them.

[5] For the praise-name Seoehla, see line 4 above.

[6] Lines 132–3 merely indicate the time of year, namely, the end of winter, when the cattle's hair begins to moult.

[7] The Agitator was Molapo, the Takers one of his regiments.

[8] The metaphor of the fawn cow now becomes mixed with those of the lightning bird with sweeping wings and the crocodile.

[9] Jonathan's sister.

[10] One of the brothers who supported Jonathan.

[11] i.e. the Buffaloes are like the very best grain, which is not eaten, but is set aside as seed for the following season.

The hornless little cow of the Buffaloes' village trampled on the
                                                    rope and removed it,
145 The hornless little cow took off the rope.[1]
Its milkers were many, very many.
In vain did the people from Joel's try to milk it,
It went on tearing their karosses:
And in vain did the people from Masopha's try to milk it,
150 It was just as if they were calling their fathers![2]
        Cow of great villages, white-faced cow,
Don't make light of the dispute:
You see that we people have gone.[3]
        The cow of the quarrellers, the Mighty Warriors,[4]
155 The scorching sun, the tough hide,
The Agitator's son is something hard!
        He heard from the men of his village,
When his men, Makotoko[5] and others, reported:
'These days the cattle go to pasture with difficulty:
160 Hlasoa and Joel and their men aren't sated,
Yet they're given food from their very own pot!'[6]
        The Agitator's son is a small fierce bee.
        The wind blew, it went in among the horses,
The whirlwind went right in among the men,
165 Into the chests of some of the men:
And the Mighty Warriors and the Tongs were there.[7]
        The princes have tried in vain:
Their wretched little sticks were finished on the shield,

---

[1] i.e. Jonathan was elusive, just as a cow without horns is elusive, and he refused to be tied down.

[2] i.e. Masopha's warriors were like herdboys who, being unable to milk a cow
themselves, have to call in their fathers to help them.

[3] i.e. Jonathan must not pretend that the quarrel is of no importance, for his
warriors have gone out to do battle.

[4] One of Joel's regiments. A chief may commonly be referred to as his enemies' cow: cp. Joel, i. 97, p. 192 below.

[5] Nathaniel Makotoko, son of Makhabane, had been Molapo's counsellor at
first, but was now Jonathan's. He was also one of his most celebrated military
commanders.

[6] i.e. although they have cattle of their own, Hlasoa and Joel and their followers try to capture Jonathan's when they go out to graze.

[7] The Mighty Warriors were one of Joel's regiments, the Tongs were one of
Hlasoa's. For the significance of the name Tongs, see Masopha, iii. 51–4,
pp. 125–6 above. This stanza may refer to the fighting in May 1883, or to the
final defeat of Joel and his allies in November 1885.

They've been finished on the shield of RaNtahli.[1]
    The heavens of the chief's son flashed,   170
Out they hurled their lightning:
Here on the plain, at Mathokoane,
People have caught glittering flashes on the plain.[2]
    The mist closed down as far as Mathokoane,
It ended when it came to Kolojane.[3]   175
    Devour the treasure, but leave the herdsmen:[4]
The devourers of the treasure are simply standing,
Seshophe and his men and Hlasoa and his men.[5]
    The men who began this tough quarrel have pouted,
Pushing out their lips.[6]   180
How did you think it would be?[7]
    The boys in the court were arguing,[8]
When one a little older than the others said:
'You've always been speaking of the Glarers.[9]
The men of our village no longer talk,   185
They're even afraid of sitting in the court!'[10]
    A woman heard in her courtyard,
She went outside, and clapped her hands,
She heard the warrior's children ask:
'Show us the Glarer of the Buffaloes!'   190
    This is the one that's a strong, tough bull,
You too with your eyes can see it for yourselves:
The young bulls it stabs in the armpits,
It tears through the skin on their little ribs.
    All you little princes, be quiet,   195

[1] i.e. Jonathan, Ntahli being one of his daughters.
[2] i.e. people have been struck by lightning at the village of his brother, Hlasoa, at Mathokoane. Once again the reference may be to the events of May 1883 or of November 1885. The following stanza suggests the former.
[3] i.e. the fighting went as far as RaManella's villages at Kolojane, as was indeed the case in May 1883. The mist here suggests the smoke from the guns.
[4] i.e. capture the cattle, but do not kill the herdsmen.
[5] 'The devourers of the treasure' were Seshophe, son of Lesaoana, and Hlasoa, for they had evidently captured some of Jonathan's cattle on a previous occasion: now, however, they were powerless to prevent their being recovered.
[6] i.e. Jonathan's enemies, the aggressors, have now been discomfited.
[7] i.e. 'Did you really expect to beat Jonathan?'
[8] The poet now depicts an imaginary scene in the court of one of Jonathan's opponents.
[9] i.e. you have always been boasting of how you would defeat them.
[10] Jonathan's enemies have been defeated so soundly that they are now ashamed to show themselves.

That the bull of the Buffaloes may bellow.
The blazing veld fire sets out from the Camp:
Those who kindled it, Khethisa and his men, rush and disappear
in the bushes ![1]
Then the White-Spotted Red One of the Locusts[2] heard,
200 He sent RaMabilikoe:[3]
'You should go to the Shining One[4] and ask:
You should go to Lepoqo[5] too and hear:
And when you pass on to Sebothoane
You should ask of the vulture above,
205 You should ask of the little white vultures too.'[6]
People have been caught by the snow at Sebothoane.[7]
It called out and bellowed, did the red white-spotted cow:
Bandy-horned cow,[8] graze at ease, cow with a blaze that covers the
face.[9]
The Buffaloes' defiant one slaughtered the wildebeest,
210 He chopped off its head and sent it to the chief's;
He gave it to the Roan One and the Magistrate,
The men who don't reward warriors:
They might also have rewarded him even in Natal.[10]
The well-horned rhino of the family of Josefa[11]
215 Keeps spoiling the houses of plenty of people:
It longs for horns, it would finish ten,

[1] This stanza probably refers to the events of May 1883, when Khethisa, Jonathan's brother, was among those chiefs who were driven from the Camp and whose villages were burnt.
[2] i.e. Letsie.
[3] RaMabilikoe was one of Letsie's most important advisers, and was evidently sent by him to try to settle affairs in the north of the country. The date of his mission is not known.
[4] Masopha's son Marthinsi.   [5] Masopha's senior son.
[6] i.e. RaMabilikoe should even make enquiries of the vultures which had eaten the bodies of Joel's warriors.
[7] i.e. Jonathan's enemies have been defeated at Sebothoane.
[8] Cp. line 4, p. 171 above.
[9] The cow here is Jonathan, who can now rest in peace after his victories.
[10] This stanza relates to the seizure of the Hlubi chief Langalibalele in 1873. The wildebeest in line 209 is Langalibalele himself. Jonathan did not in fact slaughter him and chop off his head, but merely secured his capture. The Roan One in line 211 is Captain Allison, the leader of some troops from Natal. The Magistrate is probably Major Bell of Hlotse Heights. Langalibalele's herds were divided among those who had helped to capture him, but Jonathan was clearly dissatisfied with his share.
[11] Jonathan's elder brother.

The eleventh it would place on its forehead.[1]
   Slipper away of the mighty regiments,
Slip away, slip away from the warriors here,
Slip away from Khoahlane and Lenkoane,   220
Men who are always heeded
When called upon at a meeting.[2]
   Well, why do they despise the Buffaloes' bull,
The bull with horns that are sharp?
The Buffalo of the Agitator's village,[3] the attacker,   225
The attacker attacked the white soldiers.
   Stopper who stops, young warrior,
Stop the people with enormous beards![4]
The sorcerers who come from overseas
Haven't any weapons, but hold pieces of iron,   230
Indeed they're crazy about the lightning of hands![5]
   Up on Tsikoane we claim Tšiame:[6]
Tšiame's a cow,
The son of Mokhachane is not to be passed by.[7]
   Hey! Hey! See! Hey, see!   235
You've seen: one of you the Buffalo butted,
Someone was butted by the Buffalo of Josefa,
Of the family of Mosa, of the family of Mphaphathi.[8]
Horns, thorns, spikes![9]

---

[1] i.e. the rhino is so fierce that it would wear out ten horns and then use the eleventh.

[2] In this stanza the poet turns to the second Free State war. In 1865, according to Chief 'Mako, Jonathan was still living at his father's village of Leribe, and was ordered by Molapo to remain there. Instead he slipped away to join the Sotho's main forces at Thaba Bosiu. It is known that he took part in the defence of the mountain against Louw Wepener in August 1865: Khoahlane—not Khoatsana, as in Mangoaela—and Lenkoane were two warriors who had been directed by Molapo to keep an eye on Jonathan at Leribe. Evidently they were highly respected, for people always listened to them attentively at meetings.

[3] i.e. Molapo's village, Leribe.   [4] i.e. the Free Staters.

[5] 'pieces of iron', 'the lightning of hands', i.e. guns.

[6] The poet now returns to the Gun War. Tšiame, Moshoeshoe's brother, lived at Tsikoane, and, like Jonathan, was loyal to the Cape authorities.

[7] Just as men will fight to protect their cattle rather than abandon them, so Jonathan should fight to protect Tšiame. Cp. Joel, i. 12–14, p. 188 below.

[8] According to Chief 'Mako, these lines refer to an occasion when Jonathan shot and wounded RaMatsoku Mallane, one of Joel's adherents. Mosa and Mphaphathi were Jonathan's sisters.

[9] In this final line the poet becomes so excited that he no longer formulates complete sentences, but simply throws out words which convey the ferocity of Jonathan's fighting.

(ii)

Broad-nosed man from the Agitator's, go up,
Hartebeest, go up the slope which we're climbing:[1]
Now things are different, you can't graze without clothing![2]
Crocodile, bow down as you go, servant[3] of Josefa and Lerotholi:
5 Go across streams that are full,
Go across the Orange, go across the Seate,
Even cross the Mantšonyane and others.[4]
Crocodile, cross the Seate, still bending low,
Still bending low, crawling on your hands,
10 That the Bushmen be unaware and not see.
The Ambusher who pushes through the dust
Divided up the Glarers in the passes,
And said that the Buffaloes should occupy all the hills.
Later there appeared the White-Spotted Red Ones,
15 They appeared with Mositi, son of RaMosena.[5]
Chief, please hurry and ask them
Where Soai has gone, since the cattle appear.[6]
He's gone to his lover's, at Moorosi's;
For they've intermarried with the people at Pheetla's.[7]
20 The third cow doesn't low, it's silent.
Why are you quiet, cow from Bush land?
You'll drink the Hlotse, you'll drink the Caledon,

---

[1] i.e. go up into the Maloti to attack the San of Soai.

[2] Lit.: 'It is not as usual when you graze without clothing': i.e. you are now leaving your warm and comfortable home to face the cold of the mountains and the hazards of fighting.

[3] For the use of the word *Mokone*, 'Nguni', to mean 'servant', see Maama, iv. 30, p. 166 above.

[4] The Orange, the Seate and the Mantšonyane all flow through the Maloti.

[5] Mositi, who lived at Peka, was one of Jonathan's counsellors and commanded a section of the Buffaloes called the *Lithamaha*, the White-Spotted Red Ones.

[6] The question is contemptuous. Soai, the San chief, has evidently allowed his cattle to be captured by Mositi's men. It is possible, however, that 'the cattle' here are not Soai's herds, but the four San women and their four children who were captured on this occasion. Cp. lines 24–6 below, and iii. 42, p. 185 below.

[7] There had in fact been much intermarriage between the San of Soai and the Phuthi of Moorosi, and Soai was indeed visiting Moorosi at the time of Jonathan's attack. The Pheetla (or Phetla) were closely related to the Phuthi, and during the *lifaqane* had come under Moorosi's leadership.

Then you'll go home.[1]
They jostled each other as they entered the kraal,
Afraid of the one with dark eyes, the chief;   25
The cattle are afraid of the women's din.[2]
    The women are amazed at the difference of the females,[3]
And the Agitator, the Rescuer,[4] also asked:
'Buffaloes, you've captured a crooked stick:[5]
As soon as it arrived it slipped off to the Maloti.[6]   30
Shouldn't you have killed it in the open country
That the crows of the Maloti should be sated?'
    The hyaenas give thanks for their meat, Chief.[7]
    Bushmen, you've seen, the Glarers have ascended:
In future you'll be lacking your wives,   35
The Glarers will have taken and married them.
    Have you ever captured anything to give to your parents?
I've captured for 'MaMosa[8] a little Bush woman,
Phafoli[9] has come here to work:
He'd captured pregnant women, Seoehla![10]   40

(iii)

The white-spotted red one and the white-spotted black one
    showed to each other their desire to fight:

---

[1] The third cow is Jonathan himself, the first two being his elder brothers, Josefa and Joel. To be quiet is a sign of sadness, and the poet here asks Jonathan why he is sad, since he is returning home.

[2] 'The cattle' here are almost certainly the four San women and their four children whom Jonathan had captured. They seemed to be afraid of Molapo and of the Sotho women's ululations as they entered the village of Leribe.

[3] According to Chief 'Mako, the Sotho women were amazed at the nakedness of the San women.

[4] i.e. Molapo.   [5] i.e. something odd, something defective.

[6] Soon after their capture the four San women tried to escape, but were caught at Malaoaneng. In the ensuing fight one of them was killed, and another died later of illness. Subsequently the two survivors ran away again, and this time they were not caught.

[7] The meat for which they gave thanks was presumably the body of the San woman who was killed at Malaoaneng.

[8] 'MaMosa, Molapo's senior wife, was Jonathan's mother.

[9] Phafoli was one of the four San children who were captured. He became one of Jonathan's herdboys.

[10] Cp. iii. 38–42, p. 185 below.

Then the red one stabbed with violence the red one with white
spots.[1]
They jostled each other, they filled the kraal:
The oxen are afraid of the war-song, Seoehla,
5 They're afraid of the young men's din.[2]
Go slowly, the Buffaloes' White-Spotted Red One,
Of the family of Lerotholi and the Depriver.[3]
The upward slope, the Agitator's[4] boy,
The upward slope which is climbed by the strong,
10 Which is climbed by Manoeli and Linyonyolo,[5]
Who, as they climb, go over it quickly.[6]
When the Buffaloes had shed their karosses,
Had shed them, and the Glarers were preparing skins,[7]
We realized something[8] through the arrival of a boy,
15 Of a runner with news, of a liar.[9]
When he arrived he said: 'Greetings, Chief!
You've been ordered to go there to your father.[10]
The message is: don't leave the Buffaloes behind,
They are the ones who're your arms.'
20 The cow that is black with white spots has had food for the
journey prepared for it,
The food's been prepared for the Glarers to eat,
That the Buffaloes may drink the Seate's water,[11]
That they drink the water to remain in the stomach.

---

[1] This stanza has nothing to do with the attack on the San, but relates to
Jonathan's struggles with Joel. Jonathan himself is 'the white-spotted black
one' in line 1, and 'the red one' in line 2: Joel is the red one with white spots.
Cp. i. 13–15, p. 171 above.

[2] For this stanza, cp. ii. 24–6, p. 183 above. 'The oxen' here are almost
certainly the four San women and their four children whom Jonathan had
captured.

[3] i.e. Letsie.   [4] The Agitator, i.e. Molapo.

[5] Two of Jonathan's followers.

[6] As Jonathan moves rapidly into the mountains, he himself is described as a
slope which his warriors ascend quickly.

[7] i.e. when Jonathan and his men were at ease, and were engaged in their
normal peaceful pursuits.

[8] Lit.: 'We saw', i.e. we realized that something was afoot.

[9] Messengers were commonly referred to as liars, apparently because they
were often afraid to tell the truth when news was bad. Cp. Griffith, i. 25, p. 215
below.

[10] Molapo's village was at Leribe. At that time Jonathan was living at Fobane.

[11] For the Seate, see ii. 6, p. 182 above.

You'll be missing your women.[1]
When in the pass he divided up the Glarers,   25
He said that the Buffaloes should occupy the hills:
Afterwards the White-Spotted Red Ones appeared,
They appeared with Mositi of Molibeli.[2]
    The cattle are leaving without a fight,
And where has Soai gone?   30
He's gone to his lover's, at Moorosi's.
Is it because they've intermarried with the Pheetla?[3]
    Crocodile, give medicines, servant of Josefa,[4]
Give medicines to the Bushmen, that they shouldn't breed,
That the Bushmen stay barren, every single one,   35
That the Glarers take them to marry them,
Those who like marrying polygamously.
    Tell me, cow from among those of Soai's,
If you're pregnant, if you're full with a calf in your stomach,
That the Glarers may deal with you gently,   40
That the calf shouldn't kick you in the flank,
Shouldn't kick you in the stomach, my favourite.[5]
    Cow of the family of Qhoasi,[6] of the Bush woman,
Of the Bushman, give me that arrow of mine![7]
    Go slowly, White-Spotted Red One, you've arrived,   45
You're already quite close to the villages,
You're close to Sebothoane,[8] White-Spotted Red One,
You'll drink the Hlotse, you'll drink the Caledon:
Qoqolosing[9] is already near.[10]
    As for the cow, 'MaMosa[11] queried it,   50
It was queried by the Agitator, the Father of Little Vultures,[12]
Who said: 'Show me the cow of the Buffaloes' spearshafts!

---

[1] This warning is addressed to the San.
[2] For this stanza, see ii. 11–15, p. 182 above. Mositi belonged to the Molibeli.
[3] For this stanza, cp. ii, 16–19, p. 182 above.
[4] Jonathan's elder brother.
[5] The cow in this stanza is clearly one of the San women whom Jonathan had
captured. Cp. ii. 40, p. 183 above.
[6] Qhoasi was obviously a San, but further identification is impossible.
[7] This request is merely a gentle form of mockery, for the Sotho used to make
fun of the San's bows and arrows. Cp. Joel iii. 25, p. 207 below.
[8] Part of the Leribe plateau.
[9] A mountain which rises from the Leribe plateau.
[10] For this stanza, cp. ii. 20–3, pp. 182–3 above.
[11] Jonathan's mother.   [12] i.e. Molapo.

The Buffaloes are coming with a cow that's deformed,
They've captured a stick that's crooked, have the Buffaloes.
55　Shouldn't you have killed it in the open country
And shared it out among the crows of the Maloti?"[1]

(iv)

The Rhino of the Tickets[2] of Leribe,
Seoehla's[3] the Agitator's[4] confronter.[5]
The whirlwind of the regiments of Lejaha,[6]
The whirlwind flung down the people:
5　The people were caught by a downpour of spears,
A downpour of spears, a storm,
Hail with stones that were hard, very hard:
It's always been making an end of people,
Driving them into the Maloti, in the east.
10　The Buffaloes' young warrior, the pursuer,
The pursuer cut people into pieces,
The Glarer cut people into groups,[7]
The Buffalo of the family of Mphaphathi.[8]
The Buffalo with horns that are sharp has pierced,
15　It pierced with horns that were spears,
The rhino of the youngster of the Takers![9]
The heavens struck hard at the chief's,[10]
They struck, they raised up the ashes.
Take out the child, young mother of summer:[11]
20　The Tickets with the Glarers are stirring up war,
As for this little village, they're burning it.

[1] For this stanza, see ii. 27–32, p. 183 above.
[2] The name given to the 'loyalists' in the Gun War. See Lerotholi, v. 32, p. 150 above. It was still used to refer to Jonathan and his men in their subsequent struggles with Joel and his allies.
[3] See i. 4, p. 171 above.　　　[4] The Agitator, i.e. Molapo.
[5] i.e. the one who goes out to confront the enemy.
[6] RaManella's brother.
[7] i.e. Jonathan broke up and scattered his enemies' regiments.
[8] Jonathan's sister.　　　[9] One of Molapo's regiments.
[10] 'the chief's', i.e. Joel's village of Phomolong at Qalo, which Jonathan burned down in November 1882.
[11] The young mother was Joel's senior wife, 'MaMopeli, who had just given birth to a child. She was the young mother of summer, because the child had been born in summer. It was most unusual for a woman in 'MaMopeli's condition to leave her hut, but in the circumstances she was compelled to do so.

13. *Joel*

Joel (*c.* 1842–1919) was the eldest son in Molapo's second house. As indicated above,[1] the dispute over seniority between Jonathan and himself was decided by Molapo in Jonathan's favour, and thereafter he was always a man with a grievance. As one colonial officer later remarked, 'for Jonathan to take one side in any question is almost enough of itself to make Joel take the other'.[2]

His *lithoko* reveal that he took part in the defence of Thaba Bosiu against the Free Staters in August 1865, but it is almost certain that, together with the rest of Molapo's followers, he withdrew from the war in March 1866 on the conclusion of the Treaty of Mpharane. In the early 1870s he led two expeditions into the Maloti against the San of Soai. The first, in 1870 or 1871, was a failure, but the second, in 1871, which took place after Jonathan's raid, resulted in Soai's death. He played no part in Jonathan's capture of Langalibalele in 1873, but shortly beforehand, acting on his own account, he had swept off some of the Hlubi's herds as they were being driven through the mountains.

In the Gun War he rapidly emerged as one of the leading rebels in the north, being strongly supported by his brothers, Hlasoa and Khethisa, as well as by the sons of his uncle, Masopha, and by RaManella, the son of Makhabane. In combination with them he drove the loyalist Jonathan from his mountain stronghold of Tsikoane in November 1880, and led several attacks on him and on the colonial troops who were sent to defend the Magistracy at Hlotse Heights. Throughout the war he was almost the undisputed master of the whole of northern Basutoland.

After the war he fully expected Masopha and Lerotholi to reward his efforts by recognizing his claim to seniority over Jonathan, but in this he was disappointed. In the ensuing struggles with Jonathan, which lasted from 1882 to 1885, he suffered a string of heavy defeats and his authority was cut back to his own area of Qalo. In 1889 he became involved in a territorial dispute with his neighbours in the east, the Khoakhoa of Matela, and this led to petty skirmishing for several years. In the Anglo-Boer War he was the only chief of any note who gave aid and comfort to the Free State—a course of action which was determined more by the hope of gaining some advantage over Jonathan, who was loyal to the British, than by any affection for the Afrikaners. For this he was sentenced to one year's imprisonment in 1902. He died in 1919, a frustrated and embittered man to the end.

Mangoaela has recorded three of his praise-poems. The first relates mainly to his prolonged conflict with Jonathan, but also contains what appear to be references to the capture of Langalibalele's cattle (lines 116–58, 223–50) and to the attacks on the San of Soai (lines 191–205). The second too relates mainly to the conflict with Jonathan, but also

[1] See pp. 168–9. [2] *Annual Report for Basutoland, 1899–1900*, p. 26.

contains references to the second Free State war (lines 12–16, 48–50); the raids on the San (lines 22–35, 51–60); the capture of Langalibalele's cattle (lines 67–70); and finally, it seems, the dispute with the Khoakhoa (lines 71–6). The third relates solely to the attacks on the San, and is rather like the third poem of Jonathan in that a re-ordering of its stanzas could produce a fairly straightforward narrative.

In the interpretation of these poems we have been most generously assisted, not only by Chief 'Mako, but also by Chief Lepekola Joel (one of Joel's sons), Chief Lishobana Mpaki Molapo (a nephew) and Chief Jameson Qhobela (a grandson). According to them Joel did not compose his own praises, but often chanted them, and when doing so would transpose them into the first person singular wherever appropriate. The names of the poets were given as Salai, Nthootso and Tsutsubi. The evidence of the *lithoko* themselves adds nothing to this information, for in each poem the first person singular is used only sparingly.

(i)

Mohato's[1] Protector, Mokhachane's Tough Warrior,
Fortress of the old, of the men and of the children,
Of the people who remain at the ruins![2]
If you hadn't been brave, Moshoeshoe's Tough Warrior,
5 Your family's village wouldn't be here.[3]
    A certain warrior from Libenyane's[4]
Isn't normally praised;
One doesn't normally hear him extolled;
It isn't normally said: 'You're brave, clever warrior of Mokhachane,
10 Of Libe and RaMathalea,[5]
Josefa's[6] young man, Tough Warrior!'
    Don't pass by the Chief,
Don't abandon Lekena:[7]
Lekena's a cow, he's not to be passed by.[8]
15   Bravery's well named, Mokhachane's clever warrior,

---

[1] Mohato, i.e. Letsie.
[2] 'the ruins', i.e. Molapo's village at Leribe, which Joel controlled during the Gun War. For the use of the word 'ruins' to denote the village of a chief who has left it or who is dead, cp. Letsie II, line 7, p. 210 below.
[3] i.e. but for Joel's bravery the village of Leribe, or perhaps even the whole of Leribe District, would have been dominated by the Cape forces.
[4] Libenyane, 'Little Libe', was Mokhachane, Libe being his elder brother.
[5] i.e. Posholi, Mathalea being a daughter.
[6] Josefa was Molapo's senior son.　　　[7] i.e. Lerotholi.
[8] Just as men will fight to protect their cattle rather than abandon them, so Joel should fight to support Lerotholi. Cp. Jonathan, i. 232–4, p. 181 above.

Which fights with the regiments.
The crocodile fought against things that were mighty,
The lion fights against regiments that are strange,
Against Griffith[1] and the Sparkling Soldier.[2]
You fought against Major Bell,[3]   20
The mighty champion from the Cape!
  The warrior of 'MaPaki[4] fights,
Of the family of Mothibe and Mahooana:[5]
He's just gone into the Magistrate's.[6]
There was a blaze, and the doctors' houses were burnt,   25
Burnt was the house of Potse the Ndebele,[7]
Where the horns were kept in the pass.[8]
  White-spotted black one, Mokhachane's dire omen,[9]
Stabbing as if it pulls,[10] white-dappled black one of Moshoeshoe!
  White-spotted black one, the Giraffe's[11] fierce monster,   30
Violent beast with horns that are thorns.
  The child of Matlole's son[12] drives a young milk cow,
He drives a young cow which is huge,
He drove a young cow with an enormous udder
In spring, when the cows eat burnt grass in the veld   35

[1] The Governor's Agent at Maseru during the Gun War.
[2] i.e. Sir Bartle Frere, the High Commissioner at the Cape. For the origin of this name, see Lerotholi, iv. 10, p. 144 above.
[3] The Magistrate at Hlotse Heights.
[4] Joel's mother, Mpaki being his younger brother.
[5] Two of his brothers.   [6] 'the Magistrate's', i.e. Hlotse Heights.
[7] Potse is said to have been one of Bell's policemen. Evidently he was also a doctor. Line 26 has been added to Mangoaela's text. The Sotho is as follows: *Ha e-cha ntlo ea Potse, Ndebele.*
[8] The horns contained the medicines which were believed to give strength and protection to the village: clearly they had been of no avail against Joel. This stanza probably relates to the attack on the Camp on 8 November 1880, when several buildings were burnt.
[9] At various crises the Sotho used to consult diviners, who would throw their 'bones' and would then examine the position in which they fell. *Mabelebetloa* was a position which portended death and disaster.
[10] Each position of the divining bones had its own praises, which the diviner would chant. The praises of *mabelebetloa* were as follows:

  'They've fallen into the death-portending position of the iron horns,
  Which stabs as if it pulls,
  Which stabs and sends to the pit.'

The image is that of the barbed spear, which kills a man as it is pulled out from his body, and so sends him to the pit, i.e. to the grave.
[11] The Giraffe, i.e. Mokhachane, who was renowned for his speed.
[12] Matlole, i.e. Motloang, was Peete's father.

And their herdsmen's eyes are dark.[1]
  As they came up from the hollow,
When in the dip where the *tooane* grass grows,
The black and white one they covered with sand,[2]
40 They covered with spittle
The pack ox from the home of the Magistrate and his men.[3]
   The Koena's warrior who is ever surrounded
Has been surrounded by all the nations:
All his kinsmen have shaken him off.
45 He's surrounded by Bushmen and Griqua,
Even the Boers have surrounded him![4]
   Lightning of the village of Mohato,[5] you who take all and leave
                                         nothing,
If you're not the moon, you're a star;
If you're not the sun, you're a comet.[6]
50   The child of the chief is like an elephant in spring,
He's like a stag that bends low as it runs,
When the canons set the flames ablaze,
And the fires take slowly, catch light, and blaze.
Here too the houses of the doctors still burn,
55 Of the Ndebele Potse and his friends.[7]
   The son of 'MaJosefa has a black heart,[8]
He's greedy for the property of the rebels,[9]

[1] This stanza probably means, quite simply, that Joel had captured a particularly good milk cow during the spring, when the old grass had been burnt off to facilitate the growth of the new shoots after the first rains. The incident alluded to cannot be specified.

[2] i.e. they attacked Jonathan, who was covered with the dust that arose.

[3] The pack-ox is Jonathan, who had taken refuge at the magistracy of Hlotse Heights in November 1880.

[4] Joel was not in fact surrounded during the Gun War, but the effect of this stanza is to indicate the difficulties with which he had to contend. The kinsmen who had shaken him off were his brothers Jonathan, Moliboea, Khabo and Seetsa, all of whom had sided with the Cape Government. The terms 'Bushmen' and 'Griqua' are probably contemptuous references to Joel's enemies, although there may also have been individuals of these races fighting against him. The 'Boers' are no doubt the Cape soldiery.

[5] i.e. of Letsie.   [6] i.e. Joel is particularly magnificent in appearance.

[7] See lines 25-7 above.

[8] Joel was not in fact the son of 'MaJosefa (i.e. of Molapo's senior wife, 'MaMosa), but may be referred to as such in his praises. To have a black heart is to be angry.

[9] For Joel the rebels were not those who rebelled against the Cape Government, but those who, like Jonathan, sided with that Government against most of their fellow countrymen.

The brother of 'MaPolane,[1]
The rhino of the family of Makhaola,[2] the Koena,
The Stopper of the oxen with the marks of the whip.[3]   60
    The son of Kholu,[4] the mighty flood,
The flood may overthrow the Khoakhoa,
It's overthrown Matela Tselanyane.[5]
    You're deluded, children of Tumane Pootsela,[6]
You're deluded about the lightning.[7]   65
The lightning's from Kholu and her kin and isn't dreamt of![8]
Whom have you ever seen dreaming of it?
For even Major Bell of the Cape
Was made to sweat
By the lightning from Kholu, Ntsuku's daughter![9]   70
    The rays of light entered the town,[10]
The flash went aside to the pastures
To go to seize the oxen of the span.[11]
    Heaven, comrade of the Kindler of Fires,[12]
Comrade of the children of the Depriver,[13] you're a cloud. 75
The cloud thundered, the comrade of Lekena[14] and Seeiso:[15]
Into the houses it sent its flash,
All the mountains were ablaze with fire.
    Son of Molapo, the Crocodiles' demolisher,
Demolish there, where it's firmly closed,[16]   80
Demolish iron houses, Mokhachane's clever warrior,
Cut through the chains of the wagons.

---

[1] Joel's sister.   [2] A son of Lerotholi.
[3] These oxen are the so-called 'loyalists', who bear the marks of their submission to their European masters.
[4] i.e. of Moshoeshoe's mother.
[5] Matela was chief of the Khoakhoa, Joel's neighbours in the east. Tselanyane was a Khoakhoa ancestor. This stanza refers to the skirmishing between Joel and Matela which began in 1889, and which went on for several years.
[6] Tumane was an uncle of Matela. Pootsela is said to be a praise-name of Tselanyane.
[7] i.e. you suffer from delusions that you can defeat Joel.
[8] i.e. one cannot dream of defeating Joel.
[9] Kholu's father was Ntsukunyane, a Fokeng chief, whose name is here abbreviated.
[10] i.e. Hlotse Heights.
[11] i.e. as Joel went to attack Hlotse Heights he turned aside to capture a span of oxen.
[12] i.e. of Maama.   [13] i.e. of Letsie.
[14] i.e. Lerotholi.   [15] Another of Letsie's sons.
[16] i.e. attack and destroy Hlotse Heights, which is strongly guarded.

The heavens of Libe's son are thundering,
They thundered, they were heard by those afar off,
85 They were heard by Moshoeshoe and others below,
Molapo and others heard too among the spirits,
For the lightning thunders, that which is mighty,
There thunders the lightning with a mighty thundering.
    'MaLekena's son[1] averts the hail,
90 He's just scared off the hail from the sea,
He calmed down the storm from the sea as it came
And was beating down, and the plains were resounding,
Grenades were firing, and canons too,
Exchanging with each other their flames!
95   Son of Molapo, multicoloured, black and white,
Like the guinea-fowl's feathers;
Cow of the Redcoats from there at the Cape,[2]
With its white-streaked back it's like a ratel, the pack-ox.
'MaLepoqo's son's cow[3] has a white-streaked back,
100 It's roan, it has hair in lines, in lines.
    What's stopped you being famous, clever warrior,
For you've just resisted as the country was going, and the people
                                                              too?

    The young warrior who's denied by his relatives,
Today he's been deserted by the Koena,
105 By Masopha and Lerotholi.[4]
    I, the bull, the Agitator's[5] child, became lost,
The men to look for me were missing:
I was found by Letšela Moojane's children,[6]
I, the chief, was simply found by Ntsoana![7]
110   The child of the chief has a manly heart,

---

[1] i.e. Joel himself. For this description of him as the son of Lerotholi's mother, cp. line 56 above.

[2] For the description of a chief as his enemies' cow, cp. Jonathan, i. 154, p. 178 above.

[3] i.e. Joel himself. Lepoqo was Moshoeshoe.

[4] After the Gun War Joel expected that Lerotholi, Masopha and others would support him in his claim to seniority over Jonathan, and was disappointed when they did not do so.

[5] The Agitator, i.e. Molapo.

[6] i.e. although Joel received no support from his own relatives, he was supported by the followers of Letšela, one of his subordinate chiefs, who was a Fokeng.

[7] Ntsoana too was one of Joel's subordinates, and was a Fokeng.

This chief at heart is very tough:
Here in the heart of the people's provider,
Of the son of Libenyane,[1]
It's just like a hammer of stone,
It's just like a ball of rock, clever warrior.   115
   Hey! Hey! Listen, Koena!
I myself don't pay homage, I'm a chief.[2]
I simply pay homage to the receiver of the black one,
To the driver of the milk cow which comes from Natal,
Which comes from Natal, through bravery.[3]   120
   The Crocodile, the inviter of the people of Mokhachane
Invited the people to come to the heifers,[4]
The infantry and also the cavalry, Mighty Warrior,
That all of his people should take their pick,[5]
The princes and the counsellors too.   125
   The cattle are shared out by the Crocodile that pounds,
The Crocodile pounds the heifers with his hand:
Why is he afraid to pound them with a spear?[6]
   The cow about which there is strife,
About which letters are continually running,   130

[1] Libenyane, i.e. Mokhachane.
[2] Lit.: 'I myself don't praise cattle, I'm a chief.' A chief is often greeted with the words *Likhomo tseo*, 'Those cattle', which indicate that he is the source of his people's prosperity. Here Joel states that he refuses to greet Jonathan as his chief, since he is the chief himself.
[3] The significance of lines 118–20 is obscure. Perhaps, even although he had died in 1880, 'the receiver of the black one' is Molapo, the only chief whose authority Joel had been prepared to acknowledge; and perhaps 'the milk cow which comes from Natal' represents the cattle which Joel had seized from Langalibalele in 1873, some of which he had no doubt given to his father. Indeed it is possible that this stanza was inspired by the Langalibalele affair, for this is clearly the subject of at least one of the following stanzas.
[4] i.e. Joel had captured some cattle, and he invited his followers to come for the sharing out of the spoil.
[5] Lit.: 'That all of his people should strike them.' The cattle would be in a kraal, and each man who was to receive a beast would be told: 'Strike a cow.' He would then enter the kraal and drive out the cow of his choice.
[6] The significance of this stanza is uncertain. It would appear, however, that many people were unlikely to receive any cattle, and so they demanded that Joel should not share them all out among his followers (pound them with his hand), but that he should kill some of them (pound them with his spear), so that everyone could at least partake of the meat. This interpretation is supported by lines 132–8 below. Alternatively, the meaning may be that Joel handles his enemies gently, whereas he should not be afraid to deal with them more severely.

Letters are running through the night, Mighty Warrior.[1]
    The lion would nod, it keeps on nodding:
But why does it nod when they've just come from trouble,
When the cattle have come from the Maloti's bitter cold?
135   Why does it nod when we at home are hungry,
In his villages, we're hungry, in all of them,
When the rhinos are hungry, and they're at the court,
When Gasebeng is hungry, and he is his herdsman?[2]
    The cattle are there in the Maloti, on high,
140   The beasts with their redness are standing,
The water pours off them, we looked at their flanks,[3]
They're in the tracks of RaThebe's horse.[4]
    The people keep capturing them, one by one;
The lion, the pioneer from Mokhachane's
145   Has fallen on the Ndebele's cattle:[5]
The chief of Maseru asks no questions![6]
    The lion of the village of the Agitator[7] arrived,
It arrived with a goodly number of cattle:
When the cattle are coming, where are the regiments?[8]
150   Word came from the Lion of the Mighty Warriors,
It came, it was distressing to the people.[9]
    The lion that jumps out at the start[10]

[1] Presumably the cow is Joel himself, who causes so much panic among his enemies that even at night they write letters to each other about him.

[2] The poet appears to be complaining that Joel (the lion) keeps on agreeing that his followers should receive a share of the plundered cattle (he keeps on nodding), so that most of his people, including even his warriors (the rhinos) and his herdsman (Gasebeng) derive no benefit from them and are hungry. Cp. lines 126–8 above. The plundered cattle are almost certainly Langalibalele's, for they had come 'from the Maloti's bitter cold', and there is a very clear reference to them in the stanzas that follow.

[3] The water poured off them because they were so sleek: their flanks were remarkable because they were so fat.

[4] i.e. in the Maloti, for RaThebe, a Fokeng, used to supervise Molapo's cattle-posts there.

[5] i.e. the Hlubi's cattle, the word Ndebele being used to refer to anyone of Nguni origin.

[6] i.e. Griffith, the Governor's Agent, does not complain.

[7] i.e. of Molapo.

[8] This question is contemptuous. The cattle have been captured, and their owners have not pursued them. Cp. Jonathan, ii. 16–17, p. 182 above.

[9] Presumably Joel had given orders about the raid on Langalibalele, and his warriors were apprehensive about the dangers that lay ahead. Cp. Griffith, i. 6, p. 215 below.

[10] Joel was the first of the Sotho chiefs to seize cattle from the Hlubi.

Jumped on the track which led up the valley:
It captured cattle in a sheltered place,
Among the dark rocks, in the Maloti.   155
    The cows that were black had been set apart:
He's brought them down, he didn't leave them.
Had he been a coward they'd have stayed.
    The child of the chief, the bird of the shields,
The heaven, the lightning, the son of Mokhachane,   160
It thundered as if it had nested among people![1]
You've caught the lightning, you from the Whites:[2]
You brought it here;
It's come and it goes on hurling its flash.
    The lion, the wanderer of Mokhachane's people,   165
As it wanders around, the kraal isn't filled:[3]
With what kind of cattle will it be filled?[4]
For you've just seized the cattle of Makhanya,
And you seized Mphohle's when they'd calved.[5]
    Child of the chief, there are three concerns: 170
One is for the cattle to chew,
The other, the heart keeps thinking it.[6]
    The Crocodile, the cattle it's done twice over:
To capture the black and the white-faced cows is good.[7]
    Its hand is open,[8] it goes on distributing,   175
The Crocodile distributes the cattle in the reed bed:
They run as they climb the flat white stone,

---

[1] i.e. it struck them often. See Lerotholi, i. 14, p. 138 above. As the following lines make clear, the poet has now turned from the raid on Langalibalele to the Gun War.

[2] i.e. the Cape authorities and their Sotho supporters have been attacked by Joel.

[3] i.e. although Joel raids far and wide, he does not capture enough cattle to satisfy his followers.

[4] i.e. with whose cattle will it be filled?

[5] Evidently Makhanya and Mphohle were two of Joel's enemies, but further identification is impossible. (For Makhanya, see also ii. 21, p. 203 below.) Evidently too the cattle which Joel had captured from them were very few.

[6] The meaning of this stanza is not clear. In line 170 reference is made to three problems, but in lines 171–2 only two of these are mentioned. Line 171 probably refers to Joel's need to capture cattle, and line 172 to the way in which he is to do it.

[7] This stanza may mean, literally, that Joel's forces have captured two cows, one black and one white-faced; or it may mean that he has defeated both his Sotho and his European enemies.

[8] Lit.: 'Its hand is light', i.e. it is generous.

They run as they climb the calabash-rock.[1]
Over there, at the stream, which cow is disputed?
180 The beast with the horns bent forward is disputed, the cow that is
red with white spots,
The cow for which the people have chosen
And are standing well with their regiments,[2]
Of which some have gone to Qalo[3] to stop.[4]
The child of the chief, the tamer, black and white,[5]
185 The black and white one is the deluge which sweeps away the
The deluge has filled the plain, Mighty Warriors.   [shields.
Some think they're droves of ancestral spirits:[6]
Others think it's the glutton[7] who attacks:
Others think it's the scarer of the Ndebele,
190 He scares the Nguni, while the Sotho remain.[8]
Commander, give commands, man from the Agitator's:
The Mighty Warrior commanded his bachelors
On the occasion of the battle of Mantšonyane.[9]
Sound your whistles[10] that the land may return,
195 Pray for the land of the Beoana,[11]

[1] This stanza may be taken literally, in which case it refers simply to the distribution of captured stock. Alternatively the cattle may signify Joel's regiments, and when he 'distributes' them he may be making his dispositions for battle. The calabash-rock cannot now be identified: neither can 'the flat white stone'.

[2] i.e. the best warriors have been chosen for the fight.

[3] i.e. to Joel's village.

[4] The disputed cow in this stanza apparently represents some of Molapo's herds which his old counsellor, Qacha, handed over to Jonathan as the heir to provide the marriage-cattle for his brother, Moliboea. Joel thereupon had Qacha 'eaten up', and it was this quarrel that was the immediate cause of the fighting in November 1882.

[5] In Mangoaela's text this line is as follows:

Ngoan'a morena, le-thapisetsa-phatšoa
'The child of the chief, the tamer of the black and white one.'

If this is correct, then 'the black and white one' is clearly Jonathan. In the following line, however, 'the black and white one' is obviously Joel himself, and so we have amended Mangoaela's text by removing the hyphen between *le* and *thapisetsa*, thus forming one word, *lethapisetsa*; by making *phatšoa* a separate word; and by placing a comma between the two.

[6] 'they' here are evidently Joel's regiments.

[7] i.e. Joel himself. Cp. line 47, p. 190 above.

[8] Joel's enemies are contemptuously referred to as 'the Ndebele' and 'the Nguni', while his own followers are referred to as 'the Sotho'.

[9] A river in the Maloti. The poet now turns to Joel's attacks on the San of Soai.

[10] Whistles were used to give commands in battles.

[11] The Beoana, i.e. the Sotho. See Moshoeshoe, ii. 5, p. 71 above.

That Molapo should know him by name,
That he be known by the Agitator, the Desired,[1]
That Jonathan should hear while at home
That the young man is still in the plain,
That the Mighty Warrior is abroad in the veld.   200
 Look, he's found people for himself,[2]
Here in the hoek, at Mantšonyane.
Two he's left, just two alone,
He's left them to go to report,
To go to tell lies to Moorosi.[3]   205
 What's the Mighty Warrior that he's always sought?
And here are the Catholics seeking him too![4]
 The lion of the Agitator's village arrived,
It arrived with cattle already disputed.[5]
 Child of the chief, bird of the shields,   210
Separate the roan bulls from the cows.
Pick out a cow and give it to 'MaKhutsi,[6]
That Motlalei and her group should take most:[7]
For the Great House there are chosen the white-spotted red ones.[8]
 Scatter the lightning, Agitator's child,   215
That the Mighty Warriors should stand,
That they stand in the form of a bodyguard for the chief,
In the form of a bodyguard for the chief to look out.
 Child, look there, and see,
Look among the cattle, there's fighting already;   220
A light is there, leaping among the milk cows;
Out came the smoke, we gave up as a bodyguard.[9]
 The black and white lightning strikes in the Maloti;
That with white feathers is simply standing still,

---

[1] i.e. by Molapo.

[2] Evidently Joel's forces captured some of Soai's people.

[3] For Soai's connection with Moorosi, see Jonathan, ii. 18–19, p. 182 above.
For the idea that messengers are liars, see Jonathan, iii. 15, p. 184 above.

[4] There is a touch of humour here. Everyone seeks after Joel because he is
such a splendid warrior. And here are the Roman Catholics, who are seeking
him out in order to convert him!

[5] The allusion is not known. [6] One of Joel's wives.

[7] Motlalei, alias 'MaTabolane, was Joel's third wife. Why she and her group
should take most is not known.

[8] The Great House was that of Joel's senior wife, 'MaMopeli.

[9] This line is unusual in that, in effect, it is an admission of defeat; but it is
impossible to identify the occasion.

225 It's still playing about with its wing.[1]
    Agitator's son, send the heifers to the chief's:
The milk cows were chosen, they were sent to the chief's,
They were sent to Josefa and to Senate too.[2]
The red and white one was captured for Molapo,
230 It was sent to the Agitator, the Rescuer:[3]
'Take the cattle of your enemy! They're there!'[4]
And when he takes a hundred, the Mighty Warrior,
His brother[5] will live off the fat of the land.
    The *Helethuma* monster[6] is fighting in the rain,
235 There being no mist on the Maloti:
The mists are to be seen among the Whites.[7]
    Charm of Mohato's[8] village, Mighty Warrior,
Won't you send a cow to pay the Maloti?
For this year they've sought for you milk cows,
240 They've sought for you sheep and oxen.[9]
    A certain man's wisdom is unending,
The Crocodile that's zealous,
The conquerer of the mountains[10] of your family, Mphaphathi.[11]
    Chief, the shields beat each other in the plain:
245 Once the little shields were too strong for the great ones

---

[1] The two types of lightning bird probably represent two of Joel's regiments, one of which went into action, while the other did nothing. Cp. Posholi, ii. 4–5, p. 82 above. The incident referred to is almost certainly the capture of Langalibalele's cattle.

[2] Josefa was Molapo's senior son, and was married to Letsie's senior daughter, Senate. The cattle referred to are no doubt some of those which Joel had captured from Langalibalele.

[3] i.e. to Molapo.

[4] The text recorded by Mangoaela is as follows:

Nka khom'a sera sa tseo!

This, however, is meaningless, and the words '*hao! Ke*' have been inserted between *sa* and *tseo*.

[5] i.e. Josefa.   [6] A fabulous monster.

[7] The only interpretation of this stanza which commends itself is the literal one. It was raining when Joel captured Langalibalele's cattle in the Maloti, but as he came down the mountain passes he could see mists over the Free State.

[8] Mohato, i.e. Letsie.

[9] The idea is that Joel has captured so much stock from Langalibalele in the mountains that he ought to pay them a cow in gratitude.

[10] He is the conqueror of the mountains because he has shown that he can fight there.

[11] Joel's sister.

That were black and had just been cut.[1]
Hearer of the news of the people at Mokhachane's,
Someone heard scoldings exchanged at the chief's:
The Boers were disputing with the Ndebele.
Then the hearer was the first to depart.[2]   250
The lion is standing on the slab at RaMpai's,[3]
It still stands alone at Qoqolosing.[4]
At the ford, at Sekorobele's,[5]
I find the hearer standing:
I speak with him, but he spurns me,   255
I keep on asking: 'Where's the Mighty Warrior?'
He says: 'Your people have all turned away from you.[6]
The people are being spoilt by the child of Makhabane.
Makotoko has fetched spears against you,
He's fetched cannons from the sea against you,   260
And up to this day they're still coming!'[7]
The lion has strolled round the people from Sprigg's,[8]
He remained as if they were his!'[9]

---

[1] Generally speaking, the Sotho used small shields and the Nguni large ones. These lines refer to Joel's seizure of Langalibalele's cattle.

[2] The significance of this stanza is obscure. If taken on its own the most likely interpretation is as follows. The hearer of the news is Joel himself, for he is sharp and alert. At Molapo's village of Leribe ('the chief's') he heard of the dispute between the Natal Government ('The Boers') and Langalibalele's Hlubi ('the Ndebele'), although, of course, he did not actually hear the two parties arguing. Thereupon he went out quickly and was the first to capture cattle from the Hlubi. However, this stanza appears to be linked with the next by the continued use of the word *leutloela*, 'the hearer', and this second stanza refers very clearly to the Gun War. Possibly, therefore, the 'Boers' are the Cape Government: the Ndebele are the Nguni chiefdoms which it had already disarmed: and Joel is to be regarded as the first of the Sotho to rebel in the north.

[3] i.e. RaMpai's Nek in the Leribe District.

[4] A mountain which rises from the Leribe plateau.

[5] Sekorobele was one of Molapo's subordinate chiefs, and his village, which is still known as Sekorobele's, was near a ford across the Hlotse river.

[6] The identities of the two speakers are far from clear. Perhaps the poet is calling upon Joel to fight and show his bravery: 'Where's the Mighty Warrior?' It seems strange, however, that Joel should reply that the poet has been deserted by his people, since it was Joel himself who had been deserted by Jonathan, Moliboea, etc. But perhaps Joel is represented as pointing out to his followers the difficulties with which they will have to contend if they want to fight.

[7] Nathaniel Makotoko, a son of Makhabane, was one of Jonathan's advisers, and also one of his military commanders. Cp. Jonathan, i. 158, p. 178 above. The cannons from the sea clearly symbolize the Cape soldiery.

[8] i.e. from the Cape Colony, Sprigg being Prime Minister during the Gun War.

[9] i.e. Joel was so bold in remaining close to his enemies that it seemed as if

Also those of our people who left here,
265   Ntjaatsana and RaMoshee,
Left before seeing that the Mighty Warrior
Was a tough, sharp grass, that he stabbed.[1]

The lion that once hurled down the soldiers,
That troubled them badly in the town,[2]
270   Burdened them with a chunk of war.

You've scolded, it's enough, Mighty Warrior,
People aren't beasts, Mighty Warrior,
They're Tickets from the village of your father:
Speak with them a little, and leave them alone.[3]

275   As they went to the Camp they were running already;
On their arrival a lean beast was killed for them,
They said it should be cooked by Jan Mokhahlane,
And, as for salting it, he didn't even salt it![4]

The poor men have run very fast,
280   Perhaps they'll cough, and be ill,
Perhaps they'll have a pain in the chest!

The one who drains all, the son of Molapo,
Yet from his kinsman he doesn't drain all:[5]
He's just drained all from there among the Mpondo,
285   There occurred an affair, it sent up Mhlonhlo.[6]

Letsie's sharp thorn bush, you stab,
You stab before you've grown old.

---

they were his followers. This thought may have been suggested by the siege of
Hlotse Heights during November and December 1880.

[1] Ntjaatsana and RaMoshee were two of Joel's followers, and they are
mocked here for deserting him before he had really distinguished himself in
battle. According to Chief Jameson Qhobela, they were Fokeng, and they
abandoned Joel at the time of the Gun War and went to live in Witzies Hoek.

[2] 'the town', i.e. Hlotse Heights.

[3] Joel is asked to be merciful towards Jonathan's followers because of their
close connection with his own people. For the name 'Tickets', see Lerotholi
v. 32, p. 150 above.

[4] This stanza refers to Jonathan's flight to the Camp after his defeat at
Tsikoane on 11 November 1880. Jan Mokhahlane was a police constable there.

[5] The phrase 'to drain all' would normally suggest the seizure of every head
of cattle, and this line would mean that Joel did not ruin Jonathan completely.
In the following line, however, it is stated that he 'drained all' from the 'Mpondo'
i.e. the Mpondomise, whom he never attacked, and who, like the Sotho, were in
rebellion against the Cape authorities. 'To drain all', therefore, may well mean
'to receive full support'.

[6] The Mpondomise of Mhlonhlo rebelled against the Cape Government in
1880, but they were quickly subdued, and Mhlonhlo took refuge in Lesotho.

Comrade of the child of Letsie,[1] wild beast,
Comrade of Lerotholi, you're deceptive:
You deceive Matela Tselanyane and his men,   290
And Matela continues deceiving too.[2]
The stone that is slippery,[3] the Koena,
Is the stone of the Mighty Warriors and the Rhinos.[4]
The one who presses deep with his claws, Mighty Warrior,
On the occasion when he tried to press deep,   295
The cattle arose and left their owners:
They arose, they left the old men on the mountain,
They left Qakithe Chabalala and his friends.[5]
Someone is standing at Sekameng and calling,
'MaKaibane continually cries.[6]   300
The comrade of Ntsoana's child is summoned:
Where is the comrade of Motloheloa being sent?[7]
He's summoned afar, at Mokoteli's.
He'll find that affairs are already concluded:
For what purpose is Migane's child being summoned?[8]   305

[1] 'the child of Letsie' stands in apposition to Lerotholi in the next line.
[2] For the Khoakhoa of Matela, see lines 61–3, p. 191 above.
[3] i.e. the chief who is elusive and difficult to control.
[4] Two of Joel's regiments.
[5] This stanza may possibly refer to the events of May 1883. In the knowledge that Joel was planning an attack on the Camp, Jonathan posted a force under his nephew, Motšoene, at Lefi's Nek, close to Leribe village, to block his path. However, in the words of the Anglican priest at the Camp, Canon Widdicombe, 'Motsuène . . . proved to be no Leonidas, and Leribe no Thermopylae.' Indeed Motšoene and his men offered no resistance at all, but moved aside: or, to use the words of this stanza,
'The cattle arose and left their owners'.
Joel was thus able to seize control of Leribe, where only the aged and the infirm had been left. Among these, apparently, were some men who were of Swazi origin, namely Qakithe, son of Chabalala, and his group. But this interpretation can only be a tentative suggestion.
[6] According to Chiefs Lepekola Joel and Lishobana Mpaki Molapo, when, in May 1883, Joel's village at Qalo was burnt, he himself fled past the mountain of Sekameng in the Free State, where a certain woman called 'MaKaibane wept aloud as she saw him go by.
[7] For Ntsoana, see line 109, p. 192 above. Motloheloa was his son.
[8] According to Chiefs Lepekola Joel and Lishobana Mpaki Molapo, Joel eventually took refuge on the farm of a Free Stater whom the Sotho called Migane. He was summoned to appear before Letsie (at Mokoteli's), but his people did not want him to go, for, they said, he would find that decisions had already been taken against him. It is known from Sekese's article in *Leselinyana*, 1 June 1892, that Migane (or Megane) was indeed a Free State farmer. It is also known that Letsie supported Jonathan's claim that he was senior to Joel.

Where are the men who started these affairs?
Makotoko and Selebalo, you're here.[1]
   Son of 'MaKali,[2] there are many little affairs:
The affair, RaMopeli,[3] you haven't been told of it,
310   From you, from the mouth of the war, it's withheld.[4]
   In that year of the War of the Guns
They said: 'Greetings, Koena!
Child of the blood of Molapo, Fierce-Visaged!'
When the war was over they said: 'You're an Ndebele!'
315   Had I known I'd never have continued fighting!![5]

(ii)

   The strong young chief is determined, the Tough Warrior,
The Tickets can never devour him entirely:
Having struck him with sticks they've then left him.[6]
   Father of Mopeli,[7] with zealous heart,
5   Cows enter in twos, they enter in threes:[8]
He's long been plundering for the household of the Chief.[9]
   Chief, give a cow that's in milk.
You see them, those that are plundered are strong:
Those that are plundered cause walks in the dew![10]
10   The Crocodile, the bur of Mohato,[11] Mighty Warrior,

---

[1] For Makotoko, see line 259 above. Selebalo was a junior son of Moshoeshoe who lived near his father's birthplace at Menkhoaneng, in the Hlotse valley. During the Gun War he was a 'loyalist', and subsequently supported Jonathan against Joel. The *seroki* blames Makotoko and Selebalo for the dispute between the sons of Molapo, and he is obviously suggesting that they should be the men to go to Letsie.

[2] 'MaKali was the mother of Monaheng, alias Kali, one of the ancestors of the Sotho royal house.

[3] RaMopeli, i.e. Joel himself, Mopeli being his senior son.

[4] The poet appears to be complaining that Joel has been summoned by Letsie without being told the reason. Joel is 'the mouth of war' because he had advocated resistance during the Gun War.

[5] This stanza refers once again to Joel's disappointment when, after the Gun War, his erstwhile allies refused to support his claim to seniority over Jonathan.

[6] i.e. Jonathan and his followers can never humble him completely.

[7] Joel's senior son.

[8] i.e. he is always capturing small groups of cattle.

[9] The Chief here is probably Molapo's senior son, Josefa.

[10] i.e. the warriors had set out early in the morning to capture them.

[11] Mohato, i.e. Letsie.

Stuck to the Magistrate's heifer.[1]
The lion which once went to fight for Moshoeshoe
Right here at RaFutho's, on the ridge:[2]
We came upon rocks, we sat down,
We came on little rocks, we stayed awhile: 15
We go in, we prepare to fire.
    The cow of the comrade of Lerotholi, the red cow,[3]
The cow of Peete's[4] comrade returned it,
It returned it, the stick to the tree.[5]
    When the lightning began to flash, 20
It flashed, it devoured the cattle of Makhanya.[6]
    The child of the chief knows the clouds:[7]
When he goes to war the mist would close down:
The mist has closed down on the snowy mountains,
On the mountains where the winds are raging: 25
There is wind, there is snow, Mighty Warriors,
There is wind, there is snow in the mountains:
Some would be fond of their pillows and stay.[8]
    The Crocodile can follow the horses:[9]
It'll go to burn the shelters among the Bushmen. 30
    The causer of repentance of those from Mokoteli's[10]
Said the Bushmen should repent with true repentance,
The Bushmen should repent of attacking you.
They refuse to allow the Chief's cattle to graze,[11]
They refuse to allow the oxen to be set apart.[12] 35

[1] The Magistrate was Major Bell: his heifer was Jonathan.
[2] This stanza refers to the defence of Thaba Bosiu against the Free Staters in August 1865. Evidently Joel was posted in the RaFutho pass on this occasion.
[3] i.e. Joel himself.
[4] The Peete referred to here is probably the son of RaManella rather than the father of Mokhachane.
[5] i.e. Joel has gained his revenge. Previously the stick had been cut from the tree: now it has been returned to its rightful position. Cp. Griffith, i. 76, p. 217 below.
[6] Makhanya was evidently one of Joel's enemies, but beyond this nothing is known of him. See also i. 168, p. 195 above.
[7] This probably means that Joel knows all about lightning, i.e. about war.
[8] In this stanza the *seroki* turns to Joel's attacks on the San of Soai.
[9] i.e. those which the San had stolen from the Sotho.
[10] i.e. from Lesotho. For Mokoteli, see p. 63 above.
[11] i.e. they plunder Molapo's cattle when they go out to graze.
[12] i.e. they plunder the oxen when they are separated off as a herd and sent to pasture.

Crocodile, refuge of the Hololo's debris,[1]
Whom do you say should present himself, Rhino,
Should present himself when he sees a wild beast
Of the family of Kholu,[2] of Mohlomi of the Locusts?[3]

40   Great vulture, young vulture of the Father of Josefa,[4]
He comes from Phale, he comes from Motengoane,[5]
The lion which once went and swallowed white soldiers.

        Migrants who migrate to the Whites,
You don't migrate to cattle, you migrate to a sjambok,[6]
45   You migrate to the hide of the sleeper in the water![7]

        We, the remnants of the Binders,[8]
Became water, we filled all the bedding.[9]

        These birds have been too strong for us people,
They refuse to allow us to greet the chief,
50   Saying: 'Hail, O Lord!' to the son of Mokhachane.[10]

        Crocodile, storm of the war on high,
Of the war of the time of the arrows, chief's son![11]

---

[1] The translation of *hoholi* as 'refuge of the . . . debris' is uncertain. According to Paroz it means 'alluvium collected on the banks of a river'. Chief 'Mako, however, suggests that it means the place at which rocks, branches etc. are deposited by a river. Thus Joel provides a refuge for people in the same way as such a place provides a refuge for the downrushing debris. Mr. Stephen Pinda, however, suggests that *hoholi* means material which is actually being swept down by a river, and which comes down with such force that it smashes everything out of its way. The Hololo, a tributary of the Caledon, flows within a few miles of Qalo.

[2] Moshoeshoe's mother.

[3] Mohlomi was the celebrated chief of the Monaheng who died *c.* 1815, and his regiment was the Locusts. The central idea in this stanza is that no one dares to appear before Joel when he is angry.

[4] Josefa's father was Molapo.

[5] Phale and Motengoane are said to be places in the Free State, but their positions are not known. The following line clearly indicates that the incident alluded to occurred during or after the Gun War.

[6] i.e. the Sotho who are loyal to the Cape authorities are not well rewarded, but are subjected to harsh European discipline.

[7] 'the sleeper in the water', i.e. the hippopotamus. Sjamboks were often made from hippopotamus hide.

[8] One of Moshoeshoe's regiments.

[9] i.e. Joel's warriors spread out and occupied all the land. For the idea of bedding being land, cp. Griffith, ii. 241–2, p. 226 below.

[10] This stanza refers to the second Free State war. After the Treaty of Mpharane in March 1866, in which Molapo made his own separate peace with the Free State, his people were not allowed to recognize Moshoeshoe as their chief.

[11] The *seroki* now turns to the attacks on the San of Soai.

The comrade of the child of Makate[1] makes iron,
He makes a stone for striking the counsellors
Among the Bushmen.   55
    Lion of 'MaPaki's,[2] demolisher,
Bring down the oxen from the plateau.[3]
    The chief, the hartebeest has appeared in the pass,
He doesn't allow the maidens to dance:
The Funny Little Rollers stay awake at night no more.[4]   60
    The entangler's the light, the great chief's child,
He's the light, he's the lamp of the chiefs.
    The cow of the clever warriors, roan and white-spotted,
Has stars all over its body.
It's just like a guinea-fowl, a grysbok, Koena,   65
It's just like the eggs of birds, Koena.[5]
    The cow of Tselane's lover, the brown one,[6]
Is raw from the ropes, the cow of the Mfengu,[7]
This fawn one of those who fix a sheath on the penis,
Of those who fix a sheath on the penis, the Ndebele.[8]   70
    The lion is fighting with a cub on its back,
With a cub on its back, the Senders'[9] Crocodile.[10]
    The warrior of the son of the chief was angry:
Cow, let me know if you've erred,

---

[1] According to Chiefs Lepekola Joel and Lishobana Mpaki Molapo, the child of Makate was Qekoane, a Maieane, one of Joel's followers.

[2] 'MaPaki was one of Joel's wives.

[3] *Sechaba*, 'the people', which appears in the sixth and seventh editions of Mangoaela, is a misprint for *sehlaba*, 'the plateau', which appears in the earlier editions.

[4] i.e. Joel has put an end to their revelries. The San are called 'The Funny Little Rollers' because of their rolling gait.

[5] This stanza merely indicates Joel's beauty.

[6] Tselane was 'MaSelomo, one of Joel's wives, and her lover was Joel himself. The lines that follow suggest that the cow is Langalibalele. For the idea of a chief being his enemy's cow, see i. 97, p. 192 above.

[7] The Hlubi who lived among the Sotho were often called Mfengu (Fingoes), and so it would be natural for the Sotho to think of Langalibalele's followers as Mfengu too.

[8] 'the Ndebele', i.e. the Nguni.

[9] The regiment of Josefa, Molapo's senior son.

[10] According to Chiefs Lepekola Joel and Lishobana Mpaki Molapo, this stanza and the following stanza refer to Joel's dispute with the Khoakhoa of Matela, which, as the contemporary records reveal, began in 1889 and went on for several years. It was at this time, say the two chiefs, that Joel's son Mopeli (the lion's cub in this stanza) had his first experience of battle.

75   That I may send you to the chiefs, in the meeting,
      That I may send you to the Whites from the sea.[1]

                              (iii)

      The lion of these days is giving trouble:
      It's cast its eyes on people's property.
      It's thus that it's seen the little Bushmen of Soai.
      It arrived, it stood on the Maloti,
5   It trod with its feet and it tapped:
      Soai it stabbed in the midst of his hairs,
      It stabbed him in the neck: he departed from his village
      And went up to reside with the Ndebele over there.[2]
      The Bushmen are very white, Mighty Warriors,
10   They're white, you'd imagine they were smeared with white clay![3]
      The son of 'MaMosa, the provoker of shields,[4]
      He's the provoker, for he comes from Soai's.
      The jackal's a man, the Agitator's son, and he's going,
      He's always going around in the veld,[5]
15   At the time of the moon, when it's dead,
      When it's gone to the end, and is dead.
      He was brave, the Mighty Warrior, the son of Nthe[6] and Molapo,
      He wouldn't allow his men to withdraw:
      'Lean against the tree: here it is!
20   I myself am the tree, the Mighty Warriors' Lion!'
      The lion of these days is giving trouble,
      Already it's been asked by those from Chabalala's:
      You're asked by Toejana in the valleys:
      He was asked about cattle, where they were,

---

¹ The cow here is said to be Matela, who is apparently being called upon to admit the error of his ways before his fellow chiefs and before Government officials.

² In their second attack on the San Joel's warriors actually killed Soai. Perhaps therefore this stanza refers to the first attack, and the *seroki* is claiming that Soai was wounded and driven away. The 'Ndebele over there' may possibly be a contemptuous reference to Moorosi's Phuthi, who were of Nguni origin.

³ Apparently this stanza has no significance beyond indicating that the San were lighter in colour than the Sotho.

⁴ Joel is 'the provoker of shields', i.e. of war, because he has attacked Soai.

⁵ i.e. Joel goes around the country like a jackal.

⁶ Nthe, Molapo's sister, was not in fact his mother, but his aunt.

He was asked about sharp arrows too!¹ 25
　Don't ask me about cattle, ask me about Soai:
Soai's been devoured by the Mighty Warriors' helper,
He was devoured by the lion of Mphaphathi's² family,
It devoured him, it slept for him in the veld.³
　The hearer of the news of the people from Mokhachane's 30
Heard the news about the Little Stutterer,⁴
He heard when told in his blankets:⁵
It was said that men were looking for the Mighty Warrior to ap-
　　　　　　　　　　　　　　　　　　　　　pear.⁶
　At the time he appeared he made the fire burn
Which came from the flint, from the steel:⁷ 35
The fire was given to the Little Stutterer,⁸
It was given to this man we once saw.
It was pointed over here that we should look:
He cowered, did the Chief of the Bushmen.
　The blower of the whistle⁹ he has knocked into the water, 40
The water boiled because of powder and the bullet,
And when it was boiling the little frogs were afraid!¹⁰
　The Bushmen are very white, Mighty Warriors,
They're white, you'd imagine they were smeared with white clay,

¹ For Chabalala, see i. 298, p. 201 above. Toejana was one of Joel's followers and was a Hlapo. Perhaps these men expected to receive some of the cattle which Joel plundered from the San. The last question has no point other than its humour: they even asked him for some of the San's arrows! Cp. Jonathan, iii. 44, p. 185 above.
² Mphaphathi was Joel's sister.
³ This stanza almost certainly refers to Joel's second attack on Soai.
⁴ i.e. Soai himself, who was the Little Stutterer because of the way in which he spoke Sotho. No doubt the news that was brought to Joel concerned the San's latest depredations.
⁵ i.e. while in bed.
⁶ This stanza is reminiscent in parts of i. 247–56, p. 199 above: unfortunately it casts no light upon the meaning of those lines.
⁷ i.e. from the gun, which was probably a flintlock.
⁸ i.e. shots were fired at Soai.
⁹ 'The blower of the whistle' is Soai himself, for evidently he used to give signals to his people by blowing on a whistle.
¹⁰ According to Chiefs Lepekola Joel and Lishobana Mpaki Molapo, Soai tried to conceal himself in a pool, but was seen when he put his nose out of the water to breathe. He was then shot by one of Joel's followers, Mochebelele, son of Tlaba, a Fokeng. According to the Sotho historian Sekese, however, the man who shot him was Lelosa Pokane, a Tloung adherent of Joel: see article in *Leselinyana*, 14 November 1924.

45 You might even think them springboks,[1] Mighty Warriors!
   Soai has been devoured by the Mighty Warriors' Lion,
It devoured him, it slept for him in the veld.
   The child of the chief was flashing like lightning,
He flashed, he intended that the chiefs should see him,
50 That Jonathan should see while at home
That the Mighty Warrior was abroad in the veld.[2]
   He took up the people in the hoek:
Two, however, he's left
That they go to tell lies to Moorosi.[3]
55   This year the lion of the family of Mokhachane roars when the
                            sky is clear,
The Crocodile of the family of Masopha and Makhobalo,[4]
The Crocodile of the family of Mpiti Sekake.[5]
   It cuts its horns sharp, the Lion of the Mighty Warriors[6] of
                            Mokhachane,
Preparing itself for events to occur:
60 Today's events are involved with old grievances.

14. *Letsie II*

Letsie II (*c.* 1869–1913), who was often known as Letsienyana, 'Little Letsie', in order to distinguish him from his grandfather, Letsie I, was the eldest son in Lerotholi's second house. Since there was no male issue in the first house, he was the undisputed heir and successor. He was brought up at Lerotholi's village of Likhoele, and remained there when, in 1891, his father became Paramount Chief and went to live at Makeneng.

By this time the Sotho were under direct imperial rule, and it was the policy of the Resident Commissioner and his officials to build up and establish the authority of the paramountcy throughout the country. Masopha had long been on bad terms with Lerotholi, and was constantly defying his orders and endeavouring to rule his people as if virtually independent. Towards the end of 1897 one of his subjects, a certain 'MaLibili, ran away from her husband and fled to the Free State. At the injured man's request her local chief, Masopha's son, Moeketsi, followed

[1] The stomach and chest of the springbok are a clear white.
[2] For lines 50–1, cp. i. 198–200, p. 197 above.
[3] For this stanza, see i. 201–5, p. 197 above.
[4] Two of Moshoeshoe's sons.
[5] For Mpiti, son of Sekake, see Masopha, iv. 131, p. 132 above, and Moshoeshoe, i. 9–18, pp. 67–8 above.
[6] The metaphor of the bull is here mixed with that of the lion.

her up with an armed band and arrested her, but was then arrested himself by the Free State authorities. He was tried and sentenced to imprisonment with lashes, but before these could be inflicted he and one of his accessories in the disturbance, Maboka, escaped and took refuge with Masopha. The Free State authorities requested that these men be surrended to them. This would have been possible in the case of Maboka, who was normally a resident of the Free State, but not in the case of Moeketsi, who was normally a resident of Basutoland, for there was no extradition agreement between the two countries. Lagden, the Resident Commissioner, demanded that both men should be handed over to him: he would then send Maboka back to the Free State, and he himself would try Moeketsi. Masopha refused.

Lagden then called upon Lerotholi to enforce obedience, and the Paramount Chief began mustering his regiments. In an attempt to avert the crisis Masopha handed over Maboka, but Moeketsi's surrender was demanded too. Eventually, on 4 January 1898, battle was joined at Khamolane, a plateau near Thaba Bosiu, where Masopha's warriors had erected fortifications. Letsie and his men provided the spearhead of Lerotholi's attack, but the young chief pressed too far forward, was almost cut off, and only escaped by jumping his horse over some rocks and then galloping for his life down to the Phuthiatsana River. On 10 January Lerotholi was reinforced by the regiments of Griffith, Letsie's younger brother; on 12 January Masopha was decisively defeated; and on 17 January Moeketsi was duly surrendered. This brief struggle was Letsie's only experience of war.

In 1905, on the death of his father, he became Paramount Chief, and moved his village from Likhoele to Phahameng, not far from Morija. His brief reign was quiet and uneventful, and on his death in 1913 he was succeeded by Griffith.

His *lithoko* consist of a single poem, which is of particular interest in that, after the first twenty-five lines, in which the chief is fulsomely praised with reference to his character, his home, his parentage and his beauty, it provides a coherent and well-ordered narrative of his part in the war against Masopha, beginning with his departure from Likhoele, and ending with his return. (For a more detailed analysis of the poem, see p. 35 above.)

It is generally agreed among Sotho authorities today that Letsie neither composed nor chanted his own praises, and this is borne out by the evidence of the poem itself, in which the first person singular is used only once, and then in direct speech. Unfortunately the name of the poet is no longer remembered.

> The hairy wild beast of the Man-Eaters,[1]
> The long-haired monster which is feared by the people,

[1] Just as Letsie II himself was named after his grandfather, Letsie I, so his regiment was named after one of his grandfather's regiments: see Letsie I, line 19, p. 108 above.

Someone was feared by all the people,
He was feared by the children and their mothers.[1]
5   The child of the chief, who towers above the people,
The heaven to the people of his father!
The chief who remains at the ruins[2]
Remains at Likhoele, the mountain of Makhatha,[3]
At the ancient ruins of Mojakisane,[4]
10   Which have long received sojourners of different nations,[5]
Close to the village with trees,
Trees which he looks at in the west,
Where the sun goes down.
RaLetšabisa,[6] the chief, begets,
15   He's begotten a ratel with a beautiful colour.
The child of the chief is a bright-coloured guinea-fowl,
The child of the chief is a wonderful monster,
He's just like a guinea-fowl hopping to the veld![7]
The cub of the lion, of the family of Letšabisa,[8]
20   The cub of the lion, how terrible it is!
The cub of the lion, with mighty shoulders,
The hairy-cheeked, bearded wild dog!
Your thigh is like an oribi's, Letsie,
Because you're the brother of 'MaGoliathe,[9]
25   The hunting leopard of Nkoebe and Seeiso.[10]
The man who heard at the ruins,
While still at Likhoele, the mountain of Makhatha,
It's said that the herdsmen of Masopha have blundered,
A blunder's been made by Maboka and Moeketsi.[11]

[1] i.e. he was feared by everyone, even the women and children.
[2] After his father, Lerotholi, had moved from Likhoele to Makeneng in 1891, he stayed near the houses, 'the ruins', which his father had abandoned.
[3] A Kholokhoe chief who lived at Likhoele, where there is still a village known as Makhatha's.
[4] It is said that the Monaheng chief, Mojakisane, a son of Mohlomi, once lived at Likhoele.
[5] i.e. over a long period people of many different groups have come to live at Likhoele.
[6] RaLetšabisa, i.e. Lerotholi, Letšabisa being his daughter.
[7] This stanza is indicative of Letsie's beauty, for the colours of the ratel and the guinea-fowl are much admired among the Sotho.
[8] Letsie's elder sister.
[9] 'MaGoliathe, i.e. Letšabisa, Goliathe (Goliath) being her eldest son.
[10] Letsie's uncles.
[11] See the introductory notes, pp. 208–9 above.

The Crocodile departed from Likhoele on horseback, 30
As a mist crept over the earth.
It climbed up the pass of Khamolane:[1]
They sent him down, did the people from Masopha's,
They appeared in all the little passes,
They appeared in the passes and on the cliffs, 35
They threw with their kerries and their spears,
They threw at him down to the Phuthiatsana.
Quickly he whipped and goaded on his horse,
Afraid that the spearshafts would dazzle him.[2]
Vague groups in the distance were standing on every side 40
With their hands on their foreheads,[3] and they said:
'The child of this country is running away!'
Crocodile, come out of the Phuthiatsana waters
That the holes stay empty![4]
He stood at Liphokoaneng[5] and gave orders 45
That they pass the night with their Sniders loaded.
Then they passed the night with their Sniders loaded.
He said: 'They show off, these people from Masopha's,
They've shown off against me with their sticks of iron.'[6]
He spoke the next morning with Lepolesa and Liphere, 50
With Mofoka, Likupa and Mokoenehi,[7]
Men of the sticks of iron.
At dawn men's eyes were heavy.
He went to ascend the pass of Khamolane,
Close to the village of his uncle,[8] 55
Where the bulls kick up dust against each other,
Showing to each other the redness of their horns,[9]

---

[1] The Khamolane plateau opposite Thaba Bosiu had been fortified by Masopha's warriors.
[2] Alternatively: 'Afraid that the wings of the army would dazzle him', i.e. by cutting him off so that he could not see his way out.
[3] i.e. shading their eyes against the sun as they looked at him.
[4] i.e. the holes by the river in which the crocodile might take refuge.
[5] A small hill near Khamolane.   [6] i.e. with their guns.
[7] Lepolesa, a son of Letsie I, was one of Letsie II's counsellors. Liphere had been one of Lerotholi's counsellors, but had remained at Likhoele with Letsie when Lerotholi had moved to Makeneng. Mofoka, Likupa and Mokoenehi were all chiefs who were subordinate to Letsie.
[8] i.e. of Masopha, who was in fact his great-uncle.
[9] Their horns were red because they had been jabbing the sandy soil.

With the white clay flying[1] and the gunpowder reeking!
It flashed, and it left a long trail of light,
60 The lightning flashed fire for people to be warmed.
It thundered, it burnt the villages at Sefikeng.[2]
Above all the villages of the doctors were burnt,
Mphu's and Khohlooa's were burnt.[3]
The lightning of Likhoele refuses the goats,
65 It refused to allow the kids to graze.[4]
The lightning struck clouds of dust at Sefikeng,
It struck the calves in the space before the kraal.
They scattered, did the people from Masopha's.
Then they appeared, and were holding a flag,[5]
70 Their lips were trembling,
They couldn't speak properly!
When they came they said:
'Greetings, Chief, Child of the Chief, Letsie!
You're a chief, child of this country of Mokhachane!
75 Masopha says, Chief, forgive him, he's erred.
Men often err and are forgiven.'
It was angry, the Crocodile of the family of 'MaNeo,[6]
It was angry, the Crocodile of the family of 'MaGoliathe,[7]
It was angry, its expression was not to be seen![8]
80 The comrade of the Black White-Spotted Regiment[9] was annoyed.
Tread gently, Great Soldier of the Beasts![10]

---

[1] Shields used to be smeared with white clay, and when they were struck this would come off in the form of powder. The allusion here, however, may be to gunsmoke as well.

[2] A mountain about 12 miles north-east of Thaba Bosiu.

[3] These men were not only doctors, but also headmen under Masopha. Their names are specifically mentioned because they are being mocked for the weakness of their protective medicines. Cp. Joel, i. 25–7, p. 189 above.

[4] Two interpretations of these lines immediately suggest themselves. (i) Letsie captured some of Masopha's goats and kids. Cp. line 67 below. (ii) The goats and kids represent Masopha's people, who had to shelter behind walls because of Letsie's guns. Cp. lines 98–9 below. However, there is a story (recounted to us by Mr. Pinda of Mafeteng) that one of Masopha's men crawled down to a spring to get some water, and there sheltered behind a rock. A goat was standing nearby. Malebanye, who was Letsie's crack shot, fired at the man, but killed the goat. It is possible that this incident is alluded to here.

[5] i.e. a white flag of surrender.

[6] 'MaNeo, i.e. Letsie's sister, Letšabisa.   [7] Another name for Letšabisa.

[8] Lit.: 'it covered its face', for its expression was so fierce.

[9] Another of Letsie's regiments.   [10] Another of Letsie's regiments.

Crocodile, spit,[1] son of Mokhachane!
As for answering, before he'd answered
They brought Moeketsi,
Driving him even with their knees:[2]   85
It even seemed they were running away![3]
    He stayed there throughout the third day,
Throughout the fourth he was burying them:
He's buried the people from Masopha's,
He's buried them because they were his.   90
He doesn't do battle with the people of his father,
He doesn't quarrel about land that's his own:
But he went to belabour the herdsmen,
Those stubborn little herdboys, Maboka and Moeketsi.[4]
    They say that we people from Matsieng are a rising cloud of dust. 95
We're a rising cloud, indeed we agree:
We arise like dust in every little pass.
    The goats at Khamolane are gelded,
For they're gelded by the Man-Eaters.[5]
    The swarthy avenger, Letsie,   100
Has avenged the head of his uncle.[6]
    Crocodile, drink water,[7] husband of Mahali,[8]
And return to your father's ruins.[9]

15. *Griffith*

Griffith (*c.* 1873–1939) was the younger brother of Letsie II, and was
named after Col. C. D. Griffith, the Governor's Agent in Basutoland at
the time of his birth. He was born at Likhoele, the home of his father,

[1] To spit on a person who has done wrong means to forgive him and treat him
gently. The man who spits thereby cleanses himself of anger and bitterness.
Cp. Posholi, iii. 163, p. 91 above.
[2] i.e. they were so anxious to hand him over.
[3] As soon as they had handed him over they fled.
[4] i.e. this was not a war between two different nations: Letsie had merely
punished his own followers.
[5] i.e. Masopha's people had been rendered powerless by Letsie's warriors.
[6] This stanza is reminiscent of Masopha's praises, vi. 22–7, p. 134 above.
But whereas Masopha could claim that in killing 'the chief of the Thembu' he
was avenging the death of Makhabane, Letsie was not in fact avenging any of his
uncles. Perhaps the *seroki* is merely conveying the idea that Letsie had avenged
his own initial humiliation at Khamolane.
[7] Lit.: 'put water in your mouth': i.e. Letsie should refresh himself before
setting out on his journey home.
[8] Mahali was his senior wife.   [9] i.e. to Likhoele.

Lerotholi, but was brought up at Masite, where his uncle Bereng had his village. In due course he was placed as chief at Phamong, in the Orange valley, in the Mohale's Hoek District. Close to his new village were the Phuthi of Mocheko, Moorosi's grandson, who bitterly resented the imposition of his authority, and who consistently refused to acknowledge it. In December 1897 Griffith and his followers attacked them, and for a short while they took refuge in the Herschel District.

In the following month, January 1898, Griffith was summoned by his father to take part in the war against Masopha. (See p. 209 above.) He arrived at Thaba Bosiu on 10 January, six days after Letsie's initial attack had been repelled. On 12 January, in combination with the rest of Lerotholi's forces, the two brothers inflicted a decisive defeat on Masopha, who then came to terms.

Soon after Griffith's return to Phamong the dispute with Mocheko flared up again, and finally, in 1902, the Government intervened and Mocheko was banished from the area.

In 1912 Griffith was baptized into the Roman Catholic Church. In the following year Letsie II died, and it was suggested that Griffith should act as regent for his young son, Tau. Griffith refused, and insisted that if he was to exercise the authority of the paramountcy then he should sit on the throne 'with both buttocks', and that his own children should succeed him. In the course of these negotiations Tau died, and Griffith's wishes were granted. He then went to live at Matsieng. After a quiet reign he died in 1939 at Maseru, and was succeeded by his son, Seeiso.

Two of his poems have been recorded by Mangoaela. The first relates exclusively to the campaign against Masopha. For the most part it is a straightforward narrative, but in the last twenty-three lines (72–94) the thread is broken. The second poem, with 443 lines, is the longest in this volume. It relates mainly to the campaign against Masopha, but also refers to the dispute with Mocheko (137–43, 307–53, 360–4); to the claims of Motšoene, Molapo's grandson, to the paramountcy (376–9); and to a quarrel with Letsie II which arose after Lerotholi's death in 1905 (416–28). Although there are several passages which may be regarded as substantial fragments of narrative, there is no clearly discernible over-all structure. The concluding stanza, however, in which the awesomeness of Griffith's anger is depicted in a series of colourful images, provides a most effective climax.

All authorities are agreed that Griffith did not compose these poems, and that he rarely chanted them, if at all. According to Mr. Stephen Pinda, of Mafeteng, the first poem was composed by Seliane Teba or Tapole Khoele, and the second by a man called Laistoko. In only one line (ii. 153) is the chief referred to in the first person singular outside direct speech.

(i)

The deluge of Mokhachane, the viper,
The hail of the little daughter of Nkoebe,

Why not say the little daughter of the Leopard?[1]
It departed from home when the rain was falling,
When the drizzle had made a mist,   5
And the warriors were afraid to ride.[2]
    He spoke with the Binders[3] on the previous day:
'Adjust the straps of your baggage in the night,
I'll ride at the first light of dawn,
When the fowls come down from their roosts.'   10
    It rode, the hail of Mokhachane,
It crossed the Maphutseng and the Makhaleng,
And how fearful was its flash!
It took the Thabana–Morena[4] road:
The child of the chief has come through the passes   15
In between Mafa and RaMabilikoe.[5]
    Crocodile, stir up the billows[6] on the veld,
Go and ascend the pass at Senei's.[7]
He met there a fugitive from battle,[8]
Went aside to him and asked him questions.   20
The fugitive reported and held nothing back:
'The child of the chief, Letsie, is overthrown:
Toi is still there, the child of Teele.'[9]
    The Binders' comrade was enraged and said:
'Lying, deceitful runaway,[10]   25
Hurry, go and report,
Put questions for me to the Chief to no purpose,[11]
Put questions for me to the father of 'MaNeo,[12]
Put questions for me to Lerotholi with care.'

---

[1] Griffith's senior wife, 'MaBatho, was the daughter of his uncle, Nkoebe. The Leopard was one of Nkoebe's praise-names.

[2] They were apprehensive because they were going to war.

[3] Griffith had given himself Moshoeshoe's praise-name of the Binder, and his regiment was therefore known as the Binders.

[4] A mountain in the Mafeteng District.

[5] Fokeng chiefs who lived at Thaba Tšoeu and Mathebe respectively. Cp. Maama, i. 37, p. 156 above.

[6] i.e. of dust.   [7] A village near Thaba Bosiu.

[8] Lit. 'one who throws away his little spears'.

[9] Toi, a Hlakoana counsellor of Letsie, evidently stood firm when his chief fled.

[10] For the idea that messengers are liars, see Jonathan, iii. 15, p. 184 above.

[11] i.e. go to Lerotholi and get an official report for me, even although there is little purpose in this.

[12] 'MaNeo, i.e. Letšabisa, Lerotholi's daughter.

30 'Binder', they said, 'Offsaddle the horses for grazing:
Most of the battle belongs to tomorrow.'[1]
When morning came we beheld the country:
The Binder, the cloud appeared in the east,
It arose as if there'd be rain.
35 He was like the moon that appears o'er snowy mountains,
He was like the stars of the morning when they appear,
Appearing at Makholo, in the mountains,
Appearing at Kokobe, at 'Malifatjana,[2]
A rosy dawn that vies with the Pleiades.[3]
40 A girl was laughing and said, 'Ha! Ha!'
Her mother was laughing and said, 'Ha! Ha!'
Her father was laughing and said, 'Ha! Ha!'[4]
They said: 'This 'MaLibili[5] has brought us trouble,
She's just called the serpent of the waters from the fields,
45 That the serpent of the waters should come to devour us!'
They fired at the Binder from the heights,
And indeed they were many.
He struck the earth, did the Chief of the Binders,
He struck the earth, and dongas were dug:
50 The little bushes were frosted in summer,
The little reed fences were burnt in the courtyards,
The leaves were shaken from the trees,
The sparrows abandoned their young in their homes,
Birds that nest in the trees![6]
55 In every direction fled all the Koena:
Some went down by Mokoallong,[7]
Some went down by Sefikeng.[8]
When the old men began to sit down,

[1] Griffith was so angry that he wanted to rush into battle at once, but his followers dissuaded him from this.
[2] Places near Griffith's village at Phamong. (Lines 37–8 have been added to Mangoaela's text: *Li hlaha Makholo, lithabeng, Li hlaha Kokobe, Malifatjana,* ...)
[3] Sometimes the Pleiades are still to be seen when dawn comes.
[4] They were laughing, apparently, because they were so confident of victory, and if this is so then the speech which follows is sarcastic.
[5] 'MaLibili was the woman who ran away from her husband into the Free State and who was captured there by Moeketsi, Masopha's son: see pp. 208–9 above.
[6] These are the fearful consequences of Griffith's anger.
[7] An area about eight miles north-east of Thaba Bosiu.
[8] A mountain about twelve miles north-east of Thaba Bosiu.

When they began to wipe off each other's sweat,
When they began to recover their breath, 60
They felt an overpowering tiredness.[1]
They brought out their snuff gourds and took their snuff,
And as they took snuff they began asking each other,
And the idiots asked each other apart,
They said: 'How tall is Griffith? 65
Griffith is nothing in that respect,
Even with your eyes you can jump over him.[2]
But his name is famous,
But he's brilliant in his pressing advance,
And he's brilliant when he stands on the brake,[3] 70
And he's brilliant in his progress onward.'
   The slow walker, the Beoana's[4] Crocodile,
The Crocodile of your family, Api and Makhaola![5]
   Someone was born in succession to Letsie,
But he's fought off the stick from his head:[6] 75
Today the stick has gone back to the tree.[7]
   The Khomphoro bird[8] of the Binders of Mokhachane
Flew and settled at the shop,
Close to the village of Senekane:[9]
There it's been seen by the red-skinned Bushman.[10] 80
   The viper, the flame of the Binders,
The one whose mouth is ever silent![11]
   The heaven of the one who towers above the people
Is that which has devoured Masopha's children,

---

[1] Lit. 'a tiredness which refused', i.e. which would not allow them to run any further.

[2] i.e. Griffith is so short that people can look over him with ease.

[3] Lit.: a drag applied to a wagon. To stand on the drag means to stand firm.

[4] 'the Beoana', i.e. the Sotho. See Moshoeshoe, ii. 5, p. 71 above.

[5] Two of his brothers.

[6] i.e., although younger than Letsie, Griffith has protected him against Masopha.

[7] i.e. Griffith has gained revenge: for the origin of this expression, see Joel, ii. 18–19, p. 203 above.

[8] A bird in a Sotho fable.

[9] Senekane, one of Masopha's sons, had his village near Khamolane, and there was a trading store there.

[10] This is probably a contemptuous reference to the manager of the store.

[11] This translation conveys the general meaning of *Ntinti le molomo tŝoanahali*, but the precise meaning is not known. Griffith was in fact a reserved and uncommunicative man.

85 It devoured its uncles, its friends,
 It devoured them and divided them among the birds.
   Lekena's[1] warrior, who addressed the Binders
 When quarrels were boiling.
   Indeed Tsangoane pulled out his man,
90 Tapole too came with his,
 Khajoane too came with his.[2]
   Masopha's children were showing off:
 They kept being killed as if they were mice.[3]
 It was said: 'You blundered by firing at the Chief!'[4]

(ii)

   Griffith, the warrior of Lerotholi,
 Is the lightning, Koena,
 The lightning of the house of 'MaBatho.[5]
 The lightning has built below rocks.[6]
5 The lightning departed from the cliff of the Maloti,
 Departing from Phamong and thundering already.
   The Binder, the hand of the son of Libenyane,[7]
 The muscles of the Lion of the Axes,[8]
 The fingers of the hand of Lerotholi!
10 The Binder of Mokhachane struck the mountain with his chest,
 The enormous mountain was just like sand:
 He hurled it down, and the cliffs tumbled!
   If countries could speak,
 Evidence would already be given by Boqate[9]
15 That the child of the chief is indeed a cannibal
 When he hears the sounding of the guns.

---

[1] Lekena, i.e. Lerotholi.

[2] Evidently Tsangoane, Tapole and Khajoane, who were all warriors in Griffith's regiments, had each killed an opponent. Their victims came out from the enemy ranks, either because they fell forward as they were shot, or else because they were drawn forward as Griffith's warriors pulled out their barbed spears.

[3] Lit. 'they not being mice': i.e. they let themselves be killed in large numbers as if they were mice being hunted, and yet they were not mice.

[4] 'the Chief', i.e. his elder brother Letsie.   [5] Griffith's senior wife.

[6] Griffith's village at Phamong was situated in a mountainous area. The image here is that of the lightning bird which builds its nest in the rocks.

[7] Libenyane, i.e. Mokhachane.   [8] i.e. Lerotholi.

[9] Boqate is part of the Berea plateau, and the area of Thaba Bosiu is clearly visible from it.

You're fearful, a wild animal, Chief;
You're just like a lion, son of Lerotholi,
Heaven of Peete and Mokhachane,
Lightning of Letsie,[1]   20
Crocodile, helper of Mohato,[2] Binder !
   Petty Chiefs and Chiefs, you've been amazed,
You've known the lightning of Lerotholi,
You've seen it blazing and thundering too,
Continually shaking out its flashes,   25
And the mist it carries on its shoulders !
   Binder, the lightning thundered in the Maloti:
Grandchild of Letsie, you're the lightning,
For the lightning departs from the Orange[3] and is angry,
As it goes it consumes the leaves of the trees.   30
All these countries are filled by the fire:
When we see the rocks ablaze
Thuathe and Boqate[4] are glowing red.
   You're always saying that the Koena are warlike:
Moshoeshoe once begat warriors,   35
And Letsie too begat warriors,
But today someone outstanding has appeared.
   At the time when the Koena left the village
He left with an angry heart,
His heart and his lungs were fighting as he left,   40
The sky and the earth were scolding each other.
The hail is leaving, having made a haze,
Its flash can be seen preceding the rain.
   He passed Senei's,[5] there was no one there.
Then anger itself arose within him,   45
The anger of courage, Mokhachane's Binder:
For his heart is small, but is full of courage ![6]
   The Binder, the Crocodile of the family of Makhaola,[7]
The crocodile-serpent of Lekena,[8] the rhino,
The buffalo of Libe and RaLetšabisa,[9]   50

---

[1] i.e. his elder brother.   [2] Mohato, i.e. Letsie I.
[3] Griffith's village at Phamong was in the Orange valley.
[4] Areas on the Berea plateau.   [5] A village near Thaba Bosiu.
[6] For the fact that Griffith was a small man, cp. i. 65–7, p. 217 above.
[7] His brother.   [8] Lekena, i.e. Lerotholi.
[9] RaLetšabisa, i.e. Lerotholi.

He instructed the Binders on the previous day
To adjust the straps of their baggage in the night.
 He started up when the cocks crowed,
The child of the chief became lightning:
55 It made its way along the hills,
It arrived, it climbed to the top of Boqate.
 The plateau thundered, the cliffs split away,
The trees had their leaves shaken off,
They were bitten by frost in midsummer;
60 For the hands' lightning[1] struck, Mokhachane's Binder,
The lightning gave trouble to those who begat it:
It struck the earth and made dongas appear,
The little reed fences were burnt in the courtyards,
People's houses were turned into walls![2]
65 There, you see, you people at Thuathe,
That the lightning of the hands is there, the Binder.
If you keep showing off, it'll eat you,
It's just nearly eaten both horses and people!
 Let the water-snake spit on you,[3] mend your ways,
70 And see that God too has helped you!
Heathens, today you should pray to Him,[4]
For a lion that was angry has spat on you,
And it almost swallowed you without chewing!
 The child of the chief is lightning, Koena,
75 For lightning has entered the midst of the haze,[5]
And its flash is red.
The guns became flames,
Men's faces were warmed.
 Peete's nephew[6] is just like a wildebeest,
80 He's just like a lion, the Binder, he roars,
When he jumps you might think him a leopard, the Koena!
For the Crocodile in the face is his parents indeed,

---

[1] i.e. guns. Cp. Jonathan, i. 231, p. 181 above.

[2] When huts are burnt the thatched roofs are destroyed but the walls remain standing. For this stanza, cp. i. 48–54, p. 216 above.

[3] i.e. accept Griffith's forgiveness. Cp. Posholi, iii. 163, p. 91 above; and Letsie II, line 82, p. 213 above.

[4] i.e. in gratitude.

[5] 'the haze', i.e. the battle, where there is a haze of gunsmoke.

[6] The Peete referred to here is not Moshoeshoe's grandfather, but Peete RaManella, the brother of Griffith's mother, Manella.

He resembles Peete[1] and Mokhachane,
The blacksmith of Mokhachane, the Binder,
The painted hyaena of Moshoeshoe!   85
   This day you Koena met,
You Beoana of Kali[2] and his people fought,
RaMahlolela,[3] the Chief, even clapped,
And said: 'Fight hard, my young men,
For you all belong to Mokhachane alone!'   90
   The whirlwind arose from the fields,
It came, it burned down the walls,[4]
The sparks burned the houses of the chief.
He heard the Hawks' Lion[5] in wonder say:
'What sort of child have you begotten today?   95
For me you've begotten a child with no sense!'
   The child of the chief has a heart like a rock!
Koena, your heart's like a hammer.
We see you when you leap into battle,
When you hurl yourself in among the bullets,   100
When you drive away the vultures and meerkats,
And the cats turn their backs and depart.[6]
   The lightning thundered, it gathered up its flash,
The lightning's face became wrinkled in a frown,
For its heart has remained to look for Moteki:[7]   105
The child of the Nguni is spoiling Masopha—
We don't even know Moteki's father!—
For it's he who's the starter of wars:
He begins them, and now he's afraid of them,
He keeps shrinking back into the rock-rabbit's shelter! 110
   Had you slipped away, Moteki,
Had you acted rashly and spied on the Binders,[8]
Then the birds would have eaten you,
We'd now be speaking with your spirit ended,

[1] Here Moshoeshoe's grandfather.
[2] i.e. the Sotho. See Moshoeshoe, ii. 5, p. 71 above.
[3] RaMahlolela, i.e. Masopha, Mahlolela being his daughter.
[4] i.e. the walls with which Masopha's people had fortified Khamolane.
[5] i.e. Masopha.   [6] i.e. Griffith's opponents run away.
[7] Moteki is said to have been one of those who chased Letsie over the rocks on the first day of the battle. Griffith has to return to Phamong, but he would dearly have wished to remain and to seek out Moteki.
[8] i.e. had you been so foolish as to detach yourself from the main body of Masopha's warriors.

115 Your flesh would have dried on your bones,
    Your blood would have been drunk by red ants,
    For you always pour scorn on the people from Matsieng.[1]
        This fault, Moteki, you should know,
    For even there, at the home of God, a claim will be made against
                                                                you,
120 The heads of these people will accuse you!
        Crocodile, despatch Moiloa to the Chief,
    Despatch Moiloa, the son of Mabeleng,
    To give Lerotholi a proper report;
    But Moiloa confuses affairs,
125 He quarrels when he returns from Leshoboro's.[2]
        The lightning of the family of Marakabei[3] is giving trouble,
    From the walls they fire at him when near:
    Close he has pressed, the flame darts out,
    The walls he demolishes to the ground.[4]
130   The heaven of Libe and RaMathalea,[5] the lightning of Letsie,
    The lightning appears on top of the plateau,
    At the ruins of Masopha and Makhobalo:[6]
    Its flash it planted at Tšoanamakhulo.[7]
        Lightning of the family of 'MaNeo,[8] scold,[9]
135 These people have long been Mokhachane's:
    It singed them with its flash, the bird of lightning.[10]
        Griffith, the warrior of Lerotholi,
    When in stubbornness he does a thing again,
    He does what he did before,
140 Because here, at Nte's, we receive no greetings.[11]

---

[1] i.e. the sons of Letsie I and their adherents.

[2] Moiloa, a Koena, once lived under Chief Leshoboro Majara. Then he attached himself to Lerotholi, who sent him to assist Griffith. He was placed on the Makhaleng river, at Morifi Drift, where he stirred up quarrels by demanding more land. Evidently he was a poor messenger too.

[3] One of his brothers.

[4] Lit.: 'The walls he demolishes to the drainage-holes at their base.'

[5] RaMathalea, i.e. Posholi, Mathalea being his daughter.

[6] Makhobalo was a son of Moshoeshoe's second house. The ruins of his village are said to be on the Khamolane heights. The ruins of one of Masopha's former villages are said to be in the same area.

[7] A stream in Masopha's area.   [8] i.e. his sister, Letšabisa.

[9] i.e. scold, but do no more; treat your opponents gently.

[10] Lit. 'the bird': every Sotho, however, would immediately understand that the reference is to the bird of lightning.

[11] Nte's was a village on the left bank of the Orange, opposite Griffith's home at Phamong. It was occupied by the Phuthi of Mocheko, who bitterly resented the

The lightning strikes its opponents' villages,
It strikes the villages of those who're puffed up,
It's struck Mocheko's, in amid the rocks,
It's hit Senekane's little hovel, in full view,[1]
In the sight of Mojela, Nkoebe and Seeiso,[2]   145
In the sight of Lekena and the Furious Warrior.[3]
    The news we heard from a woman of Korokoro,
Of Maama's,[4] who said as we passed:
'Whither are you riding, RaNtšebo's[5] Binder?
Sefikeng is no longer Letsie's,   150
Mateka has taken it, and so has Moeketsi,[6]
And Tsoili-Tsoili[7] is already his!'
    Now I, 'MaNthe's[8] son, became angry.
The wild beast silently moved its lips,
The white-spotted leopard of Letšabisa's[9] family!   155
At all this country it gazed around:
He's looked at Qoaling and Qeme,[10]

---

imposition of Griffith's authority over them. In December 1897, shortly before the war against Masopha, Griffith had attacked Mocheko, and the incident was described by the local Assistant Commissioner in the following terms: 'In December the young chief Griffith made a raid on the village of Mocheko, chief of the Baphuti, and looted the place; the cause of this was of long standing. It appears that Mocheko had slaughtered a stray ox, the owner of which found this out and complained to the Paramount Chief, who ordered that Mocheko was to be fined. He was called by Griffith, who was instructed by the Paramount Chief to try the case, but refused to attend court; the summons was repeated from time to time with the same result. Griffith became exasperated and took matters into his own hands and raided his village. Mocheko fled through Quthing district to Herschel.' (*Basutoland Annual Report for 1897–1898*, p. 35.) Griffith 'does what he did before', because he does to Masopha what he did to Mocheko.

[1] Senekane was one of Masopha's sons, and his village on the Berea plateau is still known as Senekane's.
[2] All three were Griffith's uncles.
[3] Lekena was his father, Lerotholi: the Furious Warrior was his uncle, Bereng.
[4] The Korokoro valley was in the ward of his uncle, Maama.
[5] RaNtšebo, i.e. Lerotholi, Ntšebo being his daughter.
[6] Mateka is said to have been one of Moeketsi's followers. Moeketsi was the son of Masopha whose surrender was demanded by Lerotholi.
[7] An area about two miles east of the Berea mission station.
[8] 'MaNthe was Moshoeshoe's senior wife, 'MaMohato, Nthe being their daughter. Griffith was not in fact her son, but her great-grandson.
[9] Letšabisa was Griffith's sister.
[10] Two extensive plateaux which are visible from the Thaba Bosiu area.

He looked at Litšoeneng, at RaTšosane's.[1]
    When the chief gives commands he acts quickly:
160 He summoned Matlabe and RaMoroko,
He summoned Lesala and Nkamohi.[2]
When he left them he was ill at ease;
The chief whose hair and forehead were unmatched,[3]
The chief herdboy looked wild and disturbed!
165   Pay attention, listen and hear,
Woman in the fields at Molibeli's:[4]
Whence comes the sound of these guns?
Are they sounding on the plateau,
Or are they sounding at Qopo?[5] Where are they sounding?
170 'This year they're sounding at Mokoallong,[6]
They sounded, they caused us grief.'
    When it burned down the villages, the fearsome beast,
It burned at Thuathe and Tsoili-Tsoili,
It burned at Mehopung and Khamolane.[7]
175   Lion, arise from the grass at the Sebapala![8]
The wild beast roars in the soft, steady rain:
The shower's made a mist.
The serpent of the waters left the Orange in cold weather,
As it left the snow was falling:[9]
180 It was like the lightning that's just thundered in the Maloti!
The lightning thundered in the summer, the Binder,
The bird-scarers cowered in their shelters!
    The son of Moshoeshoe, the young buffalo,
The hard-horned buffalo, the Binder,
185 The youth of 'MaTšoeunyane's family,
The youth of his grandmother's family,

---

[1] Litšoeneng is an area on the Berea plateau: RaTšosane, a Molibeli chief, once lived there.
[2] All these men were Griffith's adherents.
[3] i.e. his brow was furrowed in anger.
[4] 'at Molibeli's', i.e. at RaTšosane's.
[5] An area near Tsoili-Tsoili.
[6] An area on the Berea plateau, near Senekane's.
[7] All these are places on or around the Berea plateau.
[8] The *seroki* now goes back to Griffith's departure from home. The Sebapala is a river which joins the Orange not far from Phamong.
[9] It is most unlikely that snow was in fact falling when Griffith left home, for these events occurred at the height of summer. No doubt the poet is merely heightening the drama.

Of the family of his father's aunt![1]
   The star of the morning of Letšabisa's[2] family,
The star that appears with the red-glowing dawn
Appeared when the cocks were crowing.   190
   Fako,[3] the silent one of Mokhachane's son,
Doesn't Fako usually keep silent
As if he isn't listening?[4]
   The Binder's a cloud that appears over there,
The cloud appeared there, it looked towards there,   195
The fierce warrior of the son of RaThotholo,[5]
The fierce warrior of Libe and Moshoeshoe:
The Binder, the cloud appeared in the east,
The cloud appeared with the regiments, the Binder,
It inclined in a northward direction.   200
   The sweeper of the people from Mokhachane's
Swept up the Seekers and the Binders.[6]
He called to them with a mighty shout,
As he held a stick and a kerrie,
And also a bundle of spears,   205
Spears that filled the whole bag.
   He told the Binders to follow him behind,
Young men who were carrying guns around,
And among them were Matlabe and RaMoroko,
And Nkau and Mohlouoa.[7]   210
   The cloud thundered through the night, the Binder,
It moved in full view, it looked towards Sefikeng:
When facing Khamolane
The lightning thundered, its flash it concealed,
It thundered, it deepened its thunder,   215

[1] 'MaTšoeunyane was Moshoeshoe's sister, and is clearly the person referred to as Griffith's grandmother in line 186 and as his father's aunt in line 187. This use of kinship terms in Sotho is perfectly normal.
[2] Letšabisa was his sister.
[3] Fako was a name given to Col. C. D. Griffith, who was Governor's Agent in Basutoland from 1871 to 1881. The Chief, being named after the Agent, could also be called Fako.
[4] For Griffith's taciturnity, cp. i. 82, p. 217 above.
[5] i.e. Setenane, a descendant of Mokhachane's elder brother, Libe.
[6] The Seekers were the regiment of the Phuthi chief, Moorosi. The name came to be applied to Phuthi warriors in general, and when Griffith went to Phamong many of these men fell under his command. To 'sweep up' here means 'to assemble'.
[7] All these men were his adherents. Nkau was a very junior brother.

At last it could be heard at Sefikeng.
The plains trembled and so did the hills,
It seemed as if the mountains were tumbling down!
The rhino of Lekena,[1] the black cow's killer,[2]
220 The carnivore roared roars and was terrible,
The lion roared when it saw them near,
It darted out, it meant to devour them.
      They scattered, the people from Masopha's,
They scattered throughout all the village,
225 They dispersed, they behaved like finches
When they hear the switch in the field![3]
      The Binders' wild beast was disgusted,
In disgust it attempted to bring them together.
They mumbled in fear, the people of Masopha's,
230 They mumbled in fear as they tried to flee,
But in fact they were going to the ranks of his army,
Where the Binders would stab them as they turned their backs!
      The Binder, the snow fell on people in trouble
On top of the plateau.[4]
235   The Binder aroused the winter wind
That the cyclone should shatter the beams,
The ancient supports of the village of Masopha.
      There, you see, you people from Masopha's,
The Lion of the Orange is full of valour!
240 You intend it to be said that Fako[5] detests you,
But in fact he's claiming his family's cow's hide,[6]
For he's claiming the bedding of Lekena.[7]
      The warrior from there at Moorosi's[8]
Is standing with an army on top of the plateau:

---

[1] Lekena, i.e. Lerotholi.

[2] This is said to have been one of Moshoeshoe's praise-names, but its origin is unknown.

[3] Bird scarers used to be armed with long rods, from the ends of which they flicked pellets of mud. When the finches heard the swish of the rod they flew away.

[4] i.e. Griffith attacked Masopha's people on the Berea plateau. Cp. Jonathan, i. 206, p. 180 above.

[5] Fako, i.e. Griffith. See line 191 above.

[6] i.e. his family's land. Cp. Joel, ii. 47, p. 204 above.

[7] Lekena, i.e. Lerotholi. Bedding, which consists of karosses, also stands as a metaphor for land.

[8] Moorosi was the Phuthi chief who had been killed in 1879. Griffith was now living in Moorosi's country.

He objects when anyone in the distance goes aside,   245
Anyone of the enemy in the distance.[1]
  The son of Lerotholi, the giant of the Seekers![2]
  A woman laughed, a hearty laugh,
Heartily she laughed, and said:
'Look at the cloud that comes from Rakhoiti's!'[3]   250
Look, the cloud appeared at Makhoarane,[4]
Coming from Kokobe, from 'Malifatjana:[5]
Quickly it makes the rainbow[6] advance,
The Seekers and the Binders may be seen!
  The Binders have stabbed each other with answers,   255
When one says: 'I shall kill first!'[7]
The Seekers too are preparing to fight,
They bore witness that the Chief was angry.
  The great spotted beast of the son of Mohato,[8]
The great spotted beast with red ears,   260
The great spotted beast with the colours of a leopard
Devoured the duiker, but left its head![9]
  Among all the animals of the earth
The ones with great necks are not famous:
It's even the case that the lion or hyaena   265
Is surpassed by the elephant only in thickness,
And not in the fighting of war.[10]
  Fako[11] resembles the warriors of old,
He resembles Thesele[12] and Makhabane,
And Peete and Mokhachane too.   270
  The bull of the Binders is beautiful, light brown, and shot with
                      white,
The bull of you Binders and Stubborn Warriors.[13]
The bull stabs others in just the right spot,

[1] i.e. he fires at any enemy warrior who comes out of cover.
[2] For the Seekers, see line 202 above.   [3] A valley near Matsieng.
[4] The mountain overlooking Morija.   [5] Places near Phamong.
[6] 'the rainbow', i.e. Griffith's regiments.
[7] i.e. the warriors were arguing among themselves as to which one would be the first to kill an opponent.
[8] Mohato, i.e. Letsie, whose son was Lerotholi.
[9] i.e. Griffith defeated Masopha, but did not kill him.
[10] i.e. Griffith may have been short, but he was a great warrior.
[11] Fako, i.e. Griffith. See line 191 above.
[12] Thesele, i.e. Moshoeshoe.
[13] The Stubborn Warriors were another of Griffith's regiments.

It's stabbed the bull of the Leopards[1] in the shoulder,
275   That of the Leopards has even fled:
Yet still it is said that it's very courageous,[2]
That it hurled the other one[3] over the rocks!
      The Binder's a lion, the son of Lerotholi,
The lion goes around like a ghost[4] in the mists.
280   It took two steps, the Lion of the Binders,
It took two steps to cross the Tsoaing,[5]
And when it arrived at the Phuthiatsana[6]
It went up the river, and then it went down,
Hearing a row from the top of the plateau
285   When the Leopards were fighting on their own
In a wrangle about a man killed in battle,[7]
And their chief was giving commands:
'Build up the walls and make them strong,
Fako's now coming at full gallop!'
290   It was then that they felt afraid
And their hair stood on end!
      Someone spoke who was carrying a spear-bag,
With an old spliced gun, and said:
'Indeed 'MaLibili[8] has brought us trouble!
295   The warrior of Lekena[9] and of RaTšenolo[10]
Is standing exposed[11] to the bullets.
We fire at him in vain: he just stands!'
      The Kholumolumo devoured the people,

---

[1] The Leopards were Moeketsi's warriors: their 'bull' was Moeketsi himself.
[2] The reference here is to 'the bull of the Leopards'. The word 'Yet' has been added to the translation to make the sense clear.
[3] 'the other one', i.e. Griffith's elder brother, Letsie.
[4] The verb *ho poka*, 'to go about as a ghost', is derived from the Afrikaans *spook*. The idea of a ghost, being taken from the Afrikaners, is entirely different from the Sotho idea of an ancestral spirit. A ghost is angry, terrifying and mysterious.
[5] The river which forms part of the boundary between the Maseru and Mafeteng Districts. Griffith was travelling so fast that he took only two steps to cross it.
[6] The river which runs below Khamolane and Thaba Bosiu.
[7] i.e. more than one warrior was claiming to have killed him.
[8] For 'MaLibili, see i. 43, p. 216 above.
[9] Lekena, i.e. Lerotholi.
[10] i.e. Griffith's uncle, Theko, Tšenolo being his daughter.
[11] It is impossible to reproduce in English the play on RaTšenolo and *tšenoleng*, 'in an exposed position'.

The people have ended in the monster's stomach![1]
The widow there at Masopha's   300
Looks to Phamong when she weeps, and says:
'A child has been eaten by the Lion of the Binders!'
For the Binder's like a wildebeest in fighting,
He resembles a lion, and he's terrible!
   The child of the chief has a cockade for valour,   305
A cockade for driving off the Leopards.
There too, whence he comes, the Lion of the Binders
Leaves Mocheko at Moeaneng:[2]
Today he's come to scatter the Leopards.
   How fond those people are of talking   310
When they say that Fako should depart from Phamong!
At the time when Fako departs from Phamong
Their horses will stick in the mud,
They'll stick in the mud as far as their knees,
They're stuck in the blood of young men: 315
Perhaps it's then they'll remove him![3]
   Griffith no longer speaks with people,
Today Fako's colour has darkened,
He was angered by the men from Moorosi's
When they told him to leave Phamong.   320
The face of the Lion can't be regarded,
The commoners can't even look at him!
   The child of the chief, of the Lion of the Axes,[4]
Passed the night with his gun cleaned
When he heard there was now a dispute.   325
When the messenger reported to the mighty beast
The rhino called out to the Binders.[5]
   The white cliffs' hawk doesn't rest:
It only rests when there's peace.
   He created a stir by sending out his messengers,   330

---

[1] In a well-known Sotho story the monster Kholumolumo devours almost every living thing, both man and beast.

[2] For the Phuthi chief Mocheko see lines 137–43 above. Moeaneng, or Moyeni, is the headquarters of the present District of Quthing, and is now more generally known as Quthing.

[3] i.e. if the Phuthi try to drive Griffith away from Phamong many of them will be killed.

[4] i.e. of Lerotholi.

[5] i.e. Griffith began mustering his warriors when he heard that Mocheko would not answer his summons. See line 140 above.

While the men were still silent, and hadn't yet spoken.
He sent a third messenger,
Khomonala[1] went to call them; and he said:
'Please go to Mocheko, go and call him:
335   And if he refuses, come back and tell me.'
        The lightning thundered while still sitting down,[2]
It thundered, it stretched out its wings;
For the lightning strikes by choosing places,[3]
For it strikes at the villages of princes.
340   It's been doctored with powerful horns:[4]
Lerotholi's will always keep striking:
It struck at Mocheko's at first,
And then went to stab home its flash at Qiloane.[5]
        The musical bows[6] became silent in the caves:
345   Such is the lightning that's sent by sorcery!
        Yet the lightning's just scattered the Phuthi:
If Mocheko really eats the ox of Makhube,[7]
Remember:[8] a boy ate the bone of a snake,
The bone of the fish[9] then stuck in his throat,
350   Even to this day it's still with him!
        The lion that missed an Ndebele
Missed a man who'd been ordered to be brave,
Who'd been told to go and destroy.[10]
        The herdsman of the cattle of RaMahlolela[11]

---

[1] Evidently one of Griffith's adherents.

[2] This may mean that Griffith inspired terror in Mocheko even before taking action; or that he did not have to go far or exert himself much in order to defeat him.

[3] i.e. it strikes discriminately.

[4] i.e. it has been strengthened by powerful medicines (which are kept in horns).

[5] A small conical hill near Thaba Bosiu.

[6] More precisely a *thomo* is 'a stringed bow on which a calabash shell is fixed' (Paroz).

[7] Makhube was the man whose stray ox was slaughtered by Mocheko: see line 140, p. 222 above. He was one of Griffith's adherents, and lived near Maphutseng.

[8] The word 'Remember' has not been translated from the Sotho, but has been added to make the sense clear. Cp. Masopha, iv. 97, p. 130 above.

[9] The bone of the snake and the bone of the fish are not two distinct bones, but the same, since in Sotho thought the fish and the snake are closely associated.

[10] Perhaps one of Mocheko's men was sent to kill Griffith, but was almost killed himself. The incident alluded to is no longer remembered.

[11] RaMahlolela, i.e. Masopha, Mahlolela being his daughter.

Scampered away and then left them   355
When he saw the menacing long cloud appear,
When the cloud appeared and spread over the plateau.
    Lekena's[1] son's a foundation stone,
The child of the ancestors' head,[2] the Binder.
    This day he's brought harmony and friendship   360
By destroying the thorns and the stumps of reed,[3]
For he's beaten Mocheko and RaMahlolela.
    It's clear that they'd formed a plan,
Intending to capture this land.[4]
    Even in the days of long long ago   365
Chief Moorosi and his people were beaten;[5]
Even the Boers didn't take it;
Even Shaka's withdrawn from here;[6]
Even in the Battle of the Canons
They were always giving trouble to RaLetšabisa,   370
But he made them go back, they didn't take it;[7]
Neither have Matiwane and his people taken it,
For Posholi was always killing them.[8]
    The support of the pot in the fire is there in Lesotho today,
The prop of the land of Lerotholi.   375
    As for the young bull that bellows in the east,
Let the sharpeners of its horns send it here,
That Lerotholi's buffalo should stab it:
The mighty-browed buffalo stabs.[9]

[1] Lekena, i.e. Lerotholi.   [2] i.e. the ancestors' favourite.
[3] i.e. he has removed the thorns and the stumps of reed from the paths, where they might hurt people's feet.
[4] This was not in fact the case.
[5] This line may refer to Moorosi's original submission to Moshoeshoe during the *lifaqane*, or to his defeat in 1879: in neither case was he trying to take the Sotho's land.
[6] Shaka, the Zulu chief, never entered Lesotho in person, but his regiments invaded the country during the *lifaqane*. Their object was not to acquire land, but to plunder cattle, and, having done this, they withdrew.
[7] The Battle of the Canons was presumably an engagement in the Gun War in which Lerotholi took part, but it is not known which one.
[8] The Ngwane of Matiwane invaded the Sotho's country c. 1822, and stayed there until their migration in 1828. For most of this time they lived in peace with Moshoeshoe's adherents, and it was only in 1828 that hostilities broke out between them. Posholi then helped Moshoeshoe to repel them from Thaba Bosiu, and later tried to plunder some of their cattle as they departed from Lesotho.
[9] The young bull in the east was Motšoene, the offspring of Josefa, Molapo's

380   The bravery of Fako is incomparable,
       He may be likened to the lightning, the Koena,
       The sorcerer's lightning for the soldiers.[1]
           The warrior has waxed powerful on the plateau:
           They even called the Koodoo[2] to mediate
385   When Fako proved too strong for the people from Moeketsi's.
           He's white, the vulture from the family of Letšabisa,
       The vulture is beautiful when he's red:
       The hands of the vulture are red, the Binder,
       His claws have been filled with blood.
390   He resembles a hawk that has just struck the doves,
       But he himself has just struck the Leopards.
           It's always being said that the Leopard is brave,
           But[3] under the sun there's only one warrior:
       He lives at Phamong, the son of Lerotholi.
395   The sun rose, it chased off the darkness,
       The people could look around afar.
           Here is the lion on a ridge in the plain,
           Its eye is flashing with anger.
       The warriors were bereft of thought
400   When they saw the lion approaching.
       A European trader was even invited,
       It was said he should help to command the army![4]
           Here is the lion on a ridge in the plain:
           As it entered Thabaneng[5] it was running already,
405   It was thinking already of chewing the bone.

---

son, and Senate, Letsie's daughter. Had Moshoeshoe's wishes been followed
Motšoene would have succeeded Letsie as Paramount Chief, but most of the
Sotho wanted Lerotholi instead. Nevertheless some of Motšoene's adherents
still encouraged him in his pretensions to the chieftainship, and the *seroki* here
gives his reaction to this.

   [1] i.e. to his enemies he is as fearsome as lightning sent by witchcraft.
   [2] The Koodoo, i.e. Lerotholi.
   [3] The word 'But' has not been translated from the Sotho, but has been added
to make the sense clear.
   [4] The trader concerned was probably the manager of the store at Khamolane.
It is unlikely that he was invited to help in the command of Masopha's army,
and the poet is no doubt merely indicating the extent of the panic and confusion among Masopha's followers.
   [5] Thabaneng, an area about five miles south-east of Teyateyaneng, was under
Masopha's control.

The son of the Repeater[1] ignores his loads,[2]
He's utterly fearless, the son of Lerotholi,
He's fond of dashing into battle.
    The commoner avoids the dust of the bullets,
Saying he's afraid that they'll kill him: 410
He means he fears death, and where he will end,
When even Jesus, the Son of God,
Had his greatness disputed by the Jews:
They painfully stretched his arms apart.
Where will this commoner end?[3]   415
    Fish, wriggle quickly into the mud, Koena,
The water's dried up, as you see, Binder.[4]
    Ever since man appeared from the reed,[5]
The counsellors' way is to ruin plans:
In the affairs of Fako and the people of Matsieng   420
Words were spoken by Mochekoane and Mahao,
They were arrogant when all was well,
When Fako's affairs were about to be spoilt![6]
    That trick we saw from the start:
It's said that the buck should return above   425
For it's there that it's tended.[7]
    The rhino's not asleep, it's lying down:
It still wants to raise up its head.[8]
    The Crocodile of the Orange lies down at the river.
The Crocodile doesn't often go into the water,   430
It lies down outside, in a sunny place.[9]

[1] i.e. of Moshoeshoe's brother, Mohale.
[2] i.e. he is confident that he can carry out his task, in spite of the difficulties involved. Cp. Maama, iv. 72, p. 168 above.
[3] i.e. why should a commoner worry about being killed, when even Jesus Christ was killed?
[4] The *seroki* now turns to the events which followed the death of Lerotholi in 1905. When a pool dries up a fish must wriggle into the mud to save its life. Similarly Griffith must exert himself now that Lerotholi is dead and his protective influence has been removed.
[5] According to one Sotho myth the first men came out of a reed bed.
[6] Mahao and Mochekoane had been Lerotholi's advisers, and were now Letsie II's advisers. There was a boundary dispute between Letsie and Griffith, and the poet lays the blame for this on the advice given by these two men.
[7] i.e. it was suggested that Griffith's area should be confined to the mountains.
[8] i.e. although he is not fighting, Griffith is not content with his position: he still wishes to assert his claims.
[9] These lines merely describe Griffith's position at Phamong.

The water-snake's always driving off people,
Even Mocheko stays at home no more !¹
Binder, become angry, let the ocean roar,
435   Let the wind appear everywhere on earth,
Let it blow down the Phuthiatsana,
Let the frost come down, let the bushes be blighted,
Let the storm rain down, let the rivulets be filled,
Let the trees be uprooted from the ground,
440   Let the frogs be trapped by the downrushing debris,
Let the initiates' mistress² be seen by men too,³
Let the initiates' mistress turn into a rock,
Let her turn into a deep and mysterious secret !⁴

16. *Lerotholi Mojela*

Lerotholi Mojela (1895–1961) was the son of Mojela, the senior son in
Letsie's sixth house. Mojela's ward was in the Mafeteng District. During
the First World War Lerotholi was given a certain limited authority over
the 1,400 Sotho who served in France in the Native Labour Corps.
However, neither he nor any other member of the Corps was allowed to
take an active part in the fighting. On his return to Basutoland he was
awarded a medal for Meritorious Service, and shortly afterwards, in 1921,
he was placed as chief at Tebang, within his father's ward.

When Mojela died in February 1925 a dispute arose over the succession. There was no surviving male issue in the first four houses, and
Lerotholi was the senior son in the fifth house. But Molapo, who was the
senior son in the sixth house, and who had been his father's favourite,
claimed that Mojela's marriage to Lerotholi's mother had been invalid,
and that in any event he himself should be regarded as the adopted son of
'MaMakhobalo, Mojela's senior wife. The ensuing litigation was dragged
on by one appeal after another, and was only concluded in June 1928,
when the Judicial Committee of the Privy Council gave its decision in
favour of Lerotholi.

During his long exercise of authority he came to be regarded almost as a
model chief by the Government. In 1961 he died and was succeeded by

¹ Mocheko had been unable to settle down under Griffith, and in 1902 the
Government had banished him from his former home.
² A *motanyane* is a woman who wears a hideous costume and performs
certain functions in the girls' initiation school.
³ It was taboo for a *motanyane* to be seen by men.
⁴ According to Paroz, *tanka ea boliba* is a 'mysterious thing mentioned at the
initiation of girls'.

his son, Sentle. A year later his daughter, Tabitha 'MaSentle, was married to the present King of Lesotho, Moshoeshoe II.

His praises, as recorded by Mangoaela, consist of a single *mélange*, which relates to the First World War (lines 1–108); his placing at Tebang (109–29); the blessings of his rule (130–4); his dispute with Molapo (135–54); his work in the Basutoland National Council (155–7); his position near the borders of Basutoland (158–63); the fairness of his complexion (164–8); the First World War again (169–72); and finally, in the last exclamatory stanza, the 'light' which he gave to his fellow chiefs. The whole poem is of particular interest in that it is the first in Mangoaela's collection to relate to a chief who had not actually fought in battle; but so powerful was the tradition in which the *seroki* was working that he was bound to suggest that Lerotholi was a fearsome warrior—so fearsome that even the Kaiser begged for mercy when he heard that he was being sent against him.

When we visited Tebang in November 1968 everyone whom we consulted assured us that Lerotholi himself was not the composer of these praises, but no one could remember the *seroki*'s name.

The pure white star[1] of the Caster Down,[2]
The pure white star of RaMakhobalo,[3]
Of the family of Jonathan and Mofoka![4]
    At the time of the War of France,[5] at sea,[6]
The child of the chief was made a sacrifice,   5
He was made a sacrifice with a sweet-smelling savour.[7]
Moshoeshoe was amazed on high[8]
And said: 'Mojela and the Binder[9] do something amazing.
Has ever a chief been made a sacrifice?'
    The stray bullet of the Binder's children   10
Is the bullet of Bereng and Seeiso.[10]

[1] Lerotholi was noted for the lightness of his complexion.
[2] The Caster Down was Lerotholi's father, Mojela, who dislodged, or 'cast down', a European force from the mountain of Phoqoane during the Gun War.
[3] RaMakhobalo, i.e. Mojela.   [4] His brothers.
[5] i.e. the First World War.
[6] 'at sea', because this was where Europeans were believed to live. Cp. Maama, i. 32–4, p. 156 above.
[7] The idea of someone being made a sacrifice comes from Christianity, and the language of this line is taken from the Epistle to the Ephesians, v. 2, where Christ is said to have given himself to be for us 'an offering and a sacrifice to God for a sweetsmelling savour'.
[8] Moshoeshoe is thought of as being in heaven.
[9] The Binder, i.e. Griffith, who was then Paramount Chief.
[10] Griffith's sons.

When first it was taken from the bandolier
It was fired, it was sent towards the Cape and the Bay;[1]
As it went it was seen from afar, making flames,
15 We commoners followed behind,
The warriors began for it the war-song.
 The son of Mojela, who towers above the people,
The heaven to the people of Mojela's!
When first the lightning began to shine,
20 The lightning of your family, Maama and Seeiso,[2]
Of the family of Jonathan and Mofoka,[3]
It shone, it left a flashing trail;
The flash of the lightning crossed the seas!
There is thunder from the lightning of RaMakhaola,[4]
25 Of your family, Josefa[5] and Sekhonyana,[6]
Of the family of Mojela and Nkoebe.[7]
 The Kaiser begged with tears in his eyes:
'Lekena[8] and Government, forgive me!
Forgive me, Chiefs, I've erred,
30 I've stung the Government's eyes with sand!'
 The heavens of Mojela are fearsome,
The flash of the lightning enters the heart!
 The drop[9] of Mojela smells of the rain,
It smells of the rain of a mighty storm
35 That seized the Bushmen at sea:
The poor little Bushmen once ran into trouble![10]
 Mohato's[11] defender, Lekena,
The Koena defended: we were saved.

---

[1] The Cape is Cape Town. The Bay (i.e. Algoa Bay) is Port Elizabeth.
[2] Maama and Seeiso, both sons of Letsie, were his uncles.
[3] His brothers.
[4] RaMakhaola was originally a teknonym given to Lerotholi, the son of Letsie, for one of his sons was called Makhaola. Lerotholi Mojela, having been named after him, could also be referred to by his other names. Here RaMakhaola may be either the son of Letsie, or else Lerotholi Mojela himself.
[5] The senior son of Molapo.   [6] The son of Bereng Letsie.
[7] Nkoebe Letsie was one of Lerotholi Mojela's uncles.
[8] i.e. Lerotholi Mojela himself. Lekena was the most popular praise-name of Lerotholi, the son of Letsie. Cp. fn. 4 above.
[9] There is a play on words here, for Lerotholi, apart from being a proper name, also means 'a drop of water'.
[10] Lit.: 'The poor little Bushmen once saw it!' *le*, 'it', in this line stands for *letsatsi*, 'day', i.e. the day of distress. 'The poor little Bushmen' are the Germans.
[11] Mohato, i.e. Letsie.

He was fond of the guns, was RaMakhaola,[1]
Indeed he once followed the war, 40
He followed it even to Europe!
The tawny lioness of Mohato, Lekena—
Why the tawny lioness, when he wasn't a woman?—
Say a powerful spring of the Great Lake,
Of the lake of Tšakholo,[2] at the rushes. 45
    The Crocodile, the otter of Tšakholo, the child of the mighty chief,
The Crocodile, the otter of your family, Seeiso,
Of the family of Nkoebe and Maama,
Of the family of Thaabe and Sekhobe,
Of the family of Peete and Mokhachane, 50
Of the family of Moholobela and Theko,
Of the family of Masopha and Lepolesa,
Of the family of Sempe and Mohlakana![3]
    The Crocodile passed over the waters by ship,
For the letter arrived at night,[4] 55
It came to the Binder, to RaSeeiso,[5]
Saying: 'Come and help, O Koena, you're a chief!
There, on the sea, the chiefs are quarrelling,
The Kaiser's fighting even with heads,[6]
The commoners have ended in the sea!'[7] 60
    The Government hurled telegrams on every side,
The wire of Lesotho was broken!
Yet the news had already arrived at Lekena's,[8]
As we saw when the chief was gathering his strength:
The Crocodile's expression was always changing, 65
The Crocodile of the family of Maama and Seeiso.[9]
    As time went by, a little while later,
The telegram arrived at Matsieng,

---

[1] Here RaMakhaola is clearly Lerotholi Mojela himself.
[2] Tšakholo, which means 'Great Lake', was in Mojela's ward.
[3] Seeiso, Nkoebe, Maama, Thaabe, Sekhobe, Theko and Lepolesa were all paternal uncles. Moholobela (son of Seeiso), Sempe (son of Nkoebe) and Mohlakana (son of Lerotholi) were all cousins. The Masopha mentioned here is probably Masopha II, the grandson of Moshoeshoe's son, Masopha.
[4] A clear indication of its urgency.   [5] i.e. to Griffith.
[6] i.e. the Kaiser has exhausted all his weapons, and his people are now butting with their heads. An alternative translation, favoured by Mangoaela, is 'with great cruelty'.
[7] i.e. they have been drowned.
[8] 'at Lekena's', i.e. at Lerotholi Mojela's.   [9] His paternal uncles.

It was read to the Binder, to the father of Seeiso.
70   The Paramount Chief replied
And said: 'Runner of great speed,
Please go to Lesotho's protecting peg,[1]
To my father Mojela,[2] the Caster Down,
That he should send Lekena RaMakhaola,
75   For Lekena's the parent of my children,
He's the parent of Bereng and Seeiso:[3]
He's the necklace-charm[4] too at Mokoteli's.'[5]
      He arose at dawn, Makoanyane's comrade,[6]
He waited for the Pleiades to appear.[7]
80   With an angry heart rose the lion, Lekena.
      As the warriors passed, Mokhethi was grumbling:[8]
The son of Letsie[9] wasn't holding a gun,
He was thinking of France, at sea.
He passed by Mphasa's[10] without a word,
85   He went to pay homage[11] to the father of Seeiso.
      He took the ship of the Government and Seeiso,[12]
This great warship here.
The serpents in the water were torn with fear,
The fish in the water said: 'Greetings, Koena!'
90   Paying their homage to RaLetšabisa,[13]

[1] i.e. a medicated peg which is believed to ward off evil.

[2] In fact Mojela was Griffith's paternal uncle, but as such he could be referred to by Griffith as his *ntate*, 'father'.

[3] Just as Griffith called Mojela his father, so his sons could call Mojela's son their father.

[4] A *khoeetsa* is a protective charm worn round the neck by children.

[5] 'at Mokoteli's', i.e. in Lesotho. For Mokoteli, see p. 63 above.

[6] One of Lerotholi Mojela's followers was in fact called Makoanyane, and so there is no reference here to Moshoeshoe's celebrated warrior of that name.

[7] i.e. for the approach of dawn, for he was eager to set out for war at the earliest possible moment.

[8] Mokhethi, a Fokeng chief, lived within a mile or two of Tebang. According to Chief Sentle Mojela, Lerotholi's son, he was 'grumbling' because he knew that arrangements had been made for Lerotholi to be placed in his area when the war was over.

[9] 'The son of Letsie', i.e. Lerotholi Mojela himself.

[10] Mphasa's village was at Boleka, in the Mafeteng District.

[11] Lit.: 'He went to praise the cattle at RaSeeiso's.' For the origin of this expression, see Joel, i. 117, p. 193 above.

[12] Seeiso, i.e. Griffith's son.

[13] RaLetšabisa, i.e. Lerotholi Mojela himself. This name was originally a teknonym of Lerotholi, son of Letsie. Cp. the use of the teknonym RaMakhaola in lines 24 and 39 above.

The young warrior of Qibing,[1] the chief.
   Listen: when Seeiso's bullet came back,
The child of the chief was even consoled:
He was called to Maseru, to the Meja-Metalana,[2]
There, when he came, he was given a medal.[3]   95
Jealousy took hold of the mighty chiefs,
Chiefs So-and-So and So-and-So![4]
   When the fearsome beast was first born
A cheer was raised at the home of Makhobalo,[5]
While at Thaba Bosiu a war-song was sung.   100
The graves[6] sang a hymn as they sat:
The singing was led by Chief Letsie,
It was taken up by Chief Moshoeshoe!
   When the chief was first born
There was born a great chief,   105
The child of Lehloenya's daughter.[7]
A rhino, a youth, Mohato's child,
He was born a stout warrior, the eye of the land.
   The chief, the enormous bush,[8]
He was called with a mighty shout.   110
Clearly it was heard by his father's advisers:
Sariele heard while at home,[9]
And Koebu heard while at home:[10]
Quickly they sent to fetch him.[11]
   When he came to Tšakholo, the child of the chief,   115
The snakes took refuge in the cracks.

[1] A mountain in Mojela's ward, close to the town of Wepener.
[2] A small stream close to Maseru.
[3] In July 1920, during a session of the Basutoland National Council, Lerotholi received the Medal for Meritorious Service from the Resident Commissioner.
[4] The *seroki* does not mention their names for fear of offending them. Cp. Masopha, iii. 7–8, p. 124 above.
[5] Mojela's senior wife was called 'MaMakhobalo, although in fact she had no son of this name.
[6] 'The graves', i.e. the spirits of the chiefs in the royal graveyard on Thaba Bosiu.
[7] Lerotholi's mother was the daughter of Lehloenya, a Fokeng chief who lived near Matsieng.
[8] He was a bush because, metaphorically, he provided shade for his people. Cp. lines 130–4 below.
[9] Sariele (Azariel) Theko was one of Mojela's advisers, and lived near Tebang.
[10] Koebu, a grandson of Moshoeshoe's brother-in-law, Paulus Matete, was another of Mojela's advisers, and lived at Bolumatau, near Tšakholo.
[11] i.e. in order to arrange his placing at Tebang in 1921.

When he came to Tebang, Lekena,
The little old women at Tebang rejoiced.
    Sariele spoke with gladness and said:
120 'Take your chance to act thus, Caster Down,[1]
For you've long been sending them to tiny little villages:
You've sent Mofota and Lepolesa
To go to the grazing posts to look after horses !'[2]
    This year the Great One, Lekena, is being sent:
125 The Great One they've sent to Tebang,
At the front,[3] at Matšosa's,[4] in the east.
    This year, since Lekena arrived,
The old people are content at Tebang,
They've entered a tent in summer.[5]
130   The Tawny Lion has gone to the spirits,[6]
But the chief has left, having planted a tree,
He left a tree with ample branches.
Rich and poor, gather together,
Come quickly and shelter in the shade ![7]
135   You, Makopoi, who've gone to the spirits,[8]
You're now an important messenger, my sister.
Go, tell the Chiefs of Lesotho, saying:
'The orphan on earth is being oppressed,
He's oppressed since his parents are dead:
140 Maama and Seeiso are dead,
Nkoebe and Lerotholi are dead,
Mojela and the Furious Warrior are dead.'[9]
    You should start with Chief Moshoeshoe,

---

[1] Caster Down, i.e. Mojela: see line 1, p. 235 above.

[2] Mofota and Lepolesa were sons of Letsie by junior wives who had been attached to the household of 'MaMojela. Mojela was responsible for finding villages for them. Mofota he placed close to the Caledon at the village which is still known as Mofota's. Lepolesa he placed near Van Rooyen's Gate on the Caledon, at the village which is still known as Lepolesa's.

[3] 'At the front', because Tebang was close to the eastern and southern boundaries of Mojela's ward.

[4] Matšosa was a chief whose village was close to Tebang.

[5] i.e. they can live in ease and comfort under Lerotholi's rule.

[6] Mojela, the Tawny Lion, died in February 1925.

[7] The tree is Lerotholi Mojela.

[8] Makopoi, one of Griffith's daughters, also died at this time. The *seroki* now turns to the dispute which arose concerning the succession after Mojela's death.

[9] Maama, Seeiso, Nkoebe, Lerotholi and Bereng ('the Furious Warrior') were all Lerotholi's paternal uncles. Mojela, of course, was his father.

You should tell the Refuge of the Takers,[1]
The Chief of Peka, close to Botha-Bothe.[2]   145
  Water-snake, tortoise of the children of Mojela,
Of the family of the Agitator[3] and Tsekelo[4] and his group!
Go slowly, tortoise of the land:
They're here, the Makaota have returned![5]
  Speak with your heart, Nkoebe's kinsman,[6]   150
Let your heart return to its home,[7] Chief!
  Koodoo,[8] you're a crocodile, how can you be offended?
Whom do you intend the commoners to address?
A chief is a bag, son of Mokhachane![9]
  When going to Maseru Lekena races his horse: 155
Always, when returning, he restrains it,
Having just made laws among the Whites.[10]
  Lekena is the heaven that's red,
He's the heaven that's the guardian of the gates.[11]
The lion is sitting on the boundary at the Caledon,   160
The gates that he guards are in the west,
He guards those of Wepener and his people, the paupers,

---

[1] 'the Refuge of the Takers', i.e. Molapo, the Takers being one of his regiments. The translation of *Khololeli* as 'Refuge' is uncertain, and the problems that surround it are the same as those for *hoholi* in Joel, ii. 36, p. 204 above.

[2] Molapo lived at Peka for a short while during the 1840s. Botha-Bothe, which was Moshoeshoe's home before he migrated to Thaba Bosiu, is not in fact near Peka, but the juxtaposition of these two historic names has a pleasingly impressive effect.

[3] 'the Agitator', i.e. Molapo, the brother with whom Lerotholi was disputing the succession. Molapo, being named after Moshoeshoe's son, adopted his praise-names too.

[4] Another of Lerotholi's brothers.

[5] The Makaota were Sotho who had been forced to live by hunting and gathering during the *lifaqane*. Many of them settled in the area which subsequently became Mojela's ward, and which therefore received the name Makaoteng, 'the country of the Makaota'. The poet has been advising Lerotholi to proceed cautiously, and not to take precipitate action against those who had opposed him in the chieftainship dispute. Now he says, in effect: 'Look, your subjects have returned to their allegiance to you.'

[6] Nkoebe was a paternal uncle.   [7] i.e. Do not be angry any more.

[8] Koodoo was one of the most popular praise-names of Lerotholi, son of Letsie, but is here used to refer to Lerotholi Mojela.

[9] According to the Sotho proverb, *morena ke khetsi ea masepa*: 'the chief is a bag for the excrement', i.e. he has to tolerate all his subjects, no matter how worthless they may be.

[10] He was a member of the Basutoland National Council, which met in Maseru.

[11] i.e. he guards the gates of Lesotho against the Free Staters.

The warrior of the Boers of old.[1]
He's fair, the young man of the Meerkat,[2]
165 In fairness he resembles the sand,
In whiteness he resembles the stars.
But most demur, they dissent,
They say he closely resembles the dawn!
The Koena, the bullet of the son of Libenyane[3]
170 Exploded, it burned the Government's enemies;
Of the ships it made splinters;
When the Government picked up the fish, they were dead![4]
The son of Mojela, the light of the rulers,
The light of the mighty chiefs,
175 The Koena, the light of the lords,[5]
The light of Griffith and Motšoene,[6]
The light of Masopha[7] and Sekhonyana![8]

17. *Seeiso*

Seeiso (1905–40) was the only son in Griffith's third house. In 1925 he was given an extensive ward in the mountainous Mokhotlong District, and established his village at Thabang.

Since there had been no male issue in Griffith's first two houses, Seeiso would normally have had every expectation of becoming his father's heir and successor. In March 1926, however, for reasons which will be given below, Griffith announced to the British authorities in Maseru that his most senior son was Bereng, the only child in his fourth house. Seeiso immediately protested, and later that year a family council was held at Matsieng. Although the decision taken there was in favour of Bereng by twenty-three votes to ten, it was known that most of the chiefs present had really supported Seeiso, but had abstained from voting for fear of offending Griffith. Seeiso also claimed that many of those who had voted for Bereng were not 'Sons of Moshoeshoe', but Griffith's

---

[1] The town of Wepener was just across the border from Lerotholi's ward. It was named after Louw Wepener, the Free State Commandant who was killed in the attempt to storm Thaba Bosiu in August 1865.

[2] 'the Meerkat', i.e. Mojela.

[3] Libenyane, 'Little Libe', was Mokhachane, Libe being his elder brother. In this stanza the *seroki* returns to the First World War.

[4] The poet believes that even the fish in the sea are the property of the all-powerful Government of the King.

[5] Lit.: 'of the Heads'.   [6] The son of Josefa Molapo.

[7] Masopha, i.e. Masopha II.   [8] The son of Bereng Letsie.

personal advisers. When Griffith pressed the Government to confirm the decision taken, he was informed that a secret ballot would have to be held before the Government would commit itself. This he denounced as contrary to Sotho custom, and so the dispute was left unresolved. Griffith died in July 1939, and in the following month, at a specially convened meeting of the 'Sons of Moshoeshoe', Seeiso's claims were upheld by an overwhelming majority. He died after a reign of only a year, and his senior widow, 'MaNtšebo, became Regent for his infant son.

Griffith's objection to Seeiso as his heir had been inspired by his conviction that Seeiso was not his natural son. He had been on bad terms with his third wife, Sebueng, and after many arguments and quarrels she had gone back to her father, Sempe Nkoebe. When subsequently she returned to her husband he claimed that she was pregnant by another man; and the child to whom she gave birth was Seeiso. This in itself would have been no obstacle to Seeiso's succession, for according to Sotho custom any child born in wedlock is regarded as the legitimate offspring of the husband. But while Sebueng had been with her father Griffith had married one of her sisters, and this woman had given birth to Bereng. He had paid no marriage-cattle for her, and had declared that she was coming to take the place of Sebueng; and when Sebueng returned to him he did pay cattle and declared that in effect he was marrying her anew. Most of his followers, however, took the view that Sebueng had never been divorced, since Griffith had not returned the original marriage-cattle to Sempe when she had gone back home; and they also took the view that the second payment of marriage-cattle was in respect of 'MaBereng. According to Griffith, therefore, 'MaBereng had taken the place of Sebueng ('MaSeeiso) as his third wife, whereas most of his followers considered that this position was still held by Sebueng.

There was a further complication in that, broadly speaking, the Roman Catholic authorities in Basutoland supported the claim of Bereng, but for reasons which had no basis in Sotho custom. When Griffith was first seriously drawn towards Catholicism, he had more than twenty wives, and was told that before he could be received into the church he would have to put them all away except his senior wife, 'MaBatho. She, however, was a Protestant, and Griffith was therefore reluctant to do this. At this critical juncture 'MaBatho, having uttered a prayer one morning that she might be removed from earth if she was a barrier to her husband's conversion, fell down and broke her leg in the afternoon, and died shortly afterwards. Griffith, regarding this as the result of divine intervention, was then married to 'MaBereng in church.[1] In the eyes of the Roman Catholic authorities, therefore, the chief had only one son, namely Bereng, and although their views seem to have carried very little weight among the 'Sons of Moshoeshoe', their strained relationship with Seeiso is very clearly reflected in his *lithoko*.

[1] This story is still told by many Sotho today, and is related in detail by Father F. Laydevant, O.M.I., in *Bophelo ba Morena Nathanael Griffith Lerotholi, K.C.S.P., C.B.E., 1871–1939* (Mazenod, 1953), pp. 49–51.

In 1940, the year of Seeiso's death, George Lerotholi published the praises which he had been chanting during the chief's lifetime, and in 1956 these were revised. They consist of six poems, of which three are translated here. The first is entitled 'When he was Chief of Mokhotlong, in his tribulation', and is a *mélange* which relates mainly to his placing at Thabang and to his dispute with Bereng. The second is entitled 'When he took his seat of chieftainship at Matsieng, after the death of his father, N. Griffith Lerotholi'. This consists of two parts. The first is a straightforward narrative which tells how he received the news of his father's death; how he rode down into Natal; how he flew to Maseru; and how he was greeted there by the Resident Commissioner, who confirmed his right to the succession. The second begins by continuing the narrative, and we are told how Griffith's body was taken from Maseru to Matsieng, and how Bereng's supporters then started to press his claims to the Paramountcy; but the concluding lines are of a more general nature. The third poem is entitled 'When he went to see His Excellency the High Commissioner, at Pretoria'. The first thirty-nine lines are generally narrative, but in the rest of the poem there is no further reference to the visit to Pretoria. Instead the poet concentrates on the blessings of Seeiso's rule, but at the same time advises the chief to be merciful and gentle towards his followers.

As in the case of Lerotholi Mojela's praise-poems, the tradition in which the *seroki* was working was so powerful that, although Seeiso had taken no part in any serious fighting, the fiction was maintained that he was a mighty warrior who lived in times of great peril. Moreover much of the poetry is a *mélange*: since the *seroki* recorded it himself this cannot be attributed to lapses of memory, but clearly indicates the low priority which he attached to relating a coherent narrative and building up a coherent structure.

The division into stanzas is that of the *seroki*, and the criteria which he has used here are obviously different from our own. In the almost complete absence of any structured stanzas this change is of no great importance.

George Lerotholi (1905–63) was a junior son of Paramount Chief Lerotholi. He was educated at Roma, the Roman Catholic centre in the lowlands of Basutoland, and later worked in Kimberley and in Johannesburg. He was one of Seeiso's most devoted adherents and eventually became one of his most important counsellors.

(i)

The child of the bulls of the Beoana,[1] Seeiso,
Was begotten by hardy bulls,

---

[1] The Beoana, i.e. the Sotho. See Moshoeshoe, ii. 5, p. 71 above.

He was begotten by Griffith and Letsie,[1]
And so it was that he became a leopard.
He was begotten by Api and Makhaola,   5
By Marakabei and Teko,[2]
By Tau and Motsarapane,[3]
And so it was that he became a leopard!
Christians, be quiet and listen,
Quieten down, comrades of Seeiso,   10
Young men of the son of Lerotholi,
Subjects of a prince, the Renownéd,
Beyond the Orange and over here[4]—
It may be because you're afar[5]—
So that, when smoking your pipes,   15
You should know how to praise Seeiso,
Saying: 'Mokhachane's firefly, Seeiso,
Firefly of Letsie, the Renownéd!
You're the sun, the child of the mother of Lerotholi, child of the
                                        Furious Warrior,[6]
You're the sun that gives light to the nation.   20
The light of the village of Mohato,[7] Seeiso,
This man of the village of 'MaLerotholi!'
    Ratel, black with white-streaked back, of the son of Libenyane,[8]
Ratel, black with white-streaked back, of Libe and Moshoeshoe,
Ratel, black with white-streaked back, of the family of Mamello,   25
Of the family of Makopoi and Khopotso;[9]
Black white-spotted tiger of the family of 'MaTheko![10]
How fearful is the eye of the Ratel!
You might think it a lion's, son of Lerotholi,
You might think it a train's, Tšoana-Mantata![11]   30

[1] Probably the Letsie referred to here is Letsie II. In line 18 below, however, the reference is probably to Letsie I.
[2] Api, Makhaola, Marakabei and Teko were all Seeiso's paternal uncles.
[3] Tau and Motsarapane were the sons of Jonathan Molapo.
[4] Here the *seroki* conveys some idea of the extent of Seeiso's following.
[5] i.e. perhaps you are still talking because you are so far away that you have not yet heard me.
[6] 'the Furious Warrior', i.e. Bereng Letsie.   [7] Mohato, i.e. Letsie I.
[8] Libenyane, 'Little Libe', was Mokhachane, Libe being his elder brother.
[9] Mamello, Makopoi and Khopotso were all Seeiso's sisters.
[10] 'MaTheko, i.e. Mamello.
[11] Tšoana-Mantata, 'I who fetch the black cow for myself', was a praise-name of Seeiso Letsie, after whom Seeiso was named. It is used here to refer to Seeiso himself. Sometimes it is shortened to Mantata, as in the following line.

The warrior of Mokhotlong,[1] Mantata,
The lightning-ring[2] of Mokhachane, Seeiso!
The child of Nkoebe's daughter[3] is a leopard.
He says he resembles his parents,
35   He resembles Nkoebe and Lerotholi,
Being black with white spots he resembles the great one,
He resembles the Binder of Lerotholi,[4]
And Peete and Lesaoana too.[5]
  The orphan who grew as Lesotho was trembling,
40   There were troubles as the child Seeiso grew!
He was born when Lerotholi was dead.[6]
The child of the blood of Mokhachane, Seeiso,
Of the blood of Letsie and Moshoeshoe;
He was born when Lerotholi was dead.
45   The new chief of the youth,
The warrior who is loved by the Sotho;
The beautifully-horned rhino of Ntšebo's[7] family,
The young man who longs for his orders,
Who's always complaining that he wants to fight.
50   This chief, RaMoholobela,[8] is tough;
I liken him to an ox of the wagon:
He refused to listen when the letter was read,
When the letter was read at the Meja-Metalana,[9]
Being read at Maseru, in the town,
55   When the chieftainship was given to Bereng.[10]
He said that the letter should go back to RaLetšabisa's,[11]

---

[1] Seeiso was placed as a chief in the Mokhotolong District in 1925.

[2] A lightning-ring, i.e. a circle of grass burnt by lightning, is an object of awe.

[3] Seeiso's mother was a daughter of Nkoebe Letsie.

[4] 'the Binder of Lerotholi', i.e. Griffith.

[5] Lesaoana, alias RaManella, was the son of Moshoeshoe's brother, Makhabane: the Peete referred to here is Lesaoana's son.

[6] Seeiso was born in 1905, shortly after the death of Lerotholi.

[7] Ntšebo, the senior daughter of Lerotholi, was his paternal aunt.

[8] RaMoholobela, a teknonym of Seeiso Letsie, is here used to refer to Seeiso himself.

[9] A small stream near Maseru.

[10] In March 1926 Griffith sent his sons Bereng and Seeiso to see Murray, the Acting Resident Commissioner, in Maseru. Bereng took with him a letter from his father in which he was named as his successor. Seeiso protested against this, and claimed that he was the rightful successor.

[11] i.e. Seeiso insisted that the matter should be referred back to a family council at Lerotholi's, i.e. Matsieng.

It should go back to the home of Ntšebo's family.
At the time when it came to Lerotholi's
The old men who were there rushed towards it,[1]
Indeed all the Axes returned,   60
The Axes of the man, of Lerotholi.
Back came the Falcons, back came the Vagabonds,
And back came the Hawks from Masopha's too.
Finally the Man-Eaters were summoned,[2]
We Beoana of the family of Kali[3] were called   65
When a crown was placed on Seeiso's head,
When the son of Lerotholi was given a staff.[4]
    The cattle were alarmed as the Renownéd went along,
They galloped away with their yokes,
They abandoned the ploughs while tilling!   70
Even the girls in the initiation school fled;
The girls in the initiation school fled as they were dancing
When they saw Mantata on his way;
They imagined that he'd come to Phamong
And would seize the stool of the Binders' man.[5]   75
But in fact the Renownéd is travelling,
The chief is just visiting his grandfather's family.[6]
The owners of the cattle have entered the caves,
So the antbears had made them caves![7]
    The child of the heavenly lightning, Seeiso,   80
The child of the lightning that commands the nation.
Moshoeshoe begat warriors long ago,

[1] They rushed towards it because they were eager to learn its contents.
[2] The Axes were the regiment of Lerotholi; the Falcons the regiment of
Sempe Nkoebe; the Vagabonds the regiment of Makhaola Lerotholi; the Man-
Eaters the regiment of Letsie II. The reference here is not to the regiments
themselves, but to the chiefs of the families concerned and their retainers.
[3] i.e. the members of the royal family. See Moshoeshoe, ii. 5, p. 71 above.
[4] 'a staff', i.e. of chieftainship. In fact, at the resultant meeting of the 'Sons
of Moshoeshoe' in November 1926 the voting went against Seeiso, and it was
only after Griffith's death in 1939 that he was recognized as Paramount Chief.
In this stanza these events are obviously telescoped together.
[5] i.e. they imagined that he was going to remove Bereng from his chieftainship at Phamong, where Griffith, 'the Binders' man', had once been chief.
[6] The home of his maternal grandfather, Nkoebe, was in the Quthing District,
not very far from Phamong.
[7] Lit.: 'So that the antbears should make them caves.' The idea is that the
owners of the cattle were so frightened that they took shelter in the holes of the
antbears.

Letsie too begat his,
Lekena[1] too begat his;
85 The warrior begotten by the Binder[2]
You may like when the guns are sounding;
At the time when they're sounding they call him.
   Heir of Mokhachane, Seeiso,
The inheritance of cattle you'll never see,
90 You'll devour the inheritance that consists of us, that consists of
                                  us young men.[3]

Back there the people are in lines,
There on the way the people are in crowds![4]
Home come the Maaooa of Sechele,[5]
And the Bushmen from Witbooi's too;[6]
95 Even the people with goatskin girdles[7]
Are continually asking where Lesotho is
When they hear that Seeiso is paramount.
   Crocodile, the tree was pleasantly placed,
It was planted at Motete, by the Malibamatšo.[8]
100 You old men there will still live at ease
And bask in the sun in a pleasant spot.[9]
   This year the wild beast is migrating;
The Crocodile's baggage went out of the village
When Seeiso migrated to the Maloti
105 And made his way there to Lelingoana's.[10]

---

[1] Lekena, i.e. Lerotholi.   [2] i.e. by Griffith.

[3] The poet assures Seeiso that, in spite of the disputes concerning the herds which he was to inherit from Griffith, he can always rely on the loyalty of his warriors.

[4] i.e. Seeiso has so many followers.

[5] The Maaooa are the Pedi of the Transvaal: see Moshoeshoe, iii. 15, p. 73 above. Sechele, however, was a nineteenth-century chief of the Koena in what is now Botswana. Perhaps the poet has confused him with the Pedi chief, Sekwati. The idea in this line is that Seeiso is such a popular chief that even the Pedi wish to join him.

[6] Witbooi was a name commonly given to San.

[7] i.e. the Nguni.

[8] In fact Seeiso was not placed at Motete, by the Malibamatšo, but at Thabang. However the Malibamatšo valley may be regarded as being in his general vicinity.

[9] For this idea, cp. Lerotholi Mojela, lines 127–34, p. 240 above.

[10] Lelingoana was chief of the Tlokoa in the Mokhotlong District, and Seeiso was placed over him.

He says: 'You counsellors, Soko, Mabilikoe and your friends,[1]
As you keep playing about with affairs
Of our family, of the house of Lerotholi, . . .'
Know this:[2] Tšoan'a Lere[3] has already told us
That he'll never lodge an appeal,[4]   110
For ever wandering from town to town;
Let the horses sleep with their saddles,
Let the chargers spend the night saddled up,
Let the warriors have their axes in their hands;[5]
He'll lodge an appeal that will go to the spirits,   115
That will go to Lerotholi and Theko,
To Maama and the Furious Warrior,[6]
To Joel and Seetsa![7]
    Now you should start by removing the aged,[8]
The old women, mother 'MaApi[9] and her friends,   120
And the women, mother 'MaMakhaola[10] and her friends;
You should send them over there to Edward's;[11]
In the summer there'll be thunder from the bird of lightning.
Seeiso, the clouds have thundered at night!
Hear when the flash is crackling,   125

---

[1] Soko Mpiti and Mabilikoe Matete were both counsellors of Griffith. In the dispute over the succession Soko supported Bereng and Mabilikoe Seeiso. Why the poet should complain about Mabilikoe is not known. Some suggest that it was because Mabilikoe did not support Seeiso strongly enough; others that it was because, being a Fokeng, he was an outsider, and had no right to interfere in a family quarrel. Cp. lines 191–4, p. 252 below.

[2] The syntax of lines 106–9 is confused. In lines 106–8 Seeiso himself is speaking: in line 109, with his speech left incomplete, the poet begins speaking again in his own person. The words 'Know this' have not been translated from the Sotho, but have been added to make the sense clear.

[3] Seeiso Letsie was called both Tšoana-Mantata, 'I who fetch the black cow for myself', and Malere, 'The One with a Stick'. Here the two names are shortened and combined.

[4] i.e. against the decision of the Sons of Moshoeshoe in November 1926. See lines 50–67, pp. 246–7 above.

[5] i.e. rather than appeal Seeiso should fight.

[6] Lerotholi, Theko, Maama and Bereng ('the Furious Warrior') were all sons of Letsie.

[7] Joel and Seetsa were sons of Molapo.

[8] i.e. war is coming, and the old people should be removed from the area of Matsieng to a place of safety.

[9] A widow of Lerotholi.   [10] Another widow of Lerotholi.

[11] i.e. to King Edward's, to England. The reference is probably to Edward VII, even although he was long since dead, rather than to Edward VIII.

There's thunder from the lightning of the family of Makhaola,[1]
Of the family of Griffith and Letsie![2]
The spirit of Lerotholi then trembled in the grave,
And Makopoi[3] wept, now dead, saying:
130 'The orphan on earth is being oppressed,
He's oppressed, for Lerotholi's now dead!'[4]
      When you were given the chieftainship, Bereng,
Your uncles weren't summoned for you,
And so you were given it by the child of the pastor,
135 By Ephraim, son of Lebakeng![5]
When I, Lerotholi's son, was given it,
I heard my uncles being summoned for me,
Api and Makhaola,
Marakabei and Teko,
140 Nkau and Mohlakana,
Children of 'MaLerotholi's house;[6]
So that when I was given it they should wish me joy,
And say: 'The one who remains with the orphans of Lesotho,
The Beoana's commander, Seeiso,
145 The child of a junior wife,[7] Seeiso,
Whose mother's marriage was beset with troubles,
When the shadows were covering Makhoarane
And the sun was above Masite,
Then it was that his mother was married.'[8]
150   The lightning of the village of Mohato,[9] Seeiso,
When it strikes it turns red!
The lightning turns red as it's filled with anger.
Why do you cling to your name, Seeiso?[10]

[1] One of the sons of Lerotholi.
[2] The Letsie referred to here is probably Letsie II.
[3] Seeiso's sister, who died soon after the dispute had flared up.
[4] For lines 129–31, cp. Lerotholi Mojela, lines 135–9, p. 240 above.
[5] The poet complains that certain members of the royal family had not been invited to the meeting of the Sons of Moshoeshoe in November 1926, and that Bereng owed his victory there to the votes of outsiders like Ephraim Lebakeng, Griffith's counsellor, whose father was an evangelist under the French Protestant missionaries.
[6] All the chiefs mentioned were sons of Lerotholi.
[7] Seeiso's mother was Griffith's third wife.
[8] In the evening, as one looks from Matsieng, the sun sets behind Masite mountain and casts shadows upon Makhoarane mountain. The idea is that Griffith married 'MaSeeiso late, although in fact he was still a young man.
[9] Mohato, i.e. Letsie.   [10] i.e. why are you afraid to die?

The chief dies, Lerotholi's son, but the name remains,
The name remains and is given to descendants.   155
Mpiti and Lepoqo died long ago[1]
Without the nations knowing them;
But their names are still given to children even now.
The princes will remain to rule,
Men like Bofihla and Sekhobe,[2]   160
When the lightning of the village of Mohato is dead,
Having died among the cattle of Lerotholi.[3]
    Because offence has been given to Mantata
The son of Lerotholi left Maseru still weeping.[4]
Tšoan'a Lere goes to church no more;   165
This church of Rome he loves no more.
Can the chief have forgotten God?
Chief, don't throw away God.
Turn about and go back,
Rhino of the regiments of Lerotholi,   170
Of the armies of RaLetšabisa,
Of the armies of RaNtšebo,[5] Seeiso,
Lover of Sempe's girl,
Of the mother of Ntšebo, Seeiso,
I mean, above all, of the woman, of Moipone.[6]   175
Return to normal, you're a chief,[7]
As for the people, still we are yours.
Till death they're called those of the village of the Chief,
The Sotho are called those of the village of Mantata.
The traitors may possibly rebel: 180
You'll never see us in rebellion.
Bereng, remain in that land of your family,
Remain at Phamong, let it come to be home.

---

[1] Mpiti Letsie was killed in the second war with the Free State. Lepoqo
Masopha died in 1886.
[2] Two of Seeiso's brothers.
[3] i.e. having died in a dispute about his inheritance.
[4] The occasion referred to is Seeiso's visit to Maseru with Bereng in March
1926.
[5] RaLetšabisa and RaNtšebo were both teknonyms of Lerotholi.
[6] Seeiso's senior wife was a daughter of Sempe Nkoebe: she was known as
Moipone before her marriage, and as 'MaNtšebo after the birth of her daughter,
Ntšebo.
[7] i.e. do not continue to be angry with your opponents.

Let the child of a junior wife at 'MaBatho's[1] go and live far from
home,
185 Let Tšoan'a Lere leave home, let him go to live there at Lelingoana's.[2]

Go and eat leeks,
Eat the bulbs[3] of the plain,
Survive on buck, son of Lerotholi;
The cattle of your family have long been sent scampering,
190 They've married more wives for Mabilikoe and his friends![4]
Don't go on gathering Ndebele,
That is to say you're gathering Fokeng![5]
People from Maotoana's,[6] go away,
Hurry and go away, or you'll be hurt!
195 Do you think that you've come for a dance at a wedding,
Or that you've come for a song and a dance?
But the Renownéd is embroiled in a quarrel,
Saying that he desires the Beoana[7] alone,
He desires the Chief's Son[8] and the Plunderer,[9]
200 He desires that Khoabane[10] and Majara[11] should be called,
That Mashapha[12] should be called, that Sempe[13] should be
called;
For *they* are Seeiso's fathers,
Those who know his seniority.
Lapper in the water of those from Mokhachane's,
205 Lap in the water like a kingfisher;
Let the water pour over the crocodile's shoulders,

---

[1] 'MaBatho was Griffith's senior wife.

[2] For Lelingoana, see line 105 above.

[3] Lit. 'the sedge Cyperus usitatus' or 'uintjies' (Paroz).

[4] Seeiso must live as a hunter and gatherer because the cattle which should have been given to him have been used instead as marriage-payments for the junior wives of Griffith's advisers, 'Mabilikoe and his friends'. Seeiso's hardship, of course, has been fancifully exaggerated.

[5] Ndebele (i.e. Nguni) is here used merely as a term of abuse. The Fokeng referred to were some of Griffith's advisers, whose influence the poet resented.

[6] The Maotoana were a leading Fokeng clan.

[7] i.e. members of the royal family, the Sons of Moshoeshoe.

[8] i.e. RaFolatsane Letsie.

[9] i.e. Tsepinare Letsie, alias Shoaepane Letsie.

[10] The son of Theko Letsie.   [11] The grandson of Majara Moshoeshoe.

[12] A son of Letsie.

[13] Sempe, son of Nkoebe Letsie, was Seeiso's maternal uncle, and was also the father of his senior wife.

Let the water pour over his shoulders !¹
   Doesn't Griffith give appropriate names !
He's given his child the name of the leopard,
The name of Seeiso, his uncle,   210
Who's died among the cattle of Lerotholi.²
   You almost persuade us to change, Makaota,
Suggesting that we from Mokhachane's pay cattle
To buy a letter to go overseas, to go overseas to Edward and his
                                                        people.³
   We ourselves will never buy a letter,⁴   215
The letter will be bought with the blood of the Sotho,
With the blood of us young warriors.⁵
   You feed a coward, mother 'MaTšaba !⁶
Does he go on inviting crowds of people?
People can be invited after we're dead: 220
Let them be called by the smoke of young warriors.
   There, you hear, you men of deceit,
Children of junior houses, such as Loto,⁷
Of houses that are closed with wormwood !⁸
Letsie once left a cruel plight: 225
Perhaps it's because he produced no chief,
And even Seeiso was not yet a man.⁹

   ¹ In this stanza the *seroki* is merely playing with the idea that Seeiso is a
crocodile.
   ² Seeiso Letsie was a great warrior, and it was therefore appropriate that
Seeiso Griffith should be named after him. Seeiso had not in fact 'died among
the cattle of Lerotholi', although he had given Lerotholi every support during
the Gun War.
   ³ The Makaota were the subjects of Mojela Letsie. After Mojela's death in
1925 two of his sons, Lerotholi and Molapo, disputed the succession, and
Molapo lodged an appeal with the Judicial Committee of the Privy Council:
see p. 234 above. According to the poet, Seeiso was almost persuaded by this
example to lodge an appeal with King Edward against Griffith's court, but
eventually decided against this.
   ⁴ 'a letter', i.e. an appeal.
   ⁵ i.e., rather than appeal, Seeiso's warriors will fight.
   ⁶ 'MaTšaba was another name of Seeiso's senior wife, 'MaNtšebo. The
coward was Seeiso himself, for, as the following lines indicate, he kept seeking
assistance elsewhere instead of relying on his own warriors alone. It is their
loyalty, rather than the chief's cowardice, that the poet wishes to emphasize.
   ⁷ Loto, a junior son of Letsie, supported Bereng.   ⁸ A sign of poverty.
   ⁹ When Letsie II died in 1913 his only surviving son was a child, Tau, who
died shortly afterwards. Seeiso was only about eight years old at the time.
The poet still has Seeiso's difficulties in mind, for he wishes to convey the idea
that the Sotho have long been distressed.

The nation of Tšolo[1] is always being harassed,
It's been handed over to a junior child,
230   It's still being said that Leloko should thrash it![2]
     You people of the village of Seeiso are saved,
This year Seeiso's a man.
Seeiso disputed on the first of August;[3]
The young men betrayed their oaths.[4]
235   The son of Lerotholi was given a staff,[5]
We heard Mantata give thanks,
Praising the staff of RaLetšabisa.[6]
He looked at the ground and shed tears!
We Beoana of Kali and his men were stunned,
240   We marvelled at the son of Lerotholi.
Since he bought spears last year
The daughter of Sempe has been scolding;[7]
We'll eventually throw them into lairs.[8]
     Armed warriors of Letsie, the Renownéd,
245   Neck-plate of the family of 'MaApi,[9]
Of the family of Mosiuoa and Sechaba![10]

[1] One of the Koena's ancestors.
[2] Leloko, a junior son of Lerotholi, was one of Griffith's advisers, and supported Bereng.
[3] The allusion to the first of August is difficult to understand. When confronted with these *lithoko*, though not otherwise, every authority consulted declared that it was on 1 August 1926 that Seeiso made his formal complaint before Griffith's court about the decision that Bereng was senior to him. According to contemporary documentary evidence, however, this statement was made on 1 September 1926. Alternatively the reference may be to the meeting of the Sons of Moshoeshoe on 3 August 1939 after the death of Griffith, when a decision was made in favour of Seeiso. Line 234 supports the former interpretation: line 235 the latter. In either case there appears to have been a slip of memory on the poet's part.
[4] i.e. they voted for Bereng although, implies the poet, they knew that they should have voted for Seeiso.
[5] 'a staff', i.e. of chieftainship. The poet is now clearly referring to Seeiso's accession to the Paramountcy in August 1939. For this telescoping of events—if telescoping it be—cp. lines 50–67 above.
[6] RaLetšabisa, i.e. Lerotholi.
[7] The daughter of Sempe Nkoebe was 'MaNtšebo, Seeiso's senior wife: evidently she did not want her husband to go to war over the succession.
[8] Lit. 'into refuges', i.e. into the holes and thickets where animals take shelter. The spears will be thrown away for ever.
[9] 'Neck-plate', i.e. protector. 'MaApi was one of Lerotholi's wives.
[10] There were several members of the royal family with these names. Perhaps the references here are to Sechaba, the son of Teko Lerotholi, and Mosiuoa, the son of Lerotholi.

Don't go on praising mere headmen-chiefs,
Speak of the Prince of Lesotho,
The Prince of Mokhachane, Seeiso.
    If you came to be a coward, son of Lerotholi,   250
And agreed to being stripped of your chieftainship,
Then heaven you'd never discover!
I swear by Jehova of the heavens
That Jesus accepts no cowards:
He despatches Gabriel to keep them out!   255
    Son of 'MaTau,[1] driver of the ox,
Drive the red and white ox, Binder's boy,[2]
Go with it into Moshoeshoe's.[3]
The chief has the colour of stars,
The son of Lerotholi shines like the sun.   260
    Seeiso, the cloud like a wondrous tower,
The spear of the warrior in the van of the Binders
Dazzled the sun in a cloudless sky!
He said that the chiefs should all gather together.[4]
Among those who left, and who'd asked him no questions,[5]   265
Motsarapane left without speaking.[6]
He says: 'As for me, I'll give no reply,
I'm going to my father, to Ramatlamela,[7]
I'm going to Jonathan to tell him
That Seoehla[8] should speak with the Binders' man,[9]   270
He should speak with Griffith and gently persuade him.[10]
I see him destroying the bar to the kraal,[11]

[1] Letsie II and Jonathan Molapo both had wives called 'MaTau. It is impossible to say which is referred to here.

[2] The Binder, i.e. Griffith.

[3] Perhaps the idea is that Seeiso should sacrifice the ox to the shade of Moshoeshoe.

[4] The poet now returns to the meeting of the Sons of Moshoeshoe in 1926.

[5] i.e. who had supported Seeiso, and so had not cross-examined him.

[6] Motsarapane had represented his father, Jonathan Molapo, at the meeting. It is incorrect to say that he 'left without speaking', for he had been most outspoken in his support of Seeiso. Perhaps, as in the previous line, the meaning is that he had not cross-examined Seeiso.

[7] i.e. to Jonathan. This name means 'the one who binds for': see Jonathan, i. 1, p. 170 above.

[8] For this name, see the praises of Jonathan, i. 4, p. 171 above.

[9] 'the Binders' man', i.e. Griffith.

[10] Lit.: 'He should speak with Griffith to flatter him.'

[11] i.e. Motsarapane sees Griffith rendering the country defenceless by his opposition to Seeiso.

The foundation stone of the kraal[1] is falling.'
  Seeiso accepts no cowards,
275 The children of the family of Mary[2] he rejects.
On hearing: 'The chief is riding',
They usually begin to comb their hair,[3]
And I'd hear them ask: 'Where is the Teacher?'[4]
You trust in the Father[5] more than the Chief!
280   There in the battle someone takes flight,
He puts on his trousers with the back to the front,
And the buttons are shining on his buttocks![6]
Seeiso, make friends of the Christians,
But don't tell the Christians of war,
285 For of death they're very afraid,
They're always being told of it in church.
They've proved too much for your father, their master![7]
  There in the mountains, at Joalane's lover's,[8]
Cattle are slaughtered when dawn appears;
290 The chief is feeding his orphans,
Feeding the young of Lerotholi.
Round stone[9] of the son of Lerotholi,
Child of the bull, don't take things by force,
Chiefly authority is your father's by birth.[10]
295 In heaven the chiefs are quarrelling,
Letsie is quarrelling and so is Lerotholi,
They say that we've treated their child with spite,
That it's better in fact that Seeiso should be fetched
And should leave the troubles of earth.

---

[1] Lit.: 'The kraal of the foundation stone.' For this inversion, cp. ii. 45, p. 259 below.

[2] i.e. the Roman Catholics, whose leaders supported Bereng.

[3] i.e., instead of going out to escort the chief, they start getting ready to go to church.

[4] i.e. the missionary.   [5] i.e. the missionary.

[6] i.e. he is so frightened that he has not been able to dress himself properly.

[7] i.e. even Griffith could do nothing with them!

[8] Joalane was one of Seeiso's wives.

[9] Perhaps the idea is that Seeiso was a dangerous enemy, just as round stones were dangerous when rolled down from the Sotho's mountain fortresses.

[10] It would have been more appropriate to say that chiefly authority was Seeiso's by birth; for it was not his father's authority, but his own, that was being disputed.

Now Moshoeshoe refused among the spirits there,   300
Moshoeshoe refused to take hold of Seeiso.
   Then he called out, did Chief Mantata,
He called out to the hunts and the regiments,[1]
He called out to Matlere and Mabina,[2]
Who remained when the groups were divided out,   305
When Jobo and his brothers were divided out,[3]
Divided out like sheep at a feast!
   Rouse the wind, Crocodile, son of Lerotholi,
That the poor should fear even to ride,
And be frozen[4] on their horses by the wind![5]   310
   Child of the chief, thin, wispy clouds:
We know when the child of the chief will ride
By the mists when the sky is clear,
And heaven desires to pour down clouds.[6]
   The little wild beast has left Makeneng,[7]   315
Being bent on Motete and the Malibamatšo;[8]
Quietly it went, its mane it concealed.
The lion of the family of Makopoi and Khopotso,[9]
When fired at the Crocodile twists.[10]
   Warrior of Thesele,[11] avoider of the kerrie,   320
Avoid the trap, warrior of Lerotholi,
Avoid the trap and copy your parents.
At the time when the son of Lerotholi[12] was born
We saw wonders:
The sun arose as a mighty ball   325
As the mists swept over the earth;

[1] i.e. to various groups of young men.

[2] Matlere and Mabina, who were both sons of Lerotholi, followed Seeiso when he went to the Mokhotlong District in 1925.

[3] Jobo, another son of Lerotholi, went with Bereng to the area of Phamong.

[4] Lit.: 'be finished'.

[5] There was once a popular belief that the wind always blew when the crocodile came out of the water. To rouse the wind therefore means to set out from home.

[6] i.e. when Seeiso rides there are low-lying mists, like clouds that have been poured down from heaven, but the sky above is clear.

[7] Makeneng had been Lerotholi's village: it is within a mile or two of Matsieng.

[8] For Motete and Malibamatšo, see line 99 above.

[9] His sisters.   [10] i.e. it takes evading action.

[11] i.e. of Moshoeshoe.

[12] i.e. Seeiso himself, although in fact he was Lerotholi's grandson.

They came, they leapt over the Malibamatšo,
Thus bespeaking his greatness!
    Tšoana,[1] staff of Mokhachane, Seeiso!
330 The chief is the chair of Lerotholi,
The nations will sit there in time of war.
Pay cattle, son of Lerotholi,
To wash out the impurity of a woman, of Sebueng,
Of a woman who's rejected by her husband.[2]

(ii)

I greet you, Chief Mantata,
White-spotted black one of the cliff of Matlakeng![3]
Crocodile, senior of Bereng, you're a leopard.
You're just like a buffalo, Binder's boy![4]
5   Today a lion has been brought to Lesotho.[5]
When news of the death arrived in the Maloti,
Arriving at Motete, at the home of Lelingoana,
Arriving at Mosuoe Lelingoana's,[6]
The chief had already saddled up.
10   Now the Chief Mantata rode,
At dusk he was still on the way,
At the break of dawn he entered Natal.[7]
As the sun was rising he received the report:
'Today, Seeiso, RaSekopo[8] has left you.'
15   The Crocodile began by instructing Matlere,[9]
That Matlere should proceed with the herdsmen,

[1] Tšoana here is short for Tšoana-Mantata: see line 30 above. Perhaps there is a play on the use of '*Tšoana, lere . . .*', 'Tšoana, staff . . .', for Seeiso could also be called Tšoan'a Lere: see line 109 above.

[2] i.e. Seeiso should do all that he could to wipe out his mother's disgrace. Sebueng was his mother's maiden name.

[3] The mountain which overlooks Matsieng.   [4] The Binder, i.e. Griffith.

[5] People living in the Maloti refer to the lowlands as Lesotho. When Griffith died in July 1939 Seeiso left the mountains and went to live at Matsieng.

[6] For Motete and the Tlokoa chief Lelingoana, see i. 99 and 105, p. 248 above. Lelingoana died in 1934 and was succeeded by his son Mosuoe.

[7] Instead of riding down into the lowlands of Basutoland, he descended the Sani Pass into Natal, and then, as the following stanza relates, caught a plane to Maseru.

[8] RaSekopo is said to be a variant form of RaMakopoi, one of Griffith's teknonyms.

[9] For Matlere, see i. 304, p. 257 above.

Should quickly proceed to the train;
He himself would then take a flying-machine.
The Crocodile rode on a flying-machine;
He flies in the heavenly heights,   20
On the brows of the wind, the son of Lerotholi;
He's still being lifted by the kingfisher,
By the black-feathered bird of the waters!
It came and crossed over Witzies Hoek,
It came and crossed over Leribe,   25
In full view it proceeded, it faced Matsieng.
It entered Maseru as the sun was declining
In the late afternoon,
As the sun was going down behind the mountains.
    Listen, the Commissioner's greeting the Chief,   30
Richards is greeting the Chief:[1]
'Evening, Seeiso of Lerotholi!'
Today the Crocodile's on its mettle, the water-snake,
The Crocodile's ridden in a flying-machine!
    'I see you're wearing the shoes of war;   35
It's clear you're a soldier, Koena,
A soldier of the family of Makopoi and Khopotso,[2]
An officer, Seeiso of the Beoana.[3]
Crocodile, today I've come to place you.[4]
    I opposed the placing of your junior brother,   40
I opposed the placing of Chief Bereng,
It was said that Bereng, though junior, should rule you.
    I said that His Majesty would forbid, and I've forbidden,
I condemn the destruction of the bar to the kraal,
When the kraal's foundation-stone[5] falls.   45
The discussions in the Cape defeated the Binder.[6]
Let him leave the authority of the house of Seeiso,
It concerns Seeiso alone.'

[1] Sir Edmund Richards was Resident Commissioner in Basutoland from 1935 to 1942.
[2] His sisters.
[3] i.e. of the Sotho, or of the royal family. See Moshoeshoe, ii. 5, p. 71 above.
[4] i.e. as Paramount Chief.
[5] Lit. 'the kraal of the stone, of the foundation'. For lines 44–5, cp. i. 272–3, pp. 255–6 above.
[6] In November 1927 Griffith had visited Cape Town, where he had tried to persuade the High Commissioner, the Earl of Athlone, to recognize Bereng as his successor. Athlone had refused to commit himself.

The body left the town of Maseru,[1]
50 The body of the Lion of the Binders left,
The body of the son of Lerotholi left.
The body left, it was brought to Matsieng.
When it came to the home of the 'Man of the Binders'
The lamentations of our parents were loud.
55 Now it is that these troubles are begun,
Being caused by Molise and my uncle,
In particular I mean by Sekhonyana.[2]
They console me by disputing, Koena,
They'd like to seize hold of my father's authority!
60 Among them is this creature 'Mari;
And Leloko keeps intruding on every side![3]
The persistent one of Mohato,[4] Seeiso,
The Crocodile, black, white-spotted and striped;
The Crocodile doesn't swim down the stream,
65 When it swims it goes up the fords.[5]
Snatcher, you're fearsome, you're a carnivore;
You're bearlike, warrior of the Hastener's[6] family.
The Crocodile's been born to govern Lesotho,
The chief is the young men's inheritance.
70 At the time of war abroad, at sea,
The chief was desirous of slipping away,
But the nation refused, the Koena.
With presents he certainly fought,
Tšoana-Mantata bought arms.[7]
75 The cow of the house of bricks, Seeiso,
The beautiful cow comes from houses of glass.[8]

---

[1] Griffith died in Maseru hospital and his body was taken to Matsieng for burial.

[2] Molise Tšolo was one of Griffith's most influential advisers. Sekhonyana was the son of Bereng Letsie. Even after Griffith's death they both supported Bereng Griffith's claim to the Paramountcy.

[3] For Leloko, see i. 230, p. 254 above. He was also called 'Mari, i.e. Murray, after a Government official of that name.

[4] Mohato, i.e. Letsie.   [5] i.e. Seeiso has to contend with difficulties.

[6] The Hastener was Bereng Letsie.

[7] Seeiso, being Paramount Chief, was unable to serve abroad in the Second World War, much as he wished to do so. But many of his followers went overseas, and the Sotho also raised a considerable sum of money to aid the war effort.

[8] 'of glass', i.e. with windows. The idea is that Seeiso comes from a prosperous home.

The vulture of 'MaToka's[1] family flew,
Beneath its wings its feathers whirred.

(iii)

When the Chief paid a visit to the Union[2]
He went to see His Excellency Clark.[3]
He'd taken Chief Phakiso[4]
And Setebele, his younger brother;
The lion has taken the child of his uncle,   5
The Crocodile has taken Theko Makhaola,[5]
That he should clothe him in his blankets,
Arrange him, and look after him well;
Also that they should be able to arrange the affairs
Of the Beoana's government.   10
   Listen to Seeiso expounding the generations
In the presence of the Counsellor of King George:
'This day I have come to place myself;
The fifth generation has left me,
I refer to that of the Binder of Lerotholi.[6]   15
This day I shall take Lesotho,
The chiefly authority of the house of Lerotholi.
Take care of me, Your Excellency Clark,
Take care of me and the lice of my blanket,[7]
Take care of me and the Sotho of my home!   20
   I, Seeiso, am a soldier of Britain,
Of the government of England,
I mean above all of King George.
I, the Crocodile, have been given a crown,
I've also been lent a flying-machine;   25
It flies with me over the village,

---

[1] 'MaToka was one of Seeiso's sisters.   [2] i.e. the Union of South Africa.
[3] Sir William Henry Clark was High Commissioner in the Union from 1935 to 1940. Seeiso visited him shortly after his father's death.
[4] The husband of his sister, Khopotso.
[5] The son of Griffith's brother, Makhaola.
[6] Griffith could claim to be the fifth Paramount Chief of the Sotho, the first four being Moshoeshoe, Letsie, Lerotholi and Letsie II. Strictly speaking, however, he was of the fourth generation, and not of the fifth, for he and Letsie II were brothers.
[7] There is an allusion here to the story that Moshoeshoe asked Queen Victoria to look after him and the lice in his blanket, i.e. his followers.

The village of Pretoria, of chieftainship.'
The European girls were running and singing,
They filled every part of the town,
30   They imagined they'd come for a dance,
They kept calling out to the Senior Prince:[1]
'Come along, Seeiso of Lerotholi,
Hurry up, Tšoana-Mantata !'
The Binder's hero arrived and jumped down,
35   He moved around, away from the people,
Always with a frown on his face.
The Koena relaxed his expression again,
The young women of the Whites were flirting,
They thought that he'd come to court them ![2]
40   The waters of the ocean boiled, Seeiso,
The fish rose up ![3]
      This year the leopard recovers its strength,
The Crocodile of the family of Sekhothali[4] and Debora,[5]
The Snatcher of the family of 'MaLeshoboro.
45   Here in Lesotho the elephant's a young ox,[6]
Seeiso's the young men's inheritance.
The grasping tongs of Lerotholi,
The iron takes others from the fire.[7]
Mokhachane's opener of the forests,[8] Seeiso,
50   The Crocodile, the senior of Theko Makhaola,
The child of Makhaola's senior,[9] the buffalo.
Your heart's like a hammer, Koena,
It's just like iron, Seeiso of Lerotholi.[10]
      The remainer of the Sotho, Seeiso,
55   Remained when the Chief, Nkiri,[11] departed,

---

[1] Lit.: 'The One from the Senior House.'

[2] Lit.: 'They thought that they'd come to be courted !' Seeiso was notoriously attractive to women.

[3] Such was the excitement caused by Seeiso's appearance—although, of course, in travelling from Matsieng to Pretoria he never went near the sea.

[4] Sekhothali, alias 'MaBereng, was Seeiso's second wife.

[5] Debora, alias 'MaLeshoboro, was Seeiso's third wife.

[6] In several Nguni communities the chief is referred to as an elephant. Here the poet is merely indicating that the Sotho's chief is a young man.

[7] i.e. Seeiso undertakes dangerous tasks.   [8] i.e. pioneer.

[9] Just as Griffith was senior to his brother, Makhaola, so Seeiso was senior to Makhaola's son, Theko.

[10] Cp. Joel, i. 110–15, pp. 192–3 above.   [11] A variant form of Griffith.

When the son of Lerotholi departed:
When the Chief migrated to the clouds,
The Crocodile of the Sotho, Seeiso, remained.
    Please be generous, Heavenly Jehovah,
Please give the heavenly talent,   60
And sprinkle the myrrh and the hyssop,
The spices of the heavenly kingdom,
Sprinkle them over Seeiso,
Give him life that his days may be long!
    Pay attention and listen, you scoundrel,[1]   65
Listen from the cliff of Matlakeng,[2]
Listen to Chief Mantata!
    The Crocodile, Seeiso, speaks with the Sotho:
'Devote yourselves to me,[3] young men of my family,
Kinsmen of Seeiso, devote yourselves to me!'   70
The child of 'Thabo's elder brother,[4] Mantata,
The handsome one of Nkiri and Lerotholi!
    Black ox with white spots, send your weapons back home,
To the north and to the south you've defeated them.
Lesa's family's lion,[5] Tšoana-Mantata,   75
As it thundered its flashes were shaking,
In its mouth there was red!
    The Resident Commissioner heard from afar,
He heard at Maseru, at the Meja-Metalana.[6]
He sent out David, the son of Mochochoko,   80
He said: 'Go quickly, son of Mochochoko!'[7]
Tšoana-Mantata walked on his pads,[8]
The fist of Mokhachane, Seeiso,
The palm and the hand of the Government.
    I, Chief Mantata, am roaring,   85
Let the cattle of our family come back, let them come back from
                                Likhoele,
Tšoana-Mantata!

[1] The 'scoundrel' referred to may well be Sekhonyana Bereng, who was one of Seeiso's most determined opponents in 1939.
[2] The mountain overlooking Matsieng.   [3] Lit.: 'Live for me.'
[4] 'Thabo was a junior son of Lerotholi: his elder brother was Griffith.
[5] Lesa was Seeiso's sister.   [6] A small stream near Maseru.
[7] David Mochochoko was the Resident Commissioner's interpreter. The incident alluded to cannot be specified.
[8] i.e. he was gentle, for his claws were not extended.

I'm no longer the heir, the child of the chief,
I'm no longer the heir of Lesotho,
90   The Beoana's heir, Seeiso:
The heir is now Molise![1]
    Hail, child of the chief, cliff of the Sotho,
Cliff of the armies of RaLetšabisa![2]
Don't scorn people, Seeiso, you're a chief;
95   Seeiso, Kind Father, your hands are full.[3]
Wash, get ready for the road, Koena,
Go to Maseru, to the Meja-Metalana,
Tell Richards[4] to set you free
And to give you the rule of Lesotho,
100   The rule of the house of Ntšebo,[5]
That peace should come, and the Beoana rejoice.
Listen: When I, the Crocodile, first received orders,
I was given a stick with iron combined,[6]
With a knob on its shoulders;
105   At the knob, it was said, I should put in the bullets.
Where enemies fought with Lesotho
There the Crocodile of the family of 'MaApi[7] gave thanks,
The Crocodile gave thanks, and the spirits rejoiced;
Peete and Motloheloa gave thanks,
110   Mpiti and his friends among the spirits have given thanks,
Matlole and Thesele gave thanks.[8]
An anvil is there at Lelingoana's,[9]
They've placed it at the gate of the court;
If it's touched, men strip off their clothes,[10]
115   We've seen Mohlaoli strip off his clothes,

[1] Some of Griffith's cattle had been entrusted to his adviser, Molise Tšolo, whose home was at Likhoele in the Mafeteng District. After Griffith's death Molise claimed them as his own, but Seeiso sent his men to take possession of them.

[2] RaLetšabisa, i.e. Lerotholi.   [3] i.e. full of gifts for your people.

[4] Sir Edmund Richards, the Resident Commissioner.

[5] The Ntšebo referred to here may be either his paternal aunt or his daughter.

[6] i.e. a gun.   [7] One of Lerotholi's wives.

[8] Peete was Moshoeshoe's grandfather. According to D. F. Ellenberger (*History of the Basuto*, p. 378), Motloheloa was a brother of Matlole (alias Motloang), Peete's father, and was the grandfather of Mpiti. Thesele was a praise-name of Moshoeshoe.

[9] The anvil is Seeiso himself, who was placed as chief over Lelingoana's Tlokoa.

[10] i.e. Seeiso's followers will fight on his behalf if anyone offends him.

The son of Mahlelebe stripped off his clothes.[1]
   This swarthy man you see here,
Of the family of the Hastener and Leshoboro,[2]
The rhinoceros not to be fetched while sitting,[3]
If you fetch him a war will arise,   120
Perhaps you'll alight upon a leopard!
You've seen, the strong buffalo is lying down;
The Crocodile, the buffalo, may pleasantly lie,
It lay in the valley at Morija.[4]
   I shall call the Hastener,[5] that we may argue   125
That the cattle of our family should return.
I'm afraid when the mother of Seeiso starves,
When the Beoana of the family of Seeiso starve,
And Molise is fattened by the oxen![6]
   Go slowly, Chief Mantata,   130
Go slowly, Fawn One of the cattle of Tlokoeng,[7]
Go slowly, don't walk too fast,
You're close to the villages, now you're near.
A crocodile's good when it hides its fury,
The poor may be torn by fear:[8]   135
The hard-working farmers fled as they were ploughing,
The hunters fled to the rocky clefts,
The fowls were flustered as they sat on their perches,
The men didn't budge from the courts,
The women were afraid to scatter the ashes,   140
The sun rotted and went red![9]
   Listen to me, Koena, that I may tell you:

---

[1] Mohlaoli, son of Mahlelebe, was one of Seeiso's counsellors. If any incident is alluded to here it is no longer remembered.

[2] The Hastener referred to here is almost certainly Seeiso's own son, Bereng, who, being named after Bereng Letsie, also makes use of his praise-names. Leshoboro is another of Seeiso's sons.

[3] i.e. not to be provoked.

[4] Morija is only a few miles from Matsieng, where Seeiso settled after his father's death in 1939.

[5] The Hastener referred to here is clearly Bereng Griffith.

[6] This stanza refers generally to the disputes over the inheritance which arose after Griffith's death. Cp. lines 85–91 above.

[7] Tlokoeng, i.e. the Tlokoa's territory in the Mokhotlong District.

[8] i.e. they may be torn by fear if it reveals its fury.

[9] These lines depict the imaginary consequences of Seeiso's wrath. Cp. Griffith, ii. 434–43, p. 234 above.

You'll give trouble by asking the praisers.[1]
As for the Lion of Lekena's stabbing, you should say
145 That it stabs, that it pulls out the bowels.
The comrade of Matlere, Seeiso, is courageous,
The comrade of George, who fights in war;
The comrade of Mabina is eager to fight;
The comrade of Mosiuoa goes early to court.[2]
150 Comrade of the orphans of the Lion of the Makena,[3]
In particular I mean those of Lerotholi,
I mean those of the house of Ntšebo.[4]
Seeiso, if you're longing to fight,
What's wrong,[5] warrior of Ntšebo's[6] family?
155 The one who remains with the orphans of Lesotho,
The one who remains with the orphans isn't angry,
If he's angry, the Sotho grow thin.

18. *Moshoeshoe II*

In the absence of any male issue in Seeiso's first house, Constantine Bereng Seeiso, the eldest son in the second house, was his father's undisputed heir and successor. Born at Thabang in 1938, he was only an infant when Seeiso died, and from 1940 to 1960 his father's senior widow, 'MaNtšebo, acted as Regent for him. He was brought up in the Mokhotlong District, but was subsequently educated at Roma, the Roman Catholic centre in the lowlands of Basutoland; at Ampleforth College in England; and at Corpus Christi College, Oxford, where he read Politics, Philosophy and Economics. In 1960 he returned to Basutoland and was placed as Paramount Chief, taking the title of Moshoeshoe II. He is now King of the independent nation of Lesotho.

Several *liroki* have composed praises in his honour. Those printed here are the work of David RaMaema, an elderly Tlokoa from the Mokhotlong District. RaMaema, who has received only a rudimentary education, and who speaks no English, was once an evangelist in the Church of Basutoland (the creation of the French Protestant mission). The poem is

---

[1] i.e. do not ask others to praise Seeiso, for only I can praise him properly.
[2] Matlere, George, Mabina and Mosiuoa were all sons of Lerotholi who supported Seeiso. George was the *seroki* himself.
[3] i.e. of Lerotholi, the Makena being his regiment.
[4] The Ntšebo referred to here is probably Lerotholi's daughter.
[5] Lit.: 'Of what do you disapprove?' The poet implies that Seeiso has no good reason for being angry with his followers.
[6] Once again the Ntšebo referred to is probably Lerotholi's daughter.

not concentrated on any specific incidents, and is almost in the nature of a pure ode. It was recorded by Damane at RaMaema's dictation early in 1968.

I praised the stump of the wild olive tree,[1]
I praised the peg[2] of the house of 'MaBereng,
The child of the house of spears,[3] the Tough Warrior,[4]
Of the house which is closed with kerries,[5] Bereng,
The tall chief of Thakhane[6] and her kin. 5
I praise the water-snake with the black, white-spotted colour,
The water-snake that's black with white spots, the defender of
Lesotho, the Hastener.[7]
When first he was born, the Chief Bereng,
Trumpets were heard to sound afar off,
At Thaba Bosiu a paean was begun,[8] 10
The tenor was sung by RaLetšabisa,[9]
The bass was taken up by Chief Moshoeshoe.
They praised him with weapons, did the Koena,[10]
Of all these animals they took the heads:
They took the skins of a bear and a lion, 15
The child of the chief donned the skin of a leopard,
They placed on his head a snakeskin hat.[11]
The chief, Mantata,[12] begat,
The chief has begotten a falcon, a peregrine,
He's begotten a vulture, he's begotten a hawk, 20
He's begotten a snatcher-as-it-flies, a kite,

[1] The tree of Bereng's family has been cut down with the death of his father, Seeiso. Bereng is the stump which remains, and which will throw out new shoots. The wild olive is noted for the toughness of its wood.
[2] i.e. the medicated peg which is driven into the ground and which is believed to ward off evil.
[3] i.e. of a family of warriors. Cp. Masopha, i. 1, p. 117 above.
[4] 'Tough Warrior' was one of the praise-names of Bereng Letsie. Since Bereng Seeiso has been named after him it may be given to him too.
[5] i.e. of the house which is defended by warriors.
[6] Bereng is in fact a tall man: Thakhane is his sister.
[7] The Hastener was another of Bereng Letsie's praise-names.
[8] i.e. Bereng's ancestors in the royal graveyard on Thaba Bosiu also shared in the rejoicing.
[9] RaLetšabisa, i.e. Lerotholi.   [10] i.e. they gave him many weapons.
[11] Lines 14-17 refer to the custom of *lelomolo*. See Maama, ii. 45-50, p. 159 above.
[12] Mantata, i.e. Seeiso.

He's begotten a lanner, with its claws full of blood.
　　When Bereng crossed over the deeps
The fish in the waters were torn with fear:
25　　The waters burst terribly in the deep,
It seemed as if lightning had struck the deep.
The little frogs fled, they entered the water-weeds,
The frog ran away, it was trapped by the debris,[1]
The tadpole danced, danced facing the depths,
30　　The crab ran sideways in the water,
The snail even burrowed in the mud with its head,
The earthworms altered their colours,
The serpents creep, they go in beneath the stones.[2]
　　Look when the Chief crosses over the mountains![3]
35　　Hear when the jackals greet Bereng!
They were gaping as they looked above,
The jackals had emerged from their lairs.
They said: 'Mighty Ruler of Mohato,[4] Bereng!
Chief, rule over us, we're yours!'
40　　At the time when he passed the Malibamatšo[5]
He was greeted by birds
That were black with bald heads,
These black and white birds called kingfishers.
They'd begin by clapping their wings:
45　　'Hele-helele! Chief Bereng!
Chief, rule over us, we're yours!'
　　The child well sired by Thesele,[6]
This child resembles the Chief Posholi,
He resembles Lekena[7] and RaMahlolela,[8]
50　　He resembles the Repeater[9] and RaMathaleha,[10]
He resembles Griffith and Lerotholi.
　　You're double-blooded, Mohato's son:
On the right you're Chief Sekonyela,
On the left you're Mokhachane.[11]

---

[1] i.e. by the rocks and branches brought down by a river in flood.
[2] Such is the consternation which Bereng causes when he crosses the waters.
[3] i.e. in a plane.　　[4] Mohato, i.e. Letsie.
[5] A river which flows through the Maloti.
[6] i.e. by Moshoeshoe.　　[7] i.e. Lerotholi.　　[8] i.e. Masopha.
[9] i.e. Moshoeshoe's brother, Mohale.　　[10] i.e. Posholi.
[11] Bereng's mother is descended from the Tlokoa chief, Sekonyela, his father from Mokhachane.

Crocodile, govern the people with warmth, 55
Govern with warmth your father's people.
 Go slowly, father of Mohato,[1]
That we, the poor, may admire your face,
May admire your beauty, child of the chief.
Leave the lands for the commoners to plough.[2] 60
 Our tears you should gather in a blanket,
Our tears you should take to Moshoeshoe in the grave.[3]

---

[1] Bereng's eldest son, like that of the first Moshoeshoe, is called Mohato.
[2] i.e. be generous, do not appropriate them to yourself.
[3] i.e. you should intercede with Moshoeshoe for us in our sorrows.

APPENDIX

THE following texts have not been published before:
(i) the third poem of Moshoeshoe I.
(ii) the only poem of Moshoeshoe II.

(i)

Lona le ratang ho roka baholo,
Le roka hampe le siea mohale,
Le siea Thesele oa Mokhachane;
Hobane ke eena moloani oa lintoa,
5   Thesele o bohale bo matla,
Ke ho bolela Moshoeshoe-Moshaila.
   Moshoeshoe ha a qala ho busa Basotho
O qalile Botha-Bothe.
Thesele, leru la tloha bochabela,
10   La chochometsa la hlaba bophirima,
Thaba Bosiu, mokhorong oa khotla.
   Lichaba tsa utloa kaofela,
Le Bapeli ba setse ba mo utloile.
Moshoeshoe, fiela tsela matlakala,
15   Maaooa a tsamaee monateng,
A tsamaee bothakhalleng.
Ho utloile le ba ha Zulu, Matebele.
   Beha molamu, mor'a Mokhachane,
U lule fatše:
20   Motse oa molamu ha o hahe,
'U ka nketsang?' ha e hahe motse;
Motse ho haha oa morapeli, Thesele,
Moholo-holo oa Napo Motlomelo,
Moupo oa lefatše la Mabeoana.
25   Lehaha la mafutsana le marena,
Setloholo sa Peete, sekoankoetla,
O rateha ha ho tšoeroe lithebe,
Ho tšoeroe melamu ea bahlankana.
   O nkile lekoko la pholo ea Mafatle,

O le entse tširela,   30
Tširela ke ho bolela thebe,
O tla qoba ka eona har'a ntoa.
    Bana ba Napo e hlile ba ea hana,
Ba rata ha a namolela sechaba,
Ba re: ''Musetso ke oa likhomo le oa batho.'   35
    Ke tšehlana ea mara,
Ke thak'a Shakhane le Makoanyane,
Ma-besa-ka-lerole:
Lerole la tsoa ka mpa ea mohlaba,
La bonoa ke RaTjotjose oa Mokhethi.   40
    Lefiritšoane la bana ba Matlole,
Le-khatluoa-tlopo,
Le e-ja likhomo matsoele li phela.
    Khomo ea 'MaMmui, tšehlana,
E liongoana, Moshoeshoe.   45
    Ngoana e motšoana oa 'MaSetenane,
Oa sehlabisa Makhetha,
Ak'u hlabise nkhono'ao,
U hlabise 'MaSetenane,
A roale, a re khi mehlehlo   50
Ea likhomo le ea batho.
    Thesele, pharu e telele-telele ea boribeng,
Khomo li kena ka eona, li sa ile,
Batho ho kena ba litelutelu,
Khomo ho kena tse manaka a maholo.   55
    Ke ngoana e motšoana oa 'MaSetenane,
'Mopo thathalala,
'Mopo ekare oa nonyana, Lekhetha,
Hobane ke setloholoana sa RaKhokhoba.
    Basali ba lielletsa Moshoeshoe: 60
Banna ba le metatetsi ea marumo.
O rateha ha ho tšoeroe lithebe.
    RaMohato o tjeka le lelinyane,
O tjeka le ngoana ea e-so'ng ho tsebe ho tjeka:
Ekare a tjeka a re: 'Tlaitlai!'   65
    Nkemolohe, Mokhitli oa Litšoane,
Ke tsoe ke le oa letlali,
Hoba ke emere.
    Thebe e mabenyane ea RaMasopha,

70 Ekare e betsoa ea re khatsimo-mollo:
Hoa e-cha metse ea libuoa haholo.
Moshoeshoe-Moshaila ke oa RaKali, Lebeola.

(ii)

Ka roka kutu ea sefate sa mohloare,
Ka roka sethakhisa lapeng ha 'MaBereng,
Ngoan'a ntlo ea marumo, Selala,
Ntlo ea ho koaloa ka likoto, Bereng,
5 Morena e molelele oa bo-Thakhane.
Ke roka khanyapa e 'mala tololi,
Khanyapa e rolo, mosireletsi oa Lesotho, Phakane.
Mohla a qalang ho hlaha, Morena Bereng,
Terompeta tsa utloala ho luma khakala,
10 Thaba Bosiu ha phokoloa ntlolohetsane,
Tsoetse ea n'a b'e binoa ke RaLetšabisa,
Koma e lumeloa mokorotlo ke Morena Moshoeshoe.
Ba mo fapha ka lihlomo Bakoena,
Phoofolo tsena ba li nka lihloho tsohle:
15 Ba nka tlalo la bere le la tau,
Ngoan'a morena a apara tlalo la nkoe,
Katiba ba mo hloma tlhoare.
Morena oa tsoala, Mantata,
Morena o tsoetse seoli, o tsoetse leubane,
20 O tsoetse lenong, o tsoetse leitsomeli,
O tsoetse mautla-a-solla, lekholokholo,
O tsoetse phakoe, mali a tletse linala.
Bereng mohla a tšelang maliba
Tlhapi metsing tsa haroha letsoalo:
25 Metsi a qhoma habohloko bolibeng,
Eaka tlali e otlile boliba.
Nketjoane tsa baleha, tsa kena boleleng,
Nketu a matha, a tšoaroa ke mahoholi.
Oa tantša mokulubete, oa tantša o shebile koeetša,
30 Khala la matha ka lekeke metsing,
Khetla ea b'a runya seretse ka hloho,
Nohametsane tsa fetoha mebala,
Noha li hahaba, li kena tlas'a majoe.
Bona Morena ha a tlola lithaba!

Utloa ha phokojoe li lumelisa Bereng! 35
Li ne li ahlama li shebile holimo,
Phokojoe li n'e be li tsoile matšabeng.
Tsa re: 'Sebusabusane sa Mohato, Bereng!
Morena, re buse, re ba hao!'
    Eare ha a feta Malibamatšo, 40
Tsa mo lumelisa linong
Tse ntšo, tse hloho li mapatlelo,
Tse phatšoa tsena tse reiloeng liinoli.
Le ee li qale ka ho opa mapheo:
'Hele-helele, Morena Bereng! 45
Morena, u re buse, re ba hao!'
    Ngoana oa ho tsoaloa ke Thesele hantle,
Ngoana enoa o futsitse Morena Posholi,
O futsitse Lekena le RaMahlolela,
O futsitse Pheta le RaMathaleha, 50
O futsitse Kerefisi le Lerotholi.
    U malimabeli, mor'a Mohato,
Ka le letona u Morena Sekonyela,
Ka le letšehali u Mokhachane.
Koena, busa ka mofuthumela bathong, 55
U buse ka mofuthu ho batho ba ntat'ao.
    Tsamaea butle, ntat'a Mohato,
Mafutsana re u bohe tšobotsi,
Re u bohe limapa, ngoan'a khosi.
U tlohelle bafo masimo ba leme. 60
    Likhapha tsa rona u li phuthele kobong,
Khapha u li ise ho Moshoeshoe lebitleng.

SELECT BIBLIOGRAPHY

Casalis, E. *Études sur la langue séchuana* (Paris, 1841).
—— *Les Bassoutos* (Paris, 1859: English translation, *The Basutos*, London, 1861), Chapter XVII.
Cope, T., *Izibongo: Zulu Praise-Poems* (Oxford, 1968).
Damane, M., *Marath'a Lilepe a Puo ea Sesotho* (Morija, 1960).
—— 'The Structure and Philosophy of Sotho Indigenous Poetry and Its Place in the School Curriculum', in J. Walton (ed.), *The Teaching of Southern Sotho* (Maseru, 1961).
Franz, G. H., 'The Literature of Lesotho', *Bantu Studies* (1930), iv. 146–80.
Jankie, H. E., *Lithoko tsa Makoloane* (Morija, 1939). This is a collection of praise-poems composed by boys at the initiation school: Sotho texts only.
Kunene, D. P., *Heroic Poetry of the Basotho* (Oxford, 1971).
Lerotholi, G., *Lithoko tsa Morena e Moholo Seeiso Griffith* (Morija, 1940: revised edition, 1956).
—— *Lithoko tsa Motlotlehi Moshoeshoe II* (Mazenod, 1964).
Lestrade, G. P., 'Bantu Praise-Poems', *The Critic* (Cape Town, Oct. 1935), iv. 1–10.
—— 'Traditional Literature', in Schapera, ed., *The Bantu-Speaking Tribes of South Africa* (London, 1937), pp. 291–308.
Letele, G. L., 'Some Recent Literary Publications in Languages of the Sotho Group', *African Studies* (1944), iii. 161–71.
Mangoaela, Z. D., *Lithoko tsa Marena a Basotho* (Morija, 1921: 7th ed. Morija, 1965). This is a collection of Sotho texts, with no translations.
Mapetla, J., *Liphoofolo, Linonyana, Litaola, le Lithoko tsa tsona* (Morija, 1924). This contains the praise-poems of animals, birds and divining bones.
Moshoeshoe, G. T., 'Litaba tsa Mofuta oa Basuthu' (Cape Town, 1856). Unpublished manuscript in the Grey Library, Cape Town. This contains quotations from several praise-poems.
Schapera, I., *Praise-Poems of Tswana Chiefs* (Oxford, 1965).
Sekese, A. M., articles in *Leselinyana*, 1892–1925, *passim*. Many of these articles contain quotations from praise-poems and explanations.

INDEX

Names of 'Places and areas', 'Praise-poets' and 'Rivers and streams' are listed under those headings. Cultural features are listed under the heading 'Sotho'. Associative references' indicate pages on which only associative references appear.

Allison, Captain, 60, 180.
Ambrose, D., ix.
Ampleforth College, 266.
Anglo-Boer War (1899–1902), 8, 187.
Api Lerotholi, 29, 217, 245, 250.
Arbousset, Thomas, 3, 67, 68, 78, 96, 106.
Athlone, Earl of, 259.
Ayliff, John, 84.

Baatje, Carolus, 4.
Baca, 83, 129.
Bastards (of Carolus Baatje), 4.
Basutoland National Council, 235, 239, 241.
Bele, 82, 92.
Bell, Major, 58, 59, 149, 172, 180, 189, 190, 191, 203.
Berea, Battle of the, 5, 126.
Bereng Griffith, dispute with Seeiso Griffith, 24, 55, 242–4, 246–7, 249–50, 251, 253, 254, 256, 257, 259, 260; genealogy, 62.
  Associative references, 235, 238, 258, 265.
Bereng Letsie, 7, 62, 146, 154, 166, 214, 223.
  Associative references, 236, 240, 242, 245, 249, 260, 265, 267.
Bofihla Griffith, 251.
Bohosi, Alfred, 148.
Boshof, President N., 5–6, 63, 79.
Brand, President J., 6, 138–42, 146.
Brutsch, A., ix.
Bungane, 86, 87, 122.
Burnet, John, 140.
Bushmen, see San.

Casalis, Eugène, vii, viii, 3, 18, 23, 26, 64, 65, 66, 70, 72, 106.
Cathcart, Sir George, 5.
Chabalala, 201, 206–7.

Chake, 102–3.
Chopho Posholi, 88, 90.
Christianity, 16, 96, 103, 107, 110–11, 115, 139, 159, 164, 220, 222, 233, 235, 243, 245, 251, 255, 256, 263.
  Anglican Mission, 9, 16, 201; French Protestant Mission (Paris Evangelical Missionary Society), vii, 3, 9, 16, 26, 67, 106, 110, 112, 250, 266; Roman Catholic Mission, 9, 16, 197, 214, 243, 244, 251, 256, 266; Wesleyan Mission, 84, 109, 119.
Clark, Sir William Henry, 261.
Clarke, Colonel Marshall, 8.
Clerk, Sir George, 5.
Cope, T., 30, 43.
Corpus Christi College, 266.

Damane, M., viii, 65, 137, 155, 267.
David Mochochoko, 263.
Davids, Pieter, 4.
Dialect, Rolong, 102–3; Taung, 137, 151.
Dieterlen, H., 24.
Dingane, 3.
Disarmament Proclamation, 161.

Edward VII, 249, 253.
Ellenberger, D. F., 21, 67, 264.
Ephraim Lebakeng, 250.
Erasmus, Willem, 150(?), 155.

First World War, 8, 23, 234, 235–9, 242.
Fobokoane, 131.
Fokeng, enemies of Moshoeshoe's family, 63, 64–5, 67, 69–70; intermarriage with Moshoeshoe's family, 64, 74, 117, 191, 239; subjects of Moshoeshoe's family, 125(?), 139, 156, 192, 194, 200,

Fokeng—*contd.*
207, 215, 238, 239, 249, 252;
subjects of Sekonyela, 115(?).
See also Khoele Fokeng, Maotoana
Fokeng and Qhoai Fokeng.
Frere, Sir Bartle, 51, 58, 144, 145,
146, 147, 155, 189.

Gasebeng, 194.
Gcaleka, 145.
Gcina, 70, 109.
George VI, 261.
George Moshoeshoe, see T'lali
Moshoeshoe.
Germans, 59, 236.
Goliathe, 210.
Grey, Sir George, 6.
Griffith, Colonel C. D., 6, 58, 152,
167, 169, 189, 194, 213, 225.
Griffith Lerotholi, battle of Khamo-
lane, 209, 214–34; biographical
details, 62, 213–14; conversion to
Roman Catholicism, 16, 214;
death and funeral, 214, 244, 258,
260, 262–3, 265; dispute with
Letsie II, 214, 233; dispute with
Mocheko, 214, 222–3, 229–30,
231; dispute with Motšoene, 214,
231; First World War, 237, 238;
as Paramount Chief, 9, 214, 261;
relations with his sons Seeiso and
Bereng, 242–4, 248, 249, 250,
252, 253, 254, 255, 259, 260, 264.
Associative references, 29, 235, 240,
245, 246, 247, 268.
Praise-poems, 19, 24, 28, 36, 37, 41,
43, 47, 54, 55, 57, 130, 164, 168,
184, 194, 203, 204, *213–34*, 265.
Griqua, 4, 65, 116, 118, 121, 123, 136,
190.
Gun War (and continuation in fighting
between Jonathan and Joel), 6–8,
10, 14, 26, 31, 32, 33, 36, 37, 52,
59, 60, 107, 111, 116, 137, 143–
52, 154, 155–65, 167, 168–9, 170–
81, 183–4, 186, 187, 188–93, 195–
7, 199–205, 231, 235, 253.

Hammond-Tooke, Professor W. D.,
ix.
Hlakoana, 77, 160, 215.
Hlalele, 82, 89.
Hlapo, 207.

Hlasoa (identity unknown), 91.
Hlasoa Molapo, 172, 173, 176, 178,
179, 187.
Hlubi, individuals among Sotho, 63,
86, 122, 164; individuals in
Wittebergen Native Reserve, 38,
85, 87, 109; invasion of Lesotho,
2; Langalibalele incident, 7, 60,
111, 169, 180, 187, 194, 199.

Italians, 59.

Jacob (the Griqua), 116, 118, 121, 123,
136.
Jameson Qhobela (informant), 188,
200.
Jan Letele, 80, 81, 93.
Jan Mokhahlane, 200.
Jews, 233.
Joalane, 256.
Jobo Lerotholi, 257.
Joel Molapo, Anglo-Boer War (1899–
1902), 8, 187; biographical details, 62, 187; dispute with
Jonathan Molapo, 7, 36, 37–8, 59,
60, 168–81, 183–4, 186, 187,
188–93, 195–7, 199–203, 204,
205, 208; dispute with Khoakhoa,
38, 187, 188, 205–6; Langalibalele
incident, 38, 187, 188, 193–5,
197–9; Orange Free State, second war, 187, 188, 203, 204; San,
10, 38, 187, 188, 196–7, 203,
204–5, 206–8.
Associative reference, 249.
Praise-poems, 31, 32, 38, 49, 56, 58,
82, 178, 181, *187–208*, 212, 217,
226, 238, 241, 262.
Jonathan Mojela, 235, 236.
Jonathan Molapo, biographical details, 62, 168–70; dispute with
Joel Molapo, 7, 32, 36, 168–81,
183–4, 186, 187, 188–93, 195–7,
199–203, 204, 205, 208; dispute
between Seeiso and Bereng Griffith, 255–6; Langalibalele incident, 60, 169, 170, 180; Moorosi
War, 167, 169; Orange Free
State, second war, 169, 170, 181;
San, 10, 169, 170, 182–3, 184–6;
his secretary, 112.
Associative reference, 245.

Praise-poems, 23, 25, 37–8, 41, 47, 49, 50, 51–2, 53, 56, 59, 60, 61, 69, 158, *168–86*, 188, 192, 194, 199, 207, 215, 220, 226.
Josefa Molapo, 62, 168, 172, 175, 183, 198, 202, 231–2.
Associative references, 59, 127, 174, 180, 181, 182, 185, 188, 204, 205, 236, 242.
Jousse, Théophile, 25–7.
Jumba, 58, 116, 127, 129–30, 132.

Kabai, 119
'Kabékoé', 68.
Kakatsa, 76.
Kali (Koena chief), associative references, 21, 28, 40, 44, 49–50, 69, 71, 75, 76, 90, 93, 161, 171, 202, 221, 247, 254.
Kali (Molibeli chief), 4, 113.
Kamolase Mahasa, 115.
Kaptein, Jan, 4.
Katiba Moletsane, 152.
Khabo Molapo, 190.
Khajoane, 218.
Khethisa Molapo, 172, 173, 180, 187.
Khoabane (Marabeng chief), 68, 70.
Khoabane Theko, 252.
Khoabe, 164.
Khoahlane, 181.
Khoakhoa, 38, 49, 174, 187, 188, 191, 201, 205.
Khoele, 50, 117.
Khoele Fokeng, 117.
Khohlooa, 212.
Khokhoba, 75.
Kholokhoe, 101, 103, 210.
Kholu, associative references, 28, 49, 71, 74, 110, 117, 138, 139, 140, 142, 191, 192, 204.
Khomonala, 230.
Khopotso, 245, 257, 258, 261.
Koali Makhobalo, 166.
Koebu, 239.
Koena, 2, 61, 63, 74, 76, 86, 99, 160, 161, 171, 222, 254; Sechele's Koena, 248.
Associative references, 42, 43, 138, 190.
Moshoeshoe's Sotho referred to or addressed as Koena, 19, 28, 41, 46, 50–1, 54, 66, 86, 95, 106, 117, 123, 134, 143, 146, 147, 149, 151, 153, 191, 192, 193, 201, 202, 205, 216, 218, 219, 220, 221, 232, 233, 236, 237, 238, 242, 259, 260, 262, 264, 265, 267.
Kofa Marebele, 141.
Kolobe Moerane, 21, 53, 154.
Komane (Ngomane?), 82, 87.
Kora, conflicts with Sotho during *lifaqane*, 3, 14, 23, 65, 78, 96, 101, 107, 110; conflicts with Sotho during Orange River Sovereignty, 4–5, 38, 42, 58, 97, 107, 108(?), 111, 114, 118, 120–1, 123–4; conflicts with Tlokoa (1840–2), 104, 109.
Korotsoane, 93.
Krotz, Adam, 112.
Kuku, 124.
Kunene, D. P., viii–ix, 28, 40, 43, 54.
Kunene, R., 43.
Kwelela, 140.

Lagden, Sir Godfrey, 8, 209.
Langalibalele, 7, 37, 38, 60, 111, 169, 170, 180, 187, 188, 193, 194, 195, 198, 199, 205.
Laydevant, Father F., 243.
Lebakae, 167.
Lebakeng, 250.
Lebenya, 81, 93.
Lebihan Masopha (informant), 118.
Lechakola, 165.
Lehana, 83.
Lehloenya, 239.
Lejaha Makhabane, 132, 186.
Lekena, see Lerotholi.
Lekete Letsie (informant), 155.
Lelaka RaSenate, 100.
Lelingoana, 10, 145, 248, 252, 258, 264.
Leloko Lerotholi, 254, 260.
Lelosa, Jobo, 106.
Lelosa Pokane, 207.
Leluma Posholi, 91.
Lenkoane, 181.
Lenono, 86.
Lepekola Joel (informant), 188, 201, 205, 207.
Lepolesa Letsie, 28, 211, 237, 240.
Lepoqo Masopha, 174, 176, 180, 251.
Leputla, 124.
Lerotholi, battle of Khamolane, 8, 55, 116, 137, 208–9, 214, 223, 232;

278   *Index*

Lerotholi—*contd.*

biographical details, 62, 136–7, 261; death and dispute that followed, 9, 209, 214, 233, 246, 250; dispute between Jonathan and Joel Molapo, 187, 192; government of his son Griffith, 222, 223; Gun War, 7, 107, 137, 143–52, 154, 162–3, 164, 188, 231, 253; leaves Letsie II at Likhoele, 210, 211; Moorosi War, 60, 137, 152–4; Orange Free State, second war, 136–43.

Associative references, 105, 108, 127, 155, 158, 165, 171, 182, 184, 191, 201, 203, 218, 219, 226, 227, 228, 229, 230, 236, 238, 241, 244, 245, 247, 248, 249, 251, 252, 254, 255, 256, 257, 258, 259, 263, 264, 266, 267, 268.

Praise-poems, 18, 20, 29, 32, 33, 36, 38, 39, 40, 41, 42, 48, 51, 56, 57–8, 59, 60, 82, 135, *136–54*, 155, 156, 186, 189, 195, 200.

Lerotholi Mojela, 62, 234–42, 253.

Praise-poems, 19, 28, 29, 32, 41, 43, 46, 124, *234–42*, 244, 248, 250.

Lesa, 263.

Lesala, 224.

Lesaoana (Fokeng?), 70.

Lesaoana (Tlokoa), 99.

Lesaoana Makhabane, attacks Tlokoa (1848), 113; conflict with Jonathan Molapo, 169, 172, 173, 176, 187; dispute with Masopha, 115, 116, 122–3; raids Natal (1865), 140; recitation at his village, 25; relations with Lerotholi, 29, 37, 151.

Associative references, 40, 179, 186, 246.

Leselinyana la Lesotho (newspaper), vii, viii, 39, 71, 78, 97, 112, 201, 207.

Leshoboro Majara, 222.

Leshoboro Seesiso, 265.

Lestrade, G. P., 34.

Letele Mohlomi, 81, 92–3.

Letlala, 38, 109, 114–15, 117, 135.

Letlatsa, 56, 147.

Letšabisa, associative references, 55, 139, 146, 154, 155, 158, 163, 210, 212, 215, 222, 223, 225, 232.

Letšela Moojane, 192.

Letsie I, attack on Mjaluza, 108–9; biographical details, 62, 106–7, 261; conflicts with Kora, 107–8; conflicts with Tlokoa, 108, 109–10, 119; death and arrangements about succession, 8, 107, 154, 232; dispute between Jonathan and Joel Molapo, 171, 180, 201, 202; Gun War, 7, 22, 107, 148–9, 159, 160, 161; migration to Morija, 4, 106, 110, 115; Moorosi War, 152–3, 165–6; names, 40, 61, 70, 106; Orange Free State, first war, 107; Orange Free State, second war, 107, 140, 168; raid on Thembu (1835), 70, 107, 108–9, 112; relations with Masopha, 116, 122, 126, 128, 131, 132; relations with Mhlambiso, 109; relations with Molapo, 110; relations with Moroka, 108; relations with Posholi, 79, 85, 90, 94.

Associative references, 20, 21, 28, 29, 31, 33, 41, 46, 50–1, 77, 100, 117, 120, 125, 135, 136, 137, 143, 155, 156, 157, 162, 163, 167, 171, 184, 188, 190, 191, 198, 200, 208, 209, 211, 219, 222, 227, 236, 237, 238, 239, 240, 241, 245, 246, 248, 250, 251, 252, 253, 254, 256, 260, 262, 268.

Praise-poems, 23, 27, 30, 38–9, 42, 43, 44–5, *106–10*.

Letsie II, battle of Khamolane, 23, 57, 59, 208–15, 217, 218, 221, 223, 228; biographical details, 9, 62, 208–9, 261; dispute with Griffith, 24, 214, 233; succession to him, 214, 253.

Associative references, 29, 219, 245, 247, 250, 255.

Praise-poems, 23, 27–8, 35, 39, 40, 43, 59, 91, 188, *208–13*, 220.

Letsosa, 115.

Letuka Tlhabeli, 109.

Leuta, 167.

Leutsoa, 162.

Libe, 62, 63, 64.

Associative references, 22, 66, 68, 70, 95, 105, 146, 158, 160, 163, 188, 192, 219, 222, 225, 245.

Likupa. 211.
Limo, 175.
Lineo, 163.
Linyonyolo. 184.
Liphere, 211.
Lipohoana, 52, 173.
Lishobana Mpaki Molapo (informant), 66, 188, 201, 205, 207.
Loto Letsie, 253.

Maama, biographical details, 62, 154; Gun War, 7, 59, 146, 150, 154, 155–65, 166–7, 171; Moorosi War, 60, 154, 165–7; Orange Free State, second war, 154, 168. Associative references, 28, 43, 151, 191, 223, 236, 237, 240, 249. Praise-poems, 18, 20, 21, 26–7, 30, 37, 40, 41, 45, 47, 53, 59, 60, 83, 89, 92, 99, 121, 141, *154–68*, 174, 182, 215, 233, 235, 267.
Maaooa, see Pedi.
Mabeleng, 222.
Mabilikoe Matete, 249, 252.
Mabille, Adolphe, 24.
Mabina Lerotholi, 257, 266.
Maboka, 209–10, 213.
MacFarlane, Walter, 140.
Macgregor, J. C., 21.
Machakela Mopeli, 98, 101.
Maethe, 120.
Mafa, 109, 156, 163, 215.
Mafata, 131.
Mahali, 213.
Mahao, 109, 233.
Mahasa, 115.
Mahe, 137.
Mahlape, 118, 125.
Mahlelebe, 265.
Mahlolela, 120, 125, 126, 128, 151, 221, 230.
Mahooana Molapo, 189.
Maieane, 205.
Majara Moshoeshoe, 62, 252.
Majara (grandson of Majara Moshoeshoe), 252.
Makaota, 32, 78, 97, 99, 118, 136, 241, 253.
Makate, 205.
Makatolle (newspaper), 33.
Makaula, see Silonyana.
Maketekete Sekonyela, 4, 97, 117.

Makhabane, 3, 31, 62, 72, 75–9, 96, 101, 134, 170, 213. Associative references, 28, 43, 81, 92, 95, 106, 122, 132, 135, 140, 151, 169, 178, 187, 199, 227, 246. Praise-poems, 23, 40, 44–5, 49, 75–9, 158.
Makhabane Letsie, 21, 62, 155.
Makhanya, 195, 203.
Makhaola Lerotholi, associative references, 29, 191, 217, 219, 236, 245, 247, 250, 261, 262.
Makhatha, 210.
Makhetha, 76–8, 79, 93.
Makhobalo Moshoeshoe, 138, 166, 208, 222.
Makhube, 230.
Makibile, 133.
Makoala, 133.
Makoanyane (comrade of Lerotholi Mojela), 238.
Makoanyane (comrade of Moshoeshoe), 28, 43, 48, 67, 69, 74, 119.
Makoloane, 91.
Makopoi, 240, 245, 250, 257, 258.
Makoti, 86.
Makotoko Makhabane, 178, 199, 202.
Malebanye (husband of Letšabisa), 146.
Malebanye (subject of Letsie II), 212.
Maloloja, 175.
Maluke (wife of Masopha), 127, 135.
Maluke Posholi, 83, 88, 91.
Mamello, 245.
Manama Molapo, 177.
Manamolela, 81, 92–3, 101.
Manella, 40, 220.
Manganane, 81, 93.
Mangoaela, Z. D., vii, viii, 37, 38, 39, 53, 63, 64, 65, 66, 76, 80, 96, 100, 107, 111, 116, 123, 136, 137, 154, 170, 187, 214, 235; changes to his text, viii, 64, 67, 68, 69, 72, 78, 112, 162, 164, 172, 181, 196, 198, 205, 216.
Manoeli, 184.
Maotoana Fokeng, 63, 252.
Mapeshoane Posholi, 88.
Maphakela Posholi, 88.
Maphule, 68.
Maqatela, 110.
Marabeng, 68, 69, 70.
Marakabei Lerotholi, 29, 222, 245, 250.

Marebele, 141.
Marthinsi Masopha, 180.
Masakale, 125.
Mashabatela, 86.
Mashapha (a Nguni chief), 109.
Mashapha Letsie, 252.
Masoenyane, 103.
Masopha, attack on Mpondomise and Thembu (1861), 116, 126–33, 133–4; battle of Khamolane, 8, 23, 35–6, 59, 116, 137, 208–13, 214, 216–18, 221–3, 226, 227, 229, 230–1, 232; biographical details, 62, 115–116; conflicts with Kora, Griqua and Tlokoa, 106, 115, 117–21, 123, 133, 135–6; dispute between Jonathan and Joel Molapo, 37, 187, 192; Gun War, 7, 59, 116, 151, 164, 169, 173–4, 176, 178, 187; migration to Thaba Phatšoa, 115, 122–3, 135; Orange Free State, first war, 115, 123–6, 134; Orange Free State, second war, 116, 134–5, 141, 142; weak control by Letsie, 107, 116.
Associative references, 28, 29, 57, 75, 77, 104, 166, 180, 237, 247, 268.
Praise-poems, 30, 33, 40, 41, 43, 47–8, 49, 50, 58, *115–36*, 165, 178, 208, 231, 239, 267.
Masopha II, 28, 237, 242.
Masopha Letsie, 62.
Masumpa, 115.
Matabohe, 139, 142.
Matata, 133.
Mateka, 223.
Matekase, 99.
Matekoane, 88.
Matela Tselanyane, 49, 174, 187, 191, 201, 205–6.
Matete, Paulus, 109, 239.
Mathalea, 81, 89, 151, 188, 222.
Matimokanye, 88.
Matiwane, 2–3, 68, 115, 231.
Matlabe, 224, 225.
Matlake, 85.
Matlere Lerotholi, 257, 258, 266.
Matlole, see Motloang.
Matšosa, 240.
Matsoso, Samuel, 147.
Mbale, 83, 88, 96, 116, 126–30.
Mfengu, 59, 145, 205.

Mhlambiso, 38, 109.
Mhlonhlo, 145, 200.
Migane (or Megane), 201.
Mjaluza, 108, 109.
Mlanjeni, 84.
'MaApi, 249, 254, 264.
'MaBatho, 215, 218, 243, 252.
'MaBereng, 243, 262, 267.
'MaBoi, 168.
'MaBotle, 28, 81.
'MaKaibane, 201.
'MaKali, 202.
'Makhoana, 102.
'MaKhutsi, 197.
'Mako Moliboea Molapo (informant), ix, 25, 94, 112, 113, 119, 170, 171, 172, 177, 181, 183, 188, 204.
'MaLehlasoana, 123–4.
'MaLerotholi, 192, 245, 250.
'MaLeshoboro, 262.
'MaLibili, 208, 216, 228.
'MaLihlahleng, 69.
'MaLimapane, 175.
'MaLoela, 167.
'MaMakhaola, 249.
'MaMakhobalo, 234, 239.
'MaMaqampu, 91.
'MaMmui, 74.
'MaMohale, 124.
'MaMohato, 58, 109, 117, 129, 131, 223.
'MaMojela, 240.
'MaMokhachane, 66.
'MaMopeli, 186, 197.
'MaMosa, 183, 185, 190, 206.
'MaMotena, 160.
'MaMotsarapane, 175.
'MaNeo, see Letšabisa.
'MaNthatisi, 108, 109, 115.
'MaNtšebo (wife of Seeiso Griffith), 9, 54–5, 61, 243, 251, 253, 254, 266.
'MaNtšebo (identity unknown), 105.
'MaPaki, 189, 205.
'MaPolane, 191.
'MaQhoai, 64.
'Mari, 260.
'MaSeeiso, 243, 246, 250, 258.
'MaSekhonyana, 45, 113, 129.
'MaSenate, 110.
'MaSetenane, 66, 74, 75.
'MaTau, 255.
'MaToka, 261.

'Matšoana, 20, 159.
'MaTšoeunyane, 65, 86, 109, 224-5.
'Moi, 103.
'Mota, 86, 105, 110.
'Mualle, 63.
'Muso, 99.
Mochebelele Taba, 207.
Mocheko, 214, 222-3, 229-31, 234.
Mochekoane, 233.
Mochochoko, 263.
Moeketsi Masopha, 8, 35, 57, 208-10, 213, 216, 223, 228, 232.
Moeletsi Moletsane, 100.
Mofephe, 82, 87.
Mofoka (subordinate of Letsie II), 211.
Mofoka Mojela, 235, 236.
Mofota Letsie, 240.
Mohale, 62, 90, 91, 145.
Associative references, 88, 98, 120, 131, 143, 166, 232, 268.
Mohanoe Makhetha, 81.
Mohatanya, 171.
Mohatla, 165.
Mohato (son of Moshoeshoe II), 269.
Mohlabani (newspaper), 33.
Mohlakana Lerotholi, 28, 237, 250.
Mohlaoli Mahlelebe, 264-5.
Mohlomi, 1, 76, 81, 89, 106, 161, 204.
Mohlouoa, 225.
Moholobela Seeiso, 28, 237.
Moiloa Mabeleng, 222.
Moipone, see 'MaNtšebo.
Mojakisane Mohlomi, 81, 210.
Mojapo (Jacob the Griqua?), 118.
Mojela Letsie, 62, 146, 158, 223, 234, 235, 238, 239, 240, 241, 253.
Associative references, 156-7, 236, 242.
Mokali, 28, 71, 72.
Mokeke, 153.
Mokhachane, 2, 62, 63, 64-5, 67, 89, 95, 96, 101, 104, 142, 149.
Associative references, 22, 28, 30, 31, 41, 42, 43, 47, 69, 73, 74, 80, 86, 90, 92, 98, 102, 105, 108, 110, 112, 115, 120, 122, 124, 128, 134, 136, 137, 139, 146, 147, 150, 152, 153, 158, 159, 160, 164, 165, 166, 171, 177, 181, 188, 189, 191, 193, 194, 195, 199, 203, 204, 207, 208, 212, 213, 214, 215, 217, 218, 219, 220, 221, 222, 225, 227, 237, 241,

242, 245, 246, 248, 252, 253, 255, 258, 262, 263, 268.
Praise-poems, 23, *64-5*.
Mokhalong, 123-4.
Mokheseng, 161.
Mokhethi (father of RaTjotjose), 48, 67, 69, 74.
Mokhethi (subordinate of Mojela Letsie), 238.
Mokhitli, 70, 75.
Mokhoaetsi, 81.
Mokoena, 81.
Mokoenehi, 211.
Mokoteli, 63, 64.
Associative references, 68, 85, 87, 90, 114, 120, 124, 201, 203, 238.
Mokoteli (people), 2, 64, 67, 105, 132, 160.
Mokotjo, 100.
Molapo, attack on Mjaluza, 108; attacks on San, 10, 183-5, 197, 203; biographical details, 4, 62, 110-11; conflicts with Kora and Tlokoa, 106, 111, 113-15; dispute between Jonathan and Joel, 168-9, 187, 196; dispute with Masopha, 115-16, 122-3; Langalibalele incident, 7, 111, 169, 193, 194, 198; Orange Free State, first war, 111, 126; Orange Free State, second war, 6, 111, 169, 181, 187, 204; raid on Thembu (1835), 110, 112-13; weak control by Letsie, 107.
Associative references, 59, 70, 77, 135, 144, 166, 167, 170, 174, 176, 177, 182, 186, 190, 191, 192, 199, 200, 202, 205, 206, 214, 231-2, 236, 241, 249.
Praise-poems, 23, 42, 43, 45-6, *110-15*.
Molapo Maama, 21, 26-7, 154, 164.
Molapo Mojela, 32, 234, 235, 241, 253.
Molema, S. M., 102.
Moletsane, 87, 90, 94, 100, 104, 105, 123, 125, 144, 148, 152, 166.
Molibeli (people), 113, 114, 160, 185, 224.
Moliboea Molapo, 170, 174, 190, 196, 199.
Molise (Fokeng chief), 64.
Molise Tšolo, 19, 260, 264, 265.
Molomo Mohale, 88, 131.

Molulela, 83.

Monaheng (Koena chief), see Kali.

Monaheng (people), 1, 76–8, 79–82, 89–93, 95, 101.

Monyake Moletsane, 123.

Monyane, 78, 93.

Monyeke, 45, 113.

Moojane, 106.

Moorosi, battle of Dulcies Nek, 79, 84; Moorosi War, 7, 37, 60, 137, 152–4, 165–7, 169, 231(?); Orange Free State, second war, 80; raid on Thembu (1835), 112–113; relations with San, 182, 185, 197, 206, 208; submission to Moshoeshoe, 231(?).
    Associative references, 90, 115, 214, 225, 226, 229.

Mopeli, 62, 94, 96–106, 137, 141.
    Praise-poems, 39, 40–1, 43, 46–7, 56, 57, *96–106*, 125, 144.

Mopeli Joel, 202, 205.

Mophethe, 166.

Moroesi, 104.

Moroka, 4, 38, 46, 102, 104, 108, 114.

Mosa, 126, 181.

Mosaeea, 164.

Mosala, 69.

Mosi, 103.

Mosheshe, 105.

Moshoeshoe I, biographical details, 62, 65, 261; career before *lifaqane*, 1–2, 12, 13, 21, 23, 64, 67–8, 69, 73, 74–5, 132; career during *lifaqane*, 2–3, 14, 31, 63, 65–6, 68, 70–2, 73, 75–6, 79, 106–7, 108, 110, 112, 170, 231, 241; career (1836–48), 3–4; Orange River Sovereignty (1848–54), 4–5, 79, 83, 85, 87, 104, 106, 110, 111, 113, 119, 120, 123; Masopha's migration to Thaba Phatšoa (1855), 122, 123; Orange Free State, first war (1858), 5–6, 63–4, 79–80, 124; raid on Mpondomise and Thembu (1861), 131, 133; Orange Free State, second war (1865–8), 6, 45, 80, 96, 101, 111, 116, 138, 140, 141, 168, 203, 204; succession to him, 232; government, general, 7, 31–2, 66, 73–4, 80, 87, 93, 96, 99, 137, 139, 149–

150; names, xiv, xv, 13, 40, 61, 124.
    Associative references, 22, 25, 29, 36, 41, 84, 109, 115, 121, 128, 129, 130, 134, 142, 143, 145, 153, 159, 160, 165, 166, 176, 181, 188, 189, 192, 202, 215, 219, 220, 221, 222, 223, 224, 225, 226, 227, 233, 235, 237, 238, 239, 240, 245, 246, 247, 255, 257, 264, 267, 268, 269.
    Praise-poems, viii, 21, 23, 24, 27, 28, 30, 31–2, 39, 43, 44, 48, 49, 56, *65–75*, 90, 98, 147, 196, 217, 244, 248, 259, *270–2*.

Moshoeshoe II (Constantine Bereng Seeiso), 62, 235, 266–9.
    Associative reference, 265.
    Praise-poems, viii, 19, 24, 29, 33, 40, 117, *266–9*, *272–3*.

Mositi RaMosena, 182, 185.

Mosiuoa Lerotholi, 254, 266.

Mosoansoanyane, 171.

Mosuoe Lelingoana, 258.

Moteki, 221–2.

Mothibe Molapo, 189.

Motlalei, 197.

Motlejoa, 117.

Motloang, 22, 63, 71, 74, 75, 160, 166, 189, 264.

Motloang Mopeli, 141.

Motloheloa, 171, 264.

Motloheloa Ntsoana, 201.

Motonosi, 104.

Motsarapane, 29, 245, 255.

Motsetseli, 121–2.

Motšoane, see Peete.

Motšoene, 175, 201, 214, 231–2, 242.

Mpaki Molapo, 189.

Mpande, 102.

Mpangazitha, 2, 86.

Mphaphang, 68.

Mphaphathi, 172, 174, 177, 181, 186, 198, 207.

Mpharane, Treaty of, 111, 169, 187, 204.

Mphasa, 238.

Mphohle, 195.

Mphu, 212.

Mpilo, 132.

Mpinane, see Nthe.

Mpiti Letsie, 62, 251.

Mpiti Sekake, 67, 132, 208, 264.

Mpoi, 156.

Mpondo, 132, 200.
Mpondomise, 30, 35, 83, 88, 96, 116, 126–7, 130, 132–4, 145, 200.
Mthimkhulu, 86, 87, 109.
Murray, 246, 260.
Mzilikazi, 3.

Nanne, 69.
Napo Motlomelo, 32, 74, 171.
Native Labour Corps, 8, 234.
Ndebele, of Mzilikazi, 3; synonymous with Nguni, 3, 51, 73, 84, 87, 88, 90, 102, 107, 108, 128, 129, 132, 145, 147, 164, 167, 175, 189, 190, 194, 196, 199, 205, 206, 230; as term of abuse, 147, 202, 252.
Nehemiah, see Sekhonyana Moshoeshoe.
Ngubencuka, 70, 72, 96, 134.
Nguni, 1, 12, 38, 52, 73, 79, 82, 83, 84, 96, 107, 108, 109, 110, 122, 127, 129, 132, 134, 139, 164, 166, 167, 173, 182, 196, 199, 205, 206, 221, 248, 252, 262. See also Ndebele.
Ngwane, 2, 68, 115, 231.
Nkakole, 46, 113–14.
Nkamohi, 224.
Nkau Lerotholi, 225, 250.
Nkejane (Ngiyane), 85.
Nketu (newspaper), 33.
Nkhahle, 122.
Nkhehle, 132.
Nkoebe Letsie, 62, 223, 240, 247.
Associative references, 28, 32, 43, 157, 210, 214–15, 236, 237, 241, 246, 252.
Nkopane, 89, 161.
Nkopi, 28, 81, 94.
'Neheng, 173.
'Neko, 70, 112, 138.
Nqaele, 86.
Ntahli, 179.
Nte, 222.
Ntharetsane, 124.
Nthe, 43, 118, 120, 125, 129, 134, 135, 206, 223.
Ntho Mokeke, 153.
Ntisane Sekhoane, 77.
Ntjaatsana, 200.
Ntjahali, 82, 89.
Ntolo, 143.
Ntsane (Molibeli chief), 114.
Ntsane (unidentified), 119–20.

Ntsane Moshoeshoe, 148.
Ntšebo (daughter of Lerotholi), 145, 153, 223, 246, 247, 264, 266.
Ntšebo (daughter of Seeiso Griffith), 54–5, 61, 251, 264.
Ntšeke, 119.
Ntsieli, see 'MaTšoeunyane.
Ntsoakele, 172.
Ntsoana, 192, 201.
Ntšohi, 139, 142.
Ntsubise, 102, 141.
Ntsukunyane, 191.

Oetsi, 101.
Orange Free State, first war (1858), 5–6, 36, 64, 79–80, 82, 96–7, 100–101, 107, 111, 115–16, 123–6, 127, 134.
Orange Free State, second war (1865–8), 6, 14, 36, 37, 38, 80, 96–7, 111, 116, 134–5, 137–43, 154, 168, 169, 170, 181, 187–8, 203, 204.
Orthography, xiv, 53.

Paroz, R. A., 24, 204, 234, 252.
Peane, 123.
Pedi, xiv, 73, 248.
Peeka, 51, 84, 88.
Peete, 2, 40, 62, 63, 64, 105, 146.
Associative references, 22, 28, 41, 48, 71, 74, 76, 95, 101, 102, 132, 134, 139, 140, 144, 145, 159, 160, 163, 166, 171, 189, 219, 221, 227, 237, 264.
Praise-poems, 63.
Peete Lesaoana, 41, 203, 220, 246.
Pelepele, 137.
Peo, 65.
Phafane, 164, 165.
Phafoli, 183.
Phakathao Bungane, 122.
Phakiso, 261.
Pheetla, 182, 185.
Phokotsa, 56, 69.
Phuthi, 7, 90, 112, 115, 152, 166, 182, 206, 214, 222–3, 225, 229, 230.
Pinda, Stephen (informant), 94, 118, 131, 132, 204, 212, 214.
Places and areas
Algoa Bay, 85, 146, 160, 236.
Aliwal North, 82, 92, 140.
Barkly East, 112.

Places and areas—*contd.*
Berea District, 86, 114.
Berea Plateau, 99, 115, 218, 219, 223, 224, 226.
Bloemfontein, 116, 134, 150.
Boleka, 146, 156, 238.
Bolokoe (Vechtkop), 79, 83, 87, 91.
Bolumatau, 239.
Boqate, 218, 219, 220.
Boribeng, 106.
Botha-Bothe, 2, 50–1, 63, 73, 115, 117, 176, 241.
Botswana, 248.
Cana, 110.
Cape Town, 85, 96, 144, 146, 160, 236, 259.
Cathcart's Drift, 123, 124, 125.
Clocolan, 96.
Colesberg, 150.
de Villiers Drift, 173.
Dulcies Nek, 79, 82, 84–5.
East Griqualand, 96.
Elliot, 112.
Fobane, 169, 176, 184.
Fothane, 176.
France, 234, 235, 238.
Herschel District, 95, 214, 223.
Hleoheng, 176.
Hlojoaneng, 85.
Hlotse Heights, 59, 149, 169, 172, 173, 180, 187, 189, 190, 191, 200.
Hlatsing, 109.
Hoatane, 47, 173.
Johannesburg, 244.
Kalahari Desert, 99.
Kamastone, 84, 109.
Ketane, 90.
Khalise, 99.
Khamolane, 116, 137, 209, 211, 213, 217, 221, 222, 224, 225, 228, 232.
Khoalipana, 101.
Khololong (Commando Nek), 69.
Kimberley, 7, 152, 244.
Kokobe, 28, 216, 227.
Kolo, 137, 139, 142.
Kolojane, 47, 173, 179.
Kononyana, see Viervoet.
Lefi's Nek, 201.
Lentsoaneng, 78.
Leopard-That-Roars, 99.
Leribe, 23, 25, 50, 111, 112, 147, 169, 175, 181, 183, 184, 186, 188, 199, 201, 259.

Leribe District, 23, 115, 119, 169, 171, 176, 188, 199.
Leribe Plateau, 105, 106, 169, 172, 173, 185, 199.
Likhakeng, 139.
Likhoele, 43, 137, 142, 147, 148, 158, 208, 209, 210, 211, 212, 213, 263–4.
Likolonyama, 131.
Linokong, 101.
Lipetu, 119.
Liphiring, 91.
Liphokoaneng, 211.
Lithamahaneng, 124.
Litšoeneng, 93, 224.
Mabolela, 94, 96, 100, 101, 103, 141.
Mabula, 100, 101.
Machache, 127.
Mafeteng, 118, 148, 149, 158, 162, 163, 212, 214.
Mafeteng District, 79, 137, 145, 148, 161, 215, 228, 234, 238, 264.
Mahiseng, 68.
Mahlatsa, 119.
Maiseng, 172.
Majoe-a-Litšoene, 130, 165.
Makaoteng, 241.
Makate, 101.
Makeneng, 137, 208, 210, 211, 257.
Makhoarane, 140, 148, 227, 250.
Makholo, 29, 216.
Makkawaan's Bank, 102.
Makosane, 105.
Malaoaneng, 183.
Mangolo, 28, 80, 92.
Mangolonyane, 28, 80, 92.
Manyareleng, 146–7.
Maphororong (Doornberg), 102.
Maphutseng, 215, 230.
Mapoteng, 117.
Maqhaoe, 119.
Marabeng, 3, 85, 99, 108, 110, 115, 116, 121.
Marajaneng (Spitz Kop), 81, 83, 91, 92.
Marseilles, 103.
Maseru, 6, 7, 107, 148, 149, 153, 154, 155, 162, 163, 164, 169, 189, 194, 214, 239, 241, 242, 246, 251, 258, 259, 260, 263, 264.
Maseru District, 77, 161, 162, 166, 168, 228.
Masite, 109, 139, 166, 225, 250.

Mathebe (Tandjesberg), 80, 148, 156, 157, 215.
Mathokoane, 47, 173, 176, 179.
Matlakeng (Aasvöelberg), 92.
Matlakeng (near Matsieng), 258, 263.
Matsieng, 7, 33, 35, 107, 128, 137, 148, 149, 213, 214, 222, 227, 233, 237, 239, 243, 246, 249, 250, 257, 258, 259, 260, 262, 263, 265.
Mayaphuthi, 79.
Meeling, 162.
Mehopung, 224.
Mekoatleng, 87, 94, 123.
Menkhoaneng, 2, 4, 73, 78, 202.
'Male, 113.
'Malifatjana, 28, 216, 227.
'Mate, 63, 64.
Mohale's Hoek District, 166, 214.
Mohlanapeng, 157.
Mokhethoaneng, 124.
Mokhotlong District, 10, 242, 244, 246, 248, 257, 265, 266.
Mokhotsako's ford, 103.
Mokoallong, 54, 55, 216, 224.
Moliko, 97.
Molumong, 176.
Moorosi's Mountain, 166.
Morifi Drift, 222.
Morija, vii, viii, 3, 4, 106–7, 109, 110, 115, 209, 227, 265.
Motengoane, 204.
Motete, 248, 257, 258.
Mount Fletcher, 127.
Mpharane (near Ficksburg), 99, 119.
Mpharane (near Marseilles), 103.
Natal, 7, 60, 102, 111, 140, 169, 180, 193, 199, 244, 258.
Ntlo-Kholo, 75, 96, 101.
Nyaba-Nyaba, 127.
Pahong, 78.
Palmietfontein, 95.
Peka, 4, 106, 110, 182, 241.
Phahameng, 209.
Phale, 204.
Phamong, 214, 216, 218, 219, 221, 222, 224, 225, 227, 229, 232, 233, 247, 251, 257.
Phatlalla, 152.
Philippolis, 112.
Phomolong, 173, 186.
Phoqoane, 235.

Pitsaneng, 127.
Pitsi's Nek, 52, 106, 173.
Popa, 77, 130–1, 165.
Port Elizabeth, 85, 146, 160, 236.
Pretoria, 24, 258, 262.
Qacha's Nek, 78.
Qalo, 47, 169, 173, 186, 187, 196, 201, 204.
Qeme, 20, 45, 168, 223.
Qethoane, 92, 93, 95, 108.
Qibing, 239.
Qiloane, 230.
Qoaling, 31, 72, 223.
Qoing, 106.
Qopo, 224.
Qoqolosing, 50, 172, 175, 176, 185, 199.
Quthing, 229.
Quthing District, 223, 229, 247.
RaFutho Pass, 49, 116, 135, 203.
RaMatobo's ford, 103.
RaMpai's Nek, 52, 173, 175, 199.
Rand, 9.
Roma, 77, 244, 266.
Sani Pass, 258.
Sebothoane, 47, 173, 180, 185.
Sefikeng, 54, 55, 86, 212, 216, 223, 225, 226.
Sekameng, 173, 201.
Sekubu, 66, 105, 174.
Senekal, 97.
Senyotong, 114.
Seqaobe, 100.
Smithfield, 82, 92, 160.
Tebang (in Lesotho), 234, 235, 238, 239, 240.
Tebang (in Transvaal), 171.
Teyateyaneng, 132, 232.
Thaba Bosiu, 2, 3, 5, 6, 25, 29, 38, 63, 68, 72, 73, 75, 79, 96, 101, 107, 108, 112, 115, 116, 124, 133, 135, 137, 140, 141, 169, 181, 187. 203, 209, 211, 212, 214, 215, 216, 218, 219, 223, 228, 230, 231, 239, 241, 267.
Thaba Chitja, 162.
Thaba Mautse, 162.
Thaba Nchu, 108, 147.
Thaba Phatšoa, 111, 115, 122–3, 127.
Thaba Tšoeu (in southern Lesotho), 79, 156, 215.
Thaba Tšoeu (Wonder Kop), 101.

Places and areas—*contd.*
Thabana Morena, 215.
Thabana tsa Bara ba Makhetha (Beeste Kraal), 93.
Thabaneng, 232.
Thabang, 242, 244, 248, 266.
Thuathe, 219, 220, 224.
Tlapaneng, 114.
Tlokoeng, 99, 265.
Tolomaneng, 95.
Transkei, 3.
Transvaal, 147, 248.
Tšakholo, 28, 237, 239.
Tsatsa-le-'Meno, 78.
Tsikoane, 50, 112, 169, 172, 175, 181, 187, 200.
Tšoanamakhulo, 111, 132, 222.
Tsoili-Tsoili, 223, 224.
Ulu-ulu, 162.
Van Rooyen's Gate, 240.
Verkeerdevlei, 116, 134–5, 142.
Viervoet, 5, 46, 96, 97, 102, 103, 110.
Weenen, 140.
Wepener, 239, 242.
Winburg, 116, 134.
Wittebergen Native Reserve, 79, 84, 85, 87.
Witzies Hoek, 96, 101, 200, 259.
Zastron, 81, 92, 93.
Zululand, 3, 73.
Posholi, 62, 76, 79–96, 101, 130, 231.
Associative references, 29, 37, 118, 150–1, 162, 268.
Praise-poems, 18, 19, 20, 23, 28, 43, 44–5, 51, 58, 70, 74, 79–96, 99, 101, 145, 161, 164, 188, 198, 213, 220, 222.
Potse, 189, 190.
Praise-poems, alliteration and assonance, 55–6; changes of tense, person, etc., 57–9; composition, 18–23; conjunctions, relative absence of, 57; eulogues, 28, 40–52, 54, 61, 98; functions, 27–33, 59; historical value, 59–61; imagery, 54; inversion, 56; line, 52–3, 57; occasions of composition, 23–4; parallelism, 54–5; praise-names, 40, 61; puns, 63, 68, 70, 72, 84, 88, 94, 98, 99, 124, 130–1, 133, 134, 156–7, 228, 236, 258; recitation, 24–7, 52–3, 144, 154,

170, 188; rhythm, 53–4, 61; Sotho's appreciation of, 33, 39–40, 155; sources, vii-ix, 63, 64, 65–6, 76, 80, 97, 107, 111, 112, 116, 137, 154, 170, 187–8, 214; stanzas, 34–52, 244; structure, 34–40, 66, 76, 80, 97, 107, 116, 170, 209, 214, 235, 244; themes, vii, 34, 189; Zulu praise-poems, 30, 43–4.
Praise-poets, education, 22–3, 154, 244, 266; at Matsieng, 33; memory, 39; problems of identification, 18–23; rivalry, 22, 171.
David RaMaema, 24, 266; George Lerotholi, viii, 19, 24, 244, 266; Laistoko, 214; Mahasele Matekane, 170; Mokhethi Moshoeshoe, 170; Morallana Tsotetsi, 170; Nthootso, 188; Salai, 188; Seliane Teba, 214; Tapole Khoele, 214, 218(?); Tsutsubi, 188.
Privy Council, 234, 253.
Pronunciation, xiv–xv.

Qacha, 196.
Qakithe Chabalala, 201.
Qampu, 82, 89.
Qekoane, 205.
Qhoaebane, 69.
Qhoaempe, 88.
Qhoai Fokeng, 64–5, 67, 69–70.
Qhoasi, 185.
Qhoqholoane, 105.
Qoane, see Jan Letele.

RaBohoko, 105.
RaChaka, 173.
RaFolatsane Letsie, 252.
RaKhoalite (Makhabane?), 77.
RaKhoiti, 227.
RaKhosi, 104.
RaKotoanyana, 131.
RaLeotoana, 44, 78–9.
RaLetsoai (Piet de Wet), 92.
RaLiemere, 157.
RaLinkeng, 135.
RaMabilikoe, 156, 163, 180, 215.
RaMahlaela, 86.
RaMakholo, 139.
RaManella, see Lesaoana Makhabane.
RaMatiea, 22, 160.

RaMatlole, 71.
RaMatšeatsana, 67.
RaMatsoku Mallane, 181.
RaMohoere, 148.
RaMokeretla, 81, 93.
RaMokhele Montoeli, 103, 125.
RaMokoena-Seqha, see Jan Letele.
RaMonaheng, 21, 44, 69.
RaMorakane, 65.
RaMoroko, 224, 225.
RaMosala, 76.
RaMosena, 182.
RaMoshee, 200.
RaNkhoana, 64.
RaNtheosi, 28, 71, 72.
RaPakeng, 162.
RaPapali, 131.
RaPolile, 68.
RaPolo, 175.
RaPontšo, 20, 159, 161.
RaQethoane, 45, 113.
RaSheqa, 84, 94.
RaThebe, 194.
RaTjotjose, 48, 67, 69, 74.
RaTšooanyane, 48, 67, 69.
RaTšosane, 224.
Richards, Sir Edmund, 259, 263, 264.
Rivers and streams
  Caledon, *passim*
  Dulcies Spruit, 85.
  Hlotse, 2, 63, 105, 182, 185, 199, 202.
  Hololo, 204.
  Korokoro, 31, 72, 165, 166, 223.
  Kraai, 84.
  Lebabalasi, 102.
  Leqholoqha, 88, 127, 128, 132, 134.
  Lethena, 88, 132.
  Lithane (Molen Spruit), 100.
  Makhaleng, 80, 90, 91, 215, 222.
  Malibamatšo, 248, 257, 258, 268.
  Mantšonyane, 182, 196, 197.
  Maoa-Mafubelu, 105.
  Meja-Metalana, 54, 55, 162, 239, 246, 263, 264.
  Mokoallong, 112.
  Orange, *passim*.
  Phuthiatsana (northern), 110, 131, 176.
  Phuthiatsana (southern), 209, 211, 228, 234.
  Riet, 3, 65, 108.
  Sand, 102.
  Seate, 59, 182, 184.
  Sebapala, 166, 167, 224.
  Tikoe, 102.
  Tsoaing, 161, 165, 228.
  Tuke (Mopeli Spruit), 103.
  Vaal, 4, 171.
  Vet, 102.
Robinson, Sir Hercules, 146.
Rolong, 4, 38, 46, 102–3, 104, 108, 114, 147.
Ropoli, 58, 118.

San (Bushmen), devoured by Lero-
  tholi, 150; join Seeiso Griffith,
  248; loads, 168; name, xiv;
  relations with Monaheng, 81;
  term of abuse, 45, 47, 48, 92, 107,
  118, 120–1, 123–4, 133, 190, 217,
  236; wars with sons of Molapo
  (1871 and 1872), 10, 36, 38, 59,
  169, 170, 182–6, 187–8, 196–7,
  203, 204–5, 206–8.
Sariele, 158.
Sariele Theko, 239, 240.
Saunders, C., ix.
Scanlen, T., 147.
Schapera, I., 34.
Seabeng Posholi, 95.
Seara, 99.
Sebina, 99.
Sebueng, see 'MaSeeiso.
Sechaba, 254.
Sechele, 248.
Second World War, 9, 23, 59, 260.
Seeiso Griffith, 9, 62, 214, 242–66, 267.
  Associative references, 61, 235, 238, 239.
  Praise-poems, viii, 16, 19, 20, 24,
    29, 33, 40, 54–5, *242–66*.
Seeiso Letsie, 7, 62, 171, 223, 240.
  Associative references, 28, 151, 155,
    157, 159, 161, 165, 166, 171, 191,
    210, 236, 237, 245, 246, 249, 253.
Seetsa Molapo, 174, 190, 249.
Sefafe, 113.
Segoete, E., 76.
Sehohotlo Letsie, 62.
Seholoba, 123.
Sekake (chief), 71, 208.
Sekake (people), 67, 132.
Sekese, A. M., viii, 64, 71, 78, 112, 170, 201, 207.
Sekhaba 'Mapule, 65.

Sekhobe Griffith, 251.
Sekhobe Letsie, 21, 28, 155, 237.
Sekhomo, C., 117.
Sekhomo, X. 117.
Sekhonyana Bereng, 19, 96, 236, 242, 260, 263.
Sekhonyana Moshoeshoe, 45, 58, 116, 126–7, 129–30, 134, 148.
Sekoai, 148.
Sekoati Posholi, 88.
Sekonyela, conflicts with Sotho during *lifaqane*, 3, 108, 117–18; conflicts with Sotho during Orange River Sovereignty, 4–5, 19, 41, 83, 85–6, 94, 97, 99, 100, 104, 108, 109, 111, 113–15, 118–19, 121–3, 135; Sotho encroach on land, 4, 110, 113.
Associative references, xiv, 10, 268.
Sekorobele, 199.
Sekwati, 248.
Selala Lengotsoana, 91.
Sele, 87.
Selebalo Moshoeshoe, 202.
Selete Posholi, 83, 88, 91.
'Selolou', 67.
Semethe Posholi, 87.
Sempe Nkoebe, 28, 55–6, 237, 243, 247, 251, 252, 254.
Senate, 198, 232.
Associative references, 94, 126, 138, 148, 152, 153, 155, 157, 158, 160, 163, 166, 167.
Senei, 215, 219.
Senekal, F., 48, 100–1, 123–4, 134.
Senekane Masopha, 47, 217, 223, 224.
Sentle Mojela, 235, 238.
Sepechele, 51, 145, 148, 154, 155, 156, 157, 160.
Sepere, 90–1.
Seshophe Lesaoana, 179.
Setebele, 261.
Setenane, 68, 146, 225.
Setha Matete, 165.
Sethobane, 20, 159, 161, 164.
Setloboko, 119.
Setori, 84.
Shaka, 2, 3, 231.
Shakhane, 28, 43, 48, 67, 69, 74.
Shao, 81, 92–3.
Shepstone, Theophilus, 102, 140.
Siea, 38, 109, 115, 117, 119, 162.

Silonyana (Seloanyana), 58, 83, 127, 129, 134.
Sloley, H., 8.
Smith, Sir Harry, 4–5.
Soai, 10, 36, 38, 59, 169, 170, 182, 185, 187, 196–7, 203, 204, 206–8.
Sofonia Moshoeshoe, 145, 148.
Soga, J. H., 70.
Soko Mpiti, 249.
'Sons of Moshoeshoe', 242–3, 247, 249, 250, 252, 254, 255.
Sotho, cannibalism, 2, 63, 101, 117, 175, 218; charms, 32, 74, 112, 238; definition, xiv; doctors and medicines, 17, 65, 85, 89, 95, 119, 125, 133, 138, 141, 151, 173, 185, 189, 190, 192, 212, 230, 231, 238, 267; divination, 16–17, 130, 142, 189; ecology, 10–11; education, 12–13; government, 15–16; history, 1–9, 33; initiation, vii, 40, 63, 65, 71, 77, 88, 110, 120, 131, 149, 162, 164, 172, 234, 247; *lelomolo*, 159, 267; marriage, 14–15, 234, 243; *mohobelo*, 157, 236, 239; *mokorotlo* (war-song), 25, 100, 118; population, 1, 4, 9; rainmaking, 17; religion, 16 (see also Christianity); sorcery and witchcraft, 16–17, 65, 133, 136, 174, 181, 230, 232; stories, 156, 175, 198, 217, 228–9.
Sprigg, J. G., 37, 51, 143, 144, 145, 146, 147–8, 150, 156, 158, 160–1, 163, 199.
Swazi, 201.

Taaibosch, Gert, 4, 5, 38, 42, 45, 48, 97, 99, 102, 104, 107, 111, 114, 118, 121, 123, 124, 133.
Tabitha ('MaSentle), 235.
Taoma, 77.
Tapole, 214(?), 218.
Tau Jonathan, 29, 245.
Tau (son of Letsie II) 214, 253.
Taung, in conflicts during Orange River Sovereignty, 94, 100, 103, 105, 123; in Gun War, 148, 151–152; their home, 87, 102; inter-marriage with Moshoeshoe's family, 82, 104; Moorosi War, 166; Orange Free State, first war, 125; poet, 137, 151–2; praise-poems of

Moletsane, 104, 144; relations with Masopha, 123.
Teele, 215.
Teko Lerotholi, 29, 245, 250, 254.
Terminology, xiv.
Thaabe Letsie, 28, 237.
Thaane Sehlabaka, 81, 93.
Thaba Bosiu, Treaty of (1866), 6, 140.
Thabo Lerotholi, 263.
Thakhane, 40, 267.
Thamae, 68.
Theal, G. M., 64.
Theko Letsie, 28, 62, 154, 228, 237, 249, 252.
Theko Maama (informant), 168.
Theko Makhaola, 261, 262.
Thembu, conflicts with Posholi during Orange River Sovereignty, 79, 82, 83, 84, 91; Gun War, 167; Sotho attack (1829), 3; Sotho attack (1835), 3, 23, 31, 66, 70, 71, 72, 76, 108, 111, 134, 170, 213; Sotho attack (1861), 45, 96, 116, 127, 130–1, 133–4, 213.
Thesele, see Moshoeshoe I.
Tholoana, see Mahlolela.
Thulo, 166.
Tickets, 32, 150, 186, 200, 202.
Tlaba, 207.
Tlake, 133.
Tlali Moshoeshoe, vii–viii, 64, 145, 148.
Tlalinyane Moshoeshoe, 141.
Tlhabeli, 109.
Tlhakanelo, 114.
Tlhoane, 94.
Tlokoa, conflicts during Orange River Sovereignty, 4–5, 38, 42, 83, 86, 96–100, 104, 105, 108–10, 111, 113–14, 116, 117–22, 124; Gun War, 10, 145; *lifaqane*, 2–3, 14, 38, 50, 108, 117; in Mokhotlong District, 10, 248, 258, 264, 265; mother of Moshoeshoe II, 268; Orange Free State, first war, 124; poet, 266; Sotho subject, 139; terminology, xiv.
Tloung, 77, 148, 207.

Toejana, 206–7.
Toi, 215.
Tokonya, 7, 59, 164.
Tooane, 103.
Trower, Richard, 155.
Tsangoane, 218.
Tsatsi, 86.
Tsekelo Mojela, 241.
Tselane ('MaSelomo), 205.
Tselanyane, 174, 191.
Tšele, 77.
Tšenolo, 228.
Tsepinare Letsie, 252.
Tšiame (a Kholokhoe), 103.
Tšiame Mokhachane, 112, 115, 143, 181.
Tšoeu Matekase, 99.
Tšoeunyane, 65.
Tšolo, 76, 171, 254.
Tšoloane, 75, 76, 171.
Tšupane, 172.
Tswana, xiv, 150.
Tumane, 191.
Tyopho, 70, 71, 109.

Victoria, Queen, 261.
Viervoet, Battle of, 5, 46, 96, 97, 102–3, 110.
Vusani, see Ngubencuka.

Warden, Major H., 4, 79, 89, 92, 96, 98, 100, 102, 103, 104, 111, 114, 138.
Warden Line, 5, 79.
Webb, Captain R. S., ix, 127.
Wepener, Louw, 116, 135, 141, 181, 241–2.
Widdicombe, Canon, 201.
Wilhelm II, Kaiser, 235, 236, 237.
Witbooi, 248.
Witvoet, Piet, 96, 101.
Wodehouse, Sir Philip, 5–6, 25, 80, 140.

Xhosa, 70, 84, 108.

Zonnebloem College, 154.
Zulu, 2, 73, 102, 141, 231.